D•N•ANGEL

BY YUKIRU SUGISAKI

VOLUME 10

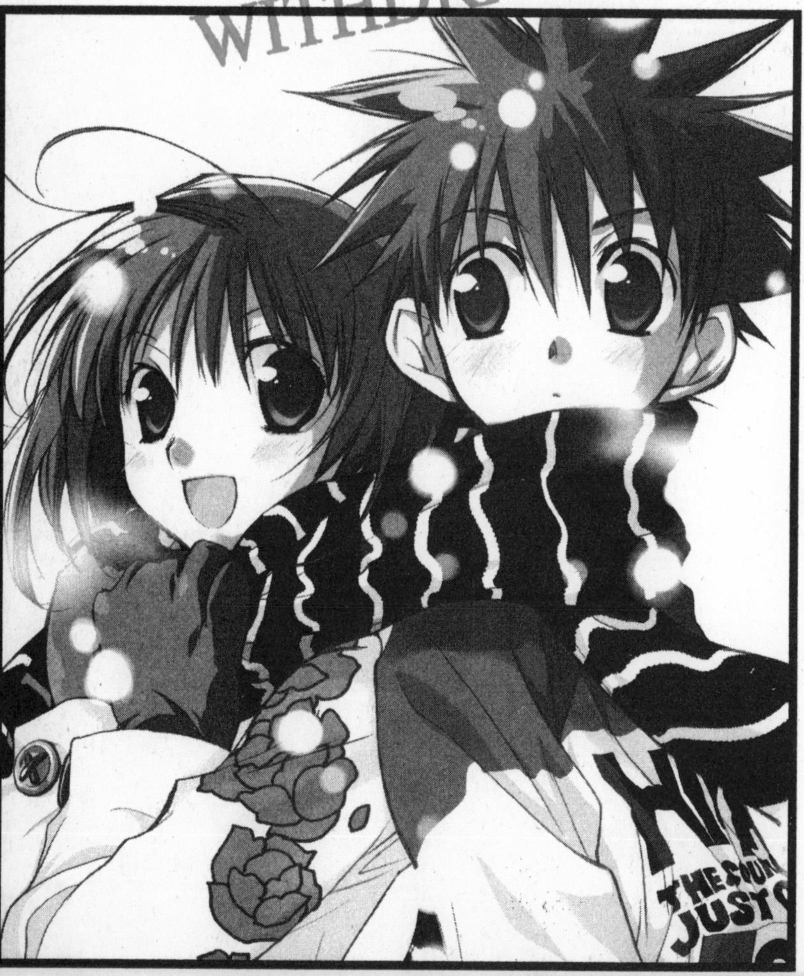

& STORY

Daisuke once had a crush on his classmate Risa, but he finally realized it was her twin sister, Riku, that he had feelings for. The two of them have now resolved their relationship and are happily in love. Meanwhile, Risa has fallen for Dark, and even tried to plant a fake warning note to get his attention. It worked, and he asked her out on a date. However, Riku, beginning to suspect that there is some connection between Daisuke and Dark, sets up a date with Daisuke at the same time and place! Wiz and Daisuke change back and forth in an attempt to keep both dates going, but...will it actually work?

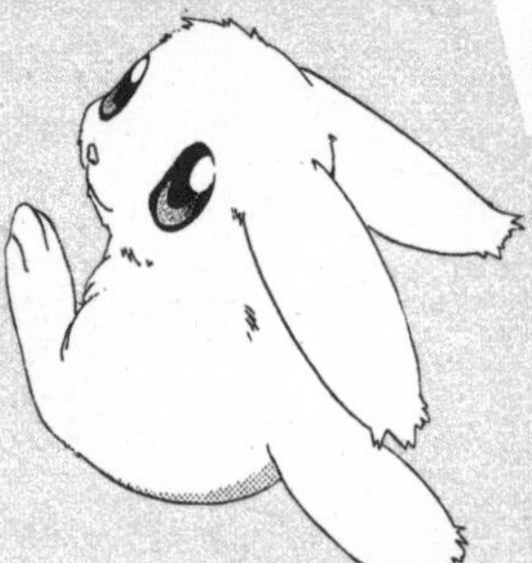

Wiz

A mysterious animal who acts as Dark's familiar and who can transform into many things, including Dark's black wings. He can also transform himself into Dark or Daisuke.

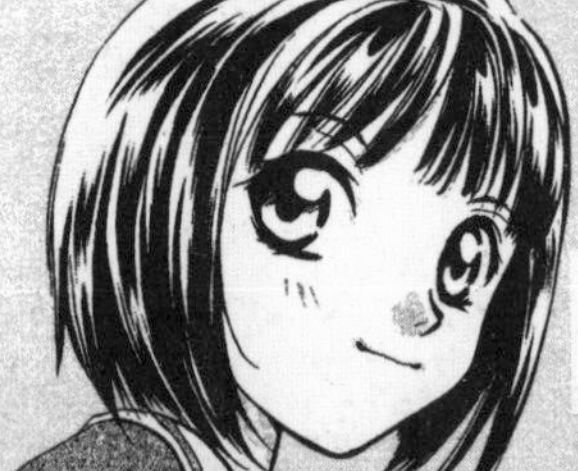

Risa Harada (younger sister)

Daisuke's first crush. Daisuke confessed his love to her...but she rejected him. She's been in love with Dark since the first time she saw him on TV.

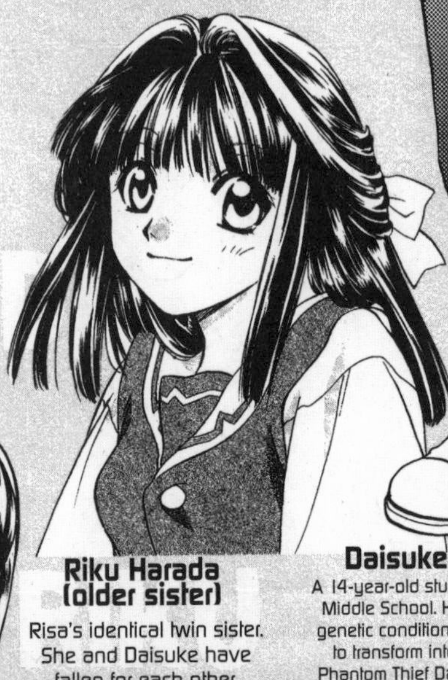

Riku Harada (older sister)

Risa's identical twin sister. She and Daisuke have fallen for each other.

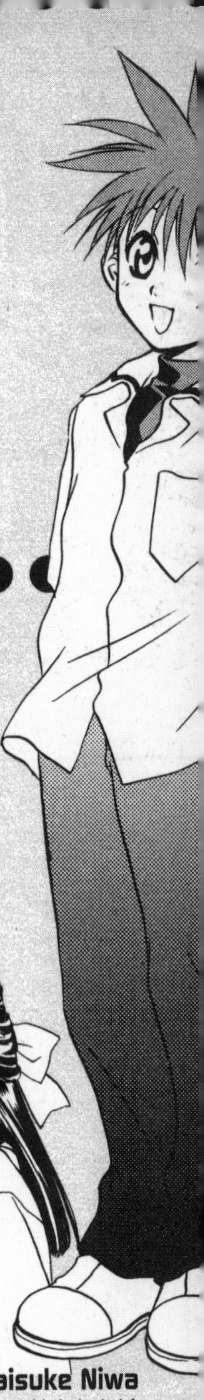

Daisuke Niwa

A 14-year-old student at Azumano Middle School. He has a unique genetic condition that causes him to transform into the infamous Phantom Thief Dark whenever he has romantic feelings.

CHARACTERS

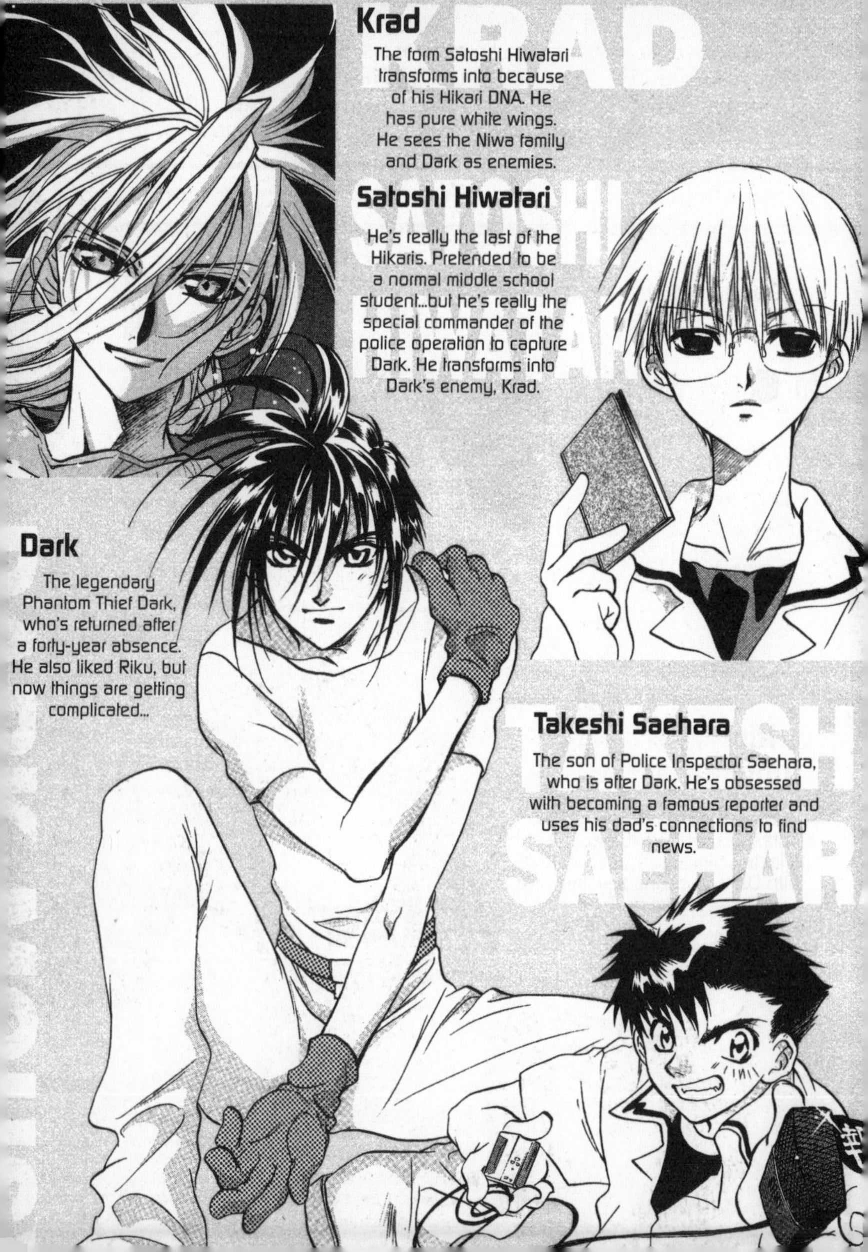

Krad

The form Satoshi Hiwatari transforms into because of his Hikari DNA. He has pure white wings. He sees the Niwa family and Dark as enemies.

Satoshi Hiwatari

He's really the last of the Hikaris. Pretended to be a normal middle school student...but he's really the special commander of the police operation to capture Dark. He transforms into Dark's enemy, Krad.

Dark

The legendary Phantom Thief Dark, who's returned after a forty-year absence. He also liked Riku, but now things are getting complicated...

Takeshi Saehara

The son of Police Inspector Saehara, who is after Dark. He's obsessed with becoming a famous reporter and uses his dad's connections to find news.

D•N•ANGEL Vol. 10
Created by Yukiru Sugisaki

Translation - Alethea and Athena Nibley
English Adaptation - Sarah Dyer
Copy Editor - Hope Donovan
Retouch - Gloria Wu
Lettering and Layout - James Lee
Production Artist - Bowen Park
Cover Layout - Thea Willis

Editor - Bryce P. Coleman
Digital Imaging Manager - Chris Buford
Production Managers - Jennifer Miller and Mutsumi Miyazaki
Managing Editor - Lindsey Johnston
VP of Production - Ron Klamert
Publisher and E.I.C. - Mike Kiley
President and C.O.O. - John Parker
C.E.O. - Stuart Levy

A  Manga

TOKYOPOP Inc.
5900 Wilshire Blvd. Suite 2000
Los Angeles, CA 90036

E-mail: info@TOKYOPOP.com
Come visit us online at www.TOKYOPOP.com

D•N•ANGEL Volume 10 ©2004 Yukiru SUGISAKI. All rights reserved. No portion of this book may be
First published in Japan in 2004 by reproduced or transmitted in any form or by any means
KADOKAWA SHOTEN PUBLISHING CO., LTD., Tokyo. without written permission from the copyright holders.
English translation rights arranged with This manga is a work of fiction. Any resemblance to
KADOKAWA SHOTEN PUBLISHING CO., LTD., Tokyo actual events or locales or persons, living or dead, is
through TUTTLE-MORI AGENCY, INC., Tokyo. entirely coincidental.

English text copyright © 2005 TOKYOPOP Inc.

ISBN: 1-59532-795-9

First TOKYOPOP printing: December 2005
10 9 8 7 6 5 4
Printed in the USA

D·N·ANGEL

Volume 10

By

Yukiru Sugisaki

CROOK COUNTY LIBRAR
175 N. W. MEADOW LAKES D
PRINEVILLE, OR 97754
541-447-7978

3CCL100113801K

HAMBURG // LONDON // LOS ANGELES // TOKYO

CONTENTS

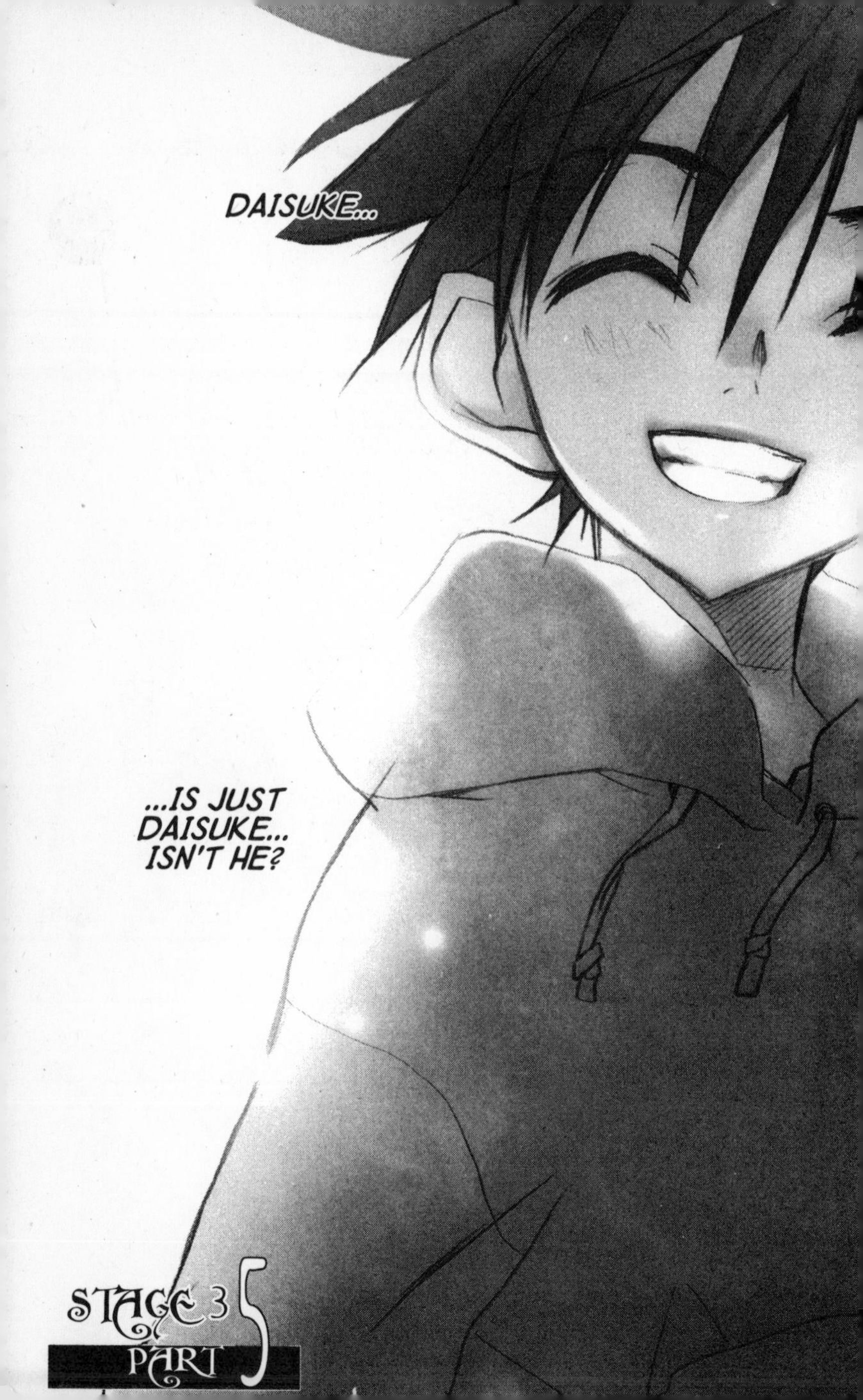
DAISUKE...
...IS JUST DAISUKE... ISN'T HE?
STAGE 3 PART 5

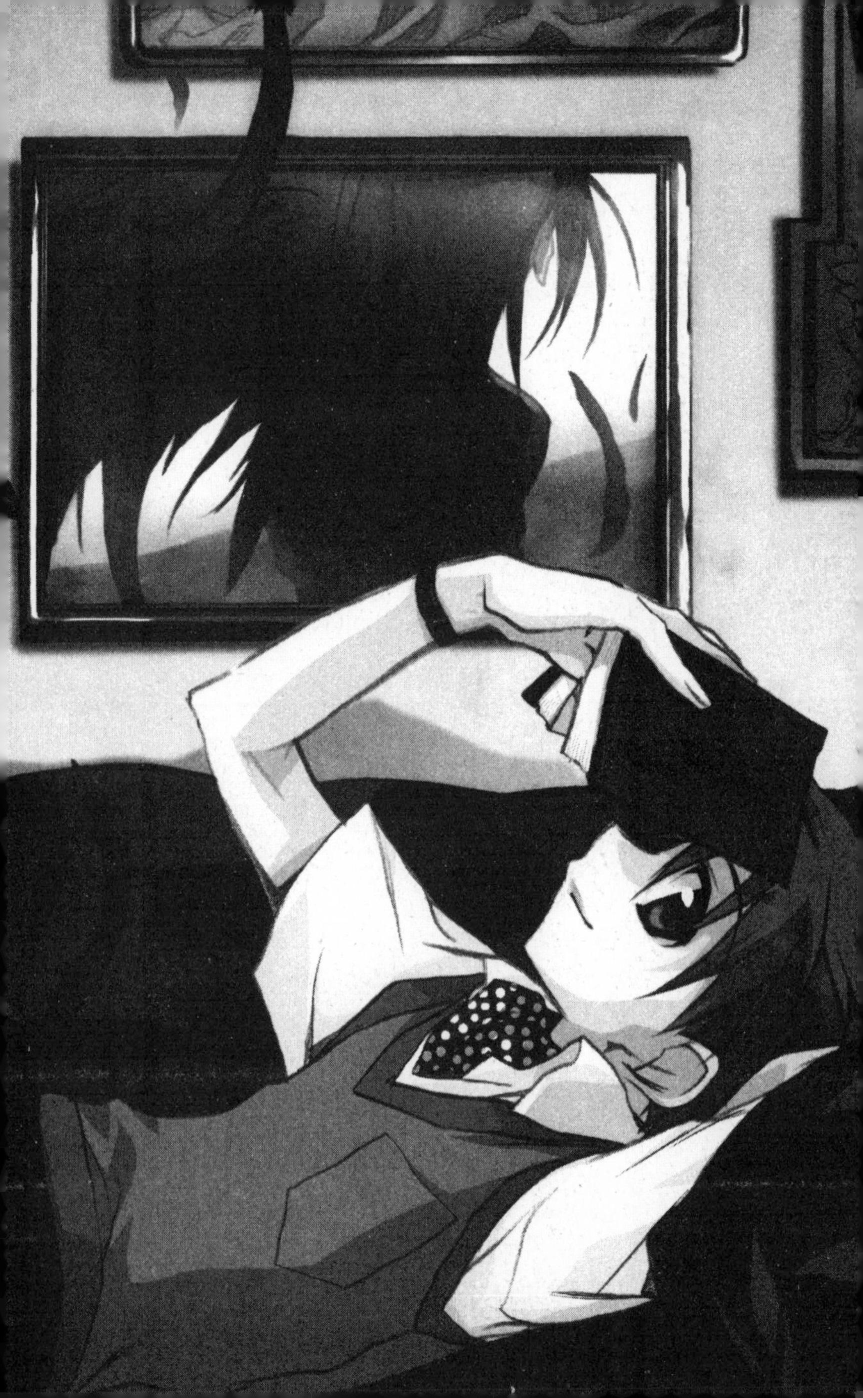

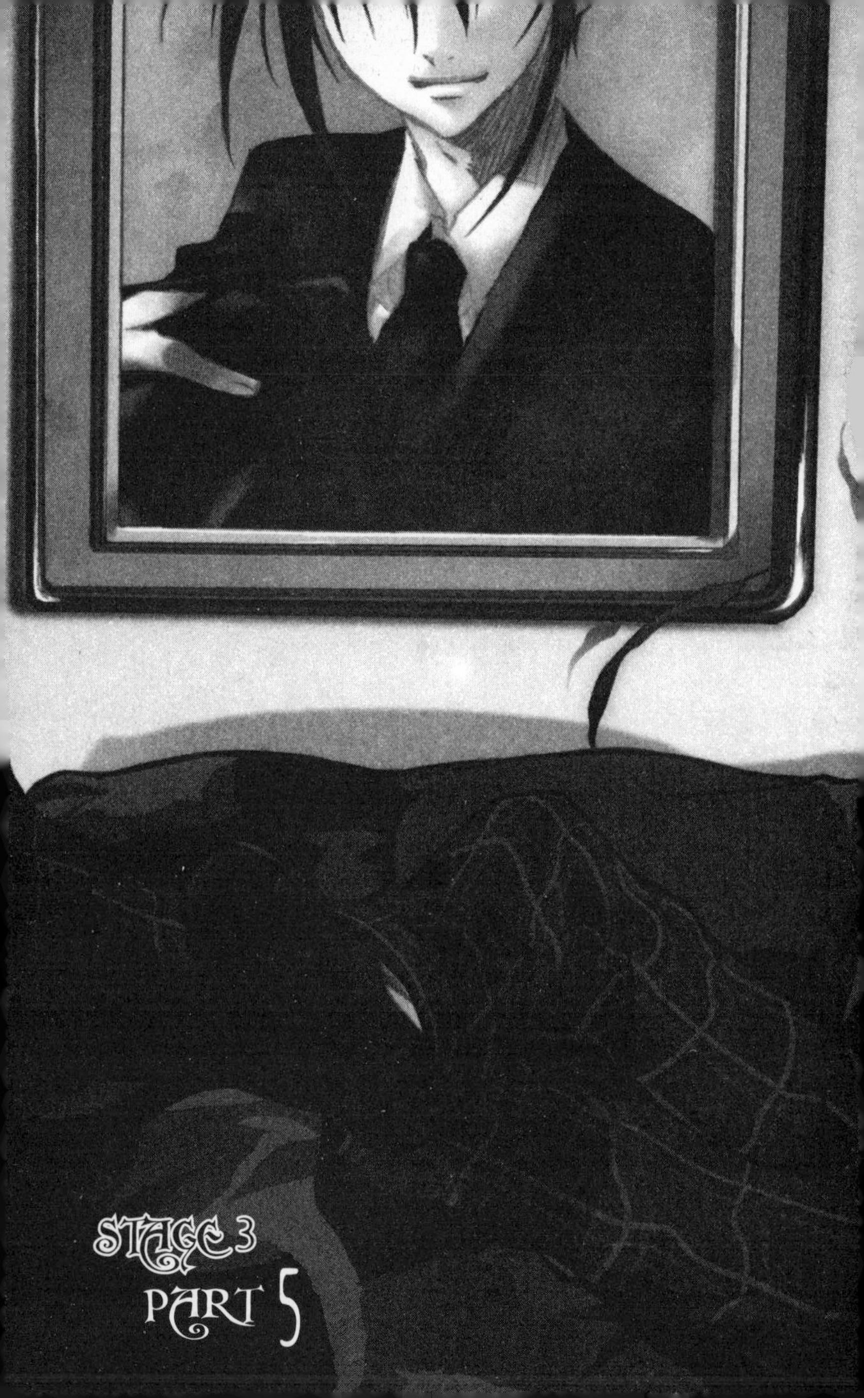
STAGE 3
PART 5

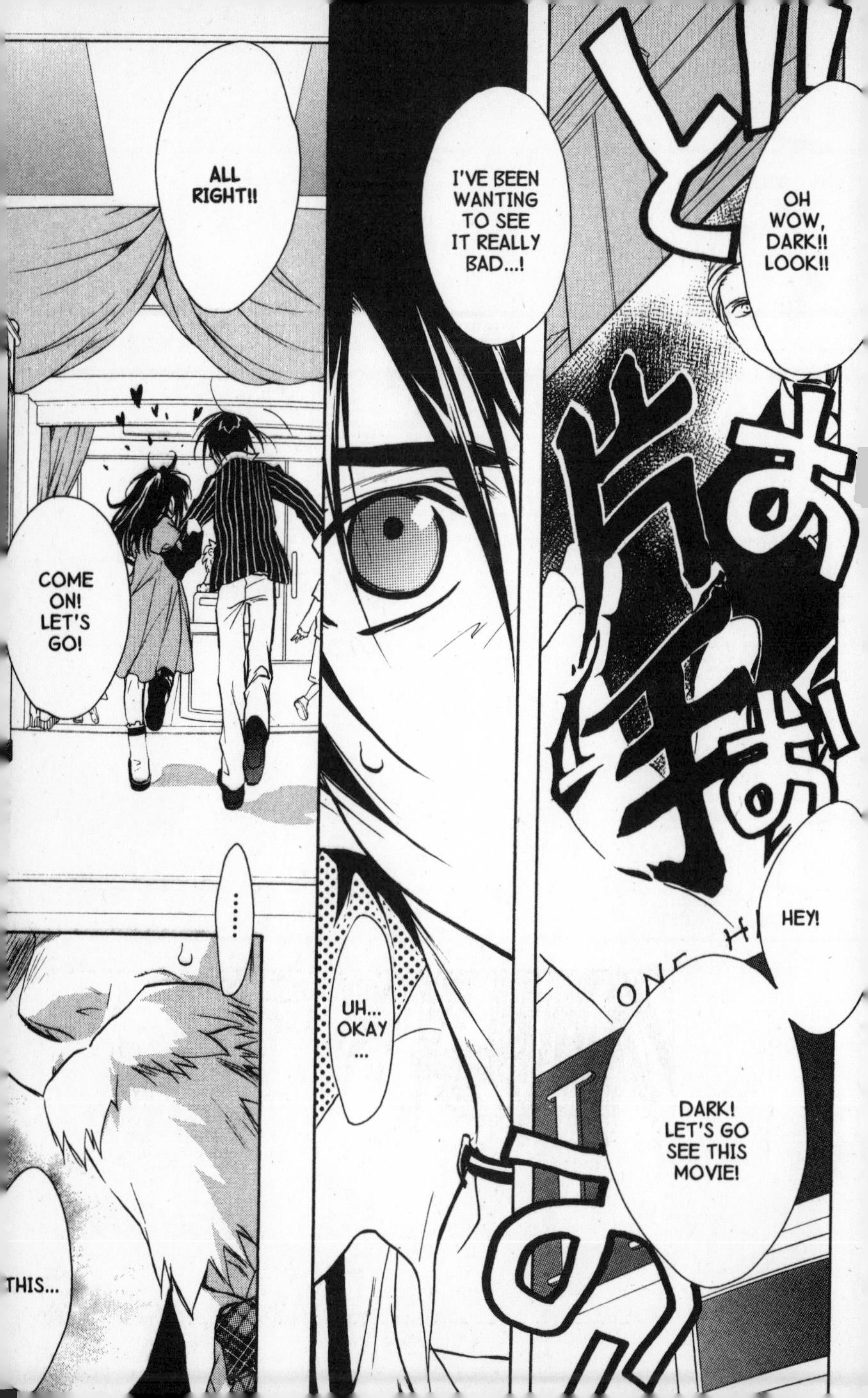
OH WOW, DARK!! LOOK!!
HEY!
DARK! LET'S GO SEE THIS MOVIE!
I'VE BEEN WANTING TO SEE IT REALLY BAD...!
UH... OKAY ...
ALL RIGHT!!
COME ON! LET'S GO!
......
THIS...

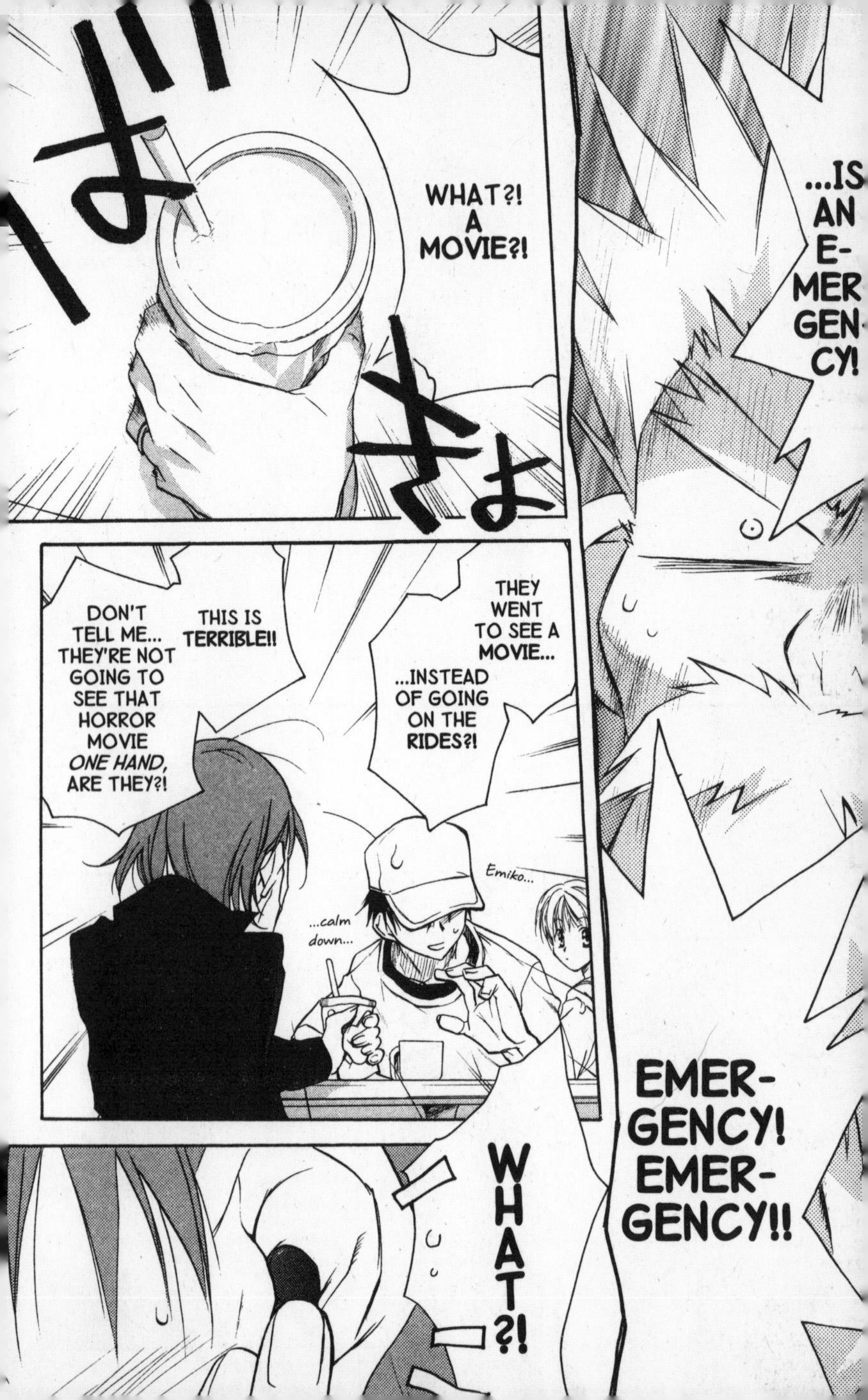
...IS AN E-MERGENCY!
EMERGENCY! EMERGENCY!!
WHAT?! A MOVIE?!
THEY WENT TO SEE A MOVIE...
...INSTEAD OF GOING ON THE RIDES?!
THIS IS TERRIBLE!!
DON'T TELL ME... THEY'RE NOT GOING TO SEE THAT HORROR MOVIE *ONE HAND*, ARE THEY?!
Emiko...
...calm down...
WHAT?!

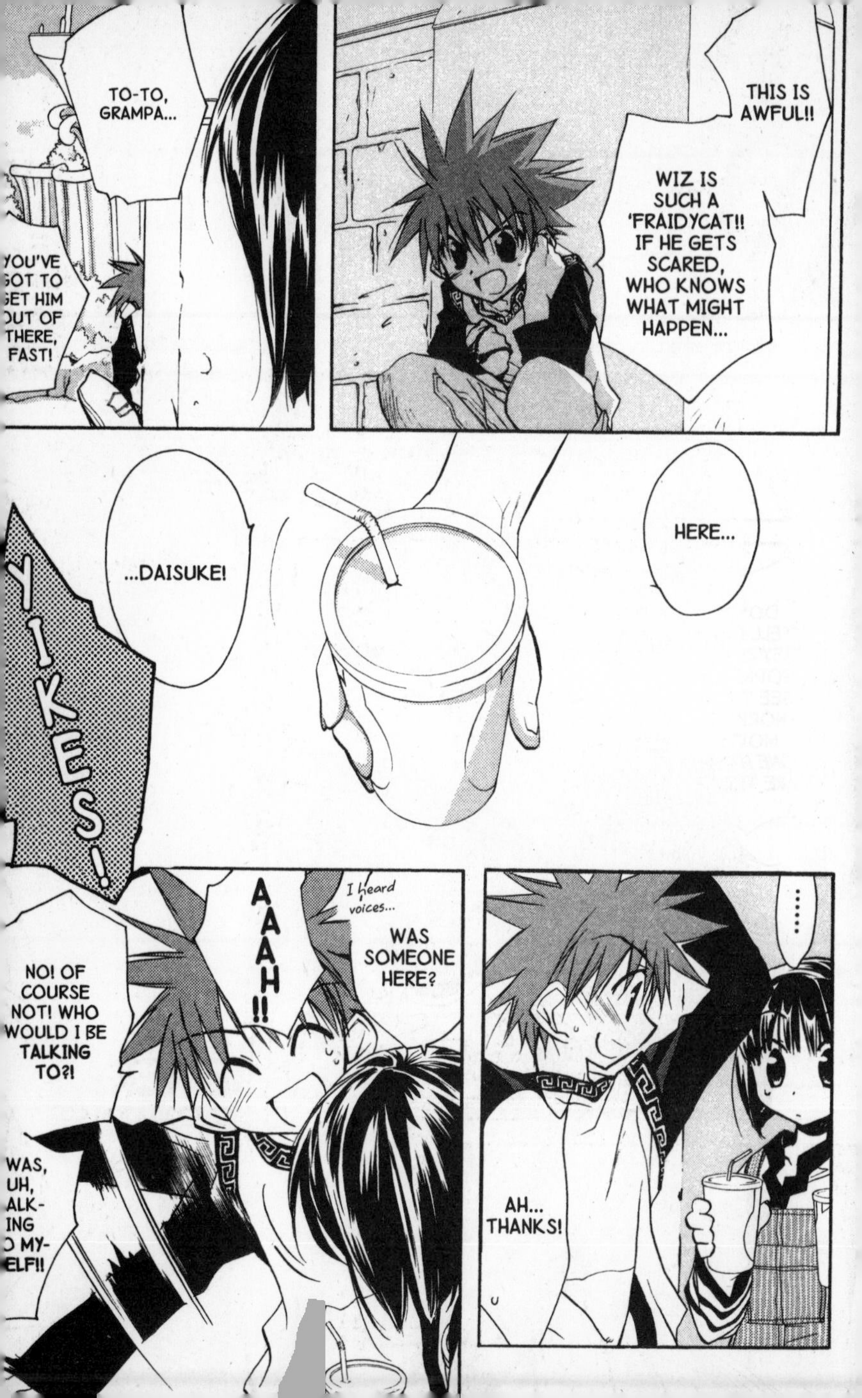
THIS IS AWFUL!!
WIZ IS SUCH A 'FRAIDYCAT!! IF HE GETS SCARED, WHO KNOWS WHAT MIGHT HAPPEN...
TO-TO, GRAMPA...
YOU'VE GOT TO GET HIM OUT OF THERE, FAST!
HERE...
...DAISUKE!
YIKES!
......
AH... THANKS!
I heard voices...
WAS SOMEONE HERE?
AAAH!!
NO! OF COURSE NOT! WHO WOULD I BE TALKING TO?!
WAS, UH, ALK-ING O MY-ELF!!

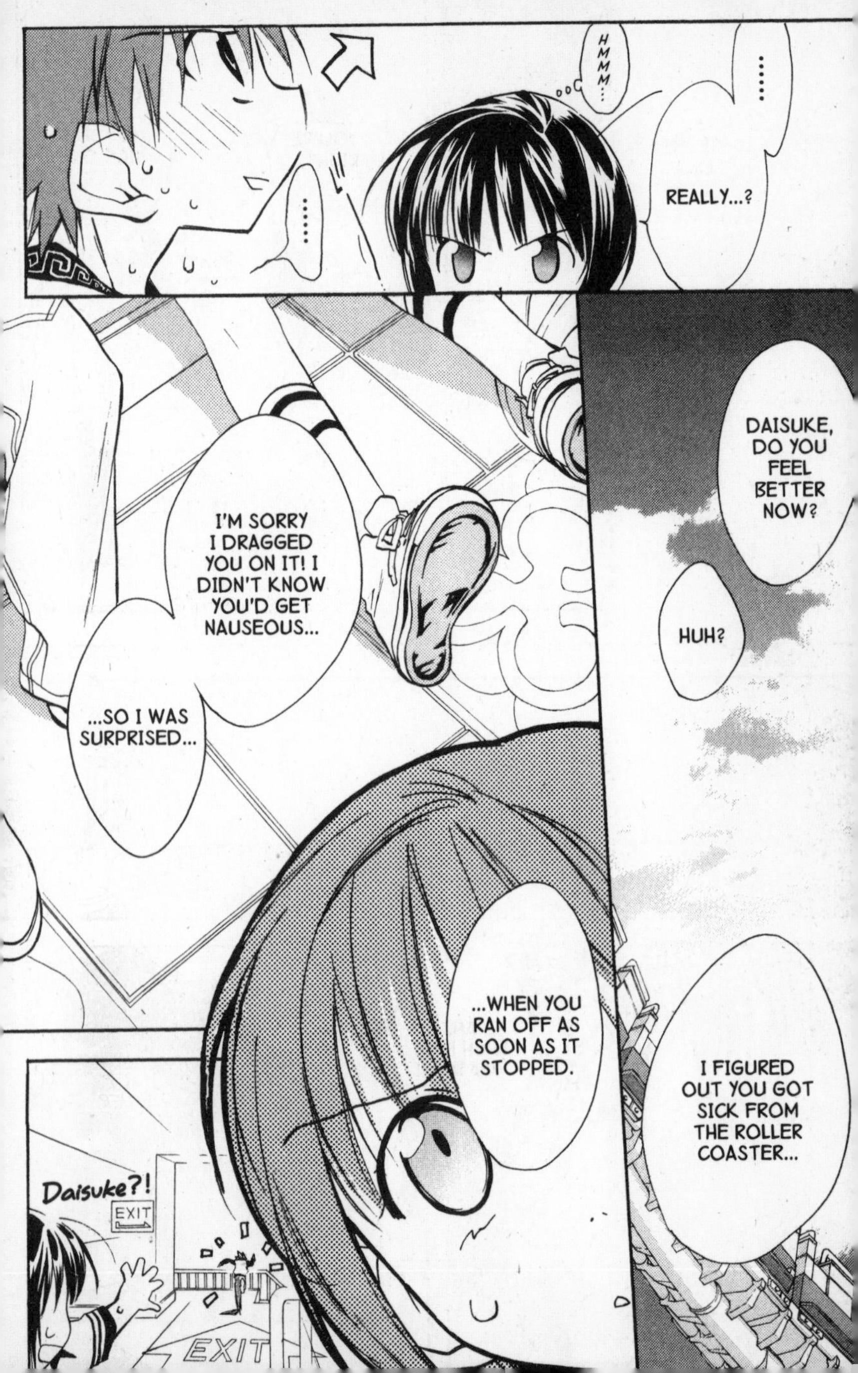
......
REALLY...?
HMMM...
......
DAISUKE, DO YOU FEEL BETTER NOW?
HUH?
I'M SORRY I DRAGGED YOU ON IT! I DIDN'T KNOW YOU'D GET NAUSEOUS...
...SO I WAS SURPRISED...
I FIGURED OUT YOU GOT SICK FROM THE ROLLER COASTER...
...WHEN YOU RAN OFF AS SOON AS IT STOPPED.
Daisuke?!
EXIT
EXIT

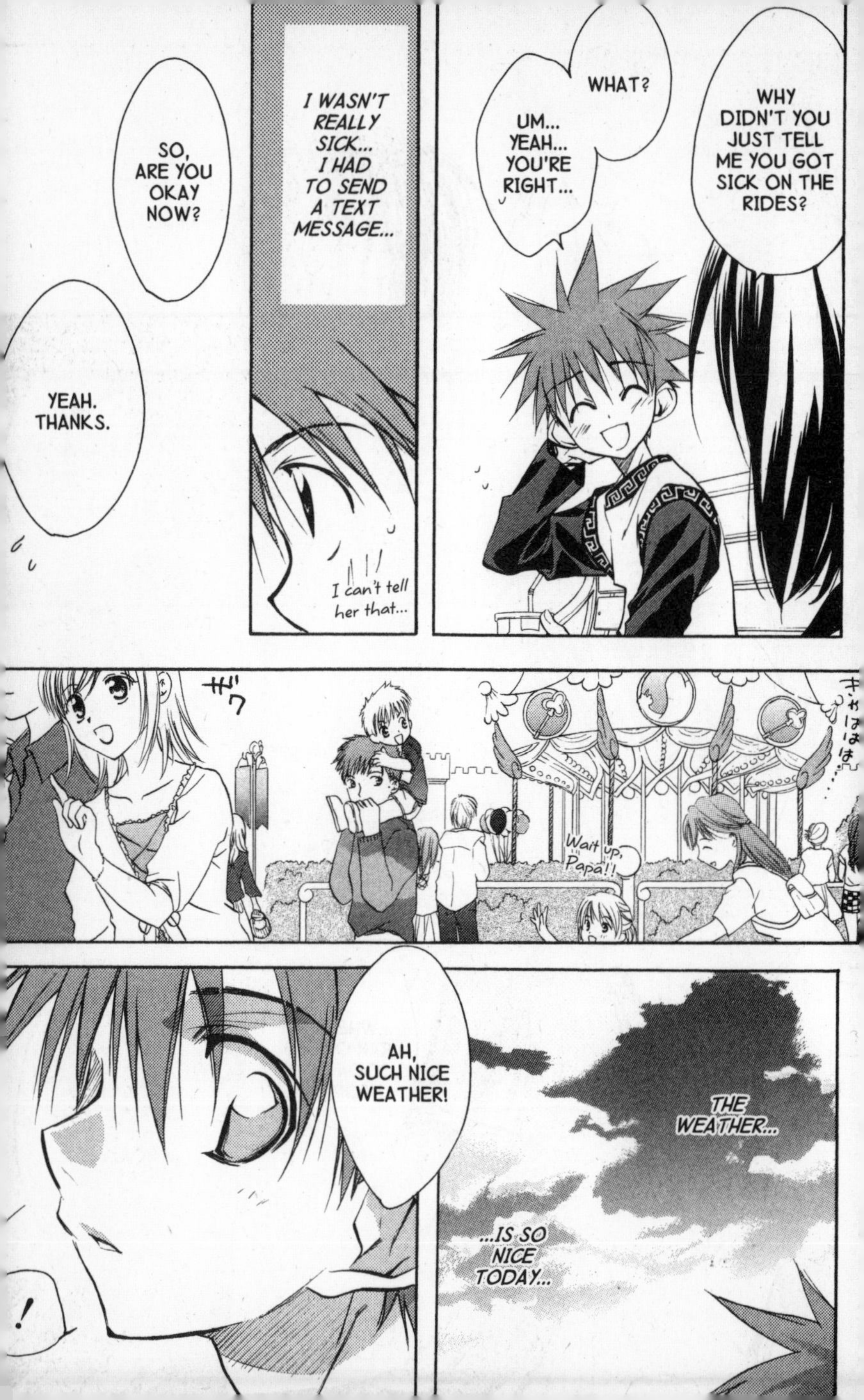
WHY DIDN'T YOU JUST TELL ME YOU GOT SICK ON THE RIDES?
WHAT?
UM... YEAH... YOU'RE RIGHT...
I WASN'T REALLY SICK... I HAD TO SEND A TEXT MESSAGE...
I can't tell her that...
SO, ARE YOU OKAY NOW?
YEAH. THANKS.
きゃははは…
Wait up, Papa!!
ザワ
THE WEATHER...
...IS SO NICE TODAY...
AH, SUCH NICE WEATHER!
!

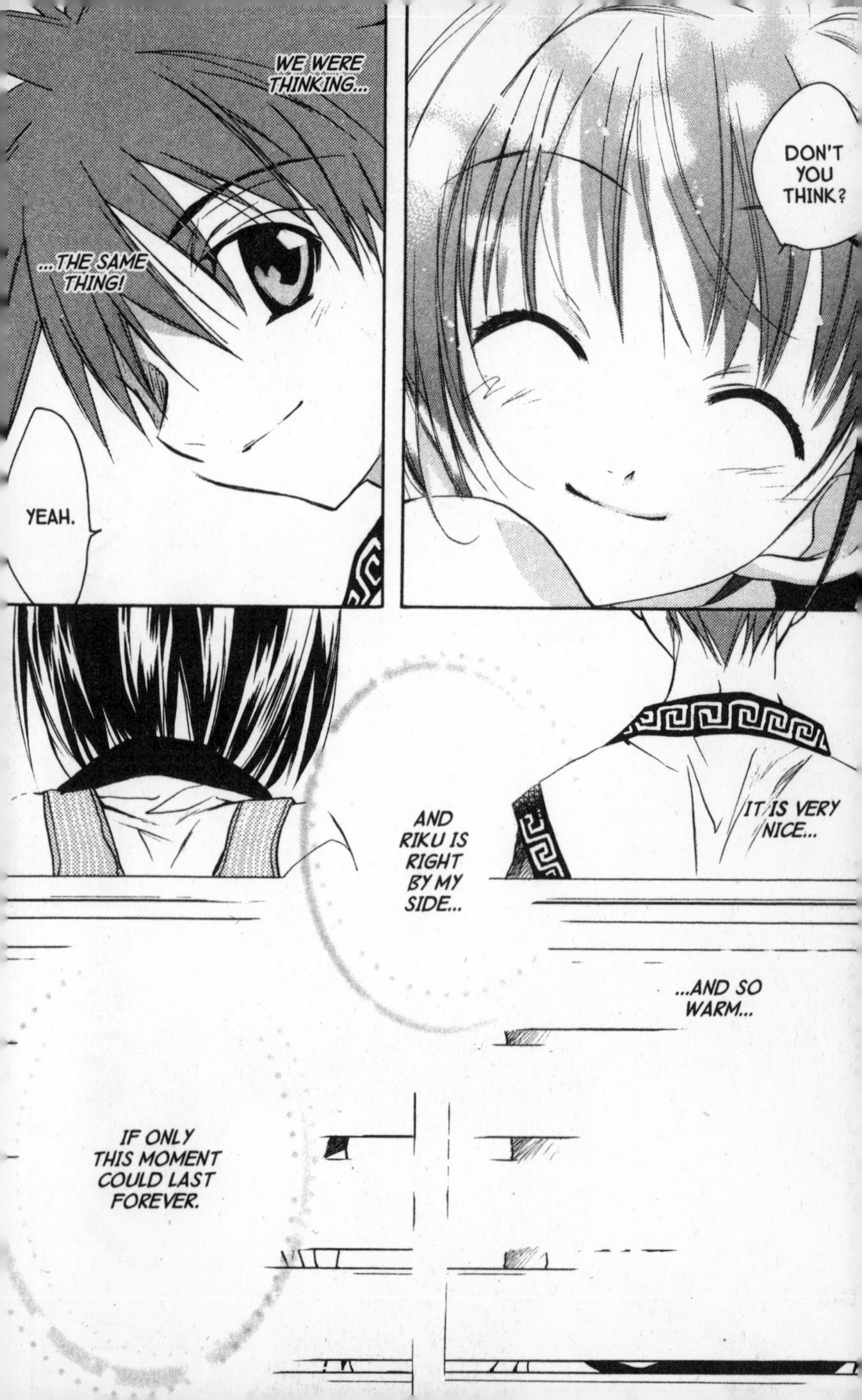
DON'T YOU THINK?
WE WERE THINKING...
...THE SAME THING!
YEAH.
IT IS VERY NICE...
AND RIKU IS RIGHT BY MY SIDE...
...AND SO WARM...
IF ONLY THIS MOMENT COULD LAST FOREVER.

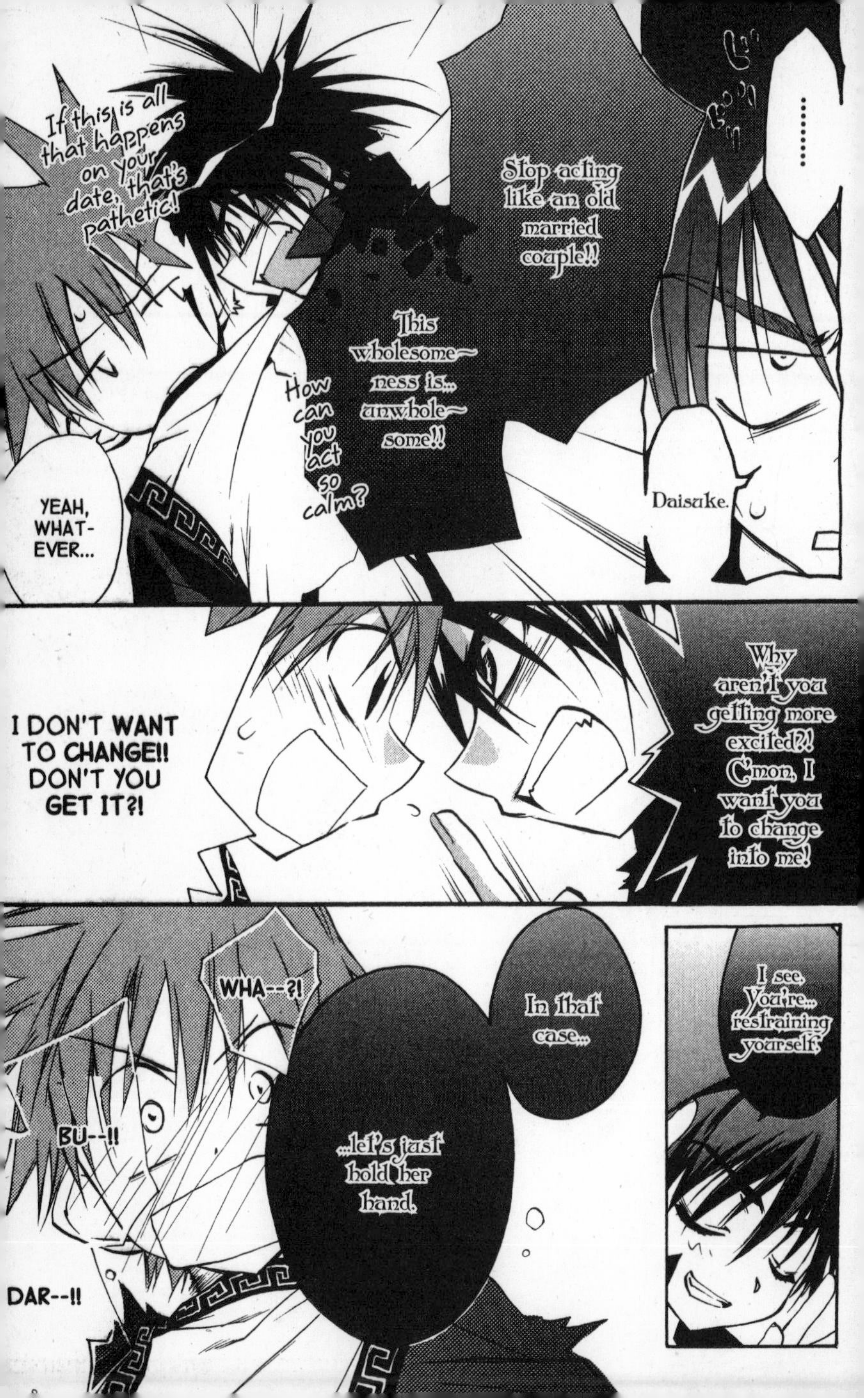
......
Daisuke.
Stop acting like an old married couple!!
This wholesome-ness is... unwhole-some!!
How can you act so calm?
If this is all that happens on your date, that's pathetic!
YEAH, WHAT-EVER...
Why aren't you getting more excited?! C'mon, I want you to change into me!
I DON'T WANT TO CHANGE!! DON'T YOU GET IT?!
I see. You're... restraining yourself.
In that case...
...let's just hold her hand.
WHA--?!
BU--!!
DAR--!!

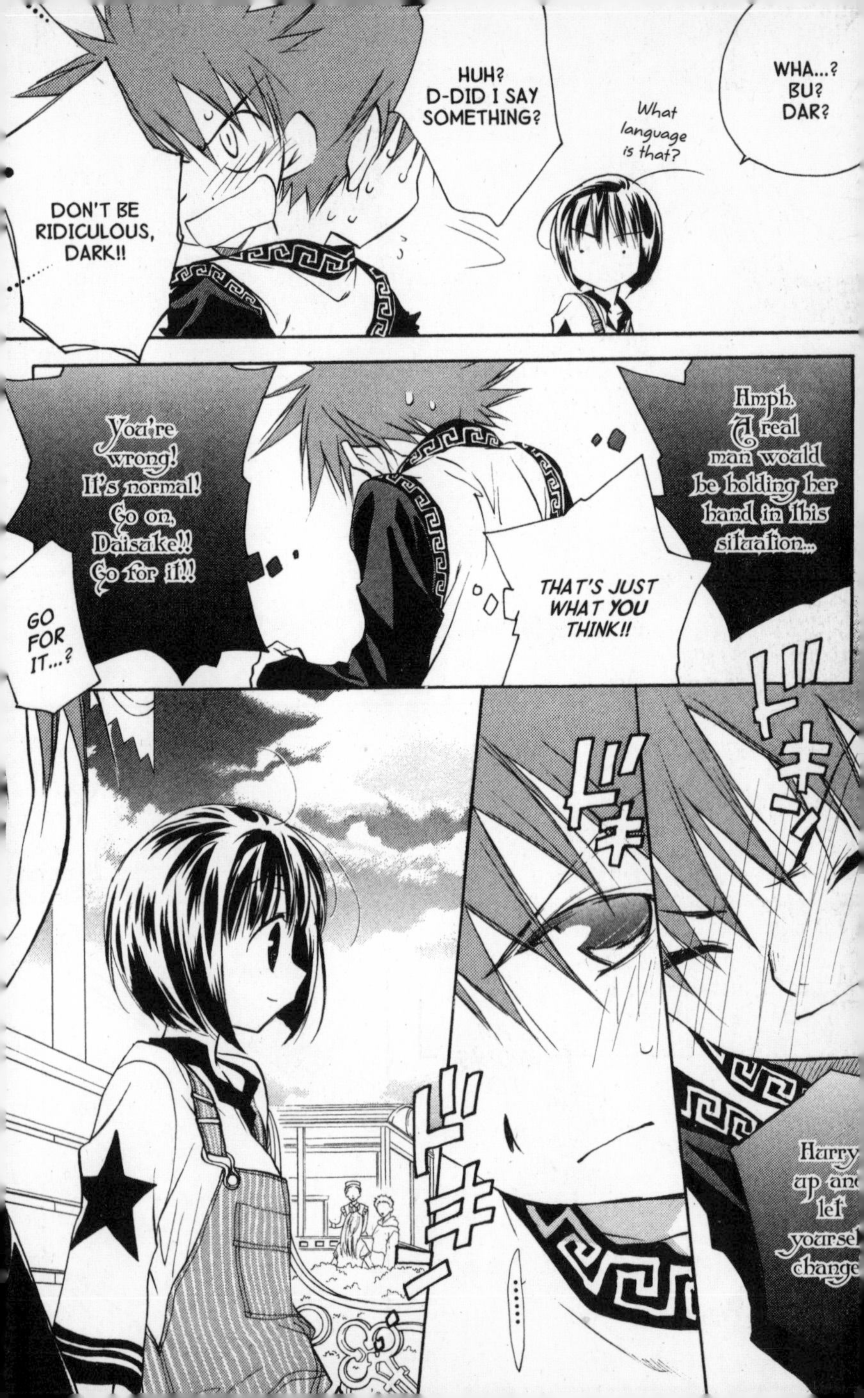
WHA...? BU? DAR?
What language is that?
HUH? D-DID I SAY SOMETHING?
DON'T BE RIDICULOUS, DARK!!
Hmph. A real man would be holding her hand in this situation...
THAT'S JUST WHAT YOU THINK!!
You're wrong! It's normal! Go on, Daisuke!! Go for it!!
GO FOR IT...?
Hurry up and let yoursel change
ドキン
ドキ
......
ドキー

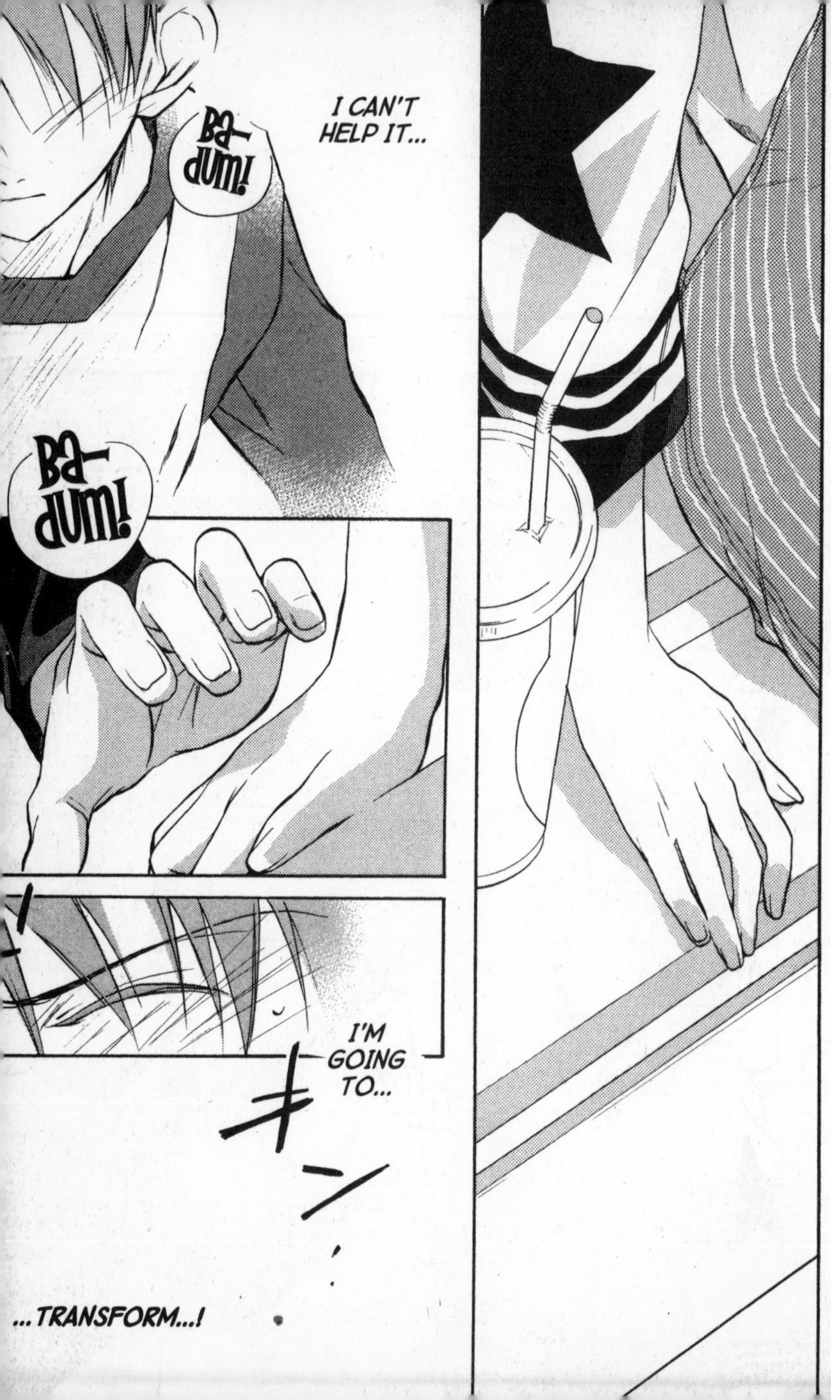
I CAN'T HELP IT...
Ba-dum!
Ba-dum!
I'M GOING TO...
...TRANSFORM...!

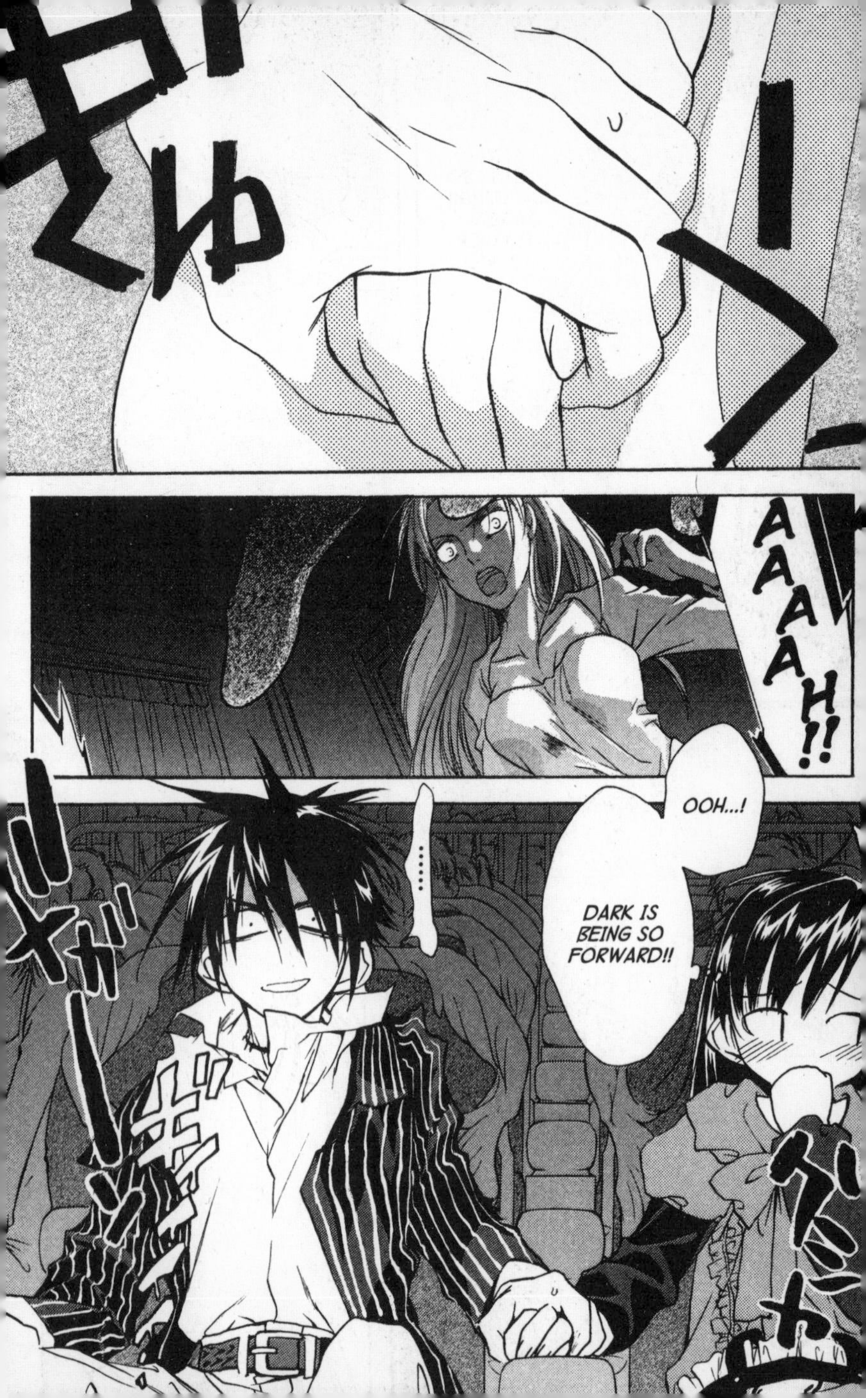
ぎゅー
AAAAH!!
OOH...!
DARK IS BEING SO FORWARD!!
......

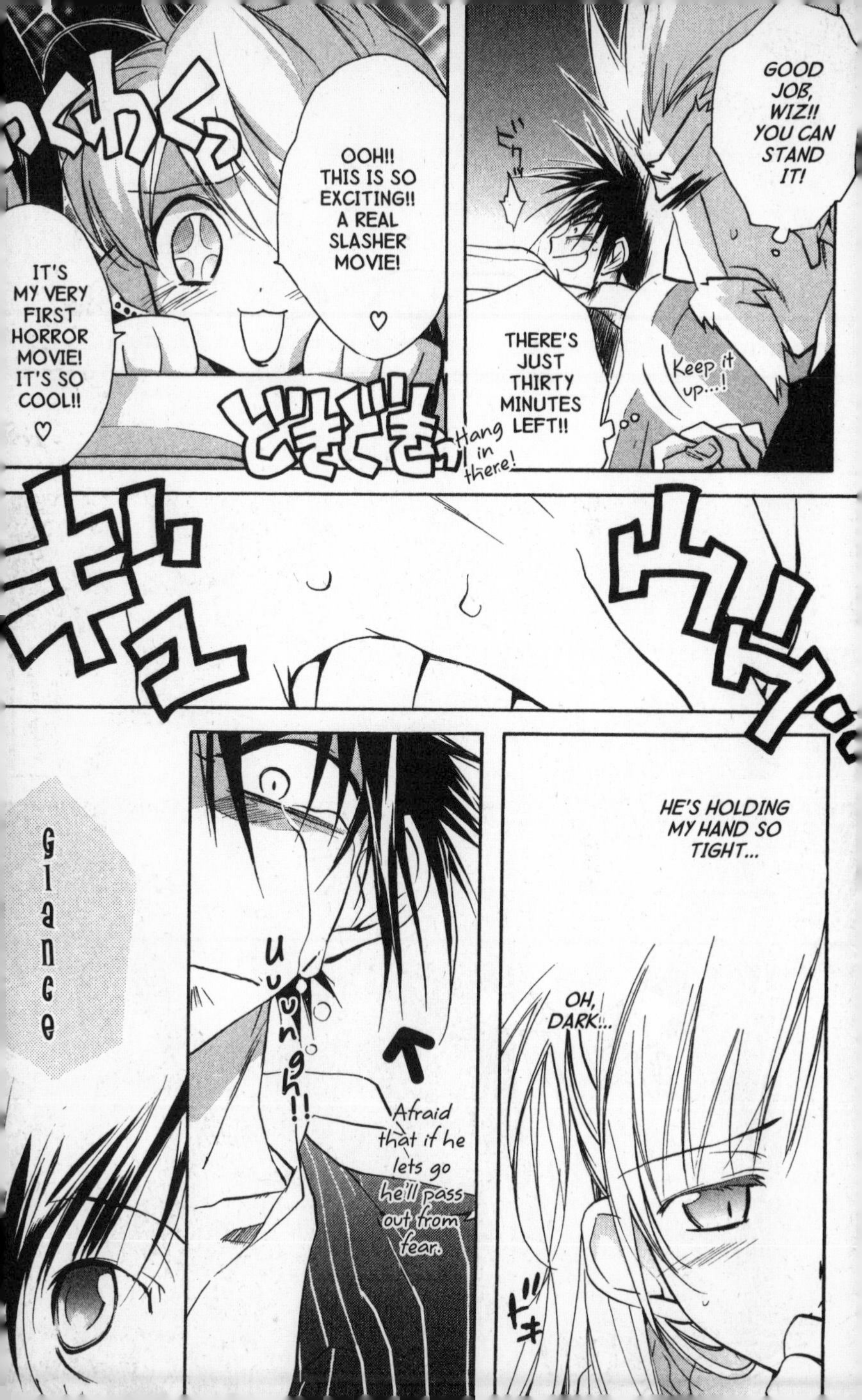
GOOD JOB, WIZ!! YOU CAN STAND IT!
Keep it up...!
THERE'S JUST THIRTY MINUTES LEFT!!
Hang in there!
OOH!! THIS IS SO EXCITING!! A REAL SLASHER MOVIE! ♡
IT'S MY VERY FIRST HORROR MOVIE! IT'S SO COOL!! ♡
HE'S HOLDING MY HAND SO TIGHT...
OH, DARK...
Uuungh!!
Afraid that if he lets go he'll pass out from fear.
Glance

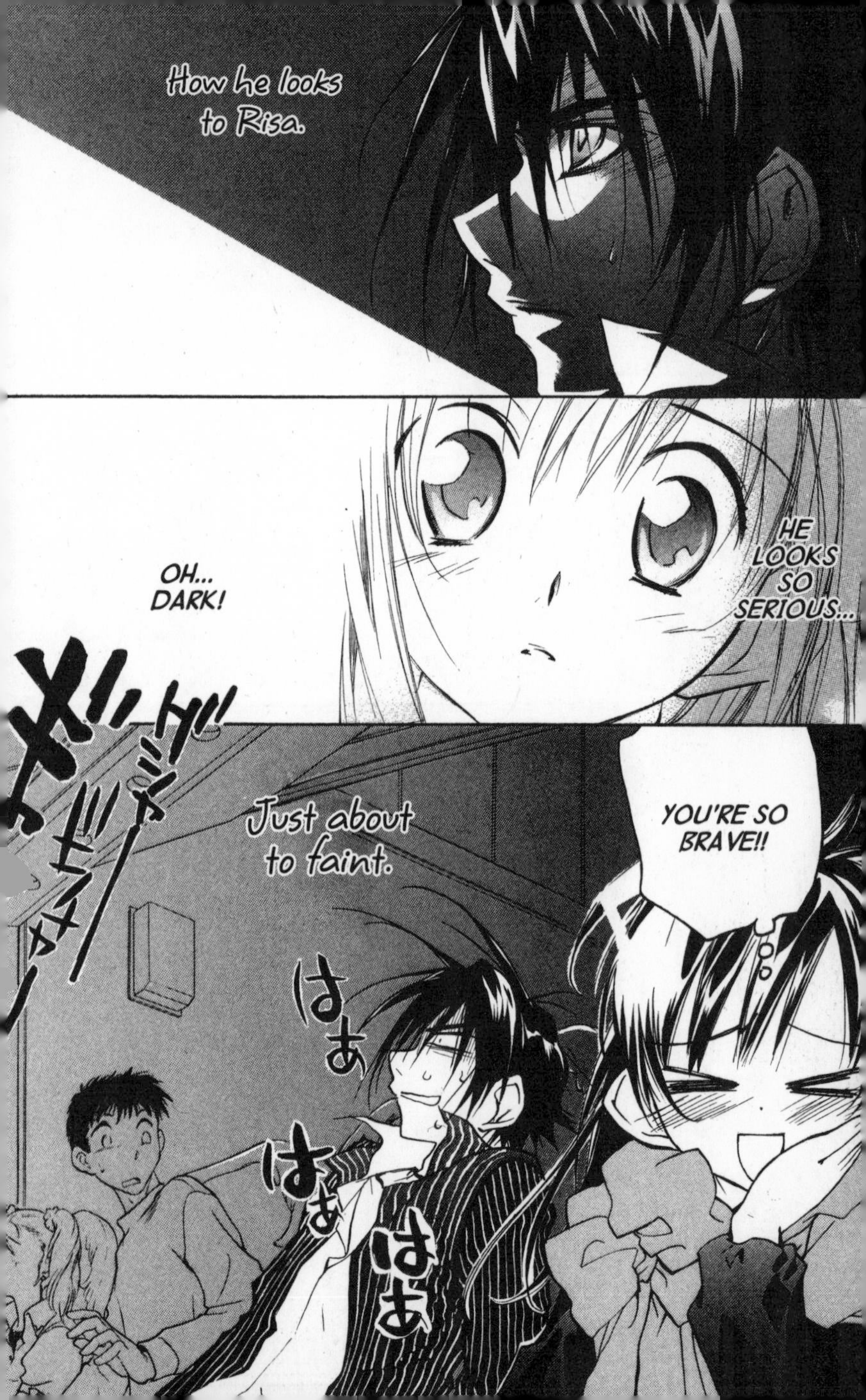
How he looks to Risa.
HE LOOKS SO SERIOUS...
OH... DARK!
YOU'RE SO BRAVE!!
Just about to faint.
はあ
はあ
はあ

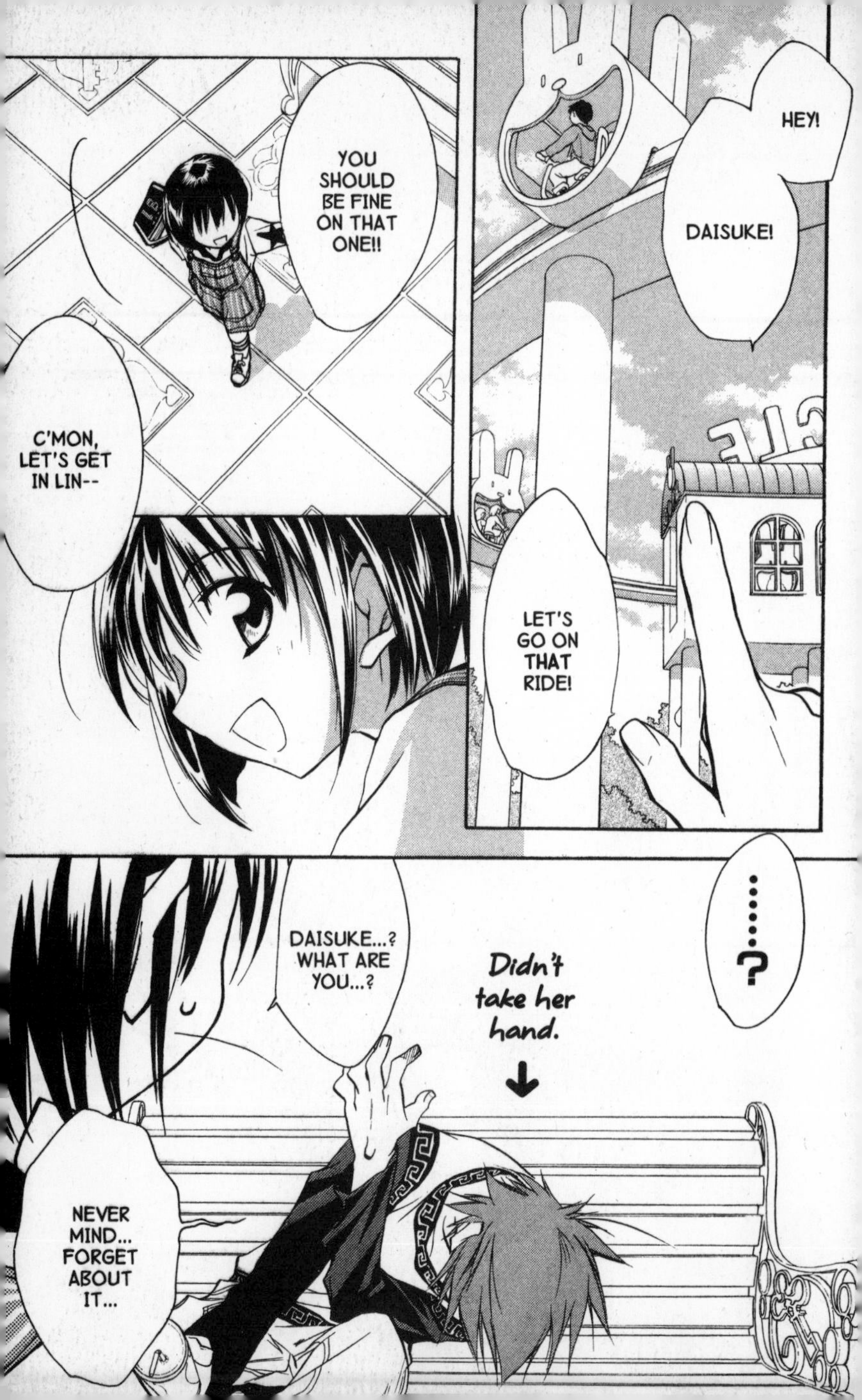

HEY!
DAISUKE!
LET'S GO ON THAT RIDE!
YOU SHOULD BE FINE ON THAT ONE!!
C'MON, LET'S GET IN LIN--
......?
Didn't take her hand.
DAISUKE...? WHAT ARE YOU...?
NEVER MIND... FORGET ABOUT IT...

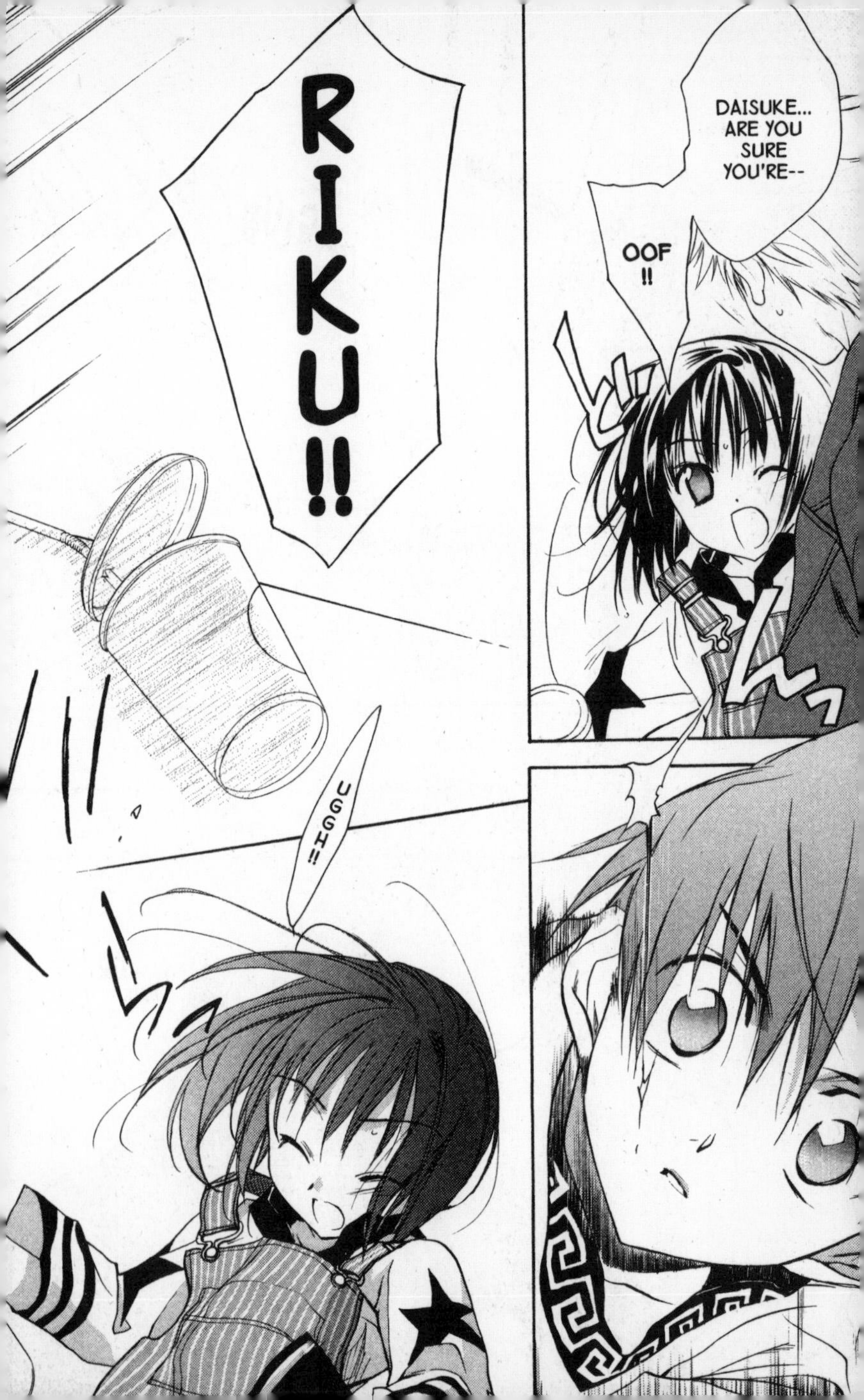
DAISUKE... ARE YOU SURE YOU'RE--
OOF !!
RIKU!!
UGGH!!

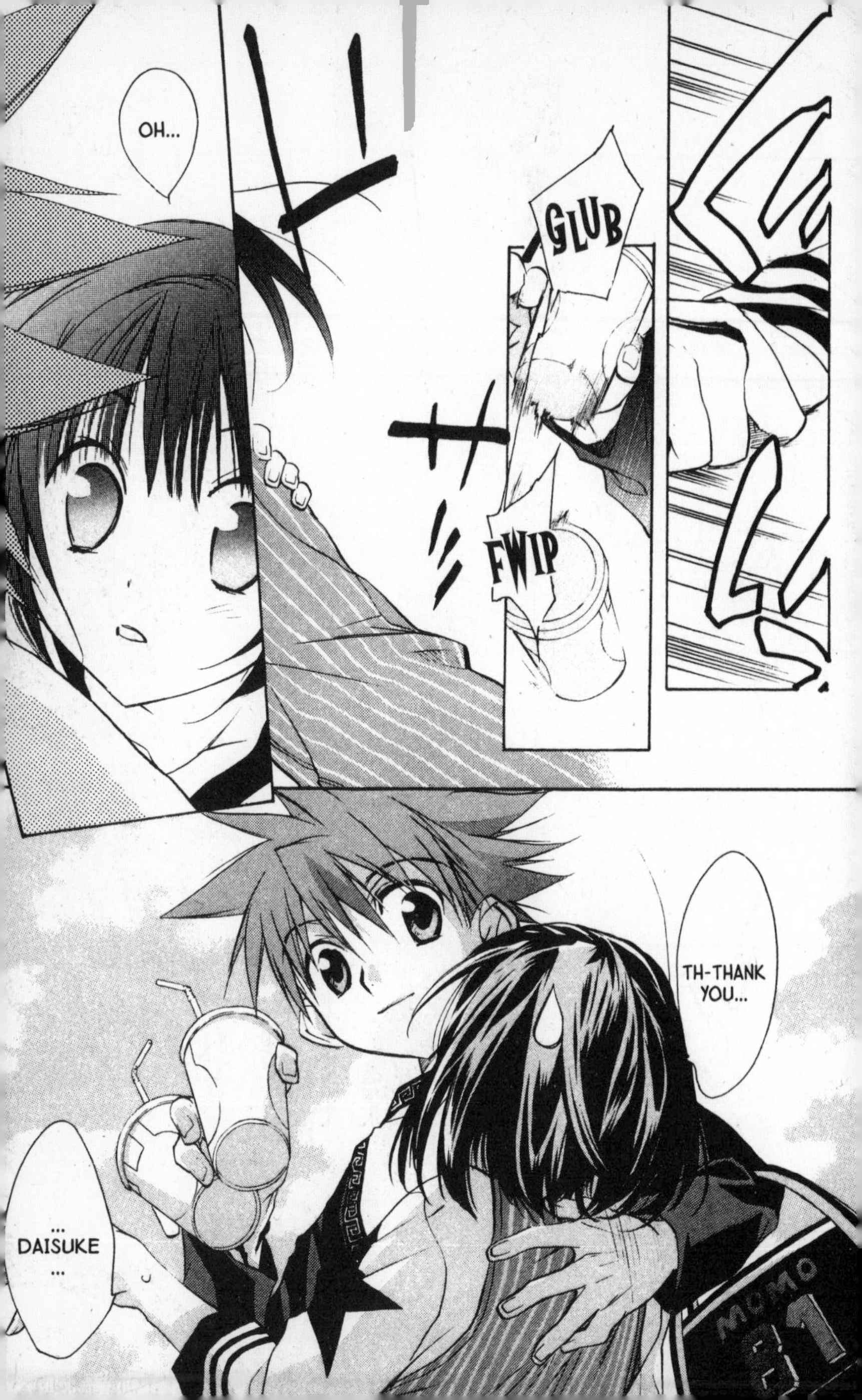
GLUB
FWIP
OH...
TH-THANK YOU...
... DAISUKE ...

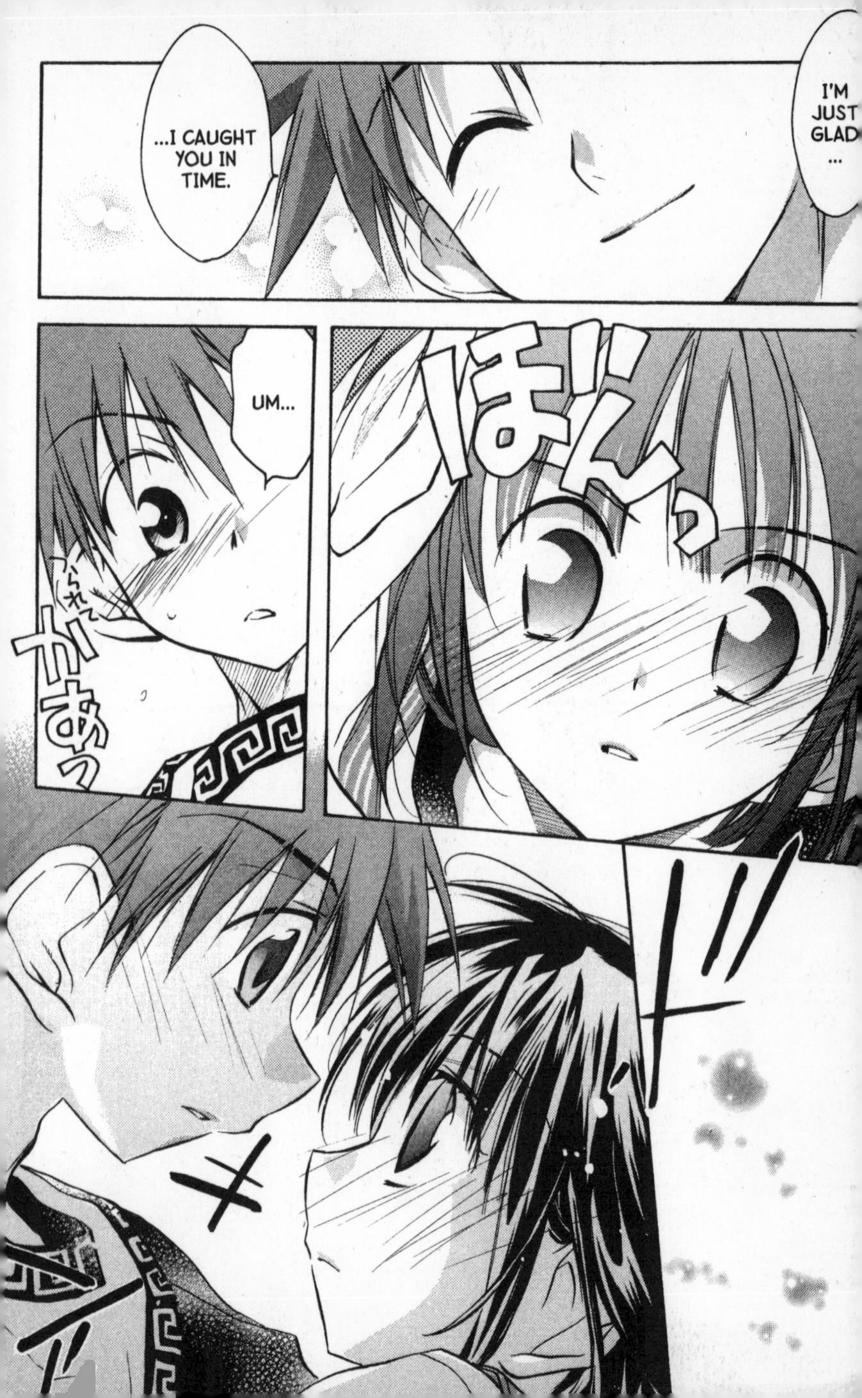
I'M JUST GLAD...
...I CAUGHT YOU IN TIME.
ぼんっ
UM...
つられて
かあっ

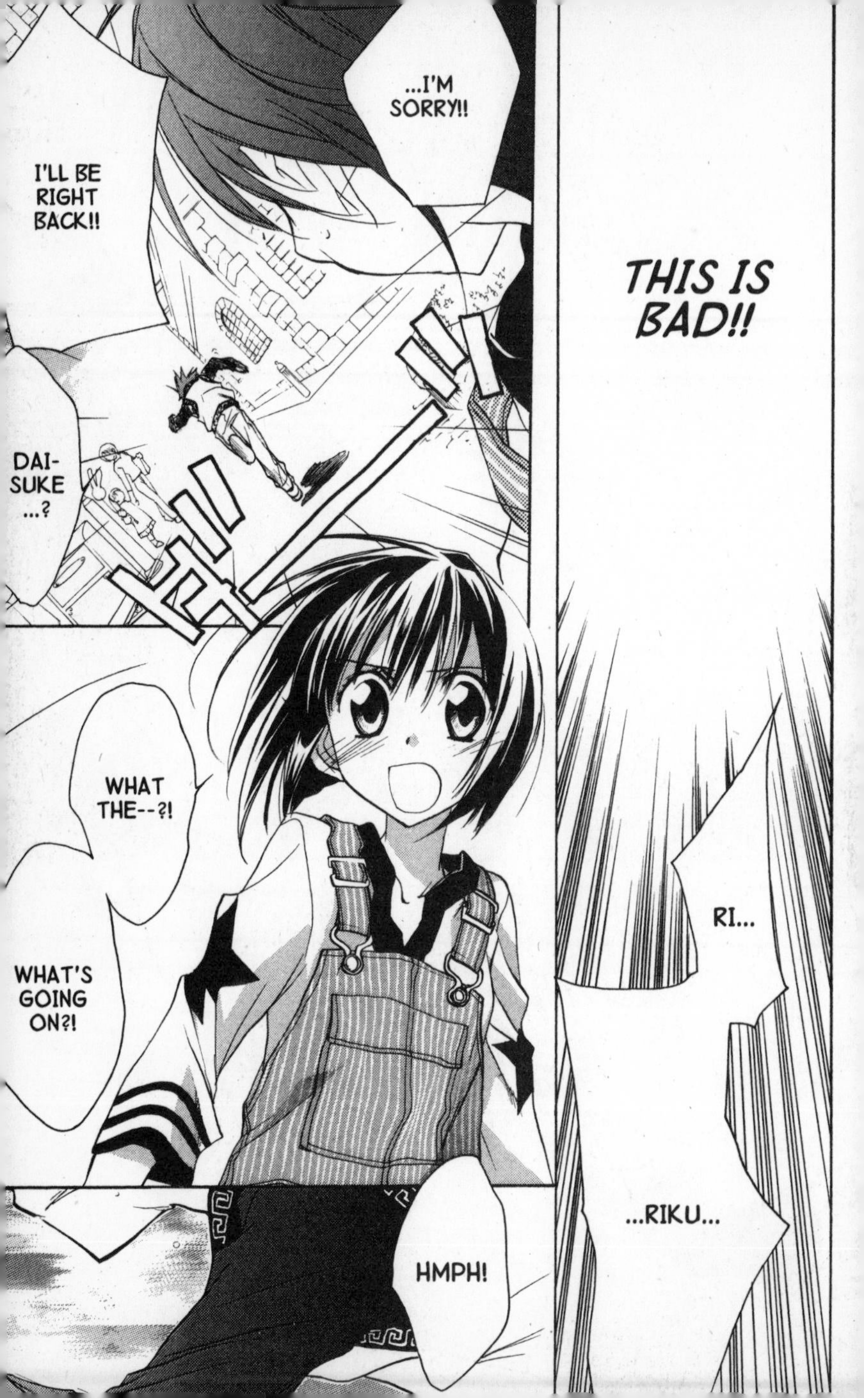
THIS IS BAD!!
RI...
...RIKU...
...I'M SORRY!!
I'LL BE RIGHT BACK!!
DAI-SUKE ...?
WHAT THE--?!
WHAT'S GOING ON?!
HMPH!

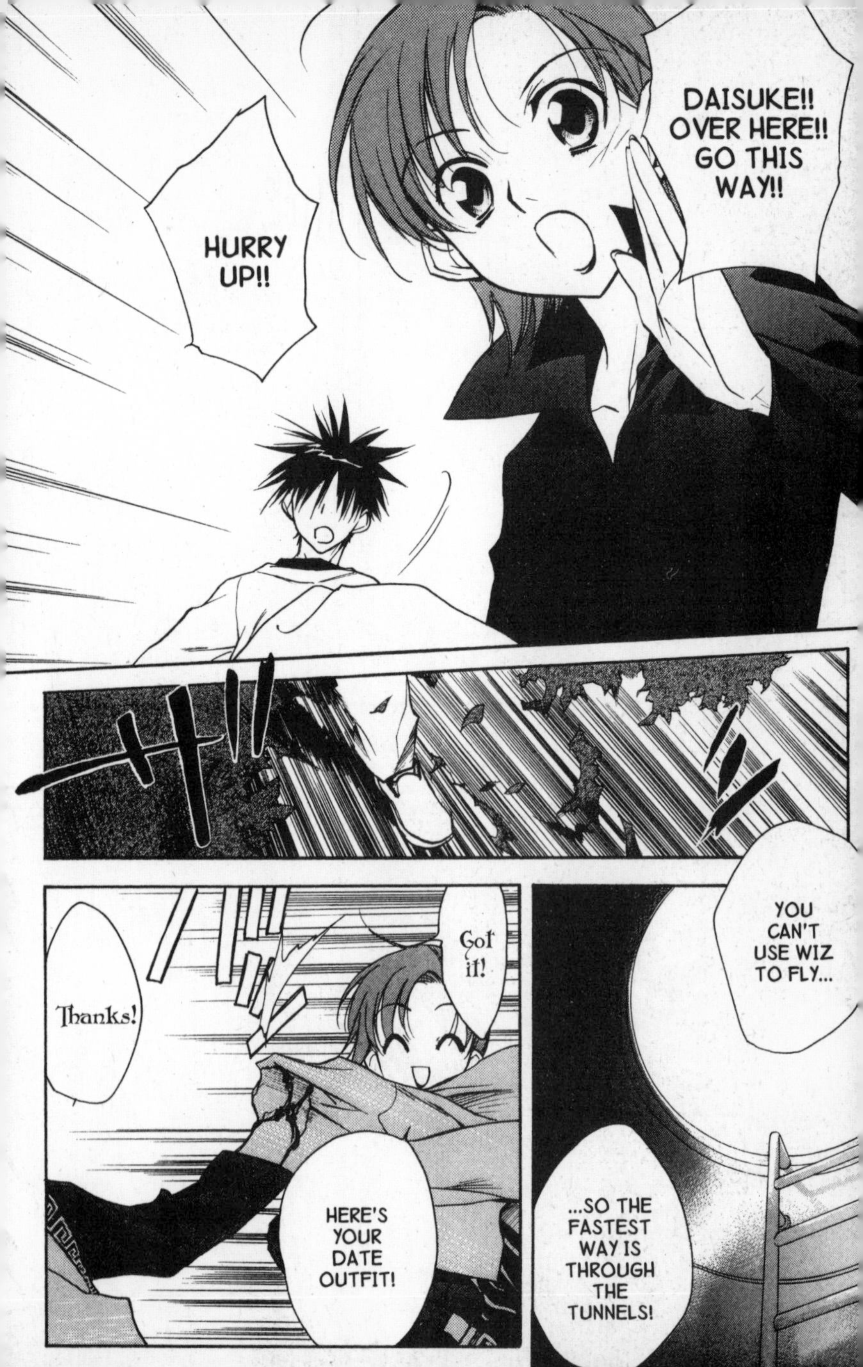
DAISUKE!! OVER HERE!! GO THIS WAY!!
HURRY UP!!
YOU CAN'T USE WIZ TO FLY...
...SO THE FASTEST WAY IS THROUGH THE TUNNELS!
Got it!
Thanks!
HERE'S YOUR DATE OUTFIT!

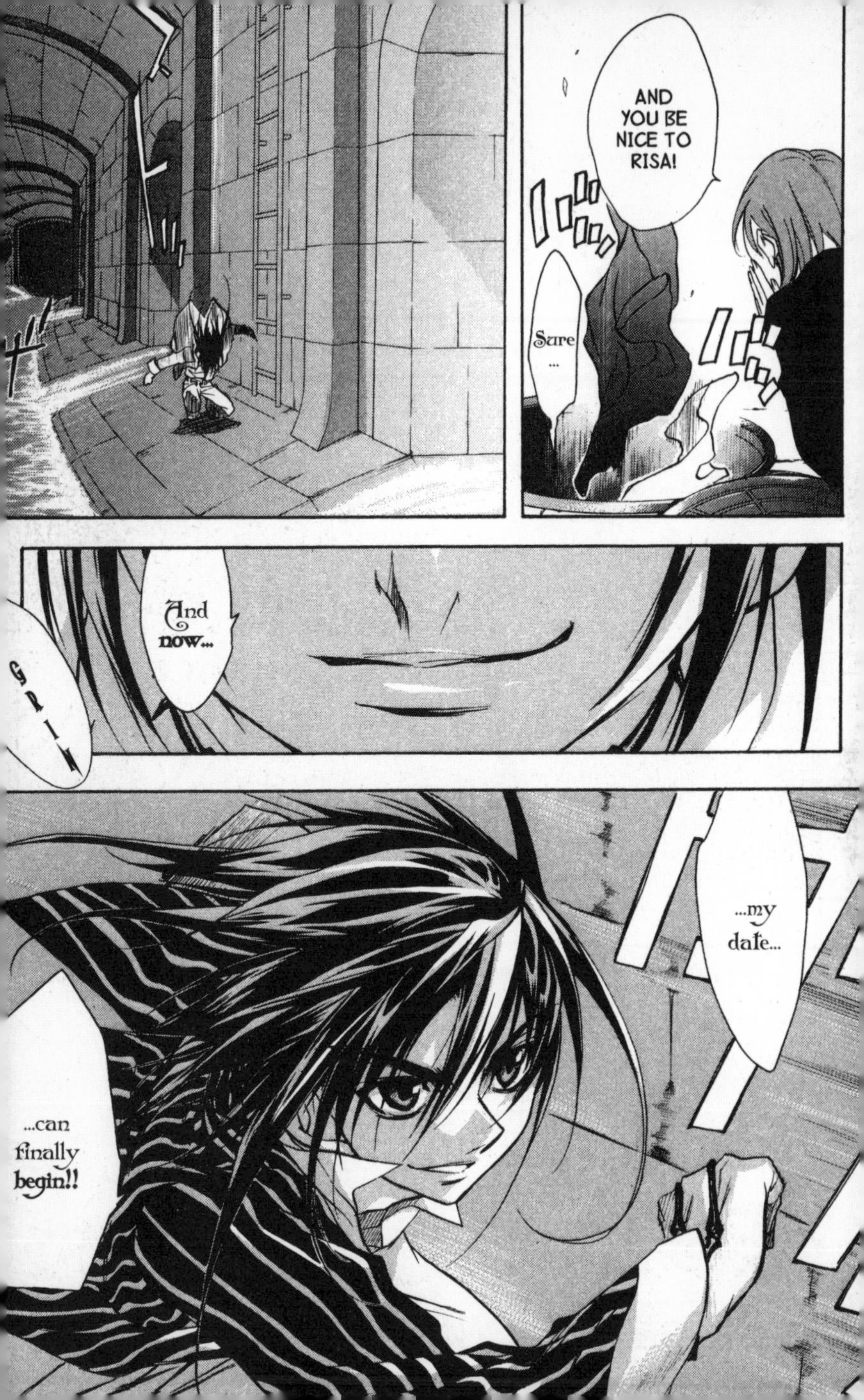
AND YOU BE NICE TO RISA!
Sure ...
And now...
GRIN
...my date...
...can finally begin!!

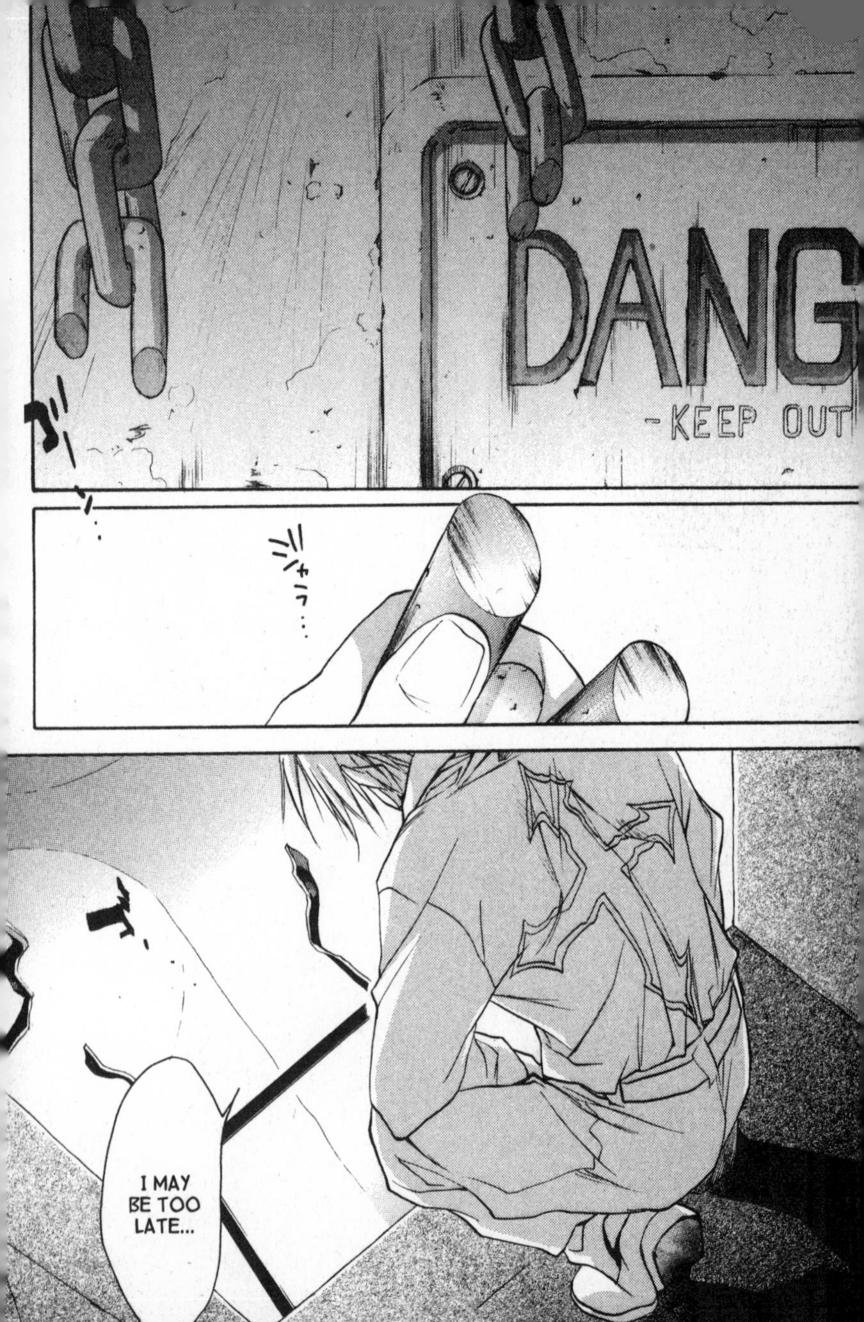
DANG
-KEEP OUT
ジャラ…
I MAY BE TOO LATE...
The End of Stage 3, Part 5

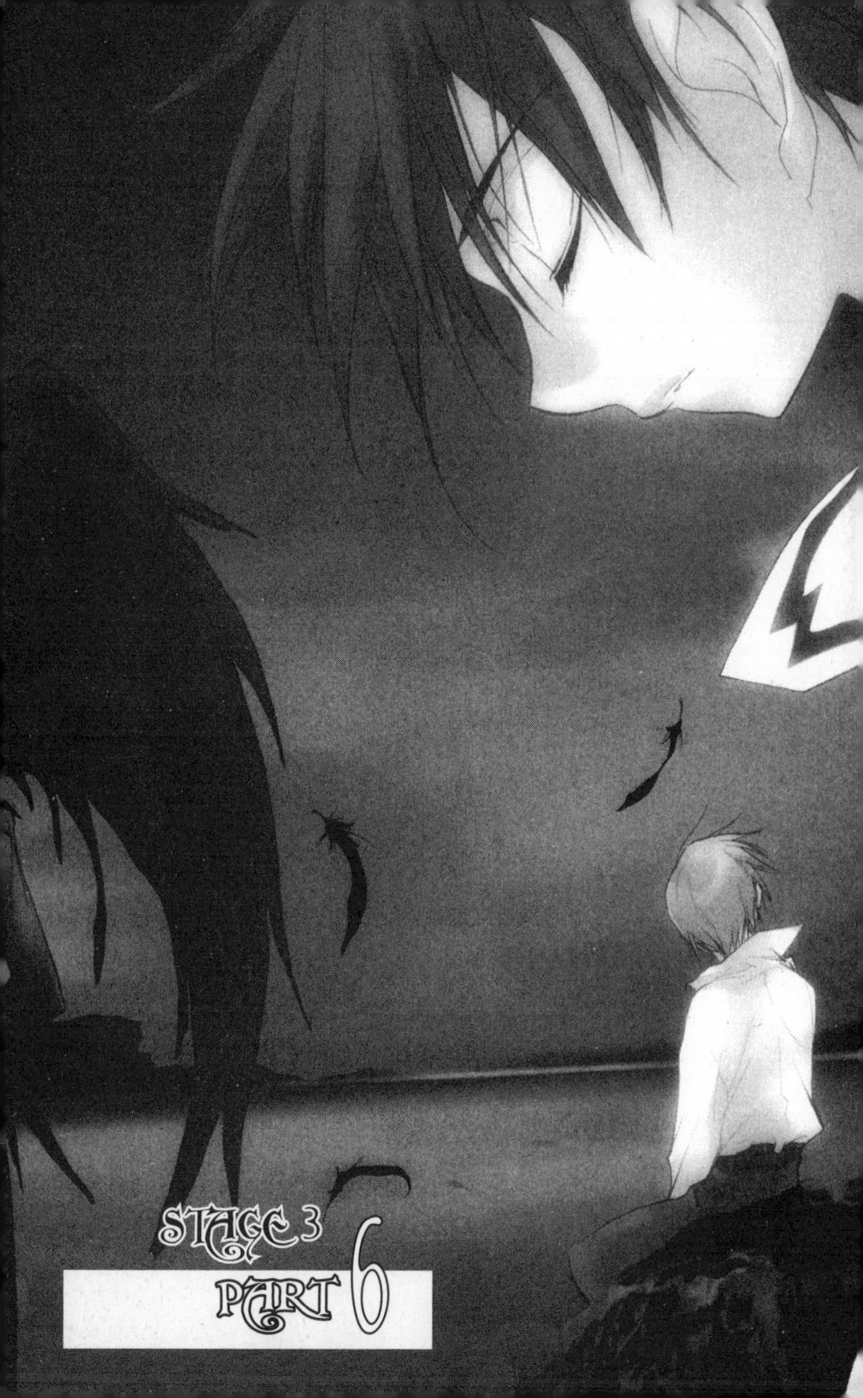
STAGE 3
PART 6

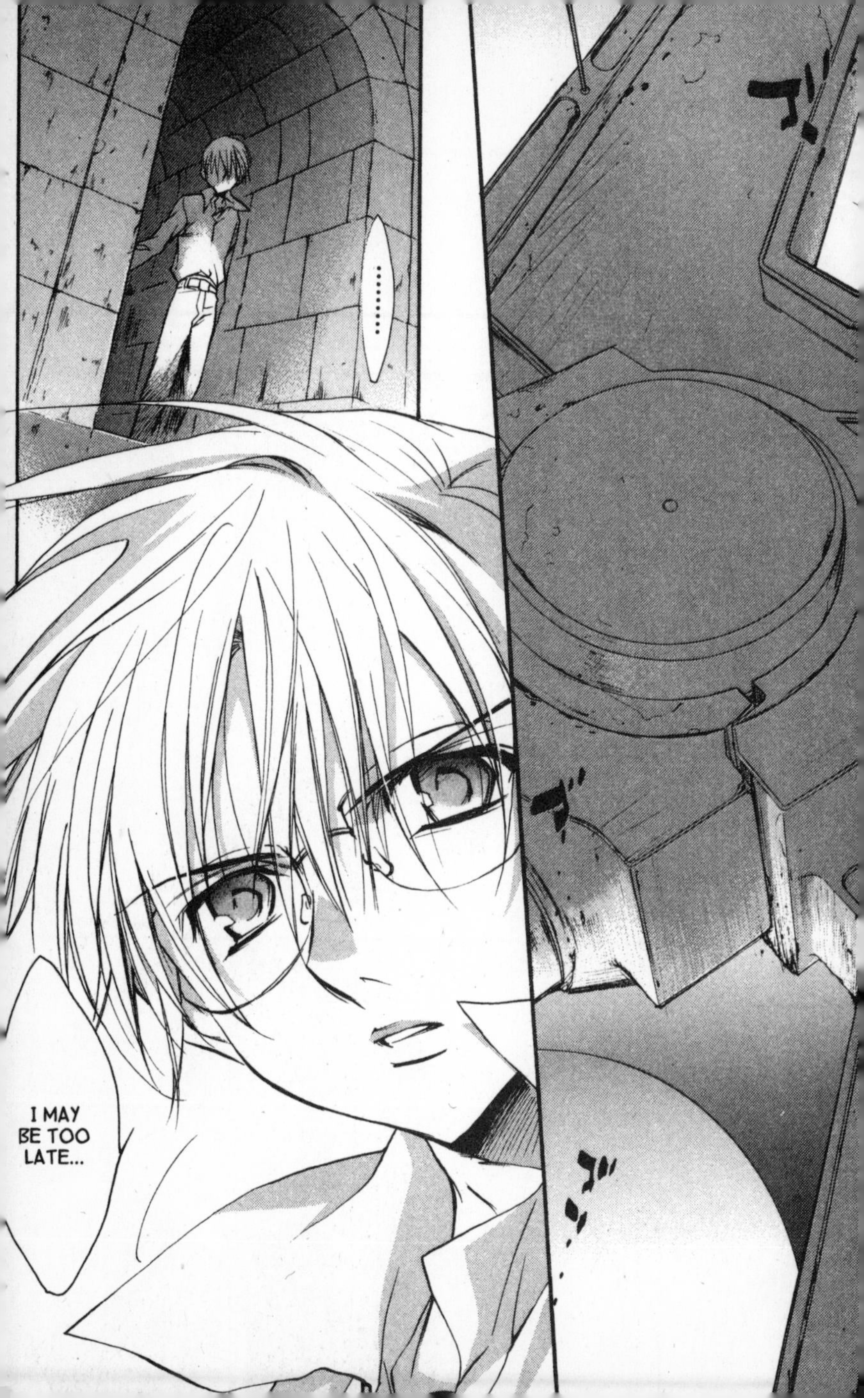
....
I MAY BE TOO LATE...

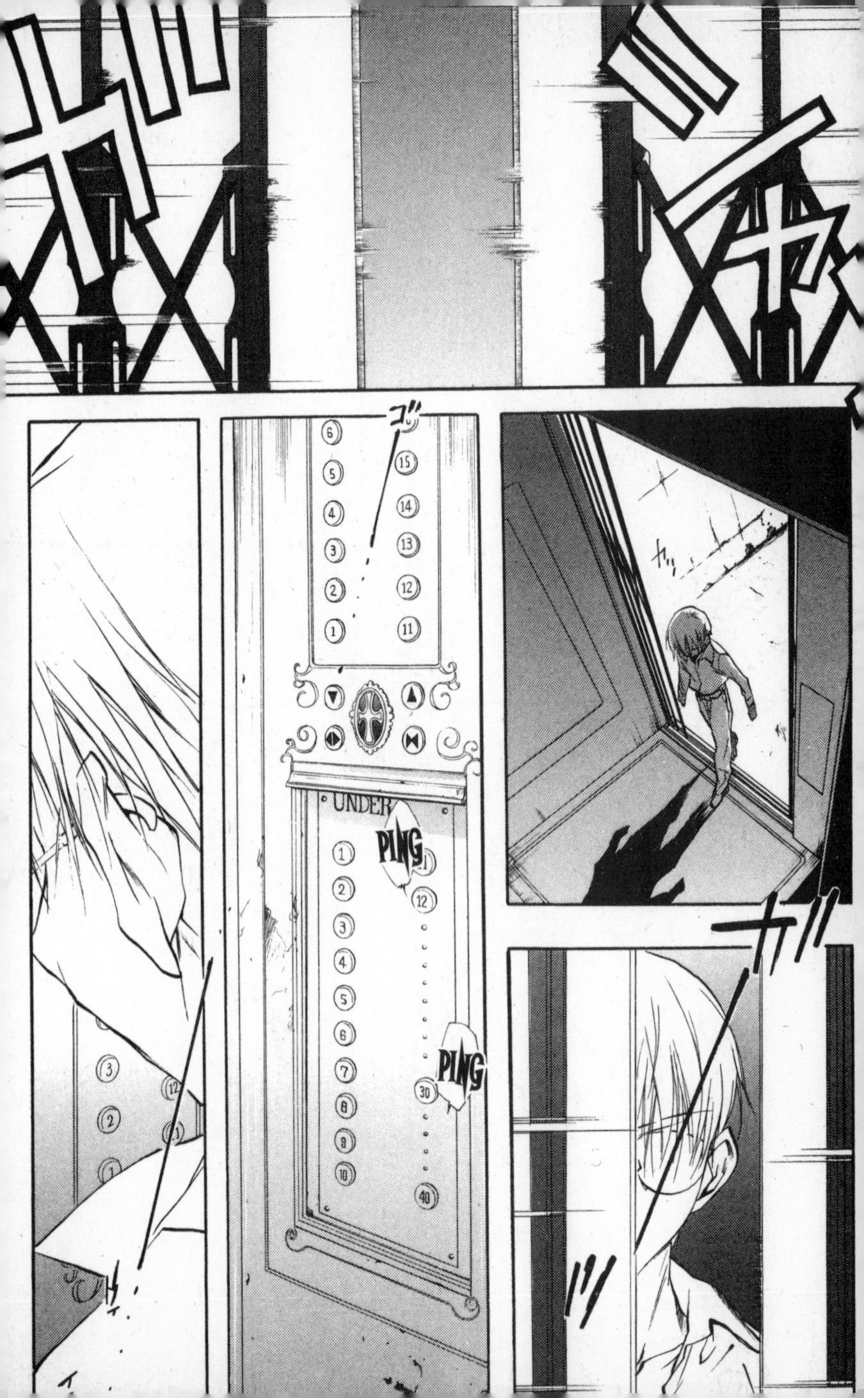
UNDER
PING
PING

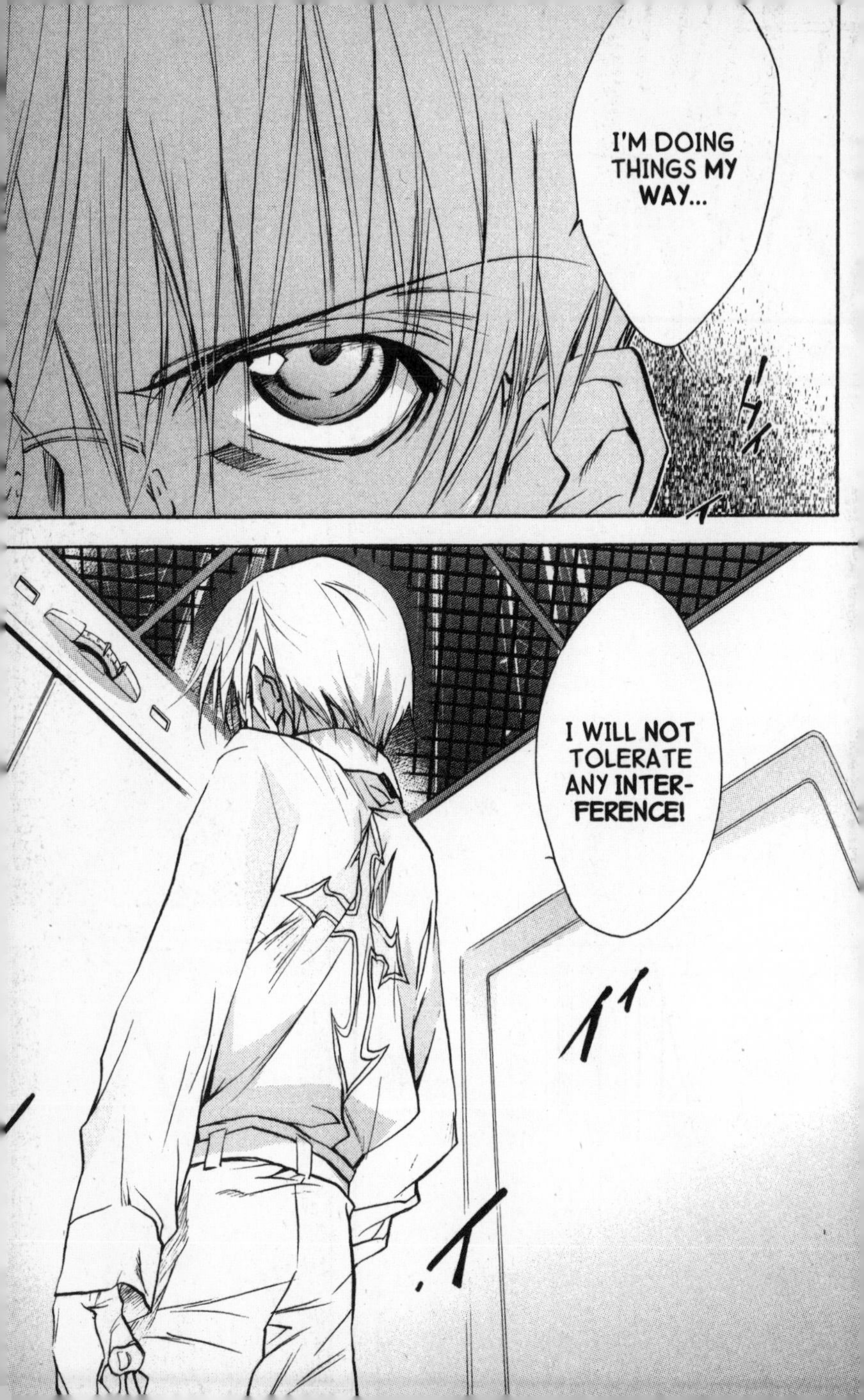
I'M DOING THINGS MY WAY...
I WILL NOT TOLERATE ANY INTER-FERENCE!

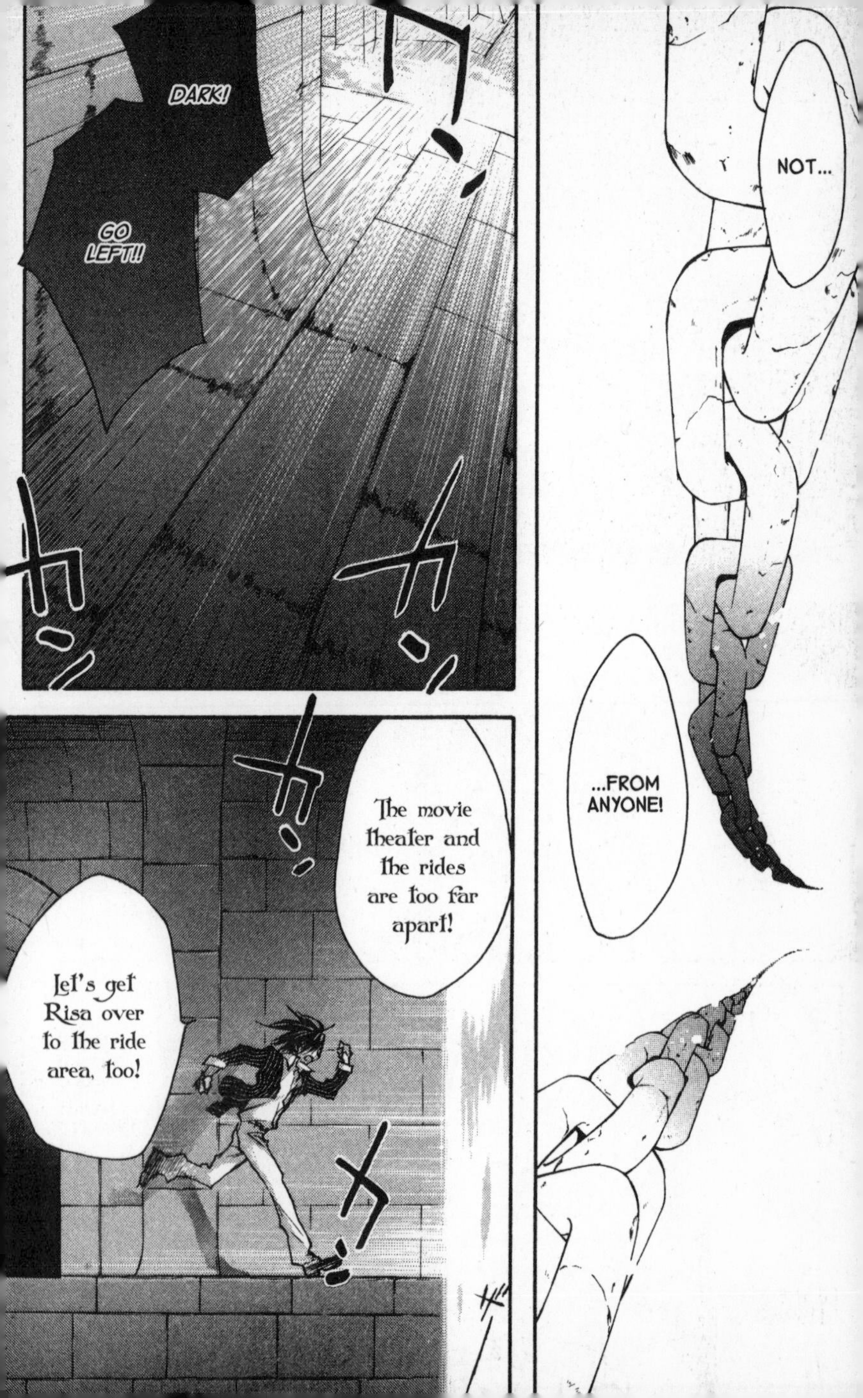
NOT...
...FROM ANYONE!
DARK!
GO LEFT!!
The movie theater and the rides are too far apart!
Let's get Risa over to the ride area, too!

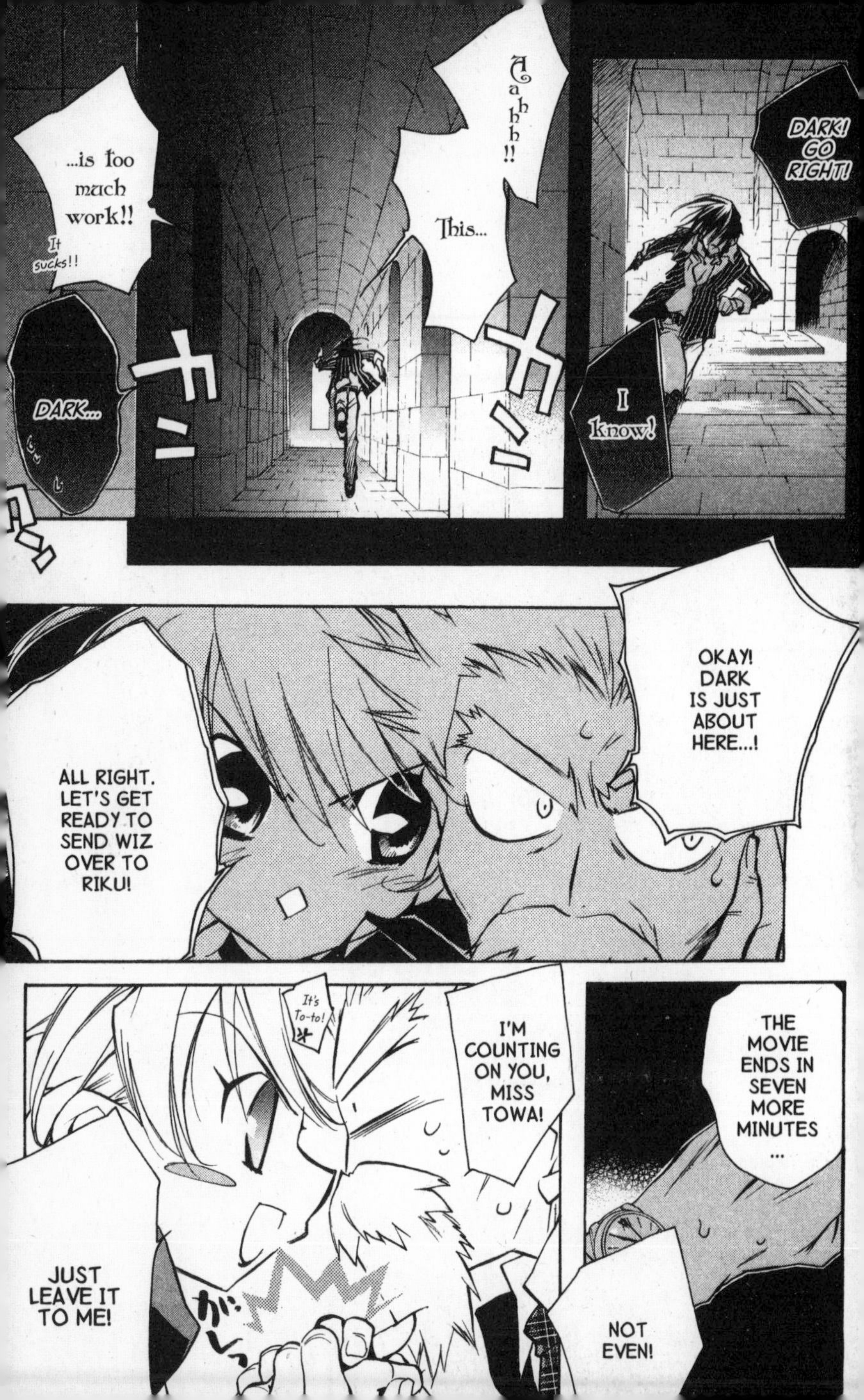
DARK! GO RIGHT!
I know!
Aahhh!!
This...
...is too much work!!
It sucks!!
DARK...
OKAY! DARK IS JUST ABOUT HERE...!
ALL RIGHT. LET'S GET READY TO SEND WIZ OVER TO RIKU!
THE MOVIE ENDS IN SEVEN MORE MINUTES ...
NOT EVEN!
I'M COUNTING ON YOU, MISS TOWA!
It's To-to!
JUST LEAVE IT TO ME!

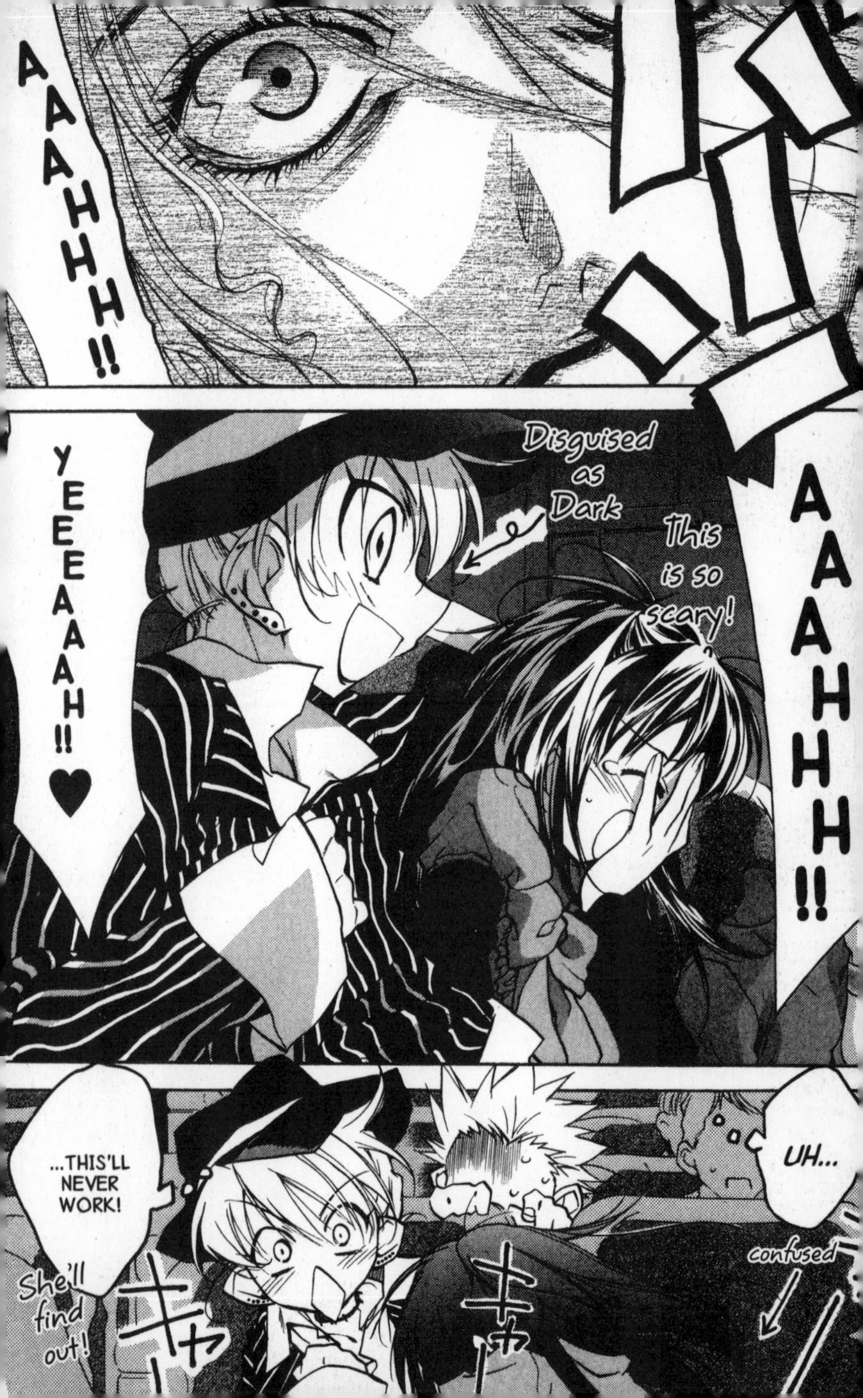
AAAHHH!!
AAAHHH!!
This is so scary!
Disguised as Dark
YEEEAAAH!! ♥
UH...
confused
...THIS'LL NEVER WORK!
She'll find out!

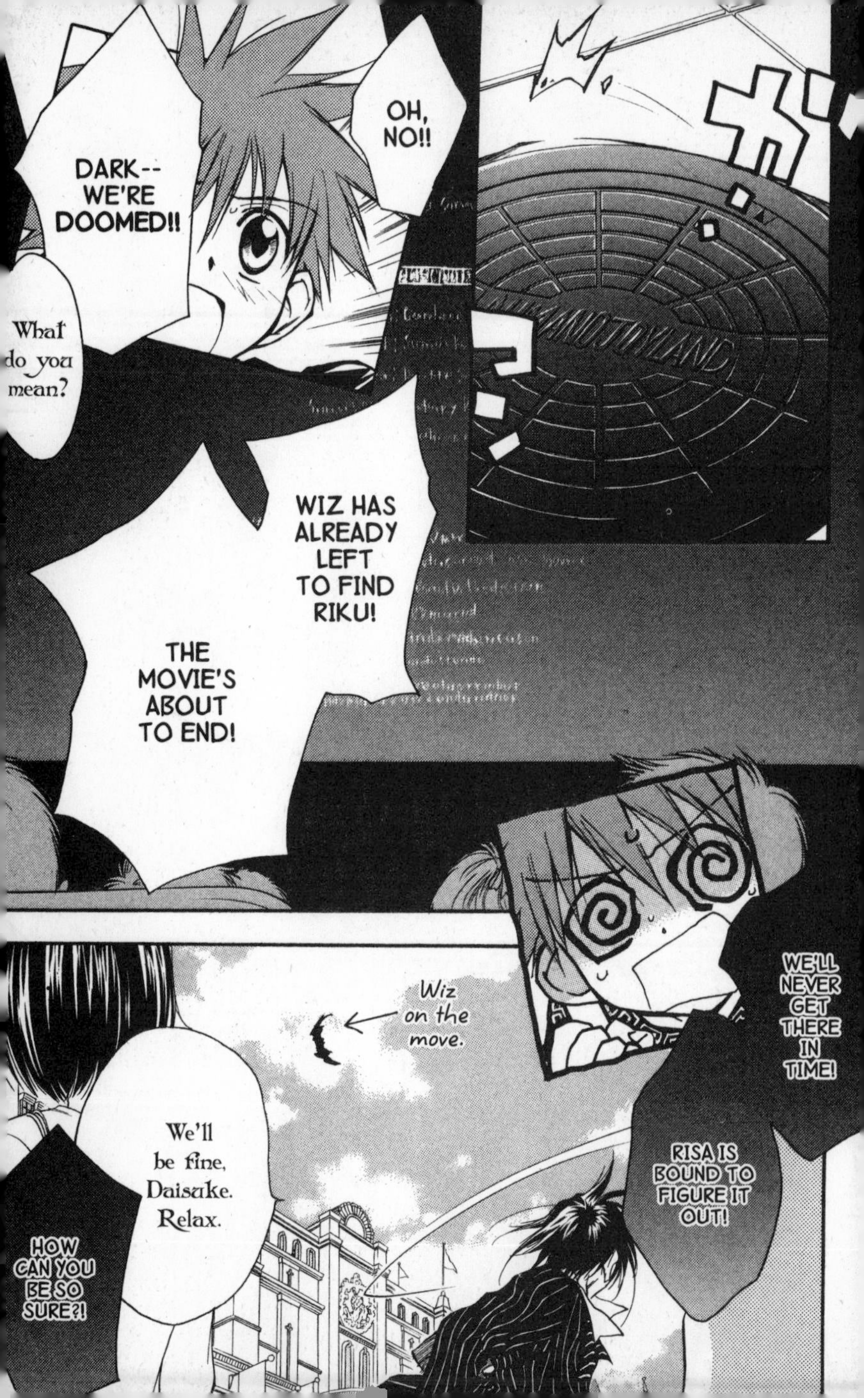
OH, NO!!
DARK-- WE'RE DOOMED!!
What do you mean?
WIZ HAS ALREADY LEFT TO FIND RIKU!
THE MOVIE'S ABOUT TO END!
WE'LL NEVER GET THERE IN TIME!
RISA IS BOUND TO FIGURE IT OUT!
Wiz on the move.
We'll be fine, Daisuke. Relax.
HOW CAN YOU BE SO SURE?!

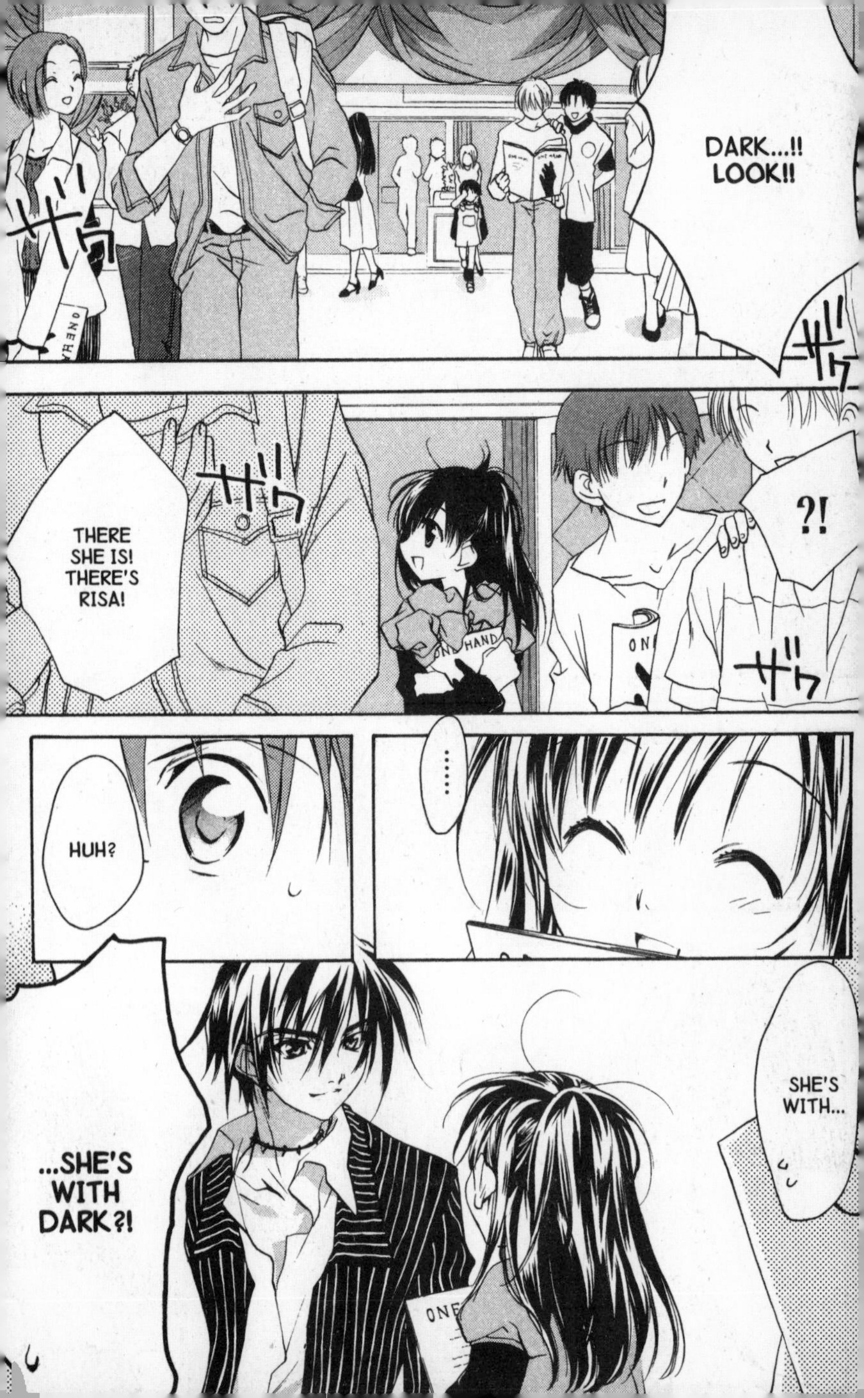
DARK...!! LOOK!!
ザワ
ザワ
?!
ザワ
ザワ
THERE SHE IS! THERE'S RISA!
......
HUH?
SHE'S WITH...
...SHE'S WITH DARK?!

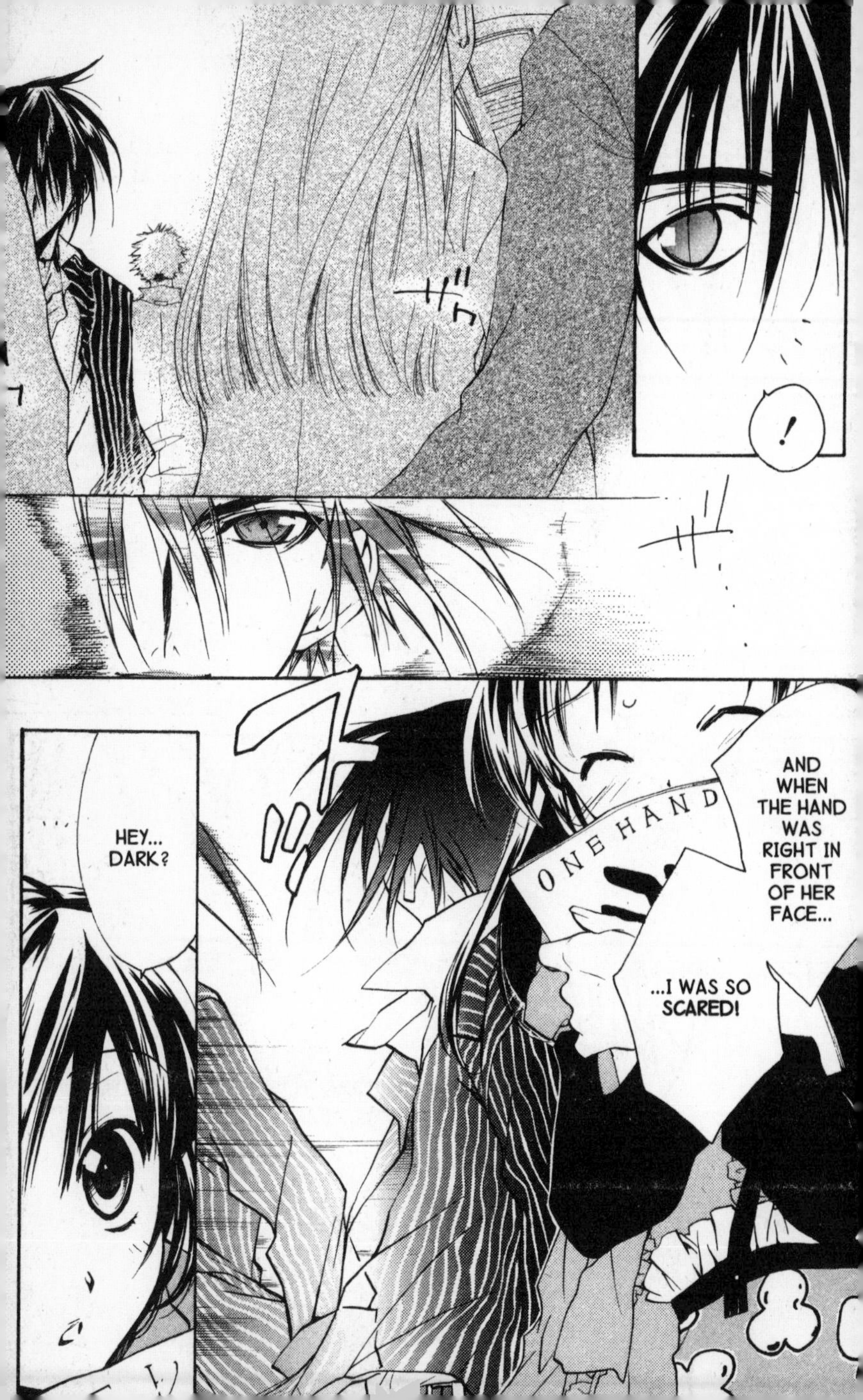
!
AND WHEN THE HAND WAS RIGHT IN FRONT OF HER FACE...
ONE HAND
...I WAS SO SCARED!
...
HEY... DARK?

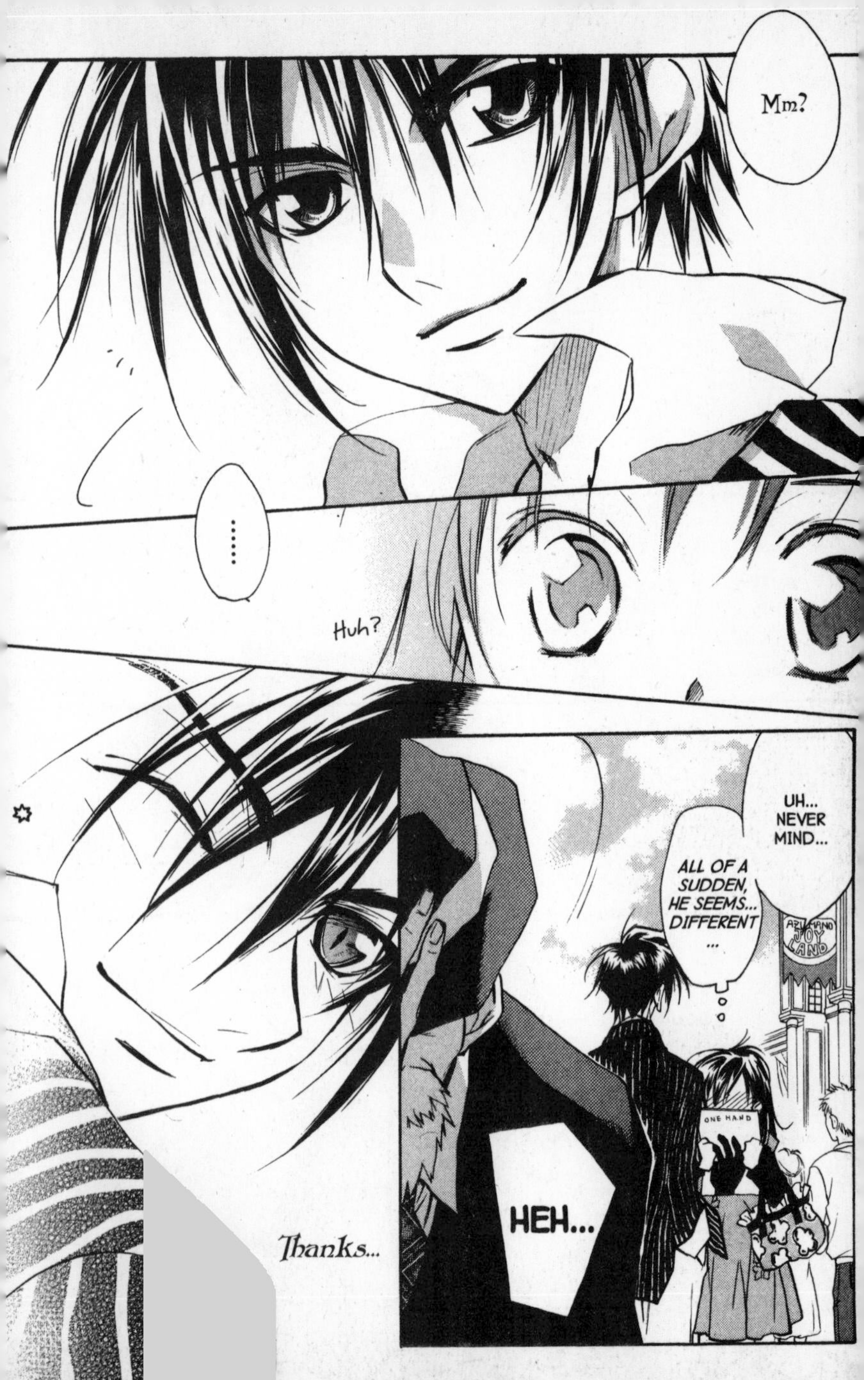
Mm?
......
Huh?
UH... NEVER MIND...
ALL OF A SUDDEN, HE SEEMS... DIFFERENT ...
ONE HAND
HEH...
Thanks...

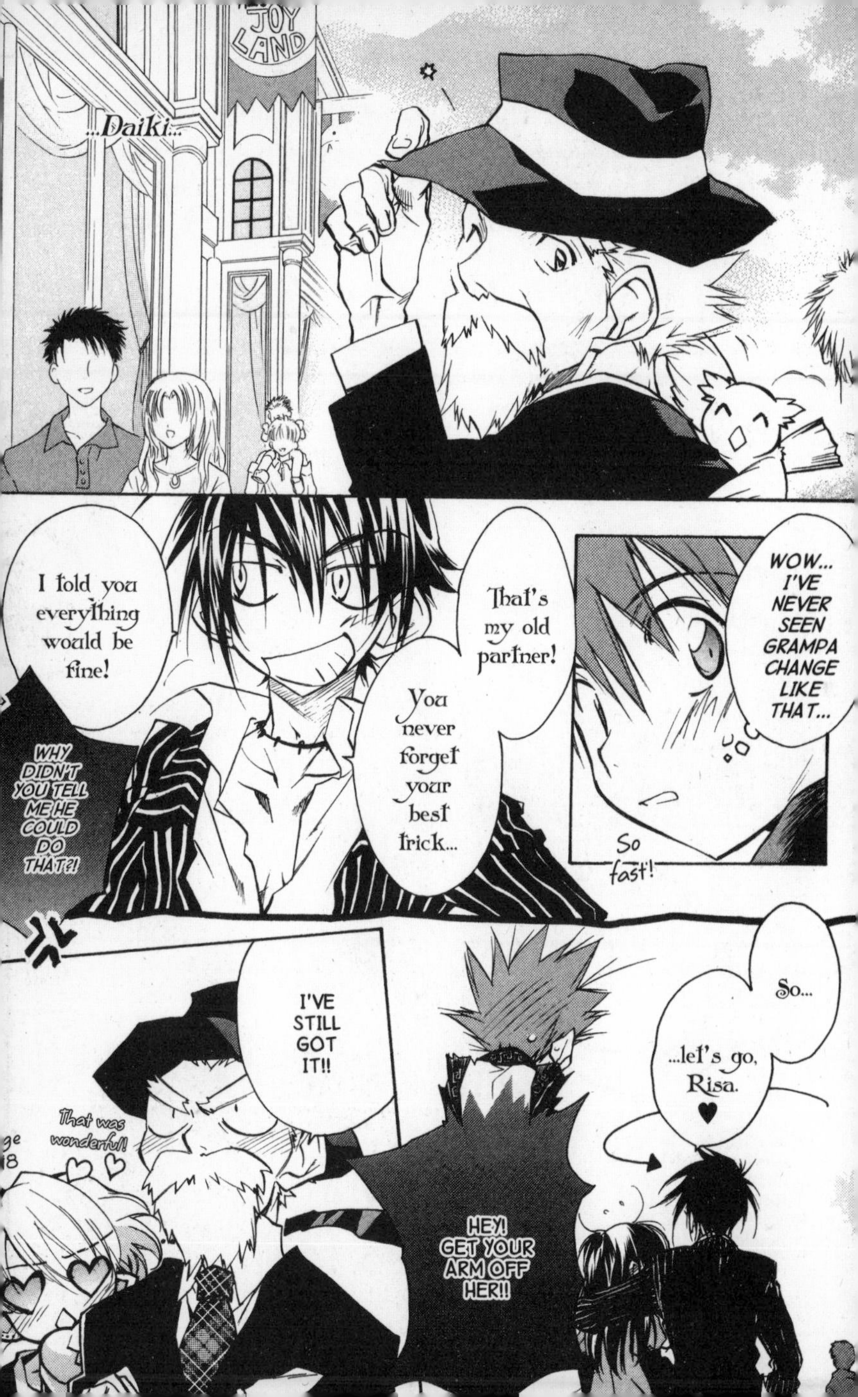
...Daiki...
JOY LAND
WOW... I'VE NEVER SEEN GRAMPA CHANGE LIKE THAT...
So fast!
That's my old partner!
You never forget your best trick...
I told you everything would be fine!
WHY DIDN'T YOU TELL ME HE COULD DO THAT?!
So...
...let's go, Risa. ♥
HEY! GET YOUR ARM OFF HER!!
I'VE STILL GOT IT!!
That was wonderful!

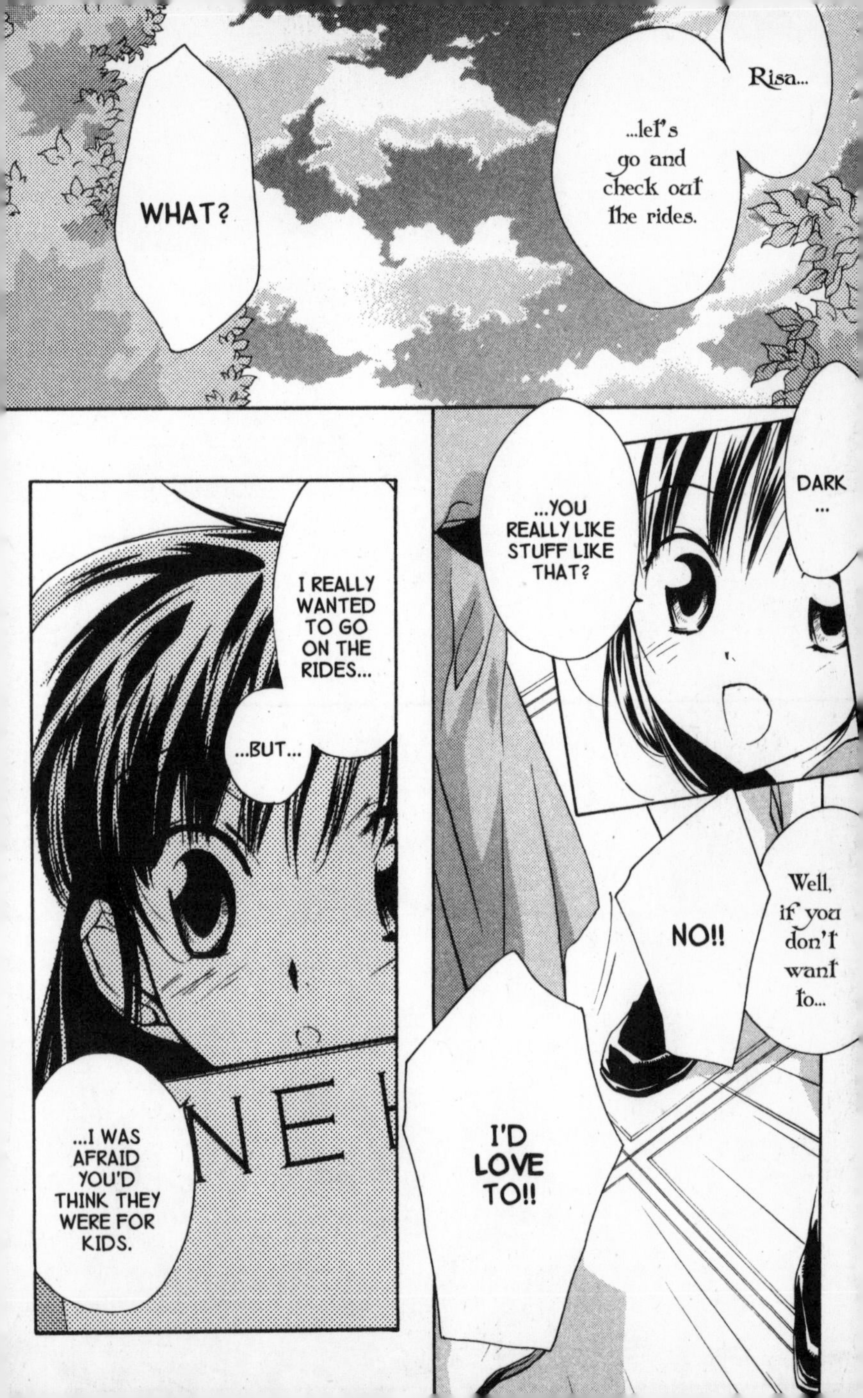
Risa...
...let's go and check out the rides.
WHAT?
DARK ...
...YOU REALLY LIKE STUFF LIKE THAT?
Well, if you don't want to...
NO!!
I'D LOVE TO!!
I REALLY WANTED TO GO ON THE RIDES...
...BUT...
...I WAS AFRAID YOU'D THINK THEY WERE FOR KIDS.

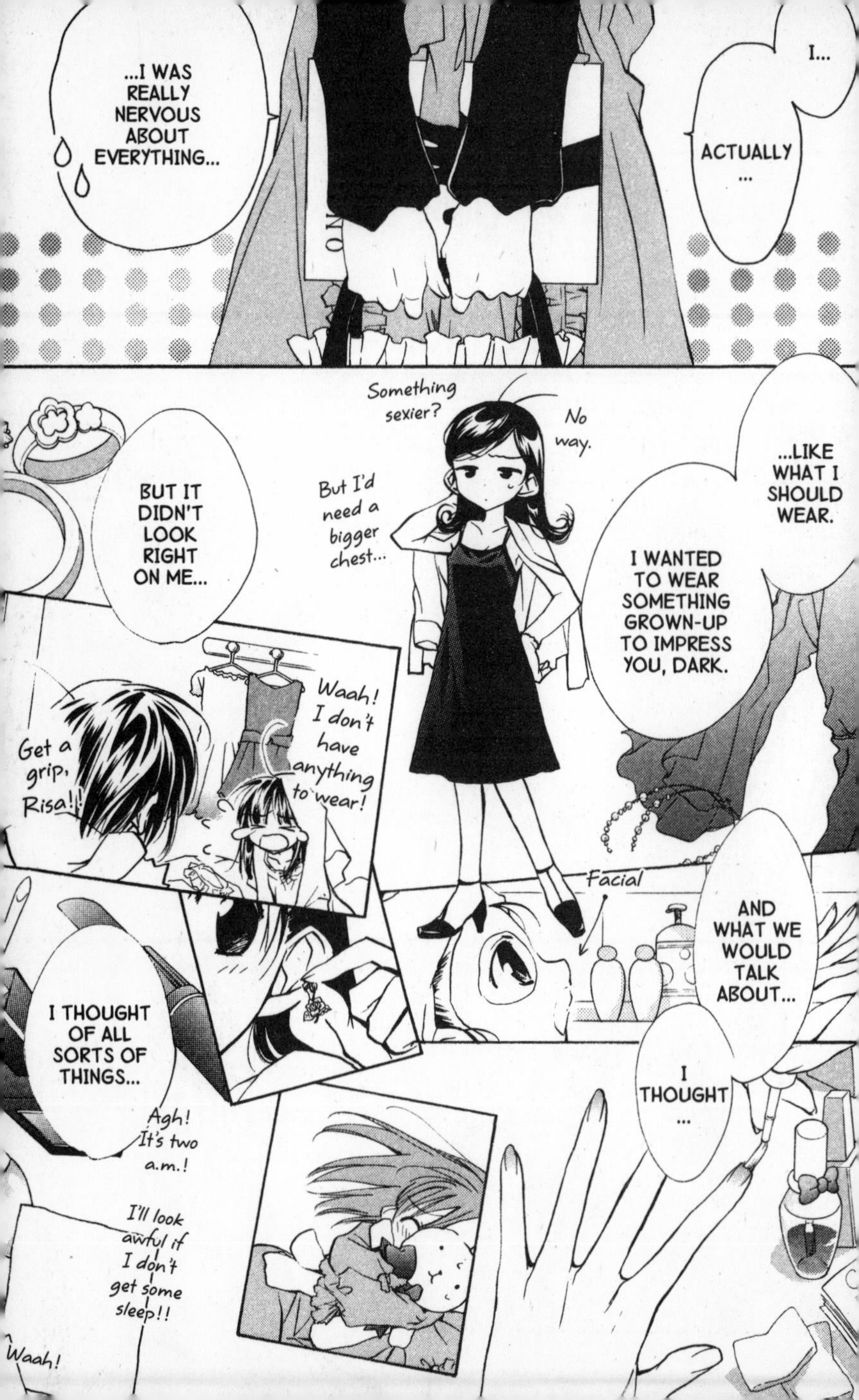
I...
ACTUALLY...
...I WAS REALLY NERVOUS ABOUT EVERYTHING...
...LIKE WHAT I SHOULD WEAR.
I WANTED TO WEAR SOMETHING GROWN-UP TO IMPRESS YOU, DARK.
Something sexier?
No way.
But I'd need a bigger chest...
BUT IT DIDN'T LOOK RIGHT ON ME...
Waah! I don't have anything to wear!
Get a grip, Risa!!
AND WHAT WE WOULD TALK ABOUT...
Facial
I THOUGHT...
I THOUGHT OF ALL SORTS OF THINGS...
Agh! It's two a.m.!
I'll look awful if I don't get some sleep!!
Waah!

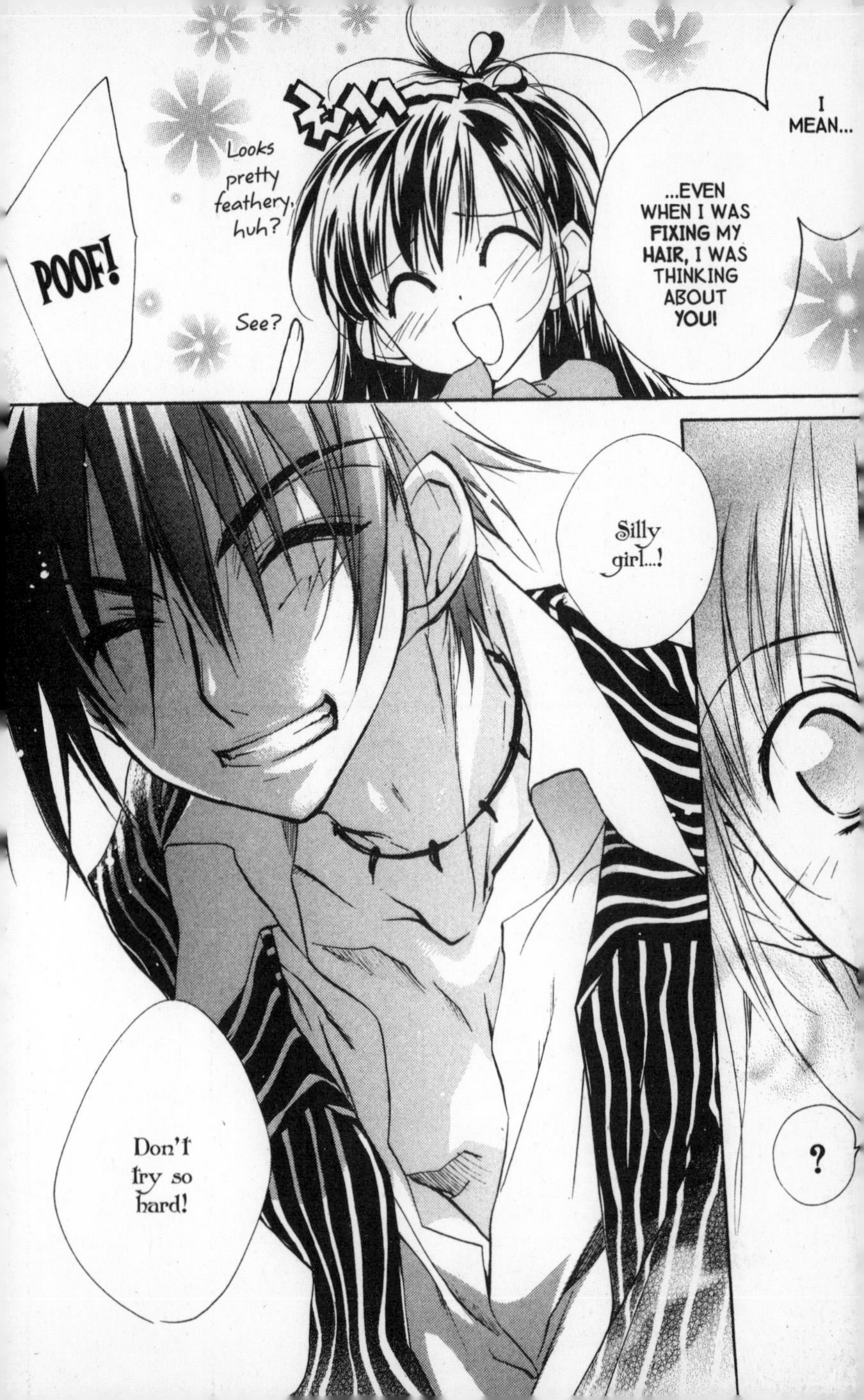
I MEAN...
...EVEN WHEN I WAS FIXING MY HAIR, I WAS THINKING ABOUT YOU!
Looks pretty feathery, huh?
See?
POOF!
?
Silly girl...!
Don't try so hard!

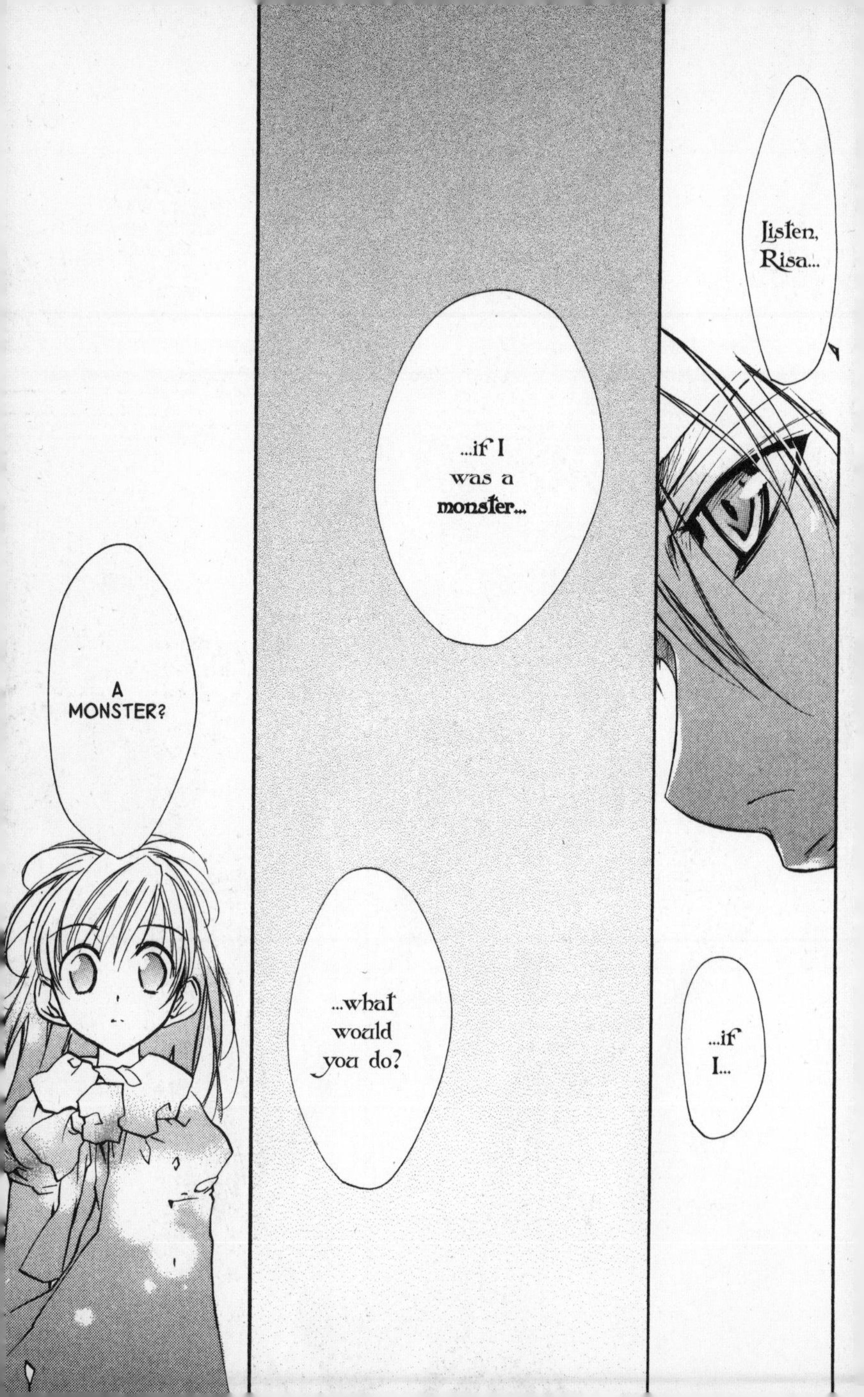
Listen, Risa...
...if I...
...if I was a monster...
...what would you do?
A MONSTER?

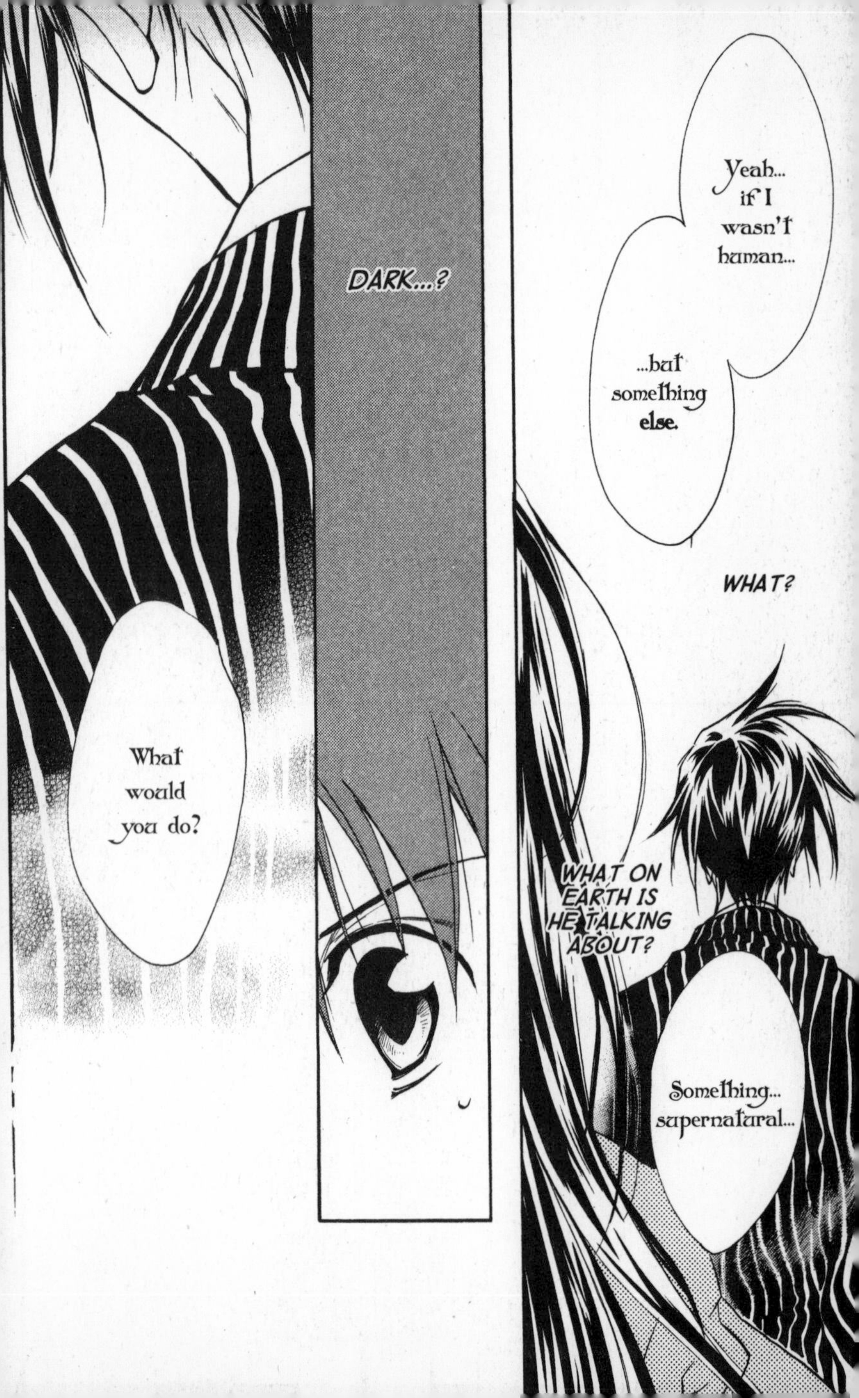
Yeah... if I wasn't human...
...but something else.
WHAT?
WHAT ON EARTH IS HE TALKING ABOUT?
Something... supernatural...
DARK...?
What would you do?

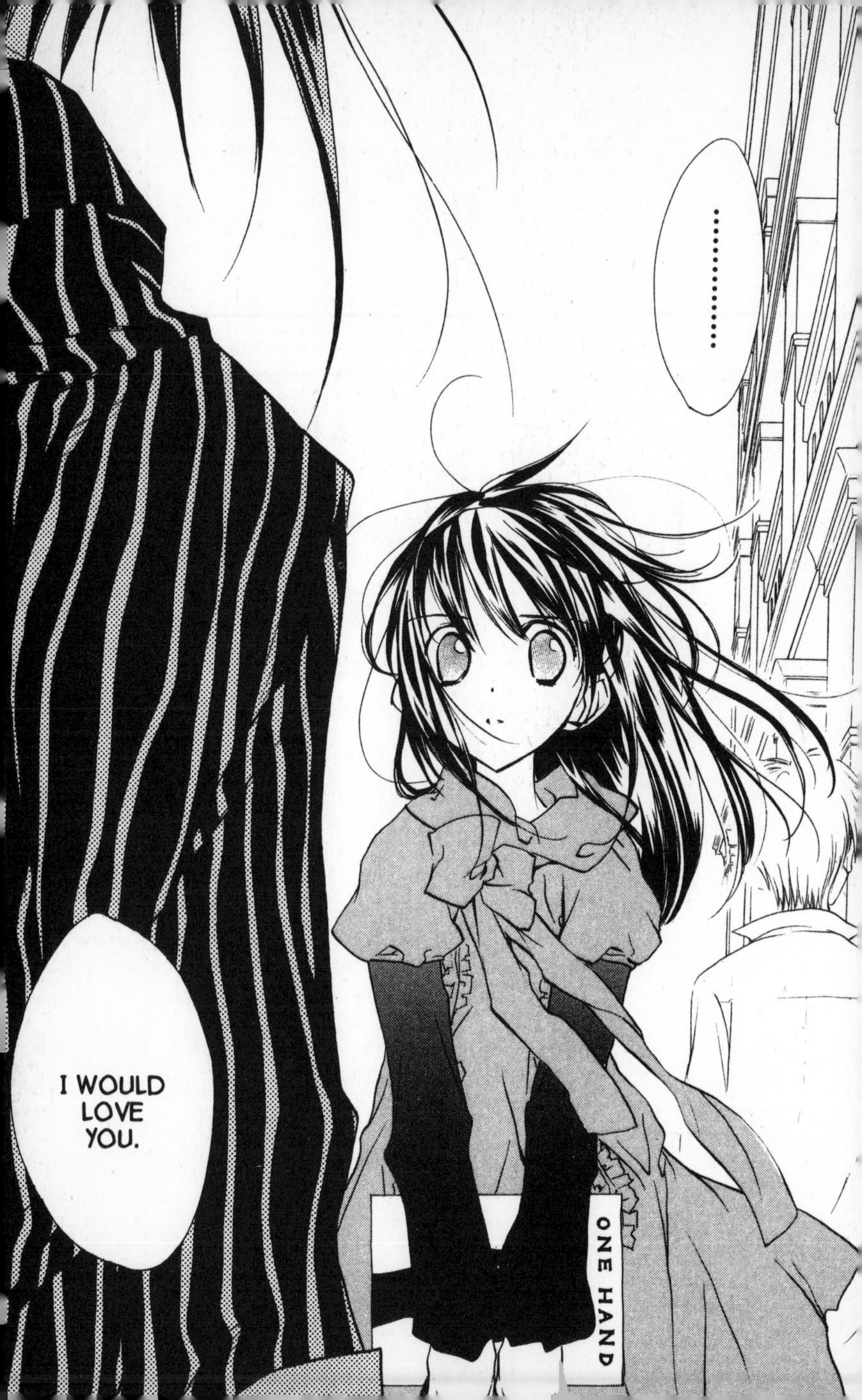
......
I WOULD LOVE YOU.
ONE HAND

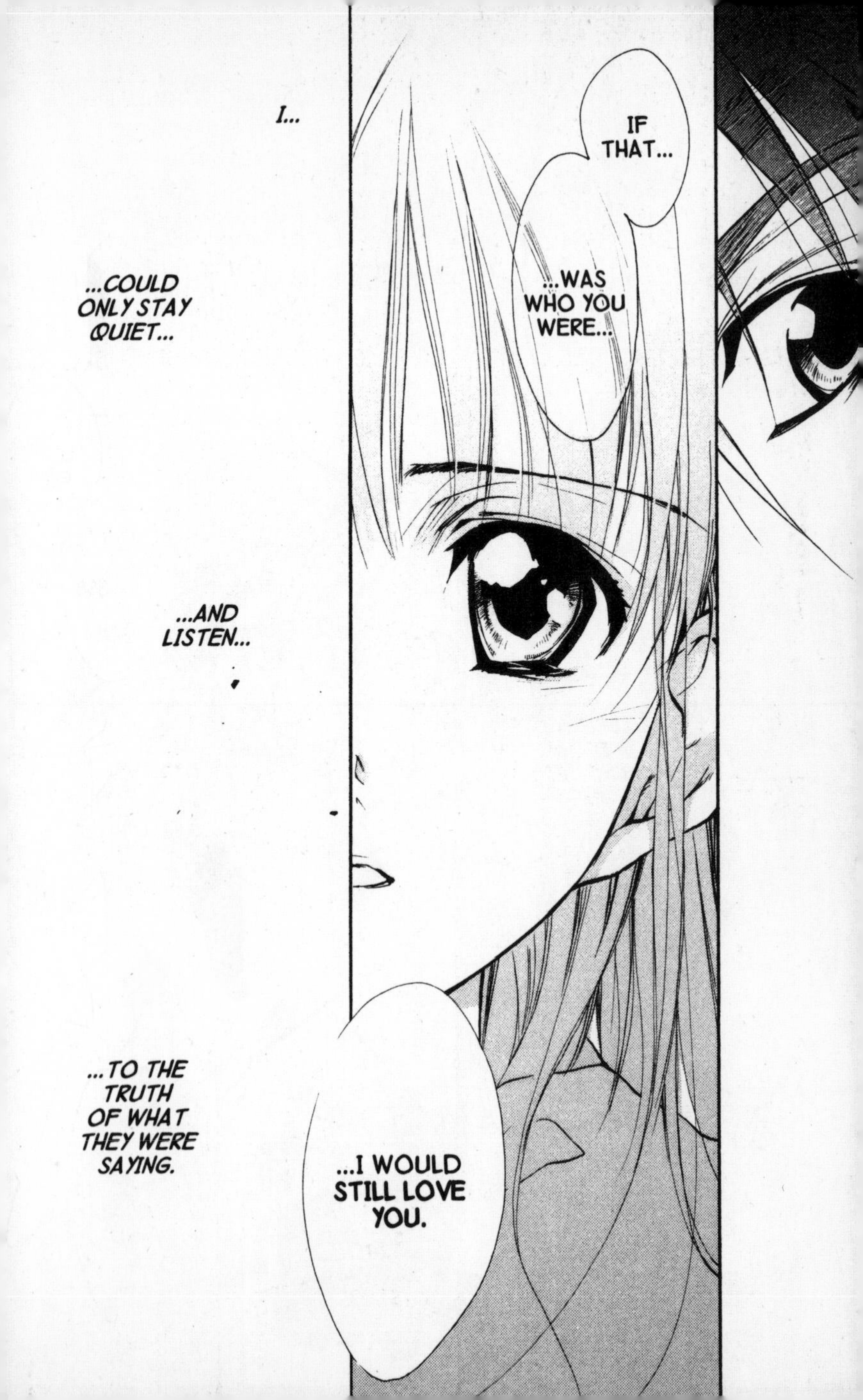
IF THAT...
...WAS WHO YOU WERE...
...I WOULD STILL LOVE YOU.
I...
...COULD ONLY STAY QUIET...
...AND LISTEN...
...TO THE TRUTH OF WHAT THEY WERE SAYING.

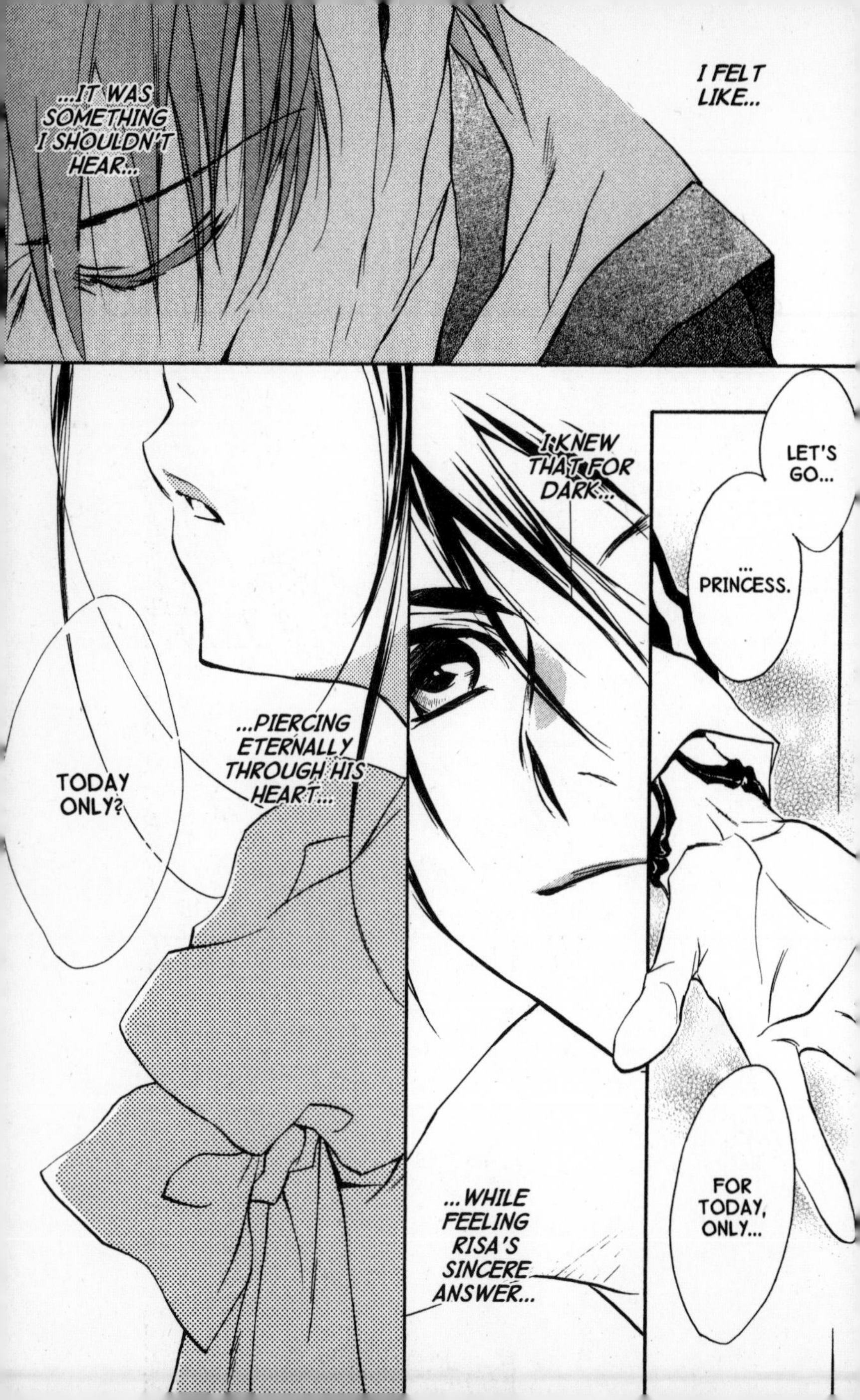
I FELT LIKE...
...IT WAS SOMETHING I SHOULDN'T HEAR...
LET'S GO...
...PRINCESS.
FOR TODAY, ONLY...
I KNEW THAT FOR DARK...
...WHILE FEELING RISA'S SINCERE ANSWER...
...PIERCING ETERNALLY THROUGH HIS HEART...
TODAY ONLY?

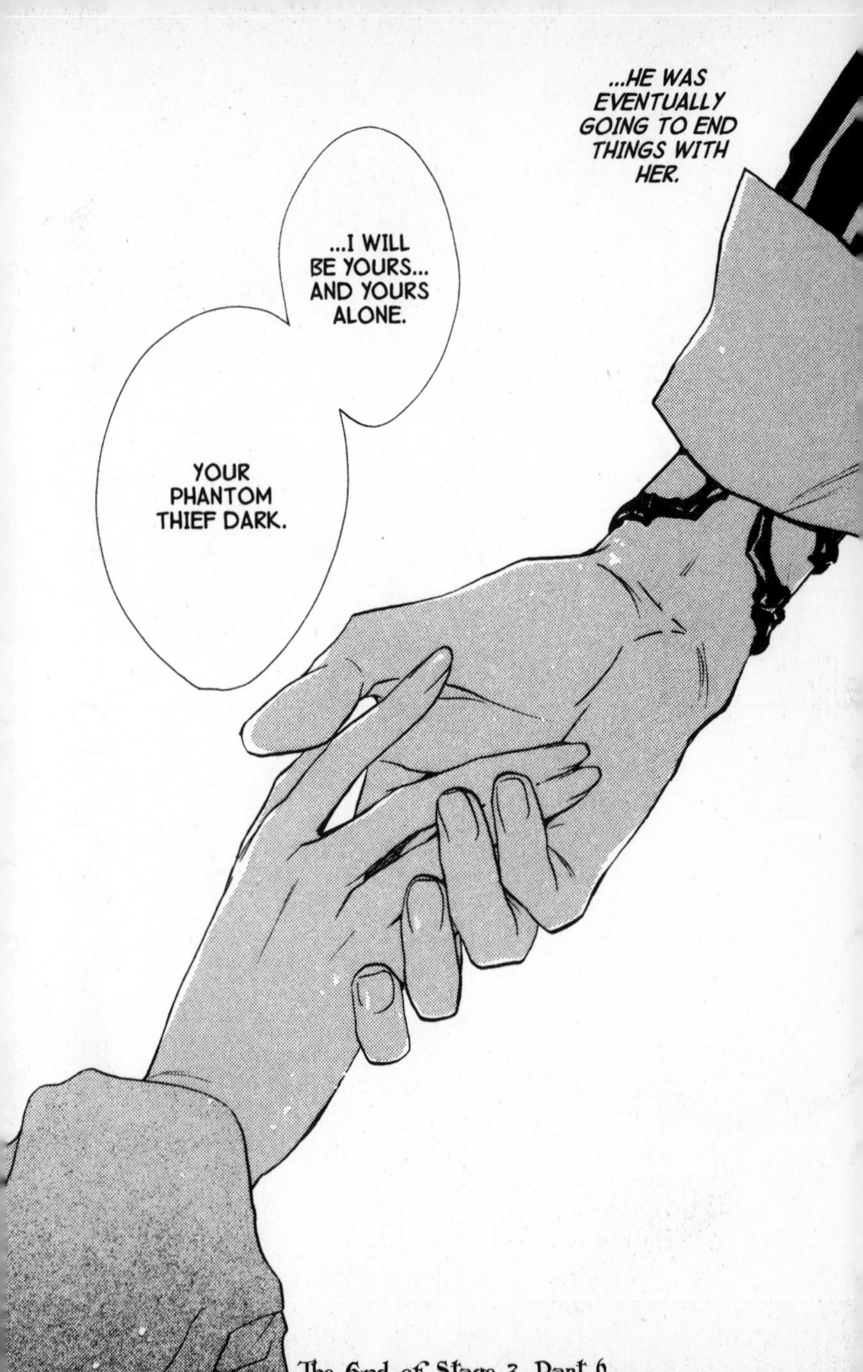
...HE WAS EVENTUALLY GOING TO END THINGS WITH HER.
...I WILL BE YOURS... AND YOURS ALONE.
YOUR PHANTOM THIEF DARK.

The End of Stage 3, Part 6

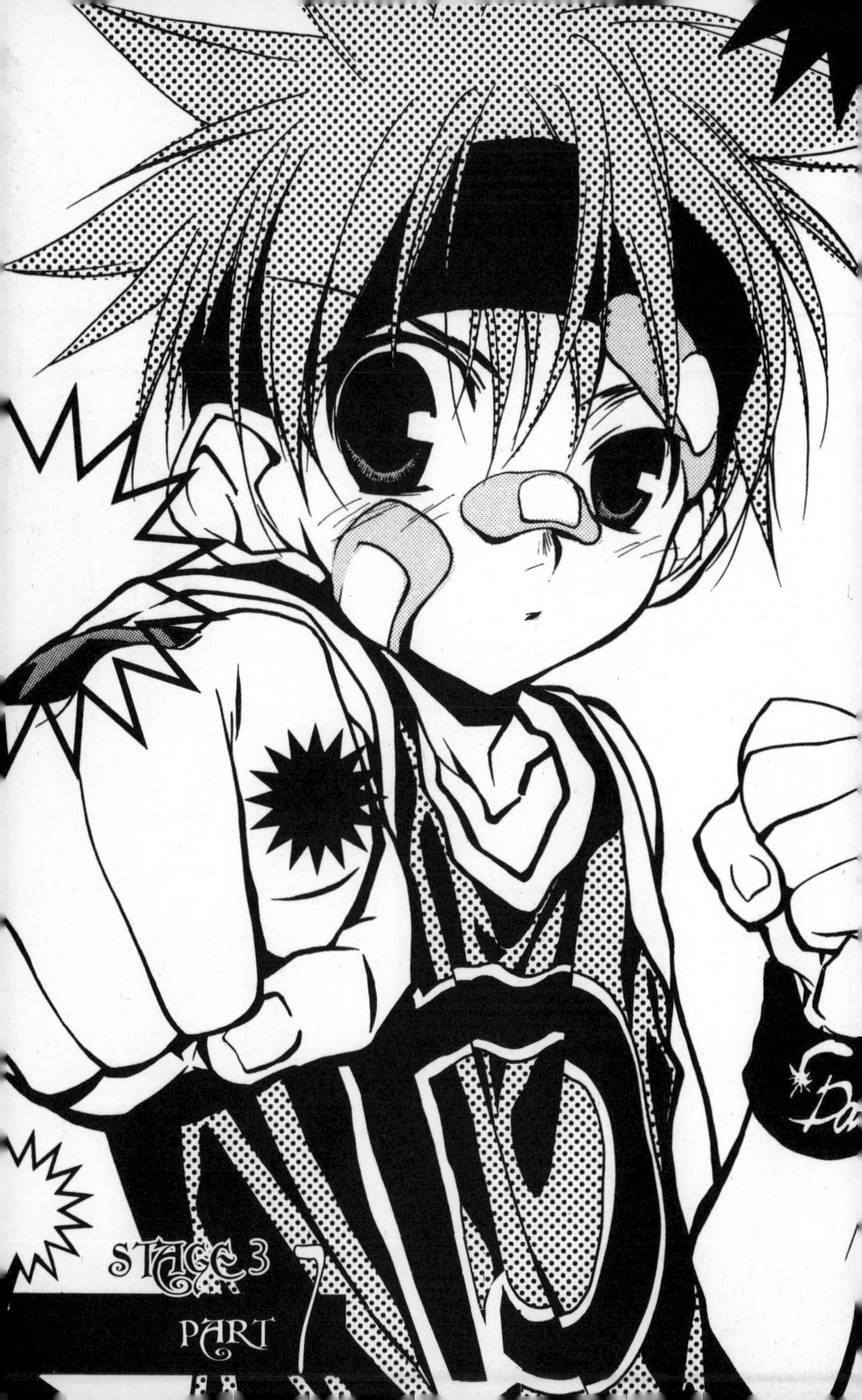
STAGE 3
PART 7

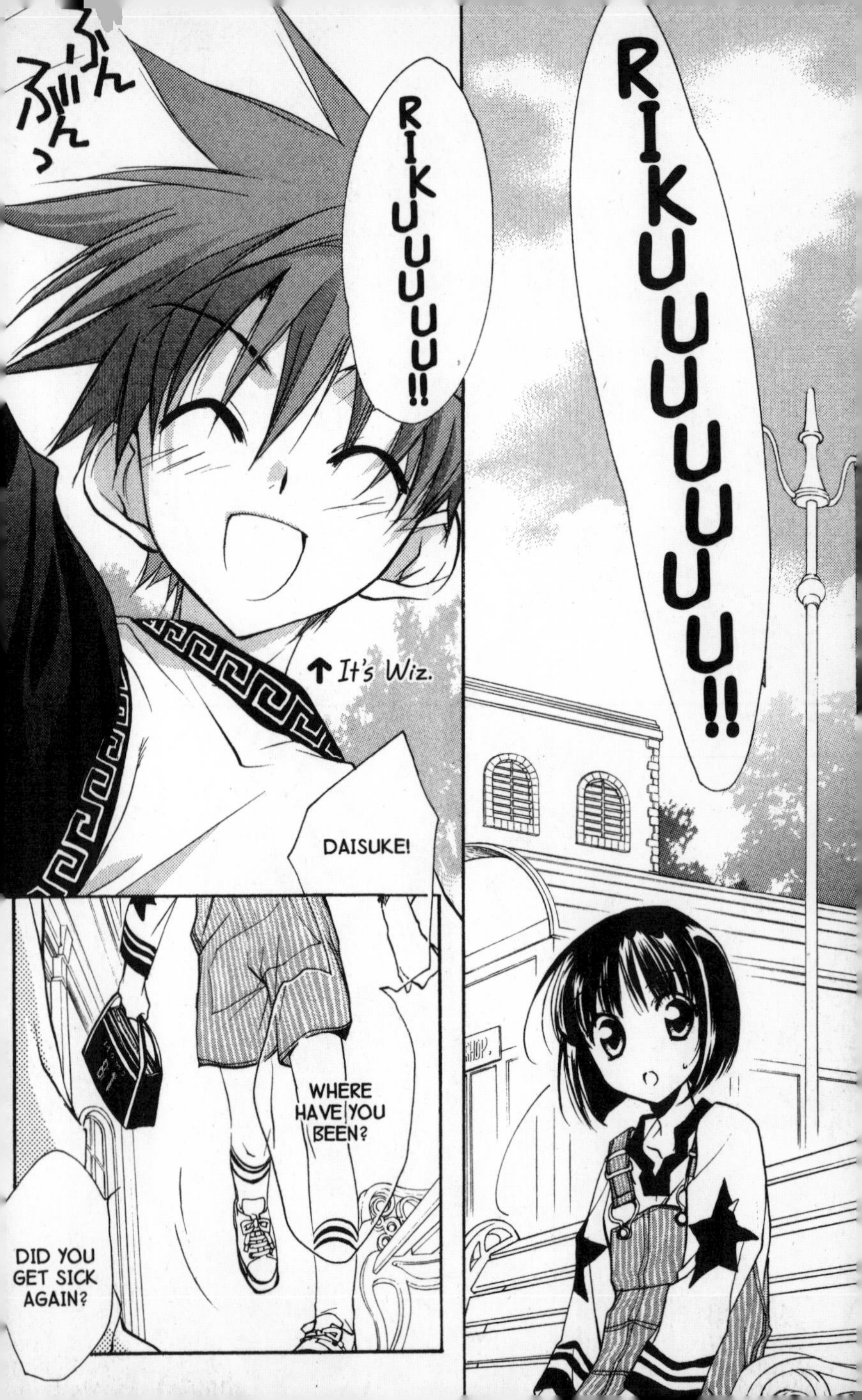
RIKUUUUUUU!!
RIKUUUUU!!
ぶんぶんっ
↑ It's Wiz.
DAISUKE!
WHERE HAVE YOU BEEN?
DID YOU GET SICK AGAIN?

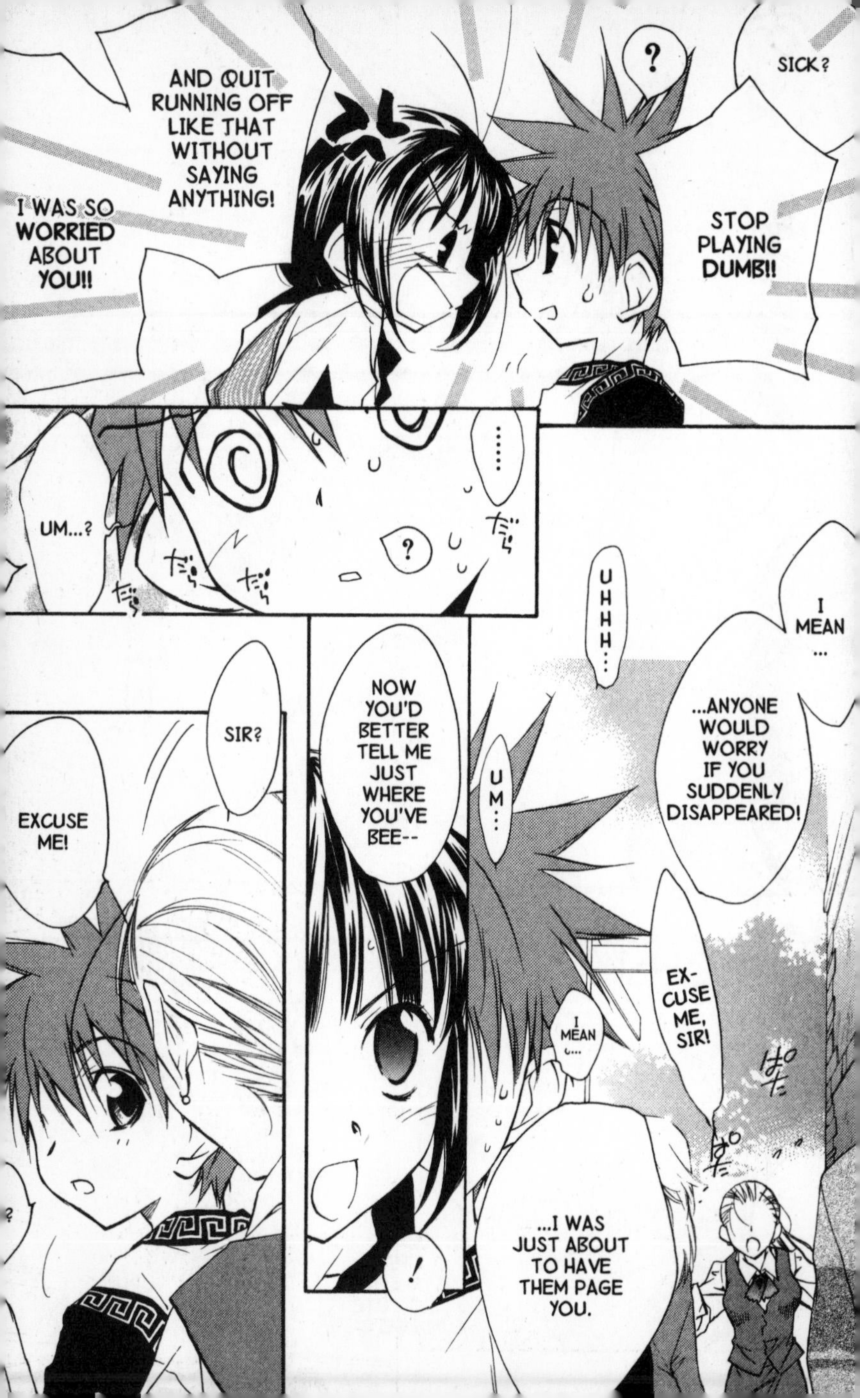
SICK?
?
STOP PLAYING DUMB!!
AND QUIT RUNNING OFF LIKE THAT WITHOUT SAYING ANYTHING!
I WAS SO WORRIED ABOUT YOU!!
......
?
UM...?
UHHH...
I MEAN...
...ANYONE WOULD WORRY IF YOU SUDDENLY DISAPPEARED!
NOW YOU'D BETTER TELL ME JUST WHERE YOU'VE BEE--
!
EX-CUSE ME, SIR!
UM...
I MEAN...
...I WAS JUST ABOUT TO HAVE THEM PAGE YOU.
SIR?
EXCUSE ME!

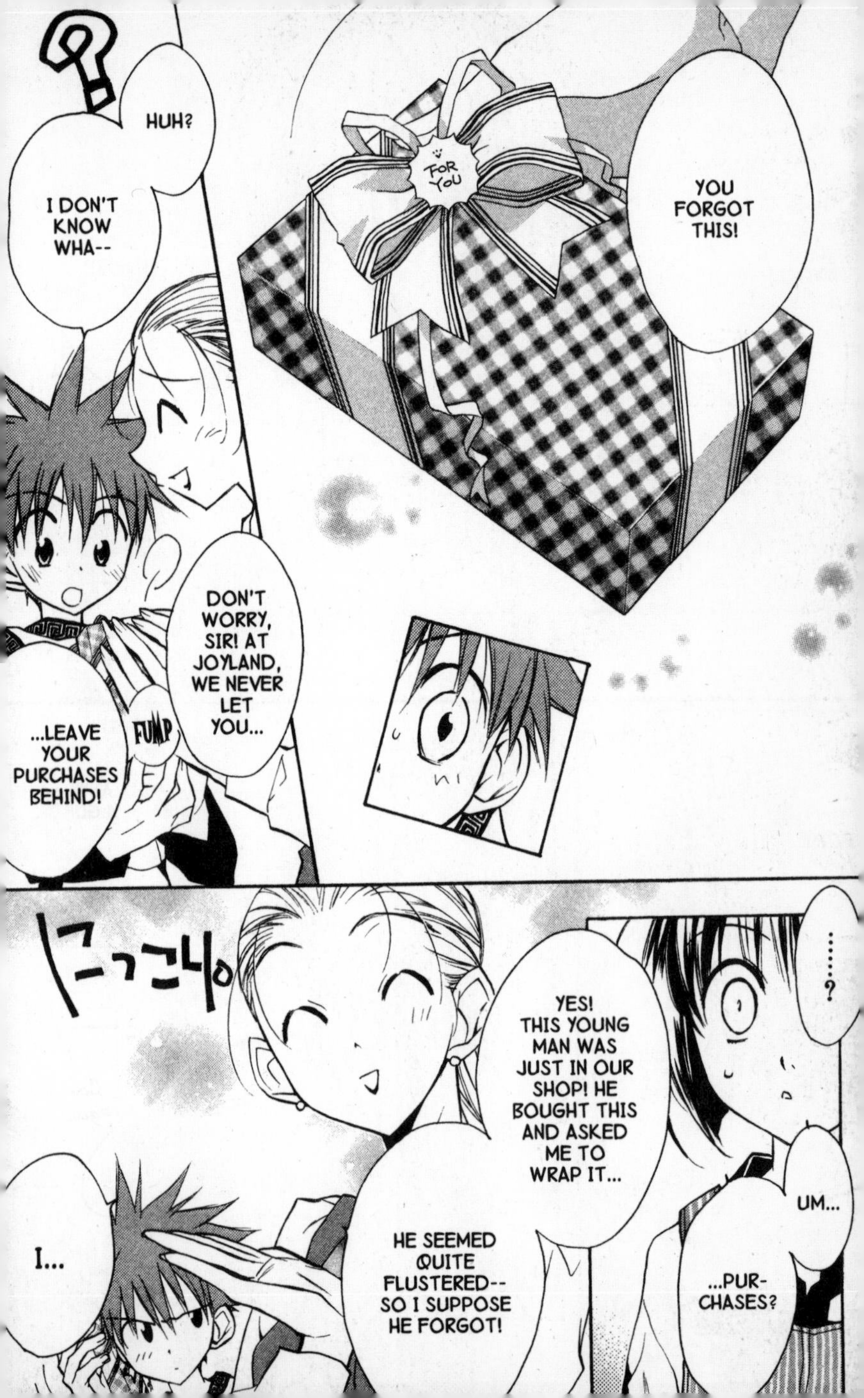

FOR YOU
YOU FORGOT THIS!
?
HUH?
I DON'T KNOW WHA--
DON'T WORRY, SIR! AT JOYLAND, WE NEVER LET YOU...
FUMP
...LEAVE YOUR PURCHASES BEHIND!
......?
UM...
...PUR-CHASES?
ニッコリ
YES! THIS YOUNG MAN WAS JUST IN OUR SHOP! HE BOUGHT THIS AND ASKED ME TO WRAP IT...
HE SEEMED QUITE FLUSTERED-- SO I SUPPOSE HE FORGOT!
I...

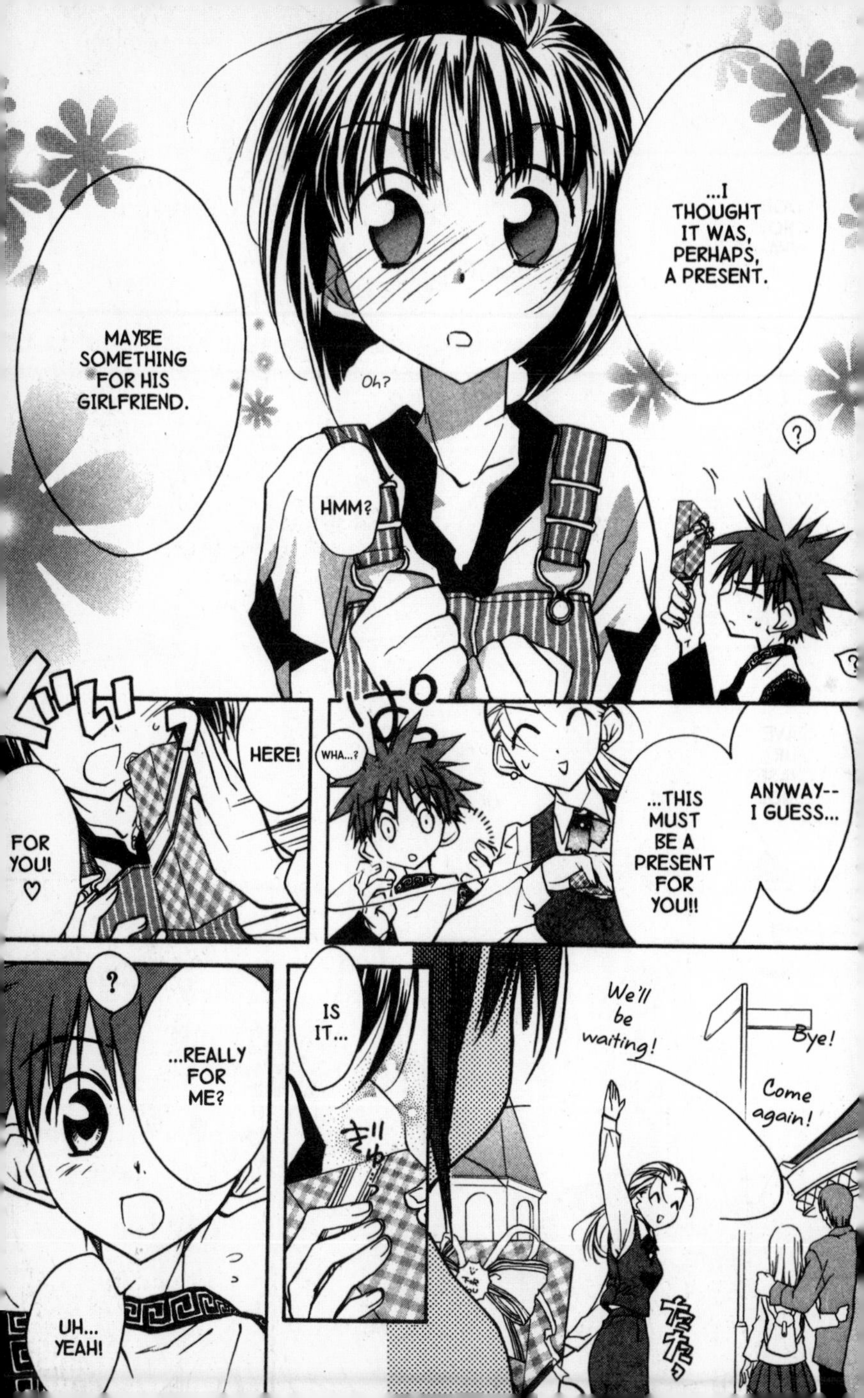
...I THOUGHT IT WAS, PERHAPS, A PRESENT.
Oh?
?
MAYBE SOMETHING FOR HIS GIRLFRIEND.
HMM?
ANYWAY-- I GUESS...
...THIS MUST BE A PRESENT FOR YOU!!
WHA...?
HERE!
FOR YOU! ♡
Bye!
Come again!
We'll be waiting!
IS IT...
?
...REALLY FOR ME?
UH... YEAH!

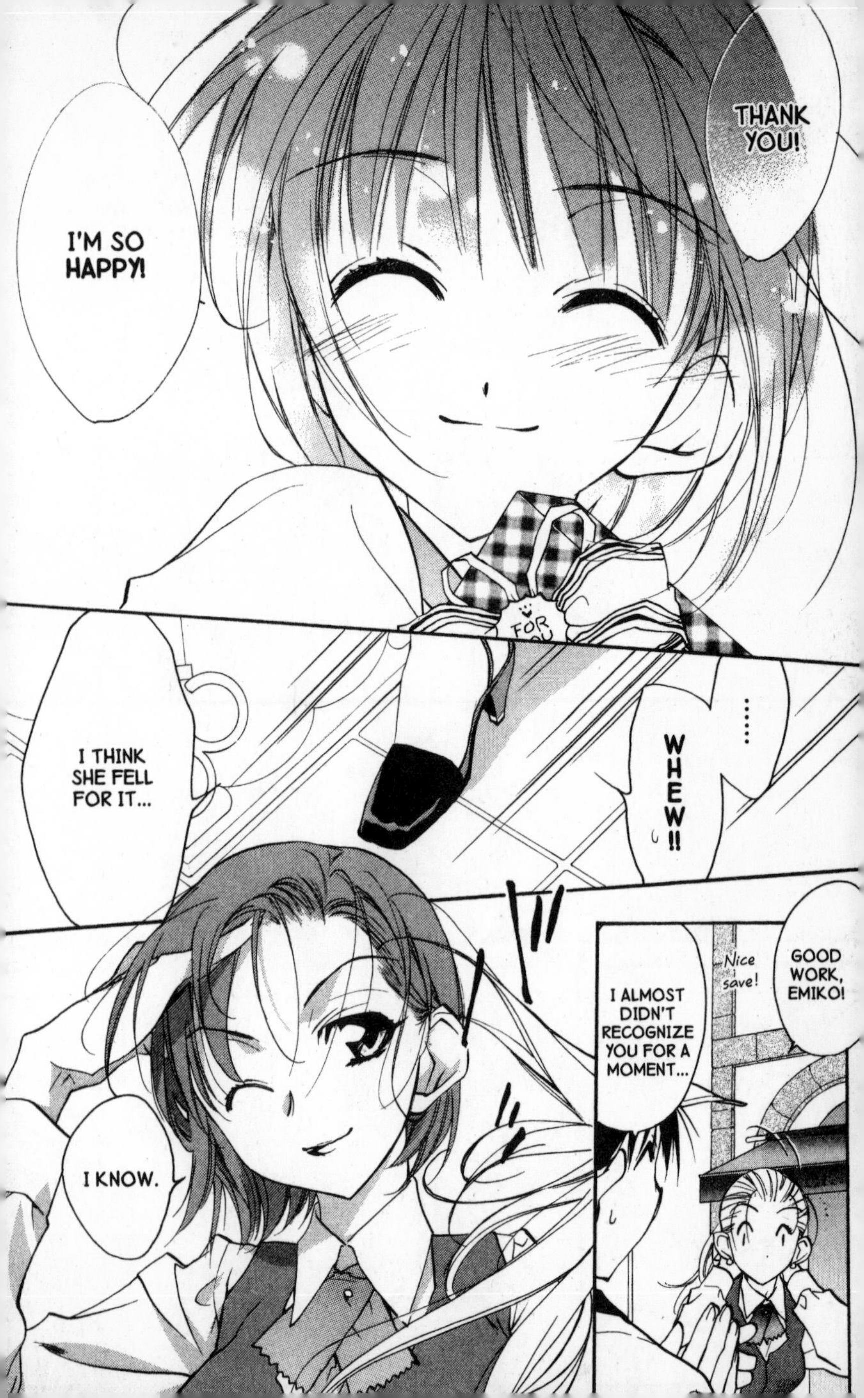
THANK YOU!
I'M SO HAPPY!
......
WHEW!!
I THINK SHE FELL FOR IT...
GOOD WORK, EMIKO!
Nice save!
I ALMOST DIDN'T RECOGNIZE YOU FOR A MOMENT...
I KNOW.

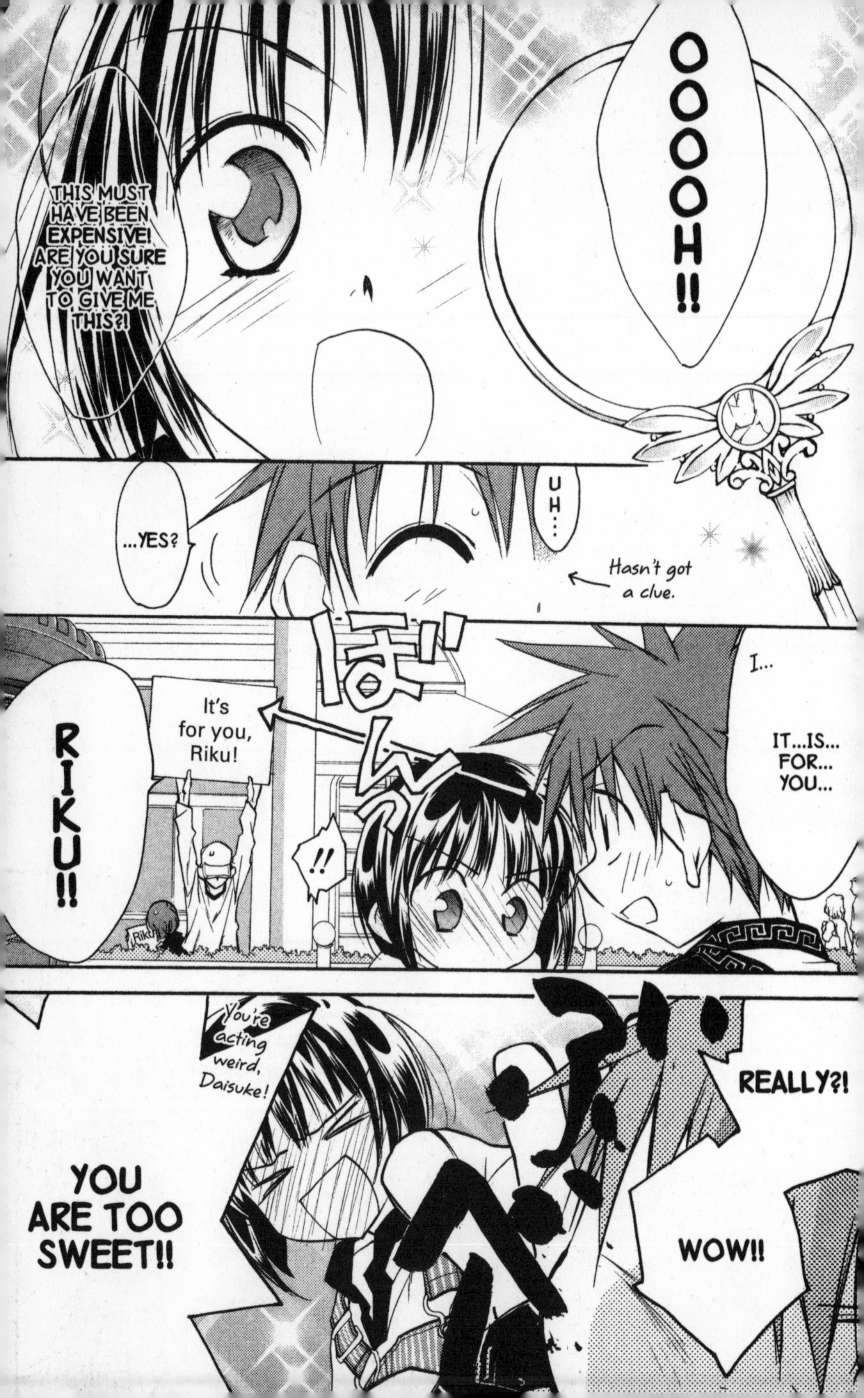
OOOOOH!!
THIS MUST HAVE BEEN EXPENSIVE! ARE YOU SURE YOU WANT TO GIVE ME THIS?!
UH...
Hasn't got a clue.
...YES?
I...
IT...IS... FOR... YOU...
!!
It's for you, Riku!
Riku
RIKU!!
REALLY?!
WOW!!
You're acting weird, Daisuke!
YOU ARE TOO SWEET!!

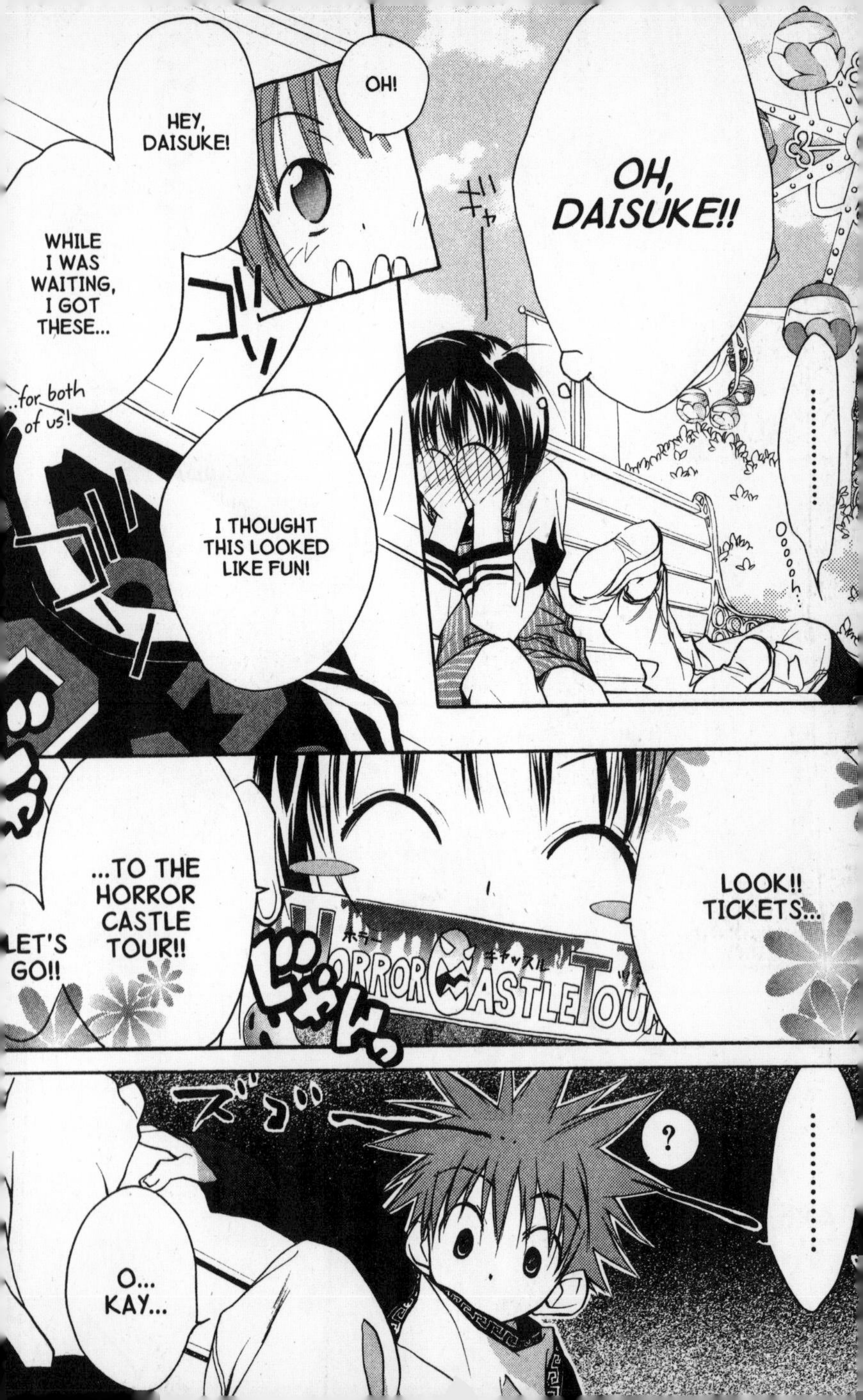

OH, DAISUKE!!
......
Oooooh...
OH!
HEY, DAISUKE!
WHILE I WAS WAITING, I GOT THESE...
...for both of us!
I THOUGHT THIS LOOKED LIKE FUN!
LOOK!! TICKETS...
...TO THE HORROR CASTLE TOUR!!
LET'S GO!!
HORROR CASTLE TOUR
......
?
O... KAY...

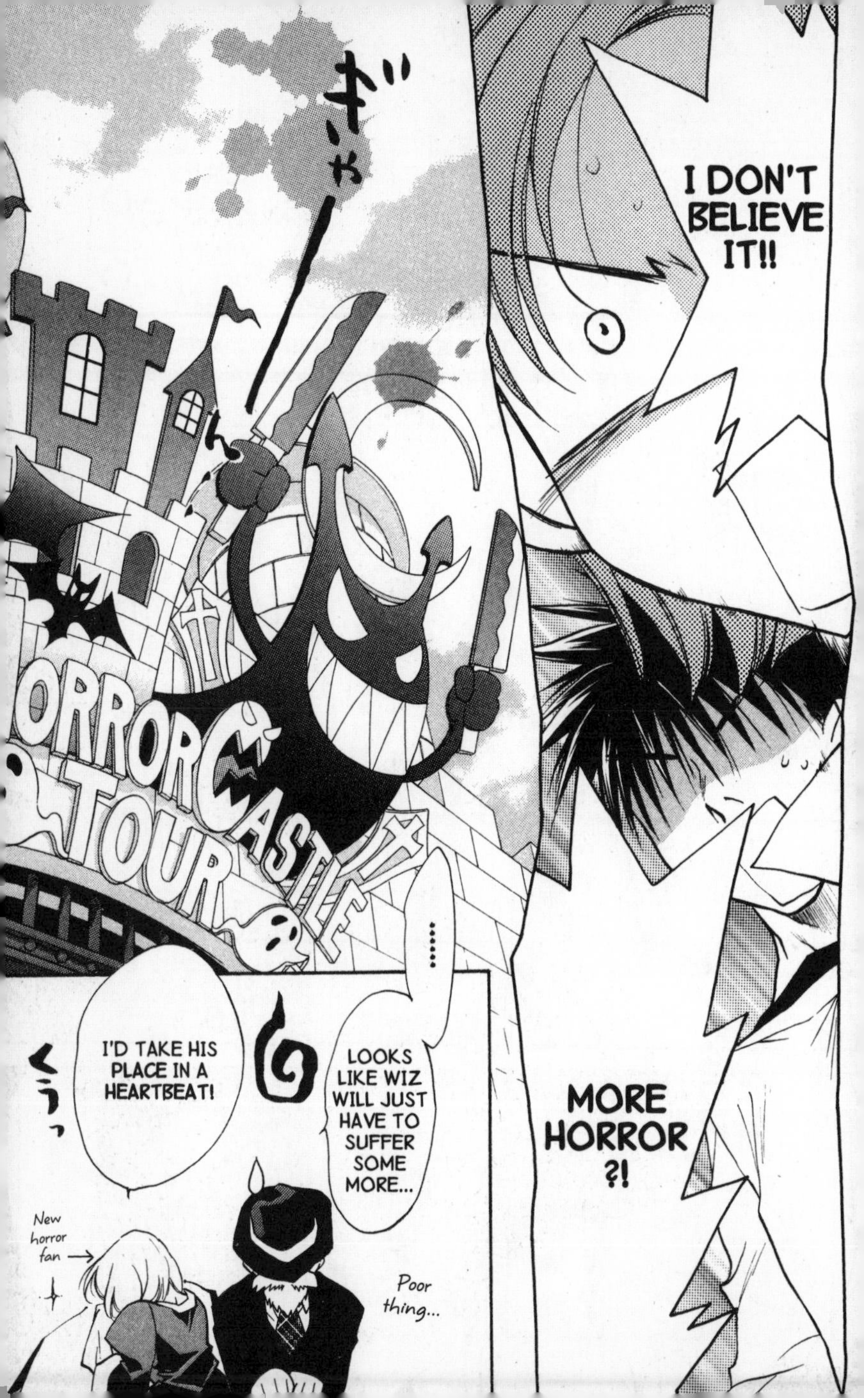

I DON'T BELIEVE IT!!
MORE HORROR ?!
ぎゃー
ORROR CASTLE TOUR
......
LOOKS LIKE WIZ WILL JUST HAVE TO SUFFER SOME MORE...
I'D TAKE HIS PLACE IN A HEARTBEAT!
くぅっ
Poor thing...
New horror fan

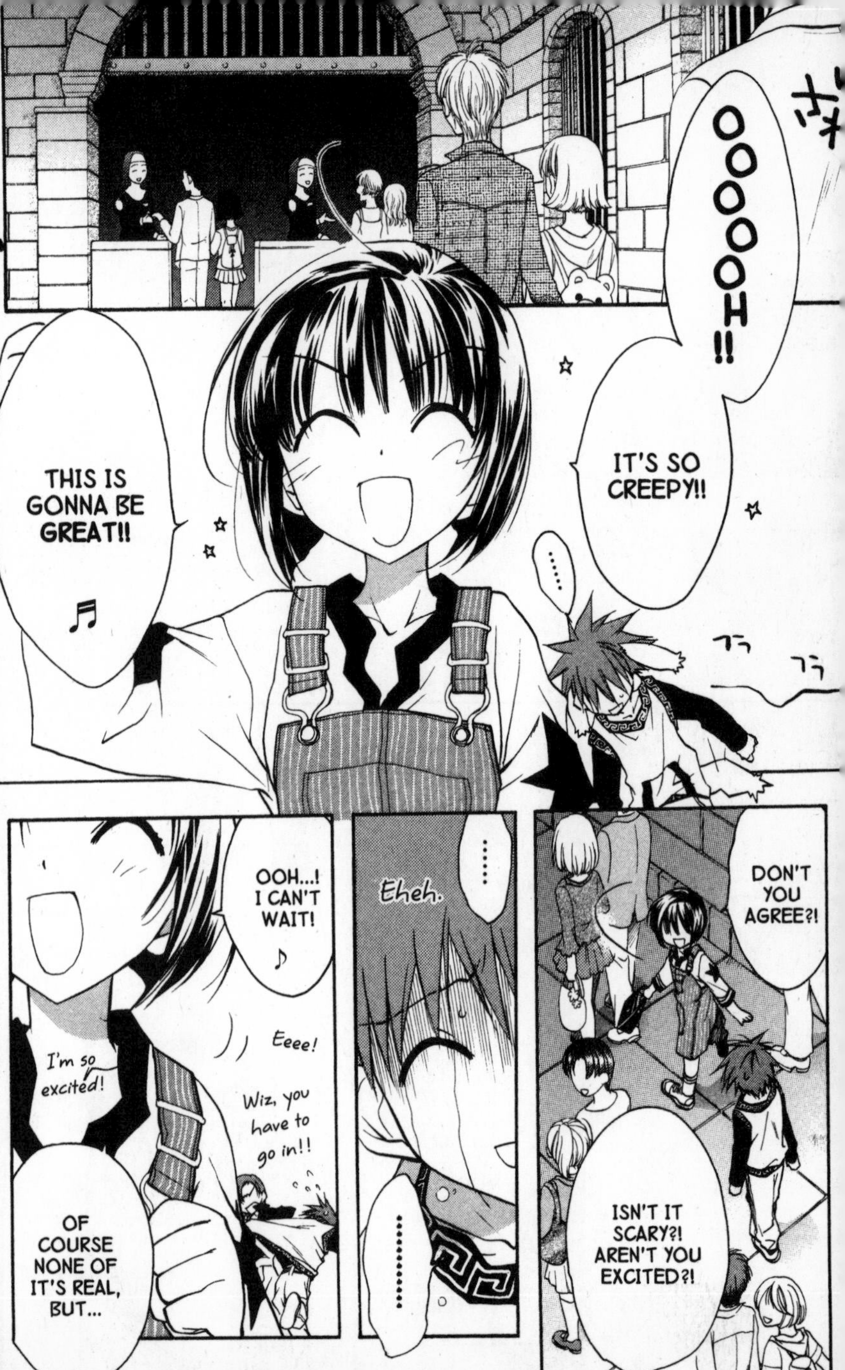
OOOOOOH!!
IT'S SO CREEPY!!
THIS IS GONNA BE GREAT!! ♫
......
DON'T YOU AGREE?!
ISN'T IT SCARY?! AREN'T YOU EXCITED?!
......
Eheh.
....
OOH...! I CAN'T WAIT! ♪
Eeee!
I'm so excited!
Wiz, you have to go in!!
OF COURSE NONE OF IT'S REAL, BUT...

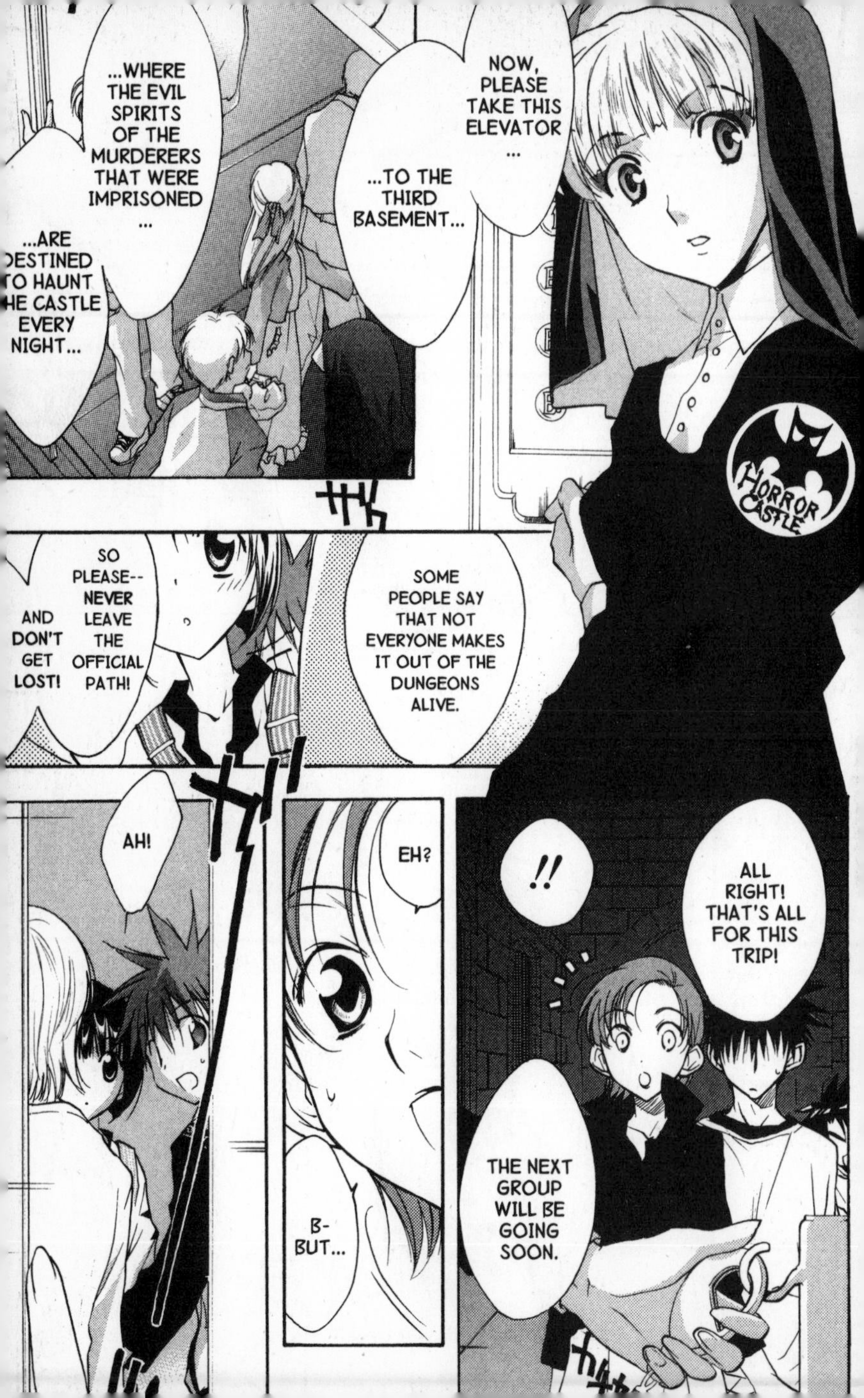
NOW, PLEASE TAKE THIS ELEVATOR ...
...TO THE THIRD BASEMENT...
...WHERE THE EVIL SPIRITS OF THE MURDERERS THAT WERE IMPRISONED ...
...ARE DESTINED TO HAUNT THE CASTLE EVERY NIGHT...
HORROR CASTLE
SOME PEOPLE SAY THAT NOT EVERYONE MAKES IT OUT OF THE DUNGEONS ALIVE.
SO PLEASE--NEVER LEAVE THE OFFICIAL PATH!
AND DON'T GET LOST!
ALL RIGHT! THAT'S ALL FOR THIS TRIP!
!!
THE NEXT GROUP WILL BE GOING SOON.
EH?
B-BUT...
AH!

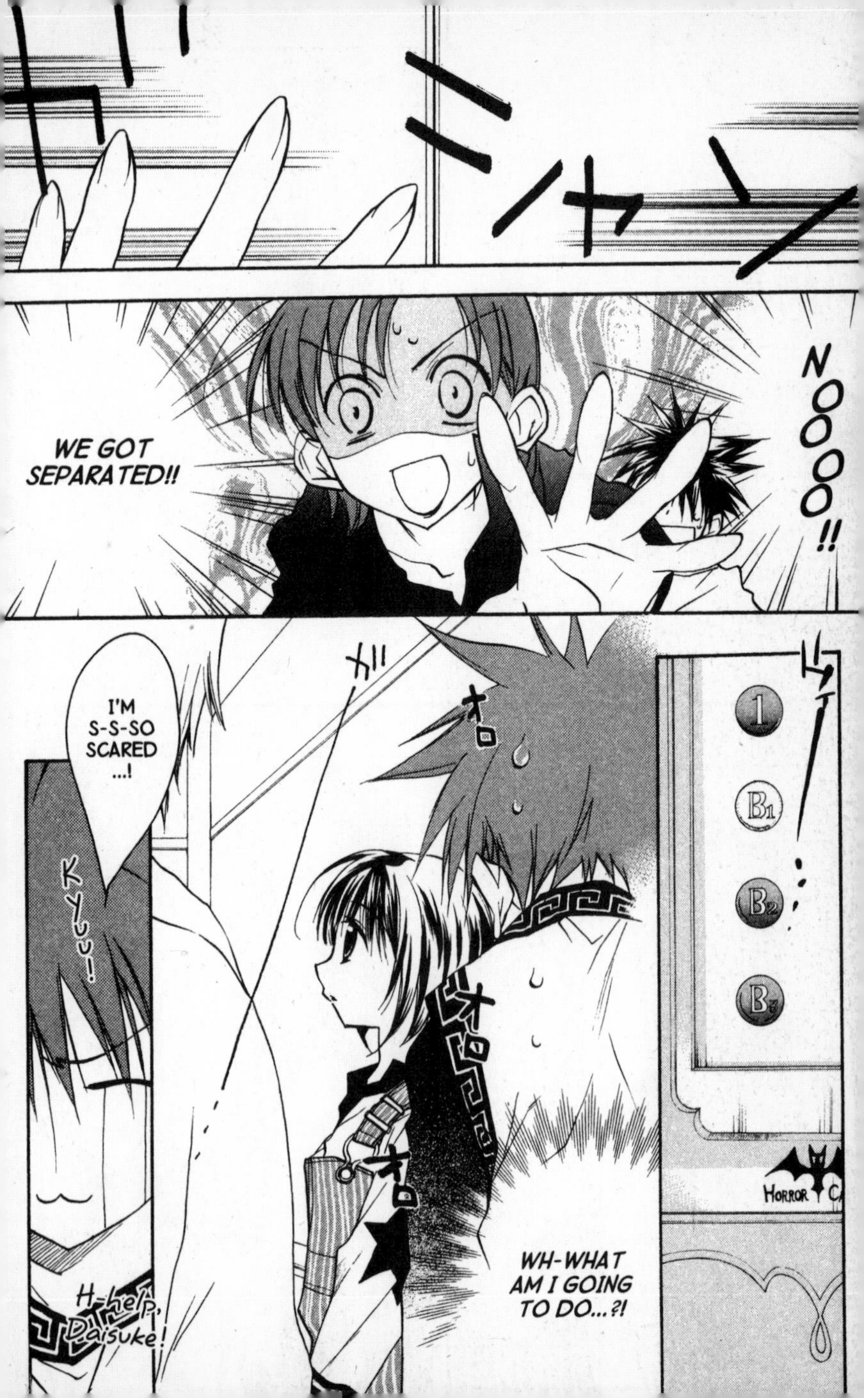
NOOOO!!
WE GOT SEPARATED!!
HORROR CA
I'M S-S-SO SCARED ...!
Kyuu!
WH-WHAT AM I GOING TO DO...?!
H-help, Daisuke!

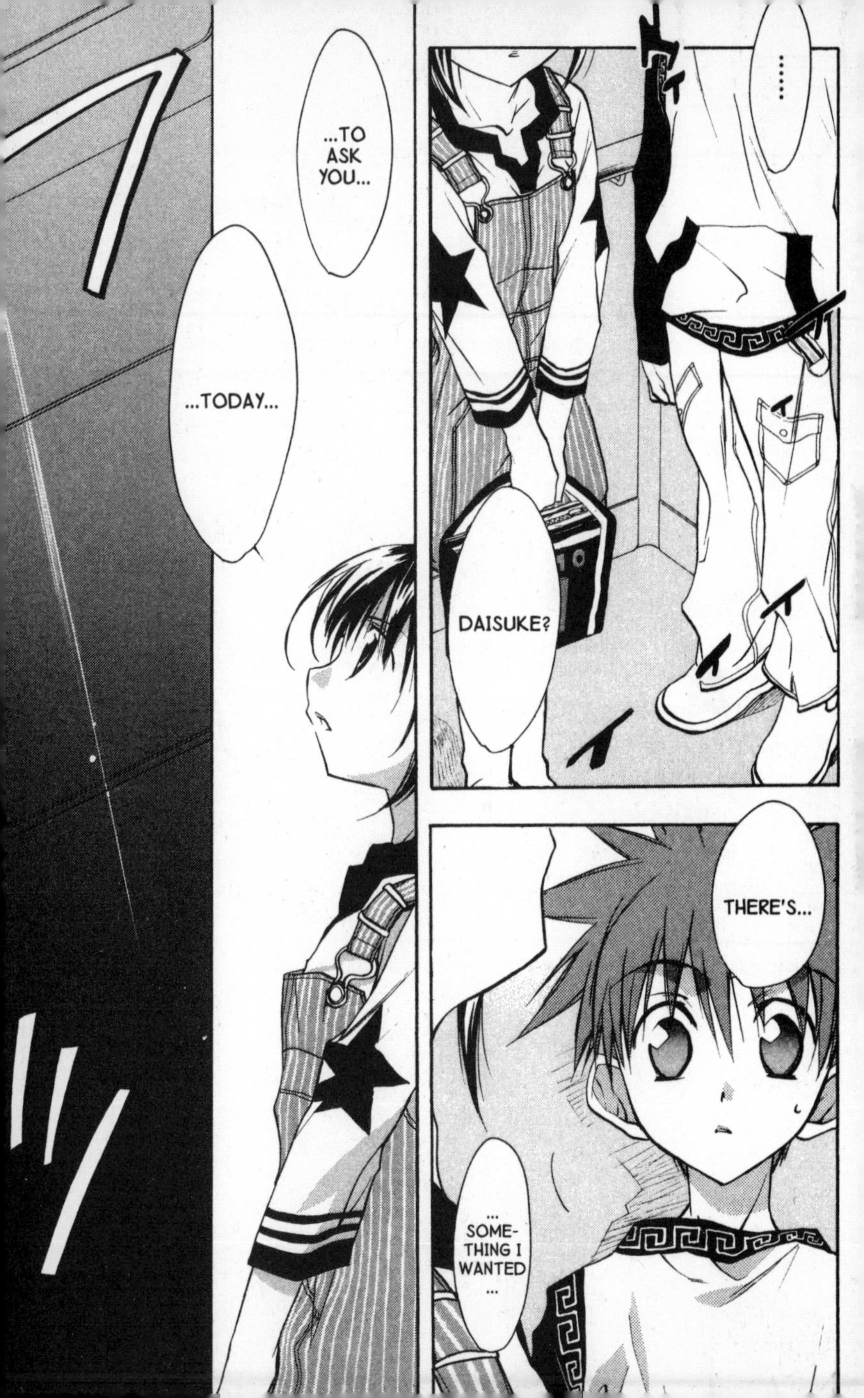
......
DAISUKE?
THERE'S...
... SOME-THING I WANTED ...
...TO ASK YOU...
...TODAY...

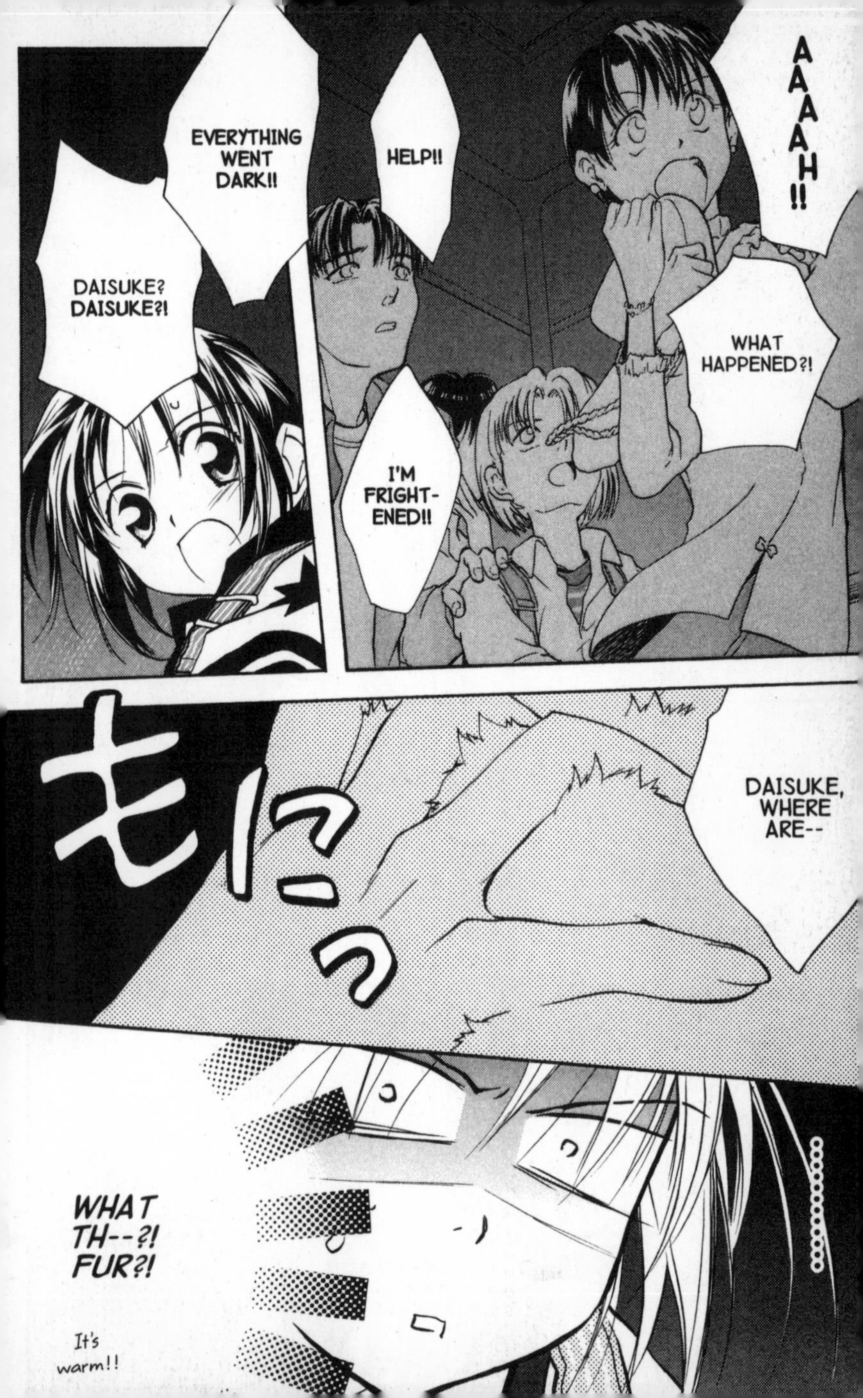
AAAAH!!
HELP!!
WHAT HAPPENED?!
I'M FRIGHTENED!!
EVERYTHING WENT DARK!!
DAISUKE? DAISUKE?!
DAISUKE, WHERE ARE--
もにっ
WHAT TH--?! FUR?!
It's warm!!

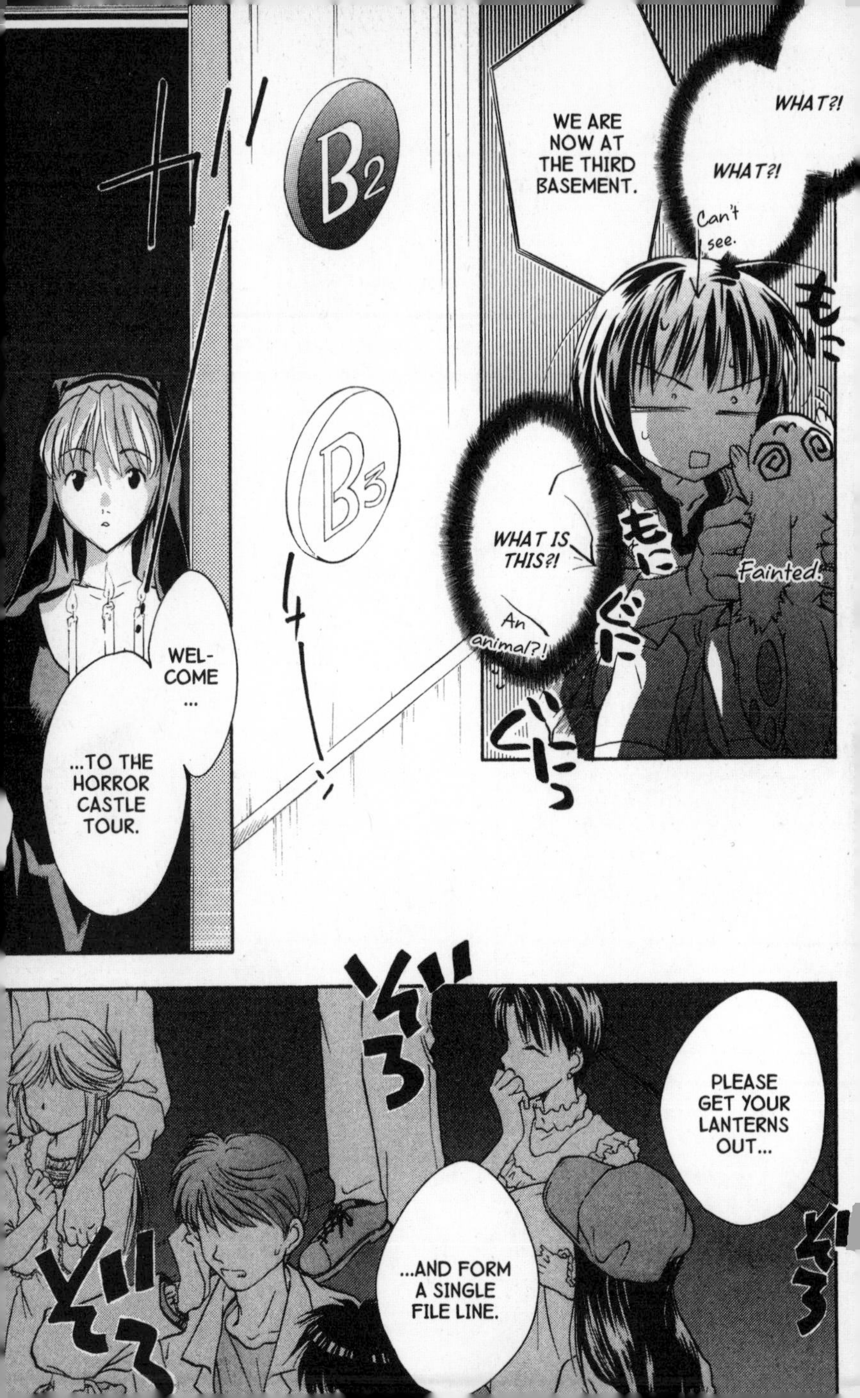

WE ARE NOW AT THE THIRD BASEMENT.
WHAT?!
WHAT?!
Can't see.
WHAT IS THIS?!
An animal?!
Fainted.
B2
B3
WELCOME...
...TO THE HORROR CASTLE TOUR.
PLEASE GET YOUR LANTERNS OUT...
...AND FORM A SINGLE FILE LINE.

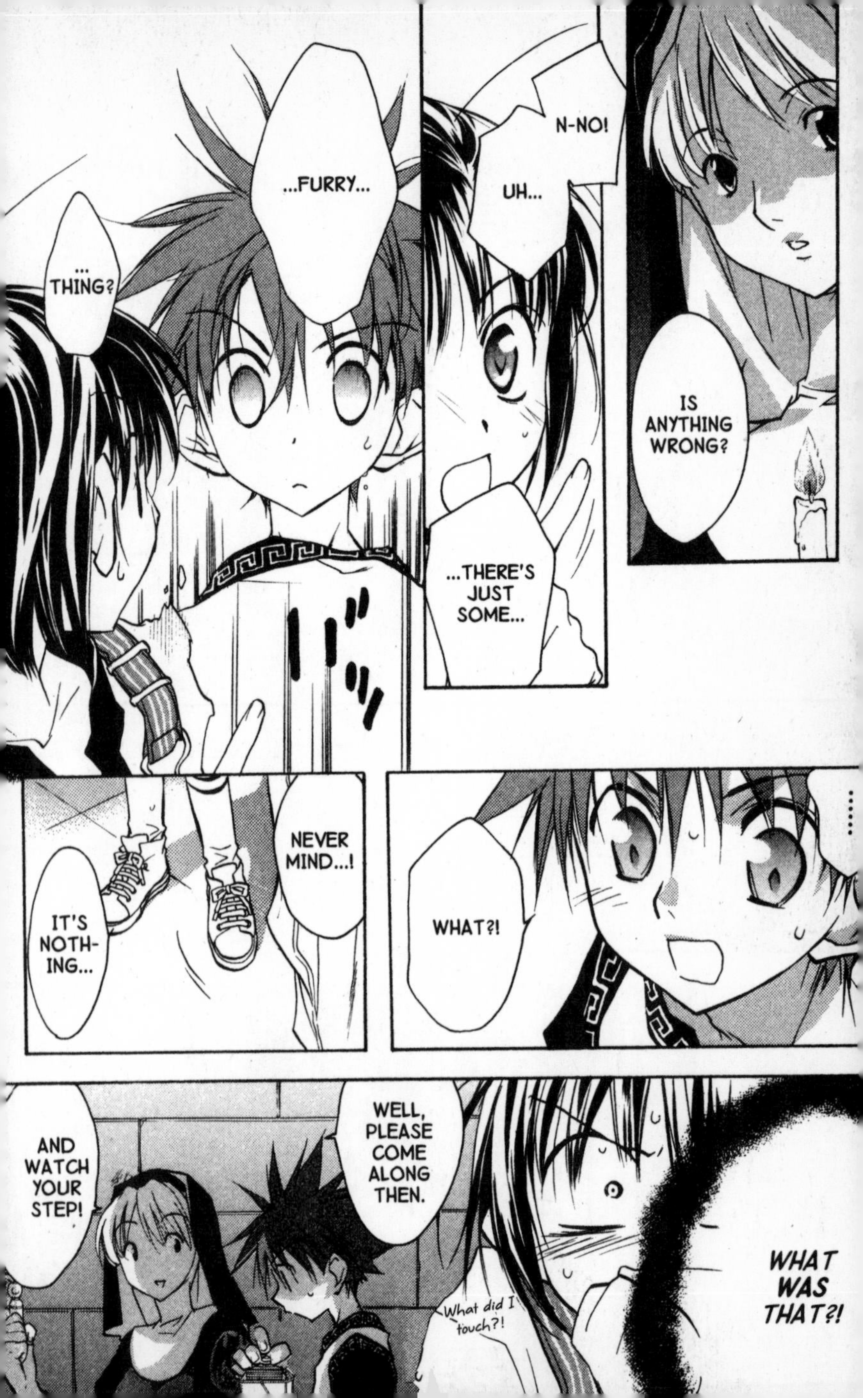
IS ANYTHING WRONG?
N-NO!
UH...
...THERE'S JUST SOME...
...FURRY...
...THING?
......
WHAT?!
NEVER MIND...!
IT'S NOTH-ING...
WHAT WAS THAT?!
What did I touch?!
WELL, PLEASE COME ALONG THEN.
AND WATCH YOUR STEP!

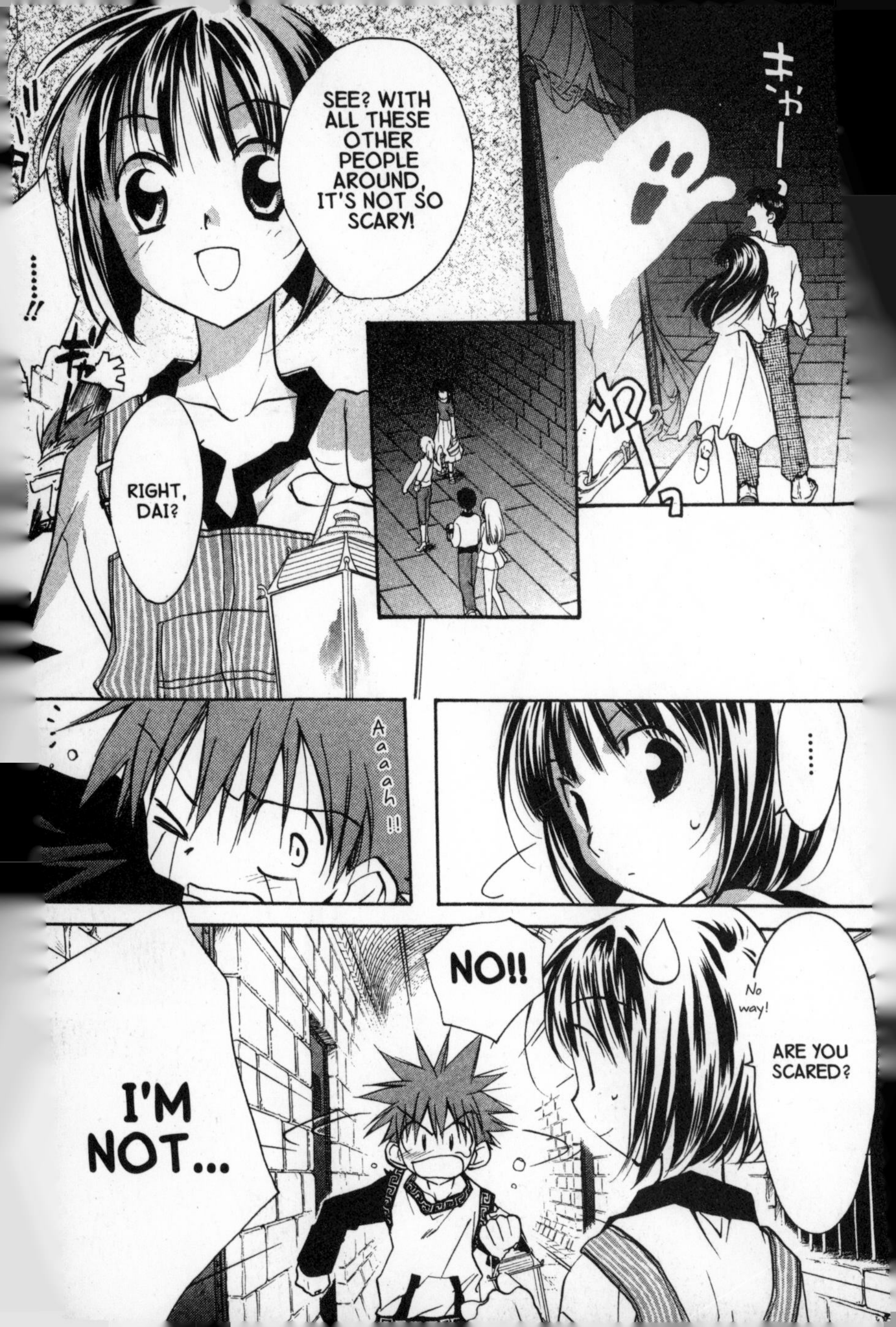

SEE? WITH ALL THESE OTHER PEOPLE AROUND, IT'S NOT SO SCARY!
RIGHT, DAI?
......!!
......
Aaaah!!
ARE YOU SCARED?
No way!
NO!!
I'M NOT...

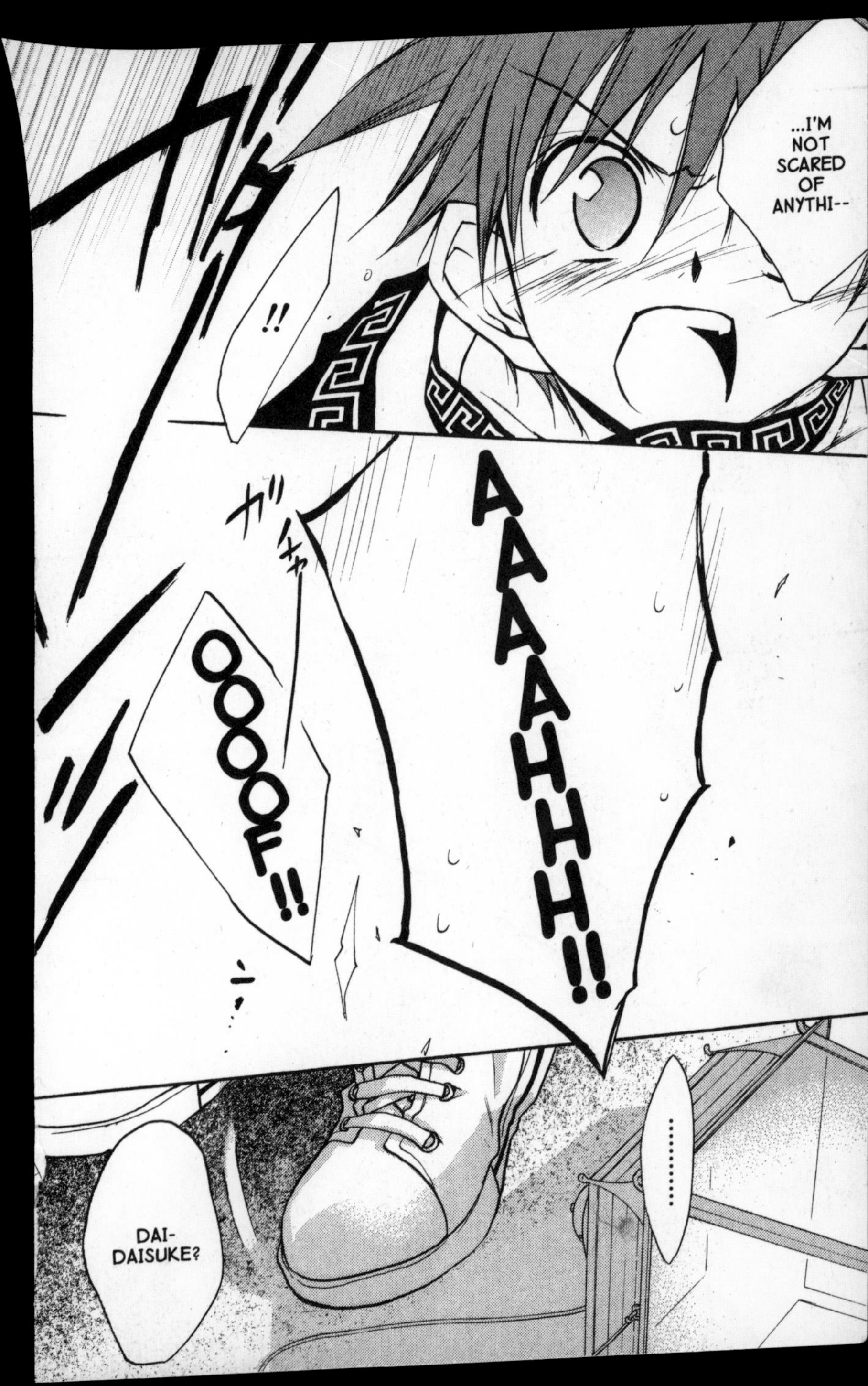
...I'M NOT SCARED OF ANYTHI--
!!
AAAAHHH!!
OOOOF!!
......
DAI-DAISUKE?

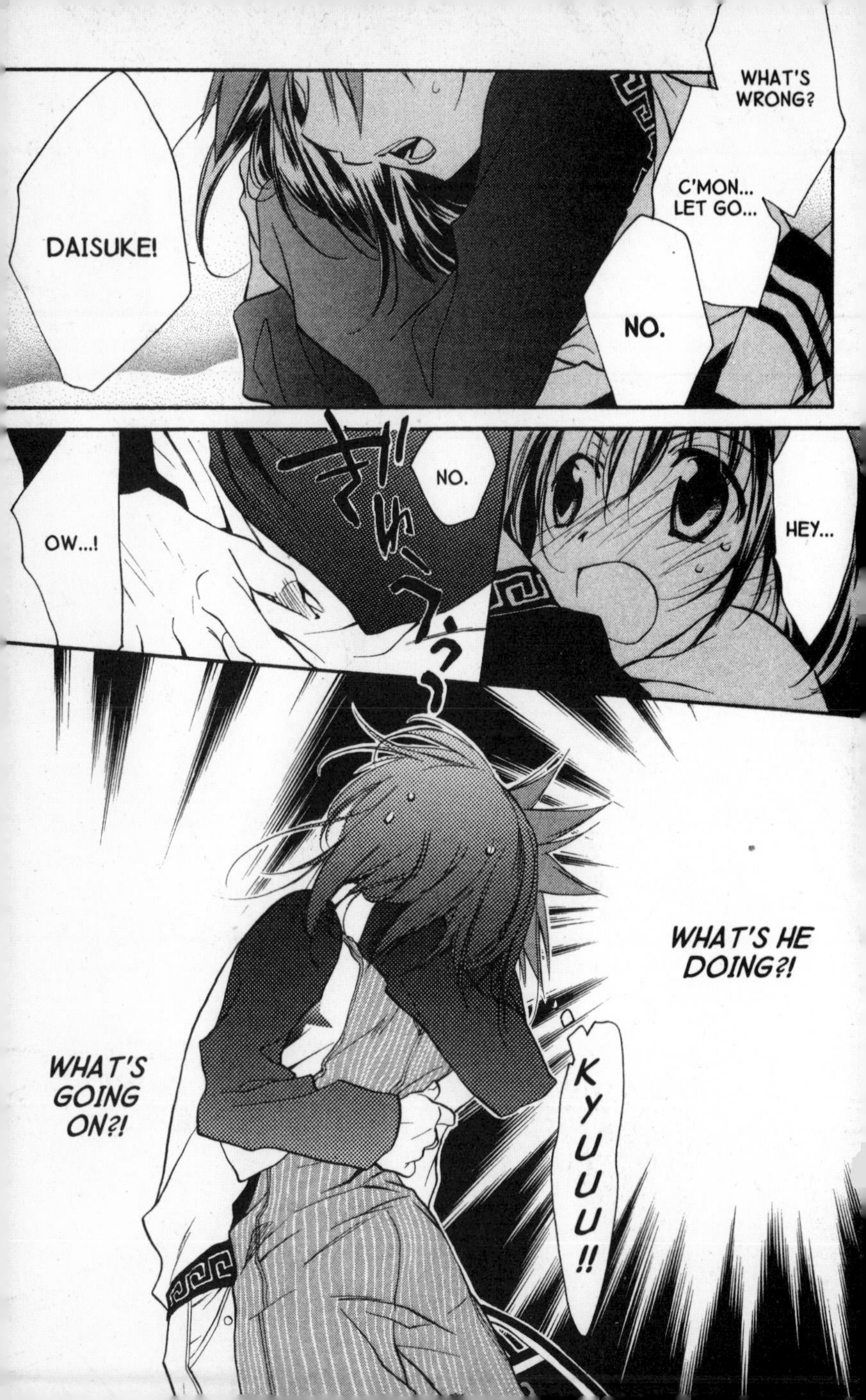
WHAT'S WRONG?
C'MON... LET GO...
NO.
DAISUKE!
HEY...
NO.
OW...!
WHAT'S HE DOING?!
KYUUUU!!
WHAT'S GOING ON?!

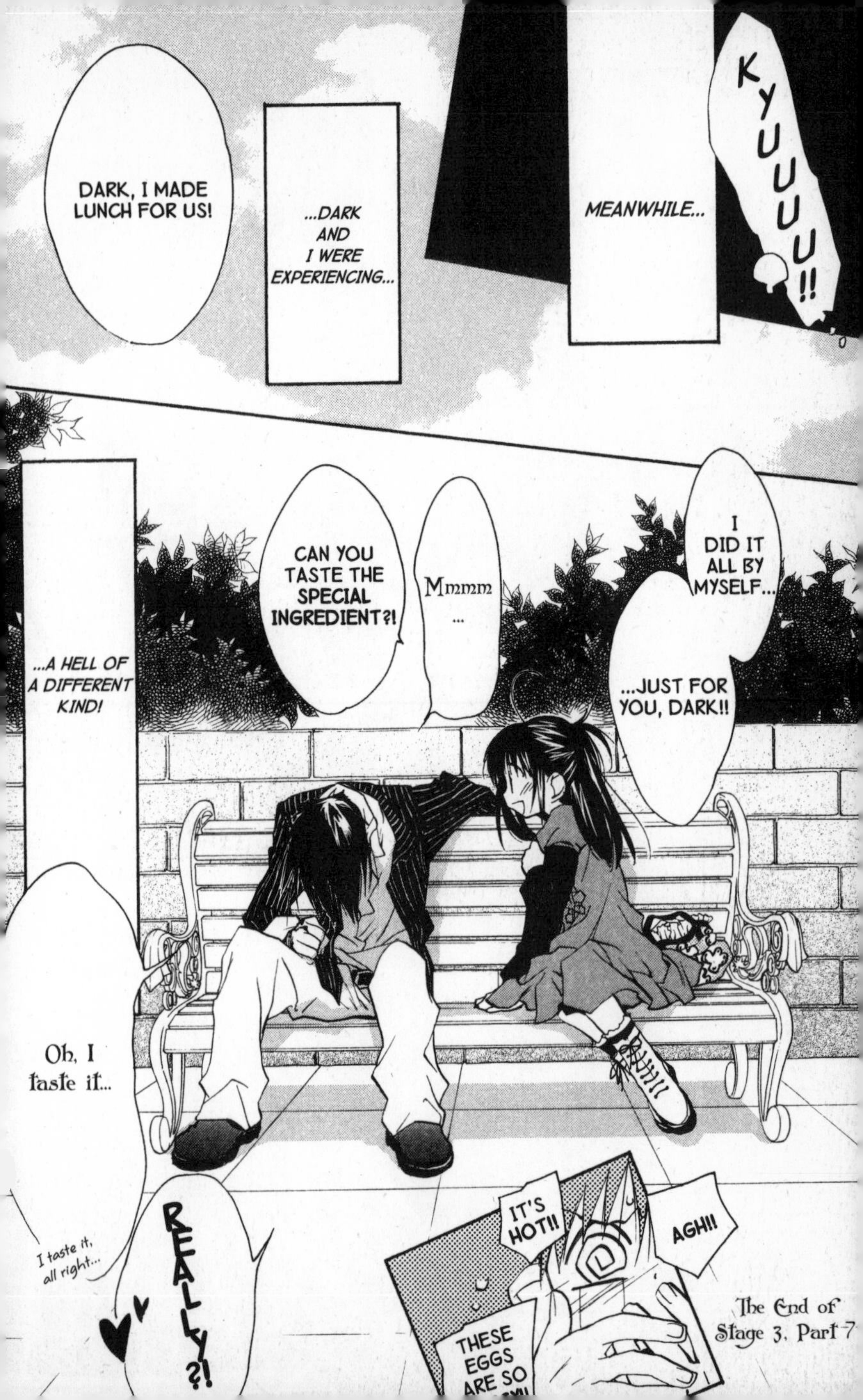
KYUUUUU!!
MEANWHILE...
...DARK AND I WERE EXPERIENCING...
DARK, I MADE LUNCH FOR US!
I DID IT ALL BY MYSELF...
...JUST FOR YOU, DARK!!
Mmmm ...
CAN YOU TASTE THE SPECIAL INGREDIENT?!
...A HELL OF A DIFFERENT KIND!
Oh, I taste it...
REALLY?!
I taste it, all right...
AGH!!
IT'S HOT!!
THESE EGGS ARE SO

The End of Stage 3, Part 7

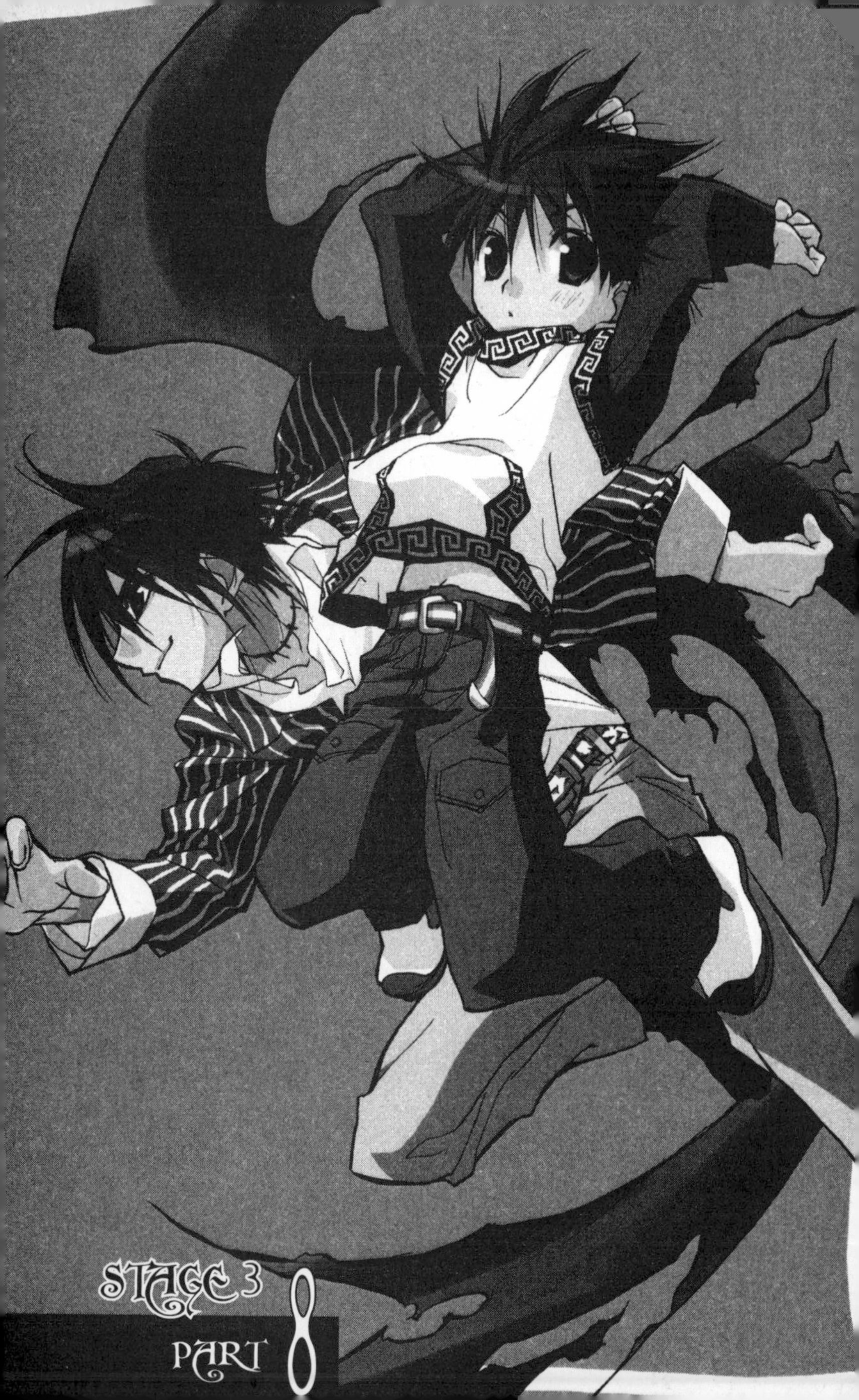
STAGE 3
PART 8

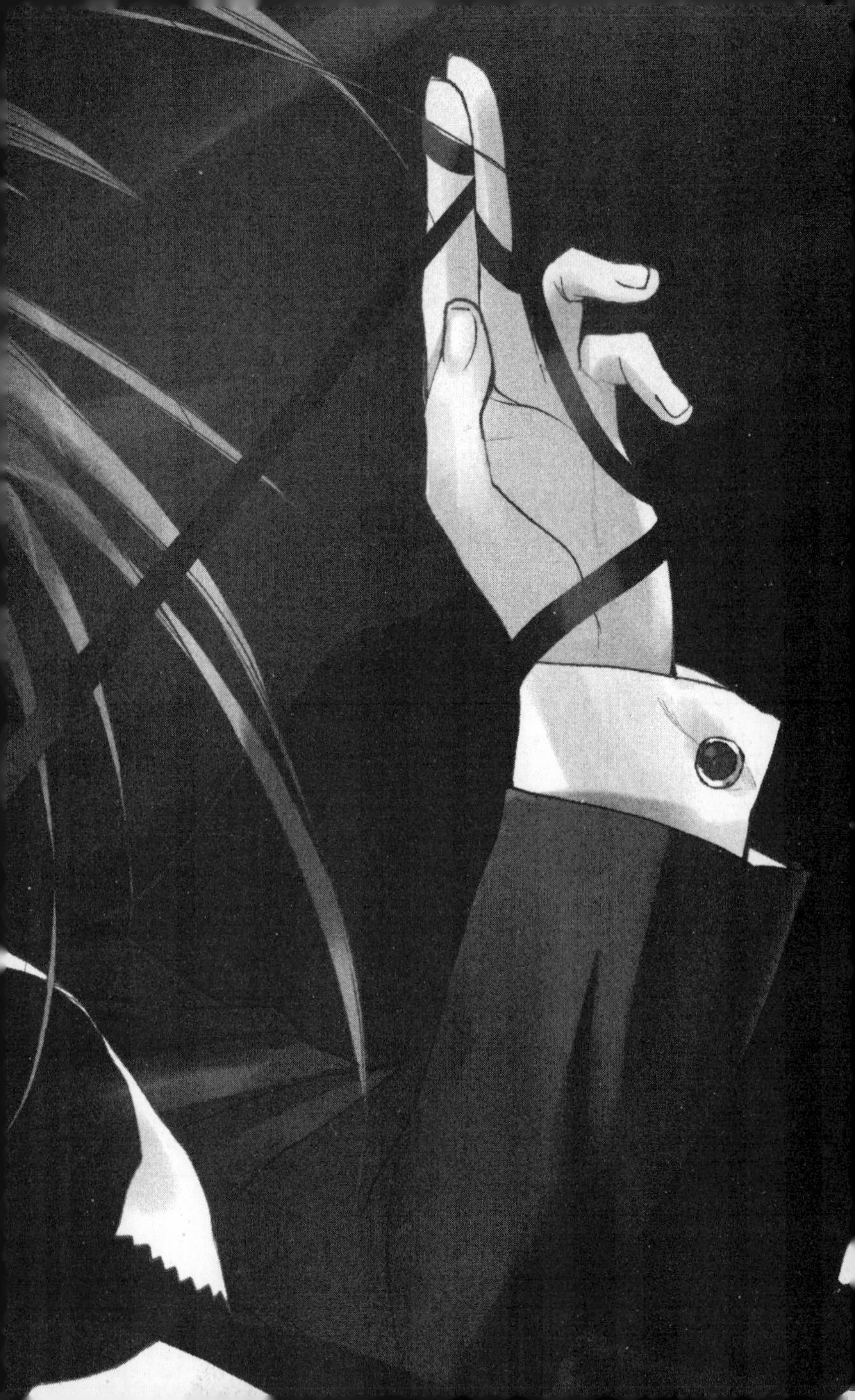

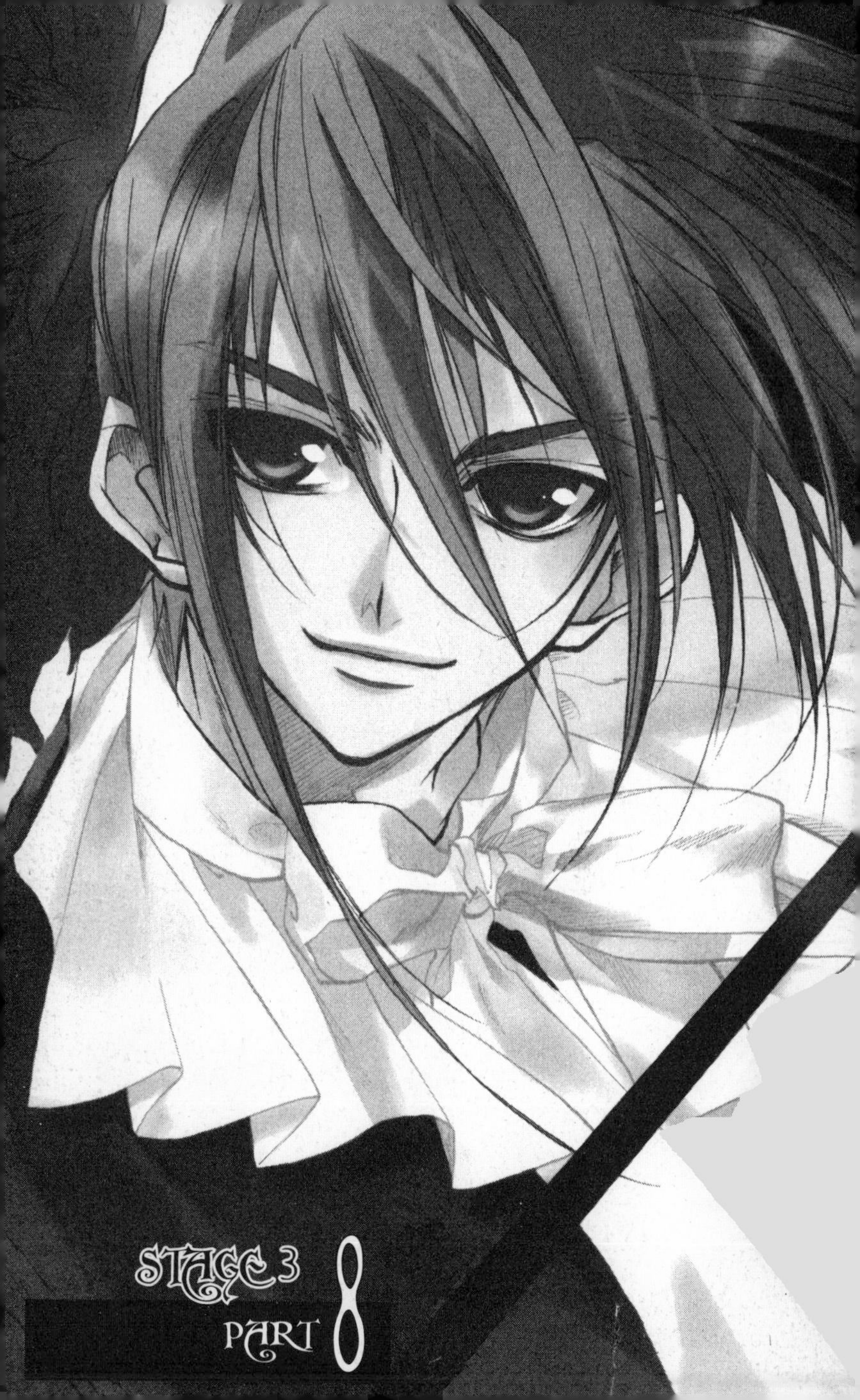
STAGE 3
PART 8

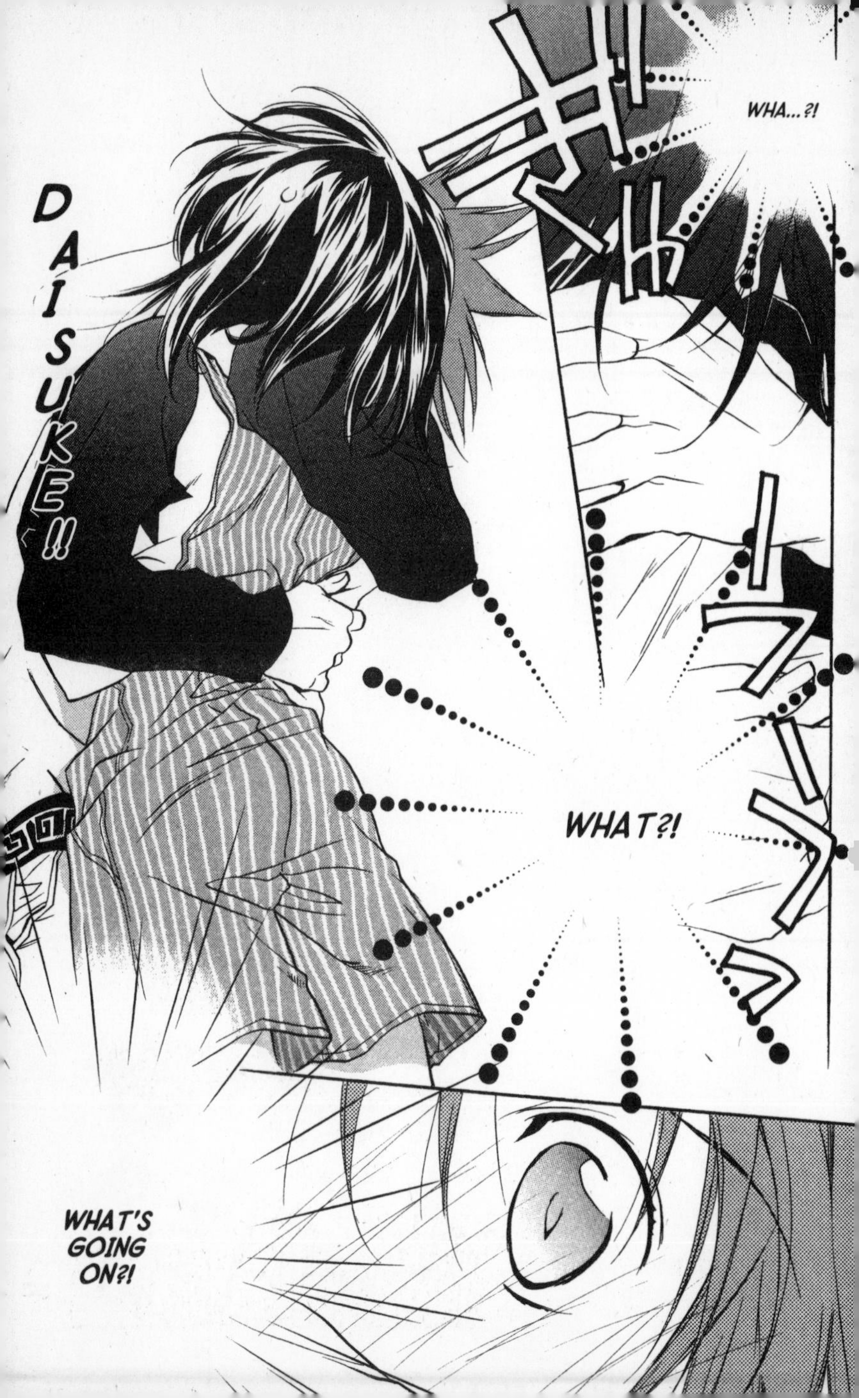
WHA...?!
DAISUKE!!
WHAT?!
WHAT'S GOING ON?!

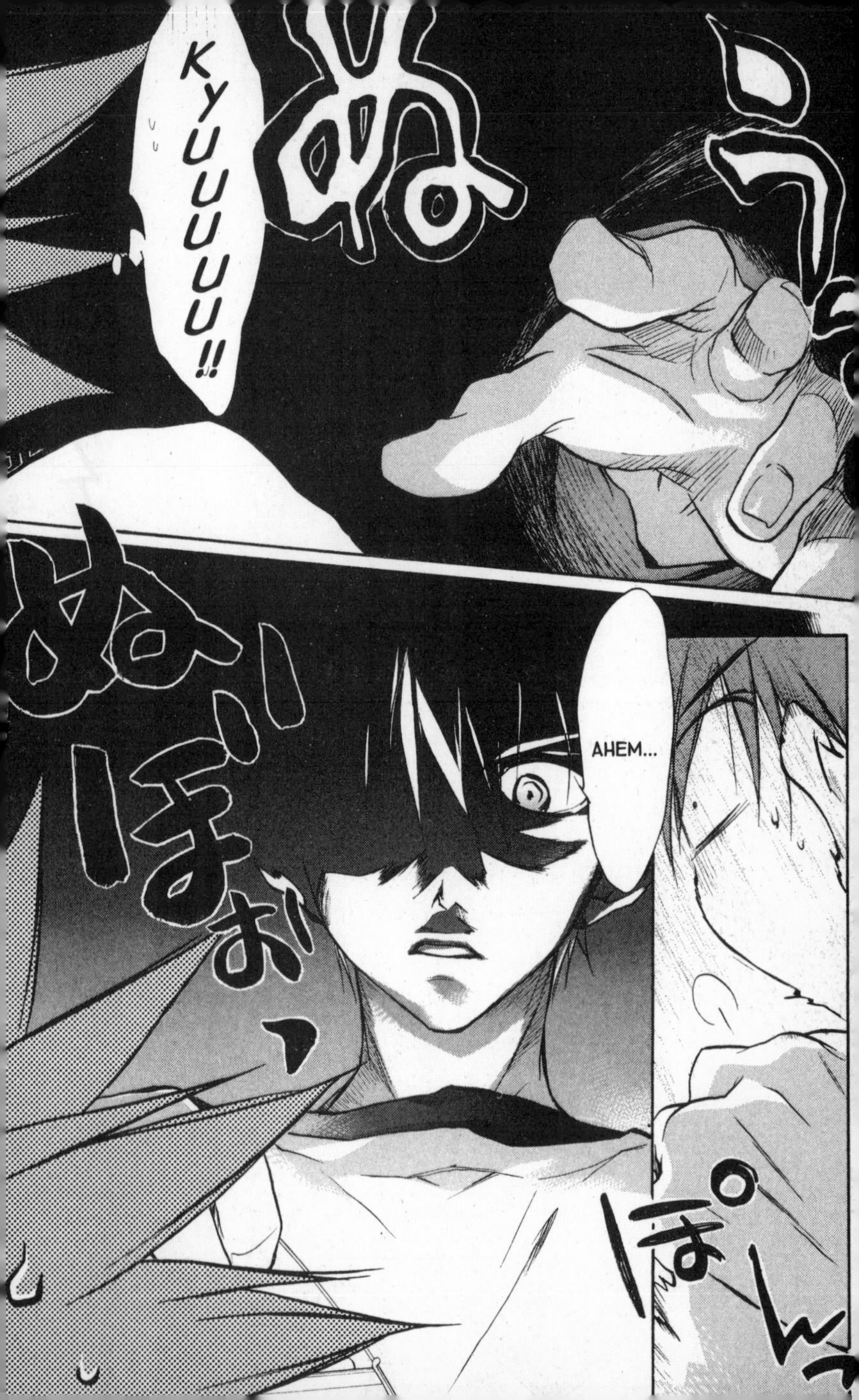
KYUUUUU!!
AHEM...

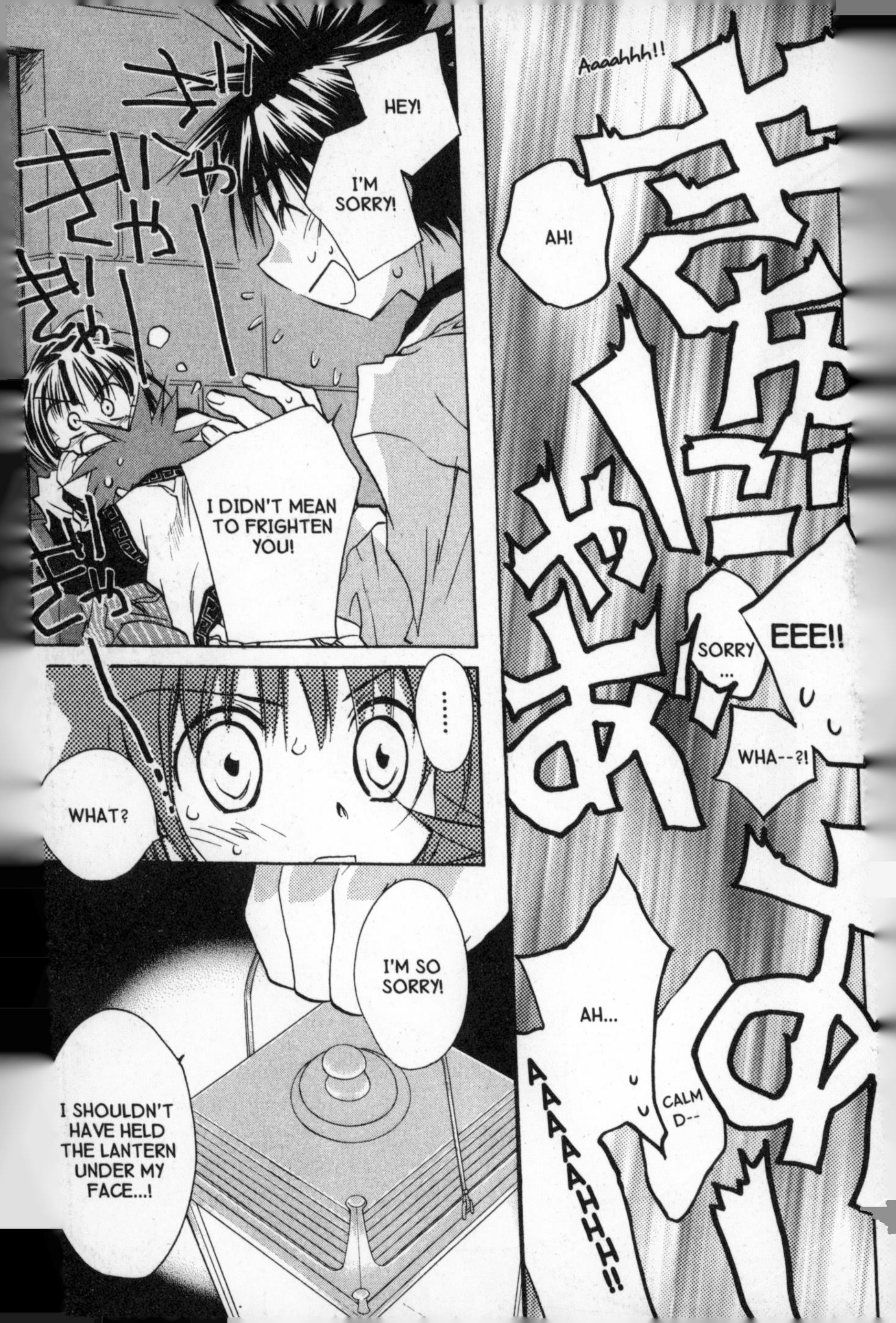
Aaaahhh!!
AH!
EEE!!
SORRY ...
WHA--?!
AH...
CALM D--
AAAAAAHHH!!
HEY!
I'M SORRY!
I DIDN'T MEAN TO FRIGHTEN YOU!
......
WHAT?
I'M SO SORRY!
I SHOULDN'T HAVE HELD THE LANTERN UNDER MY FACE...!

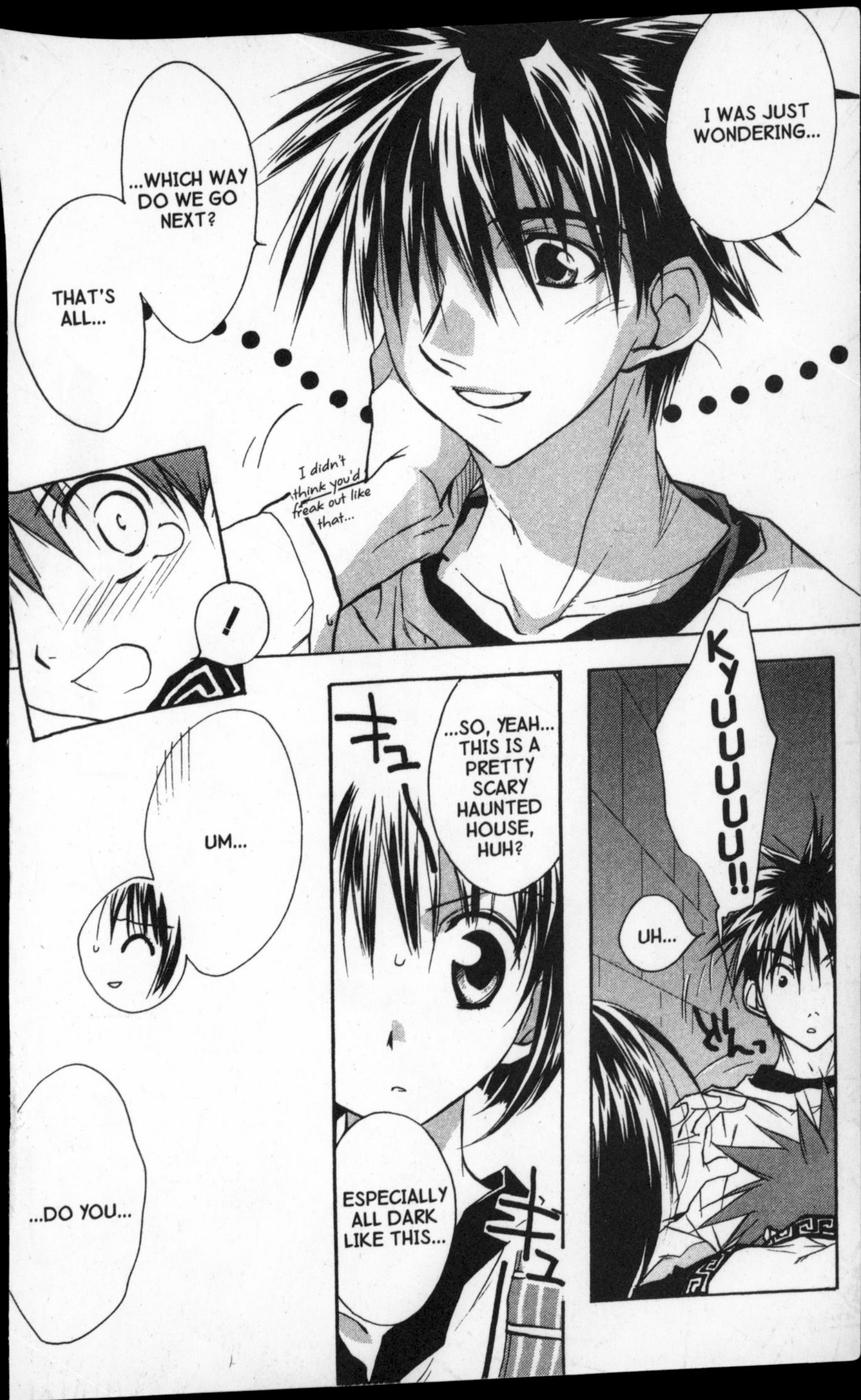
I WAS JUST WONDERING...
...WHICH WAY DO WE GO NEXT?
THAT'S ALL...
I didn't think you'd freak out like that...
!
KYUUUUUU!!
UH...
...SO, YEAH... THIS IS A PRETTY SCARY HAUNTED HOUSE, HUH?
ESPECIALLY ALL DARK LIKE THIS...
UM...
...DO YOU...

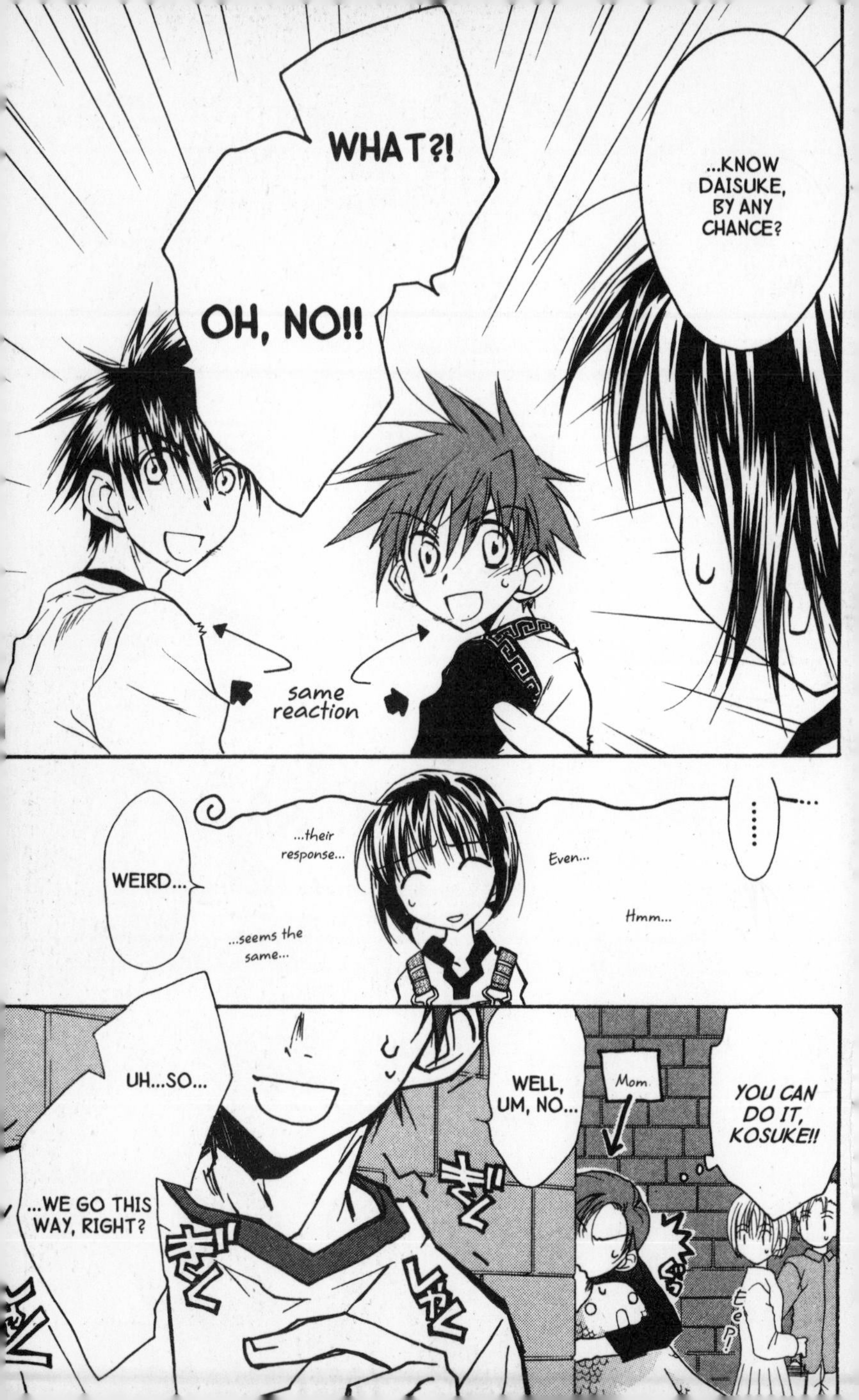
...KNOW DAISUKE, BY ANY CHANCE?
WHAT?!
OH, NO!!
same reaction
......
Hmm...
Even...
...their response...
...seems the same...
WEIRD...
YOU CAN DO IT, KOSUKE!!
Mom
Eep!
WELL, UM, NO...
UH...SO...
...WE GO THIS WAY, RIGHT?

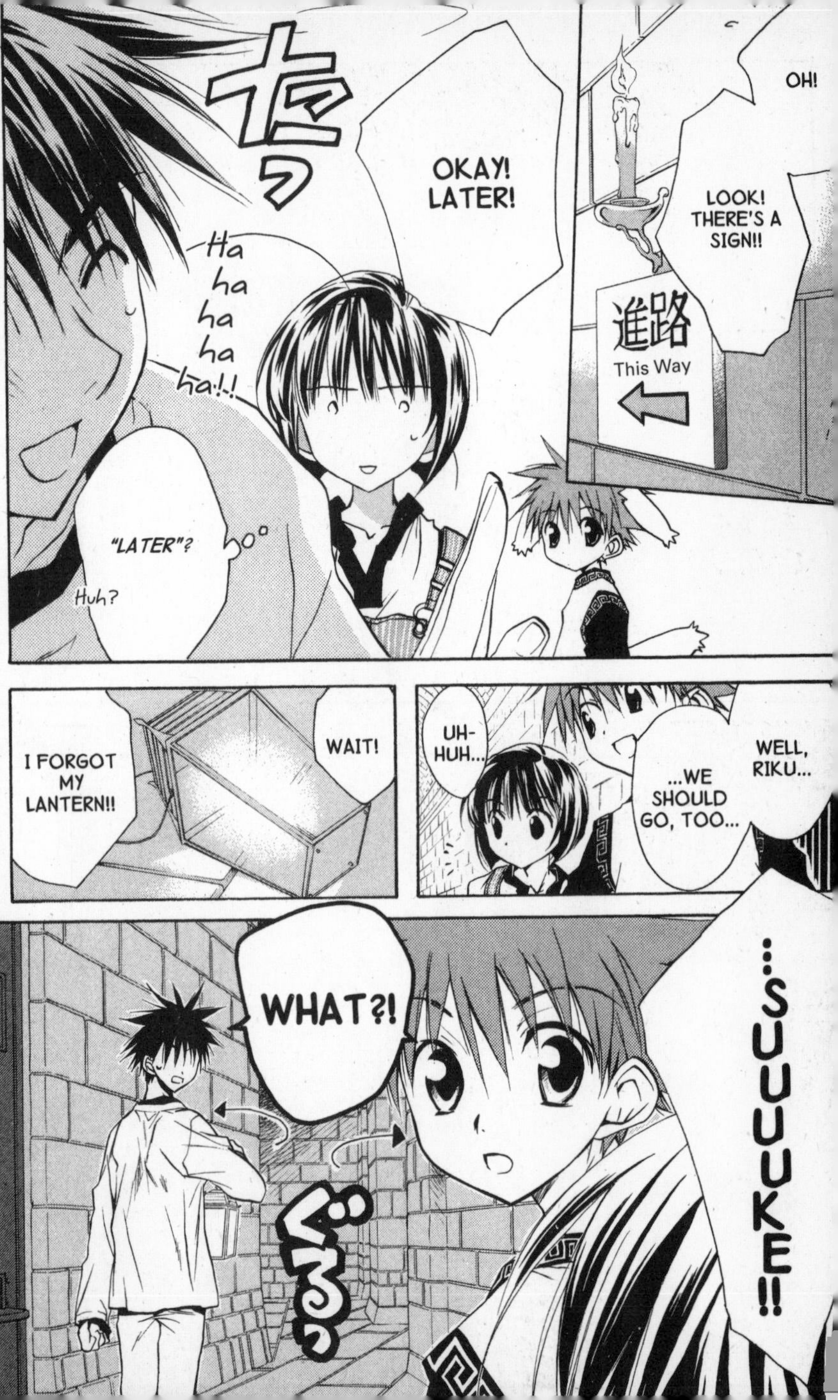
OH!
LOOK! THERE'S A SIGN!!
進路
This Way
たっ
OKAY! LATER!
Ha ha ha ha ha!!
"LATER"?
Huh?
WELL, RIKU...
...WE SHOULD GO, TOO...
UH-HUH...
WAIT!
I FORGOT MY LANTERN!!
...SUUUUKE!!
WHAT?!
ぐるっ

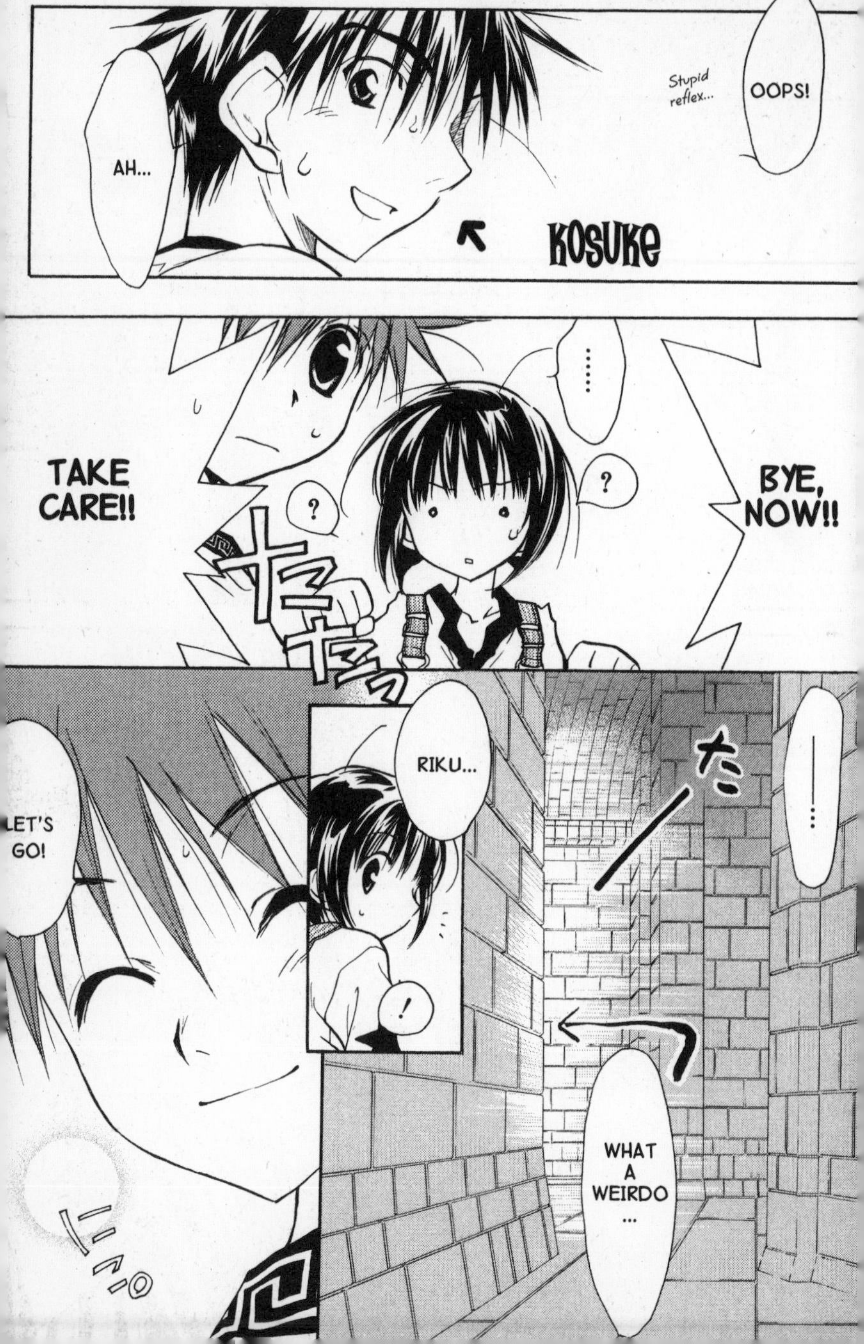
OOPS!
Stupid reflex...
KOSUKE
AH...
BYE, NOW!!
......
?
?
TAKE CARE!!
......
WHAT A WEIRDO ...
RIKU...
!
LET'S GO!

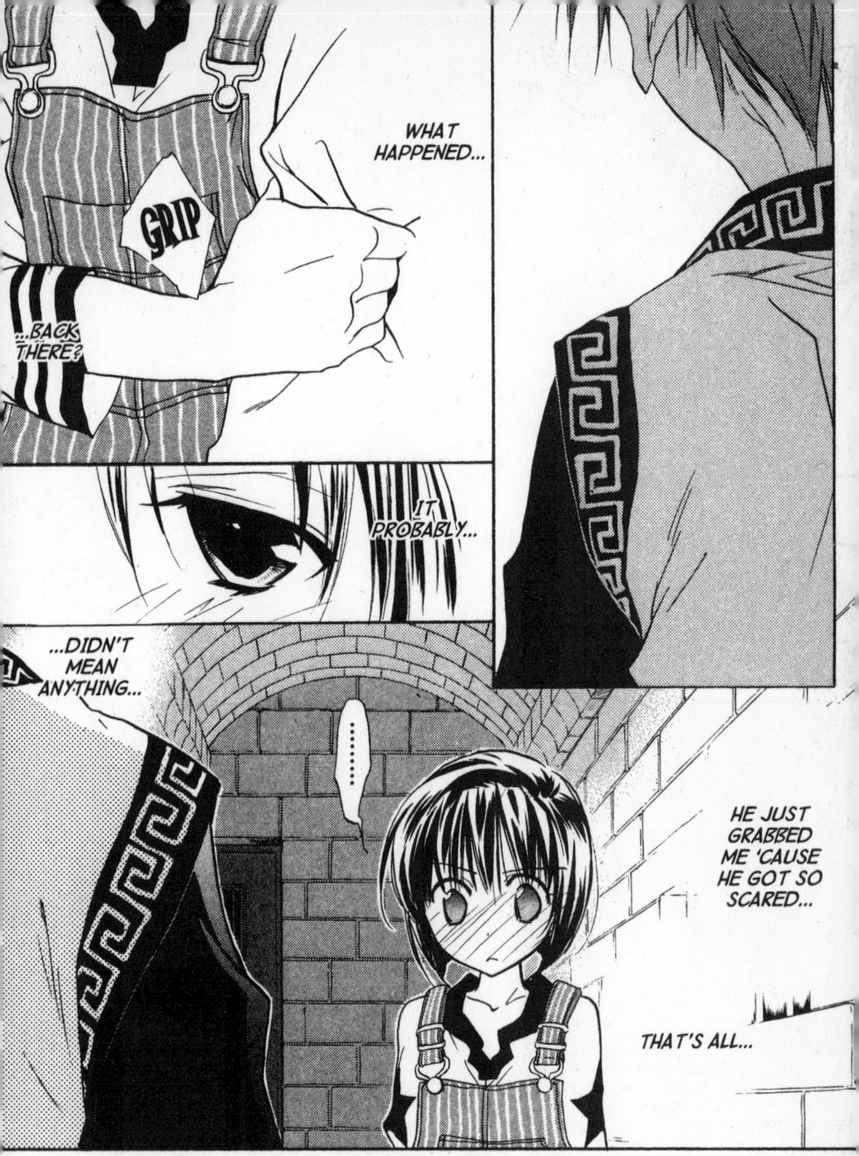
WHAT HAPPENED...
...BACK THERE?
IT PROBABLY...
...DIDN'T MEAN ANYTHING...
......
HE JUST GRABBED ME 'CAUSE HE GOT SO SCARED...
THAT'S ALL...

...RIGHT?

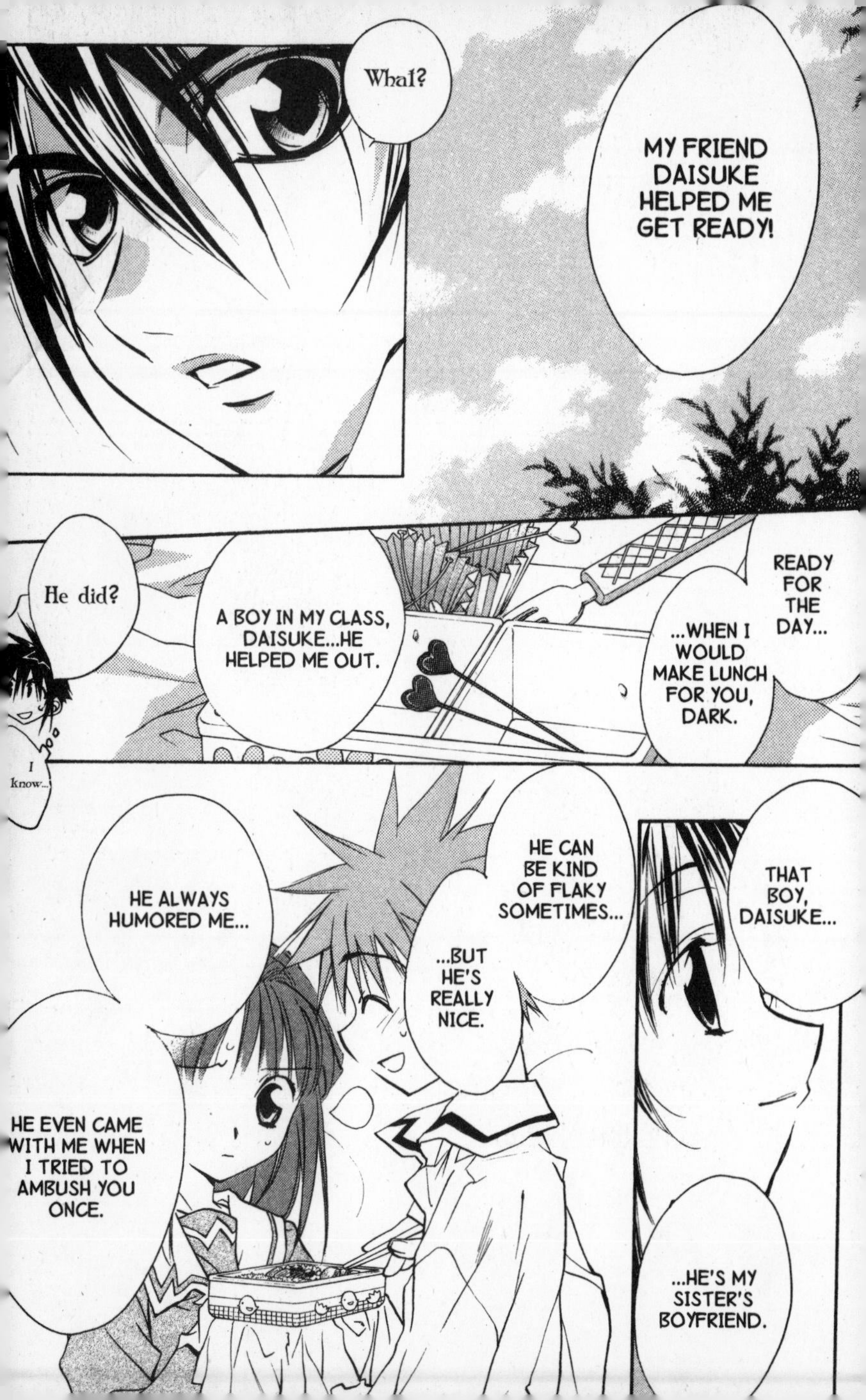
MY FRIEND DAISUKE HELPED ME GET READY!
What?
READY FOR THE DAY...
...WHEN I WOULD MAKE LUNCH FOR YOU, DARK.
A BOY IN MY CLASS, DAISUKE...HE HELPED ME OUT.
He did?
I know...
THAT BOY, DAISUKE...
...HE'S MY SISTER'S BOYFRIEND.
HE CAN BE KIND OF FLAKY SOMETIMES...
...BUT HE'S REALLY NICE.
HE ALWAYS HUMORED ME...
HE EVEN CAME WITH ME WHEN I TRIED TO AMBUSH YOU ONCE.

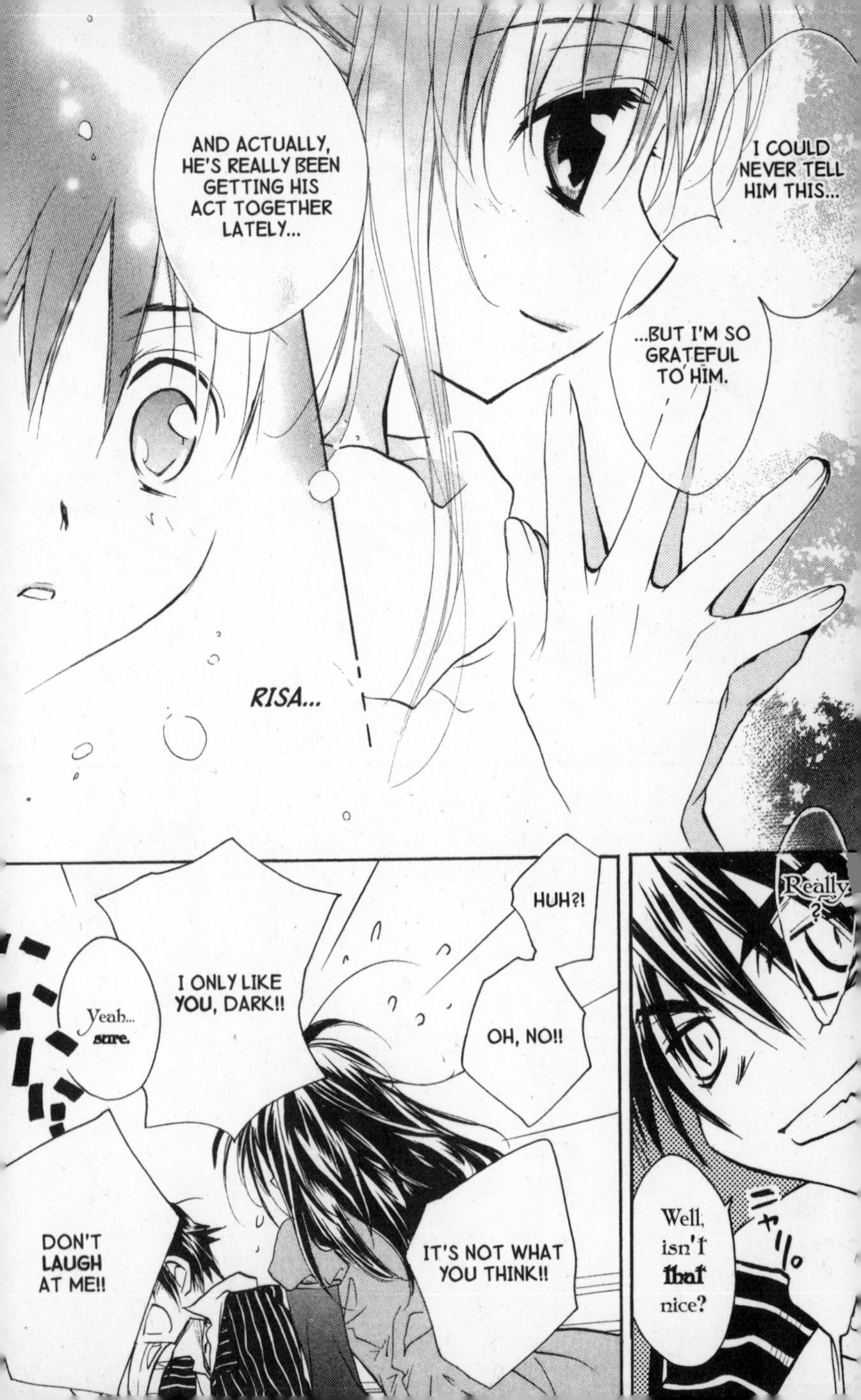
AND ACTUALLY, HE'S REALLY BEEN GETTING HIS ACT TOGETHER LATELY...
I COULD NEVER TELL HIM THIS...
...BUT I'M SO GRATEFUL TO HIM.
RISA...
Really?
Well, isn't that nice?
ニヤリ
HUH?!
OH, NO!!
I ONLY LIKE YOU, DARK!!
Yeah... sure.
IT'S NOT WHAT YOU THINK!!
DON'T LAUGH AT ME!!

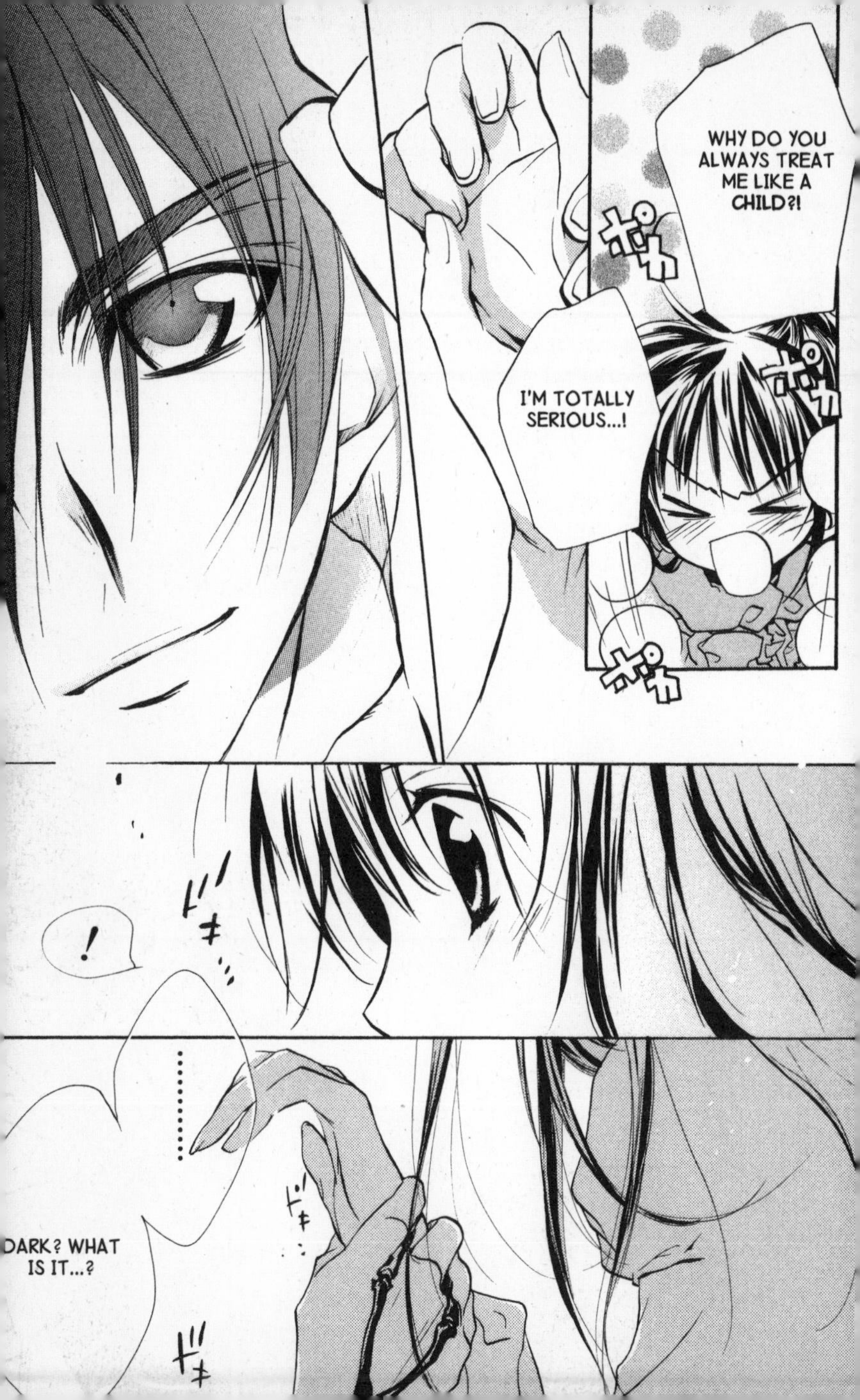
WHY DO YOU ALWAYS TREAT ME LIKE A CHILD?!
ポカ
ポカ
I'M TOTALLY SERIOUS...!
ポカ
ドキ...
!
......
ドキ...
DARK? WHAT IS IT...?
ドキ

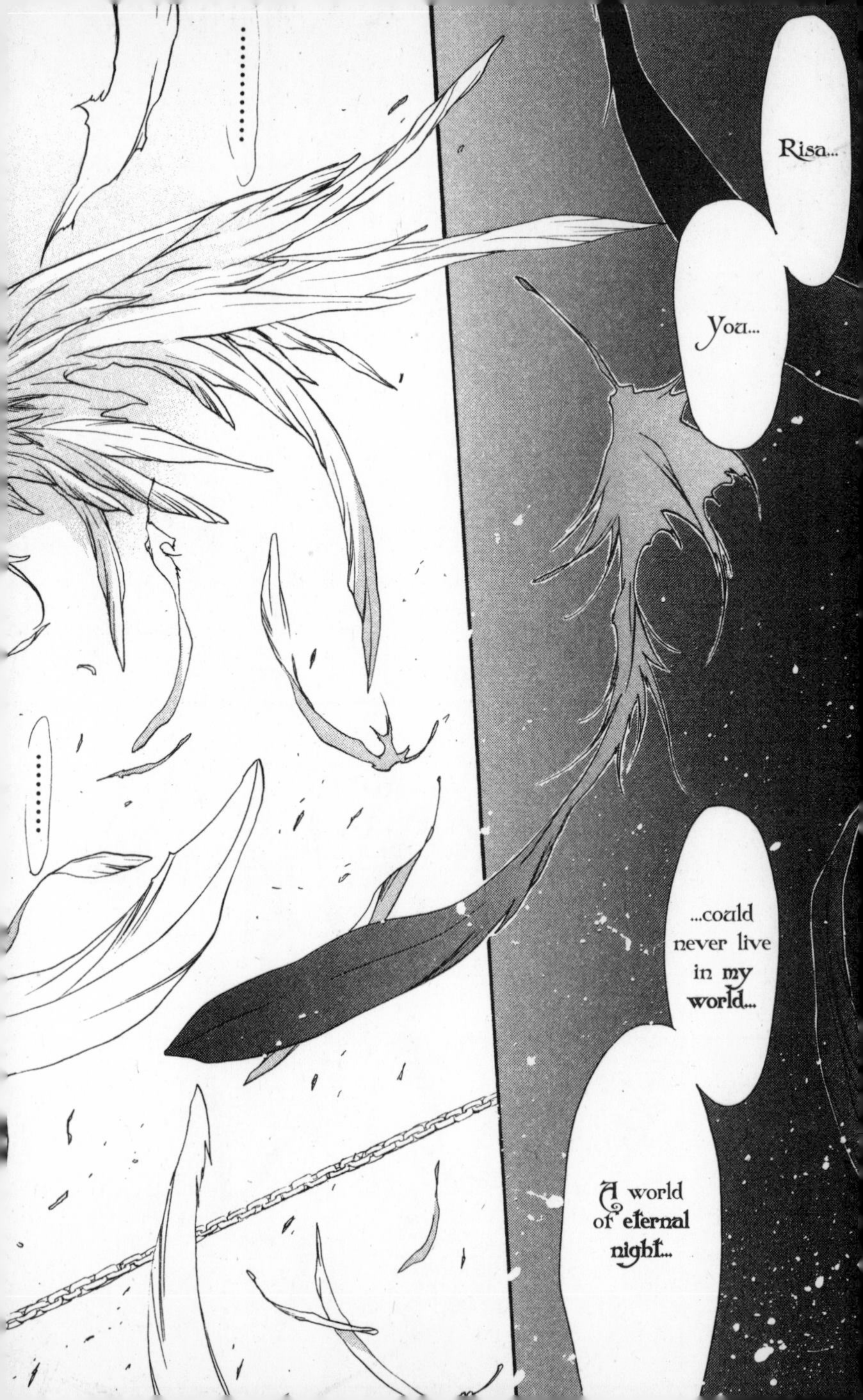
Risa...
You...
...could never live in my world...
A world of eternal night...
......
......

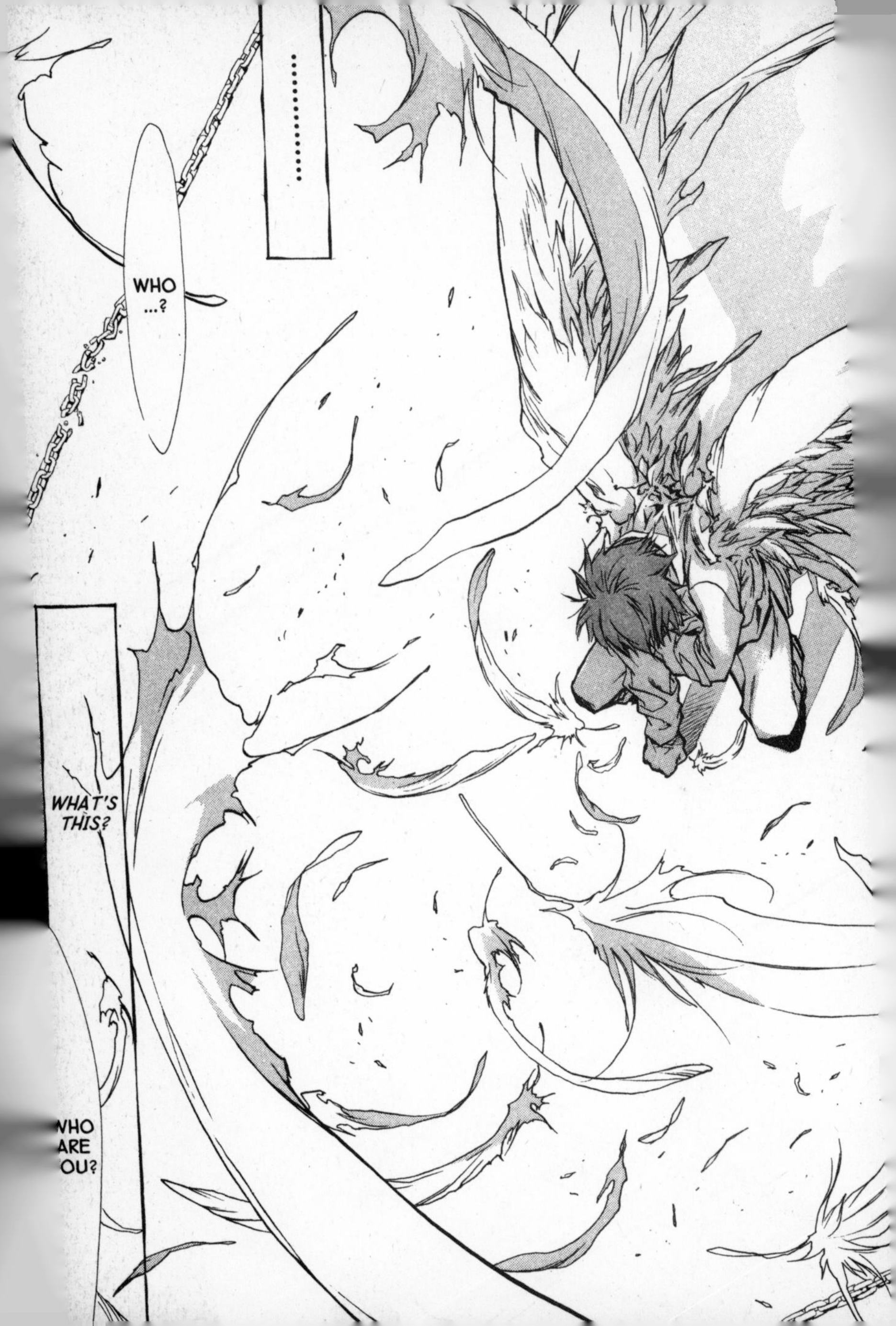
......
WHO ...?
WHAT'S THIS?
WHO ARE OU?

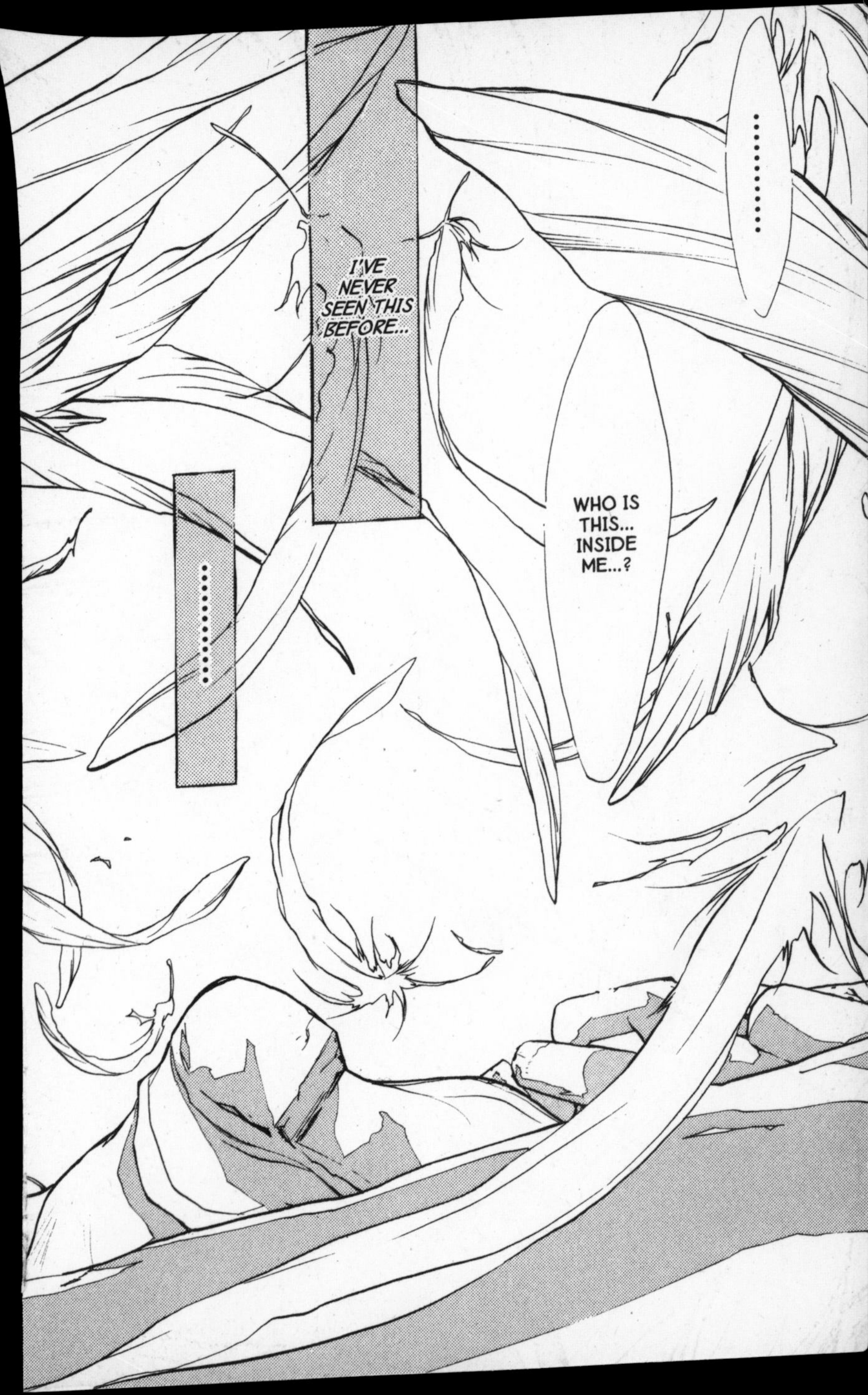
……
I'VE NEVER SEEN THIS BEFORE…
WHO IS THIS… INSIDE ME…?
……

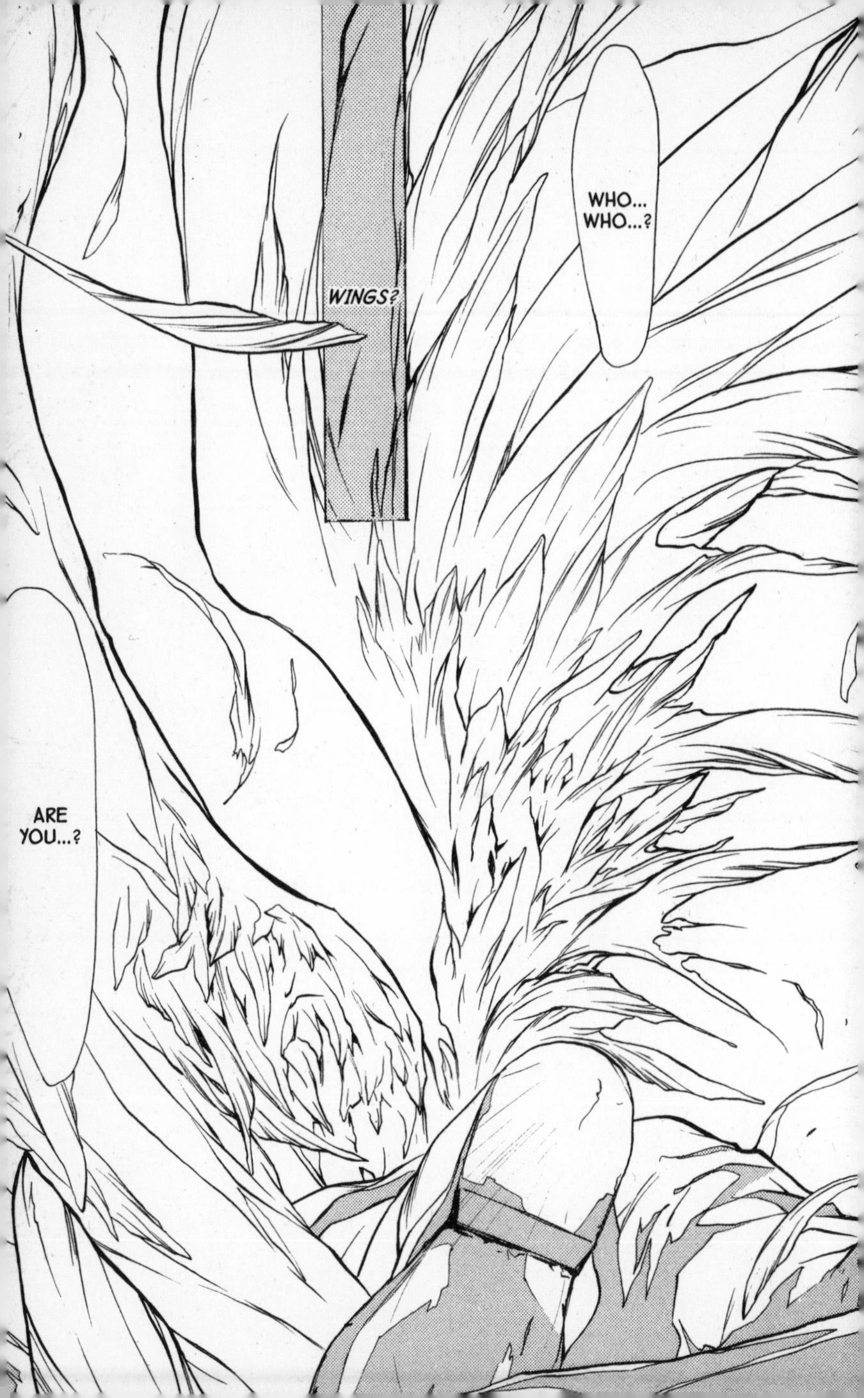
WHO... WHO...?
WINGS?
ARE YOU...?

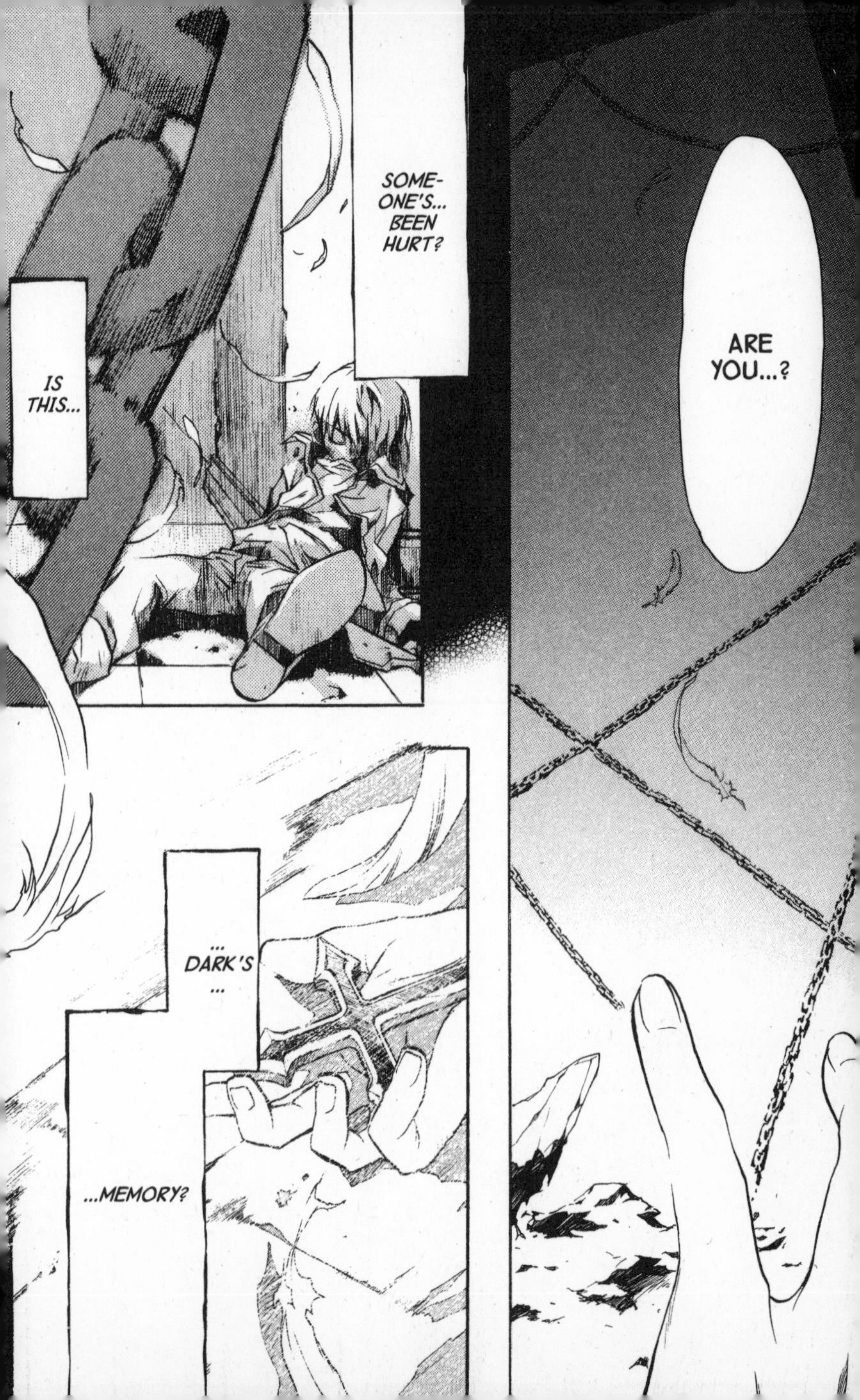
ARE YOU...?
SOME-ONE'S... BEEN HURT?
IS THIS...
... DARK'S ...
...MEMORY?

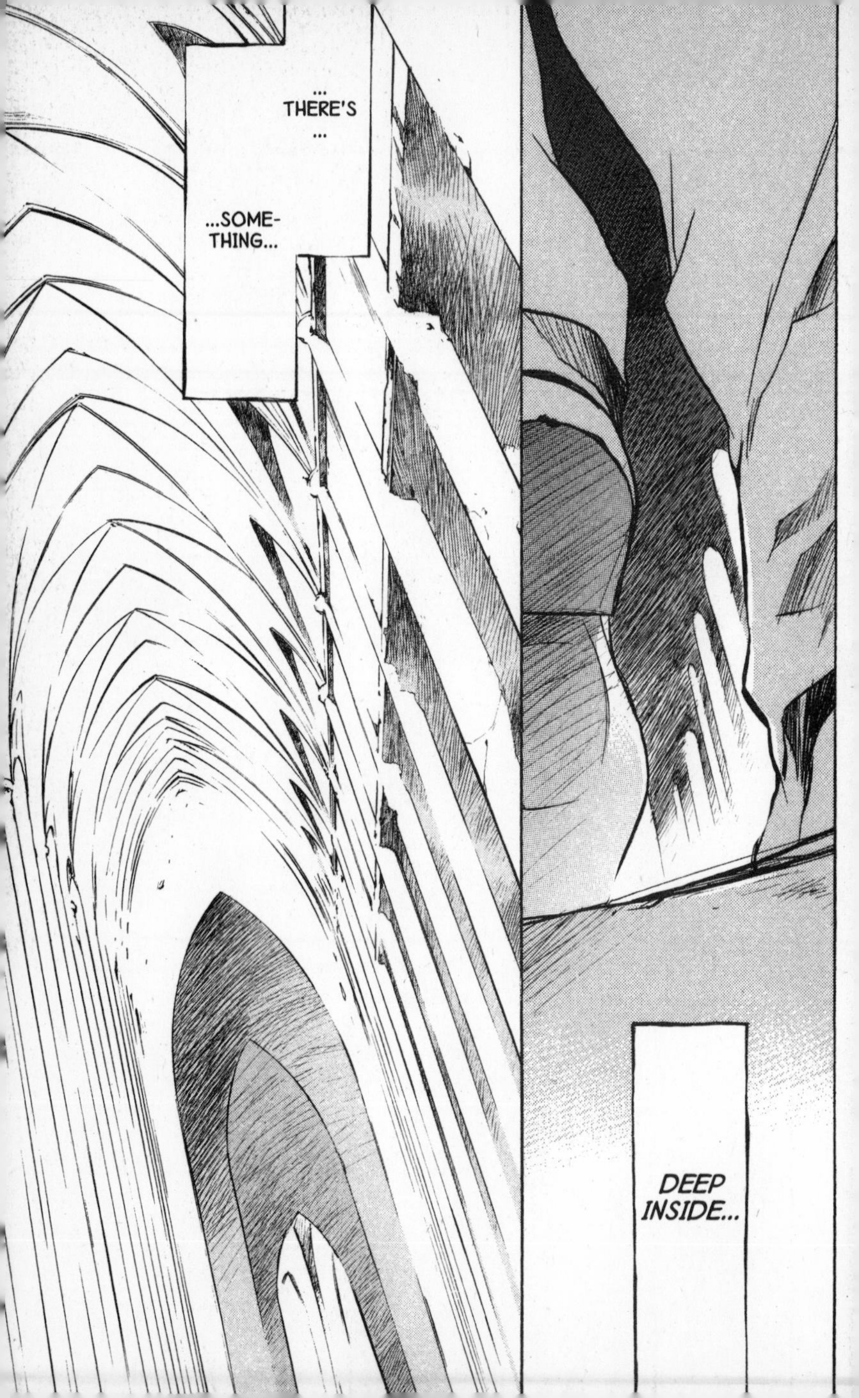
DEEP INSIDE...
... THERE'S ...
...SOME-THING...

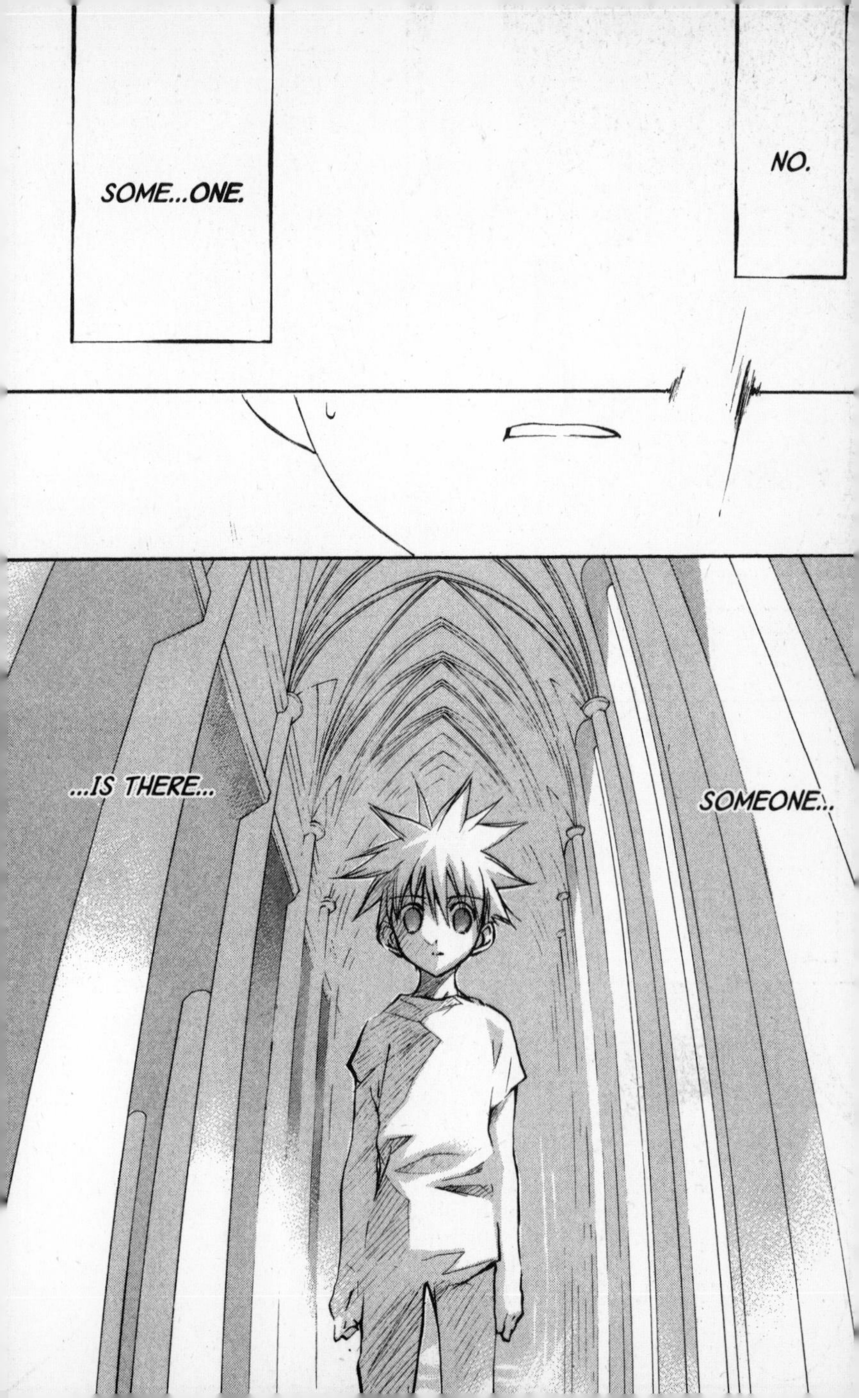
NO.
SOME...ONE.
SOMEONE...
...IS THERE...

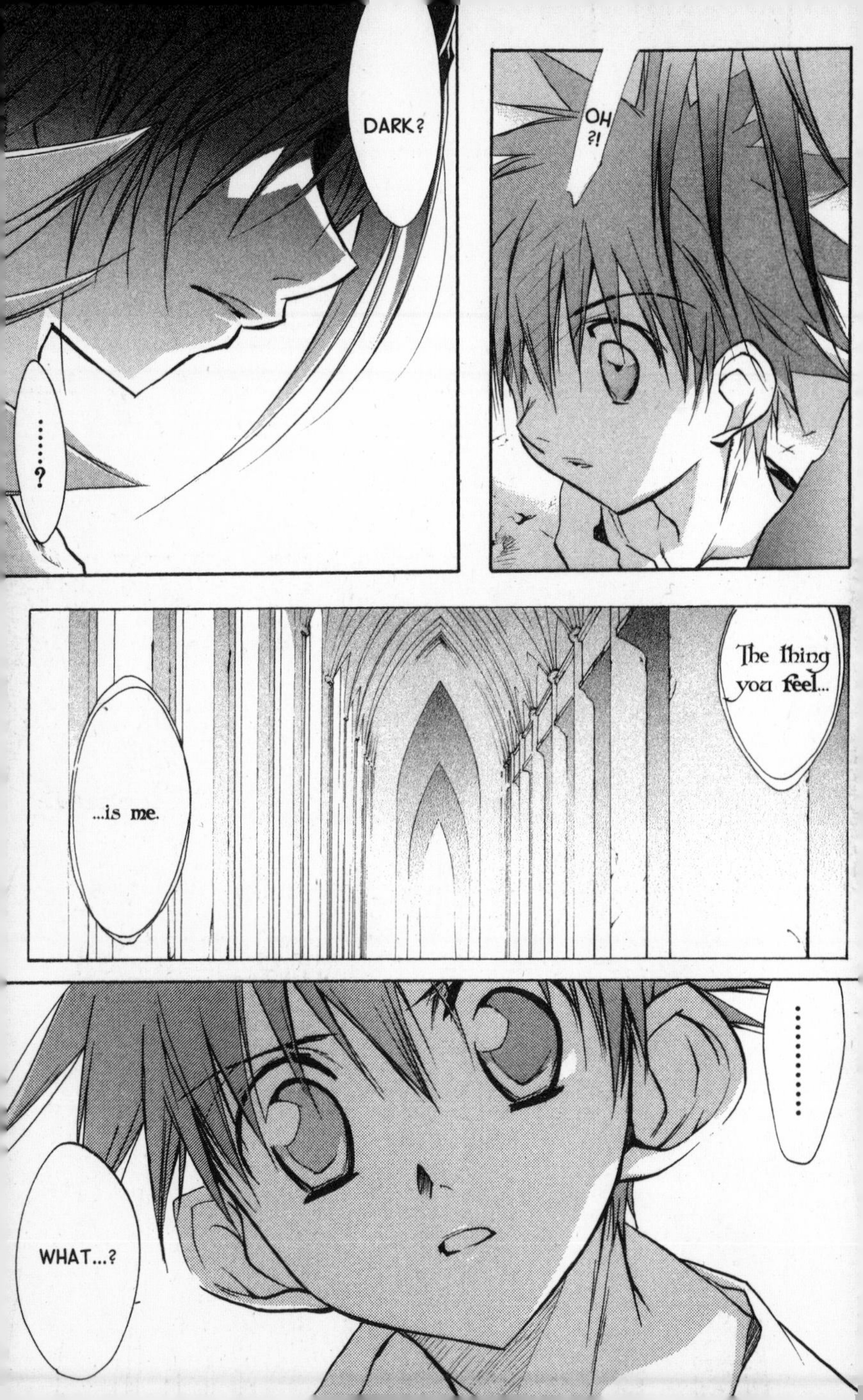
OH ?!
DARK?
.....?
The thing you feel...
...is me.
....
WHAT...?

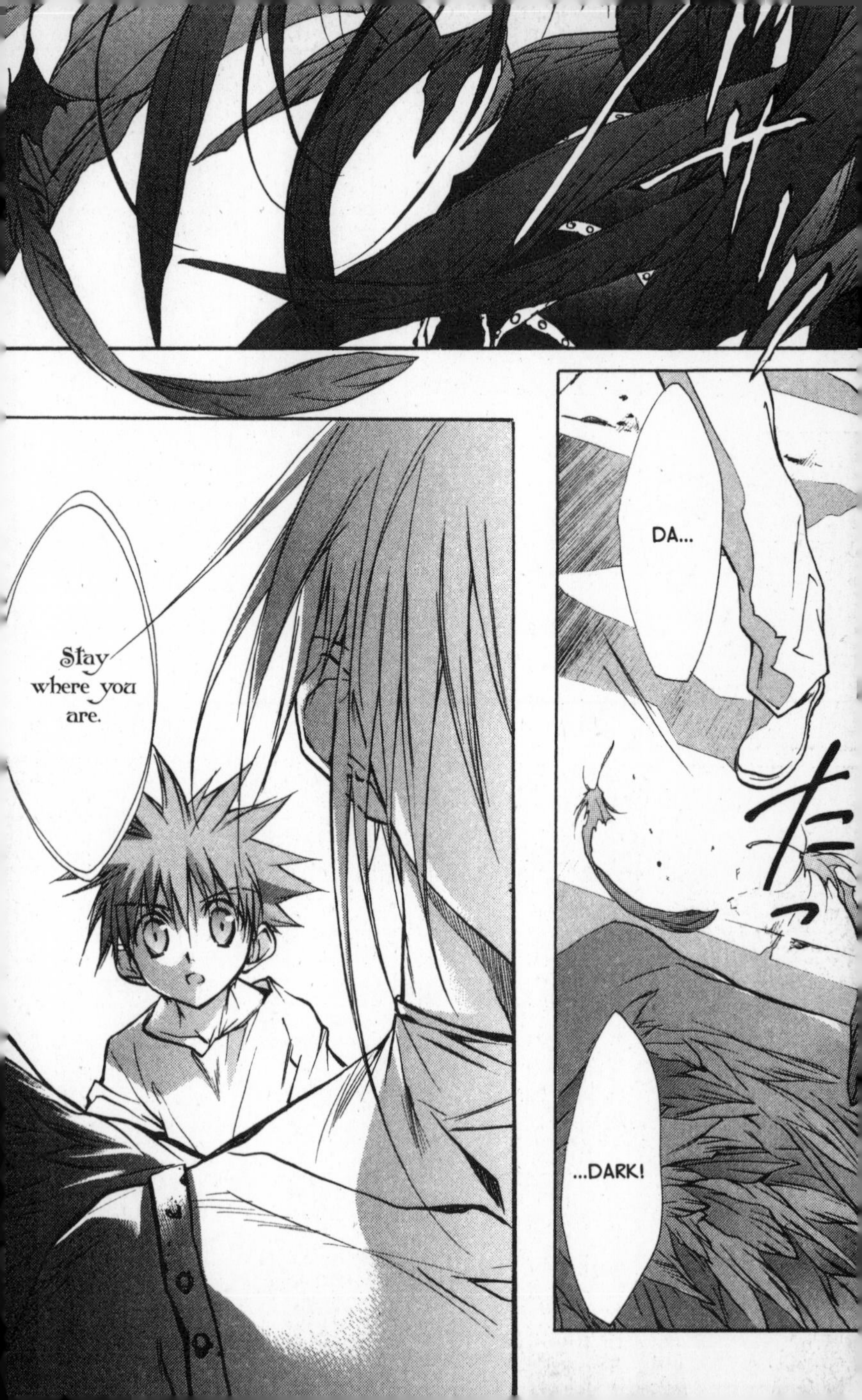
DA...
...DARK!
Stay where you are.

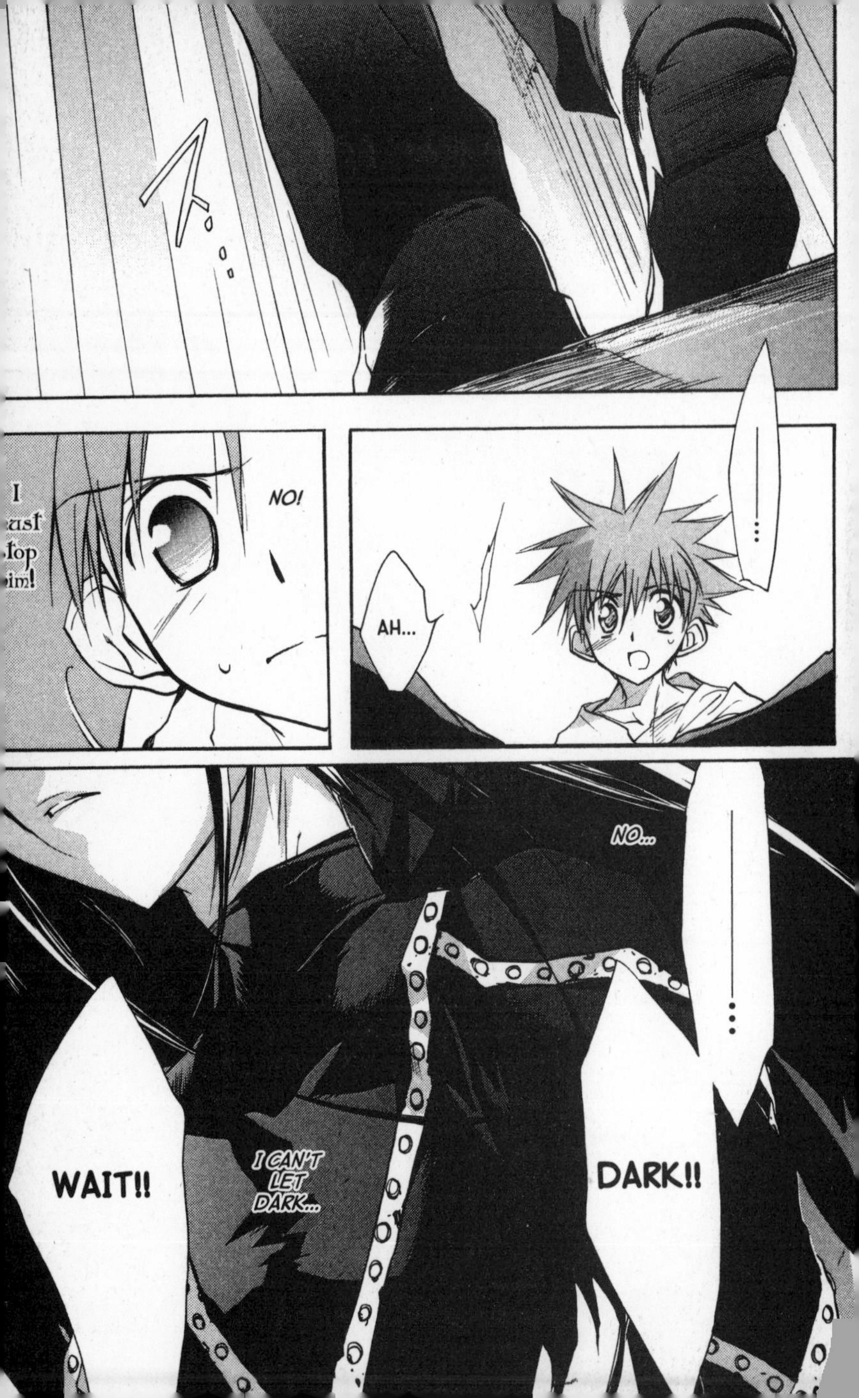

ス
...
AH...
NO!
I ust top im!
...
NO...
DARK!!
I CAN'T LET DARK...
WAIT!!

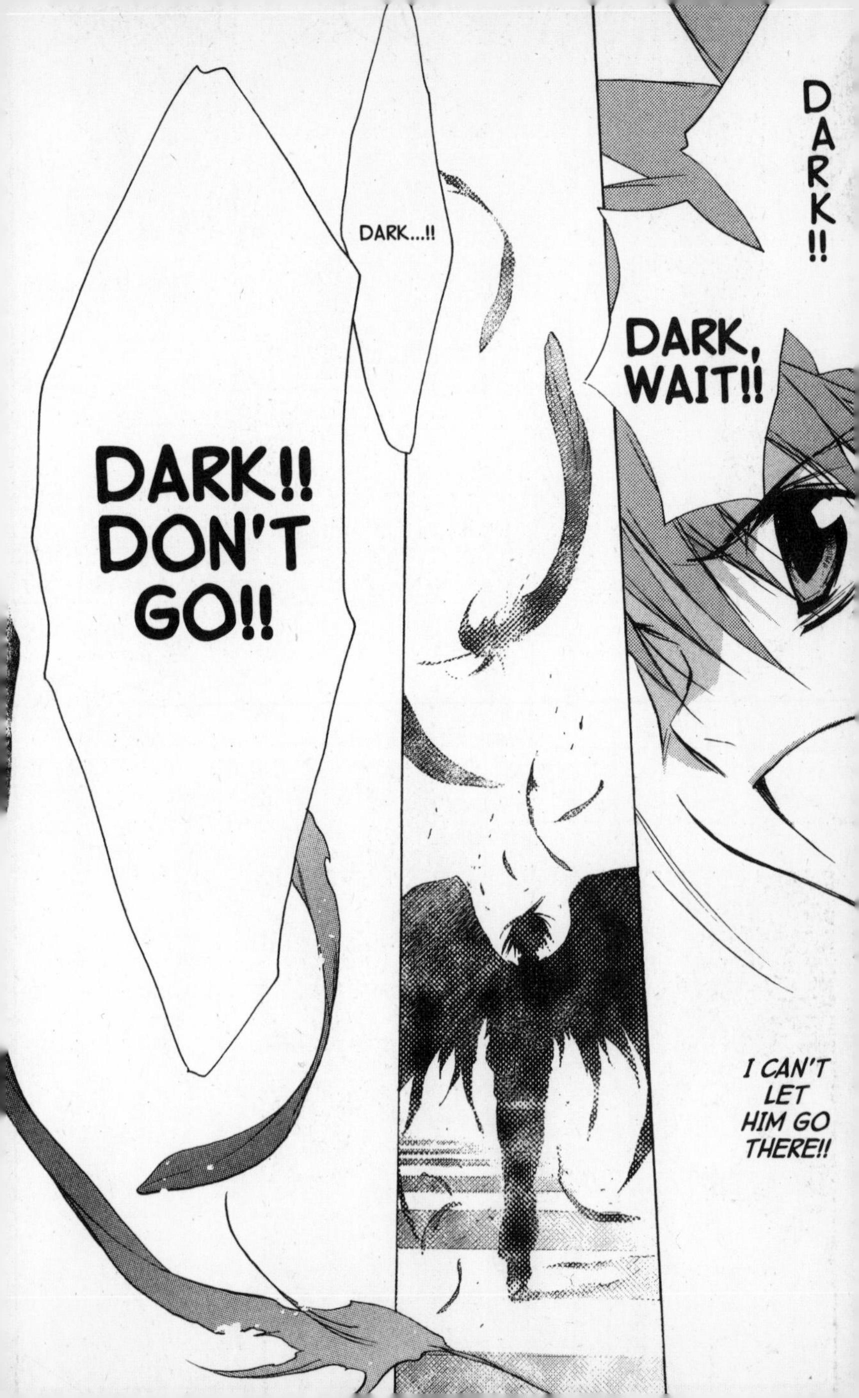
DARK!!
DARK, WAIT!!
I CAN'T LET HIM GO THERE!!
DARK...!!
DARK!! DON'T GO!!

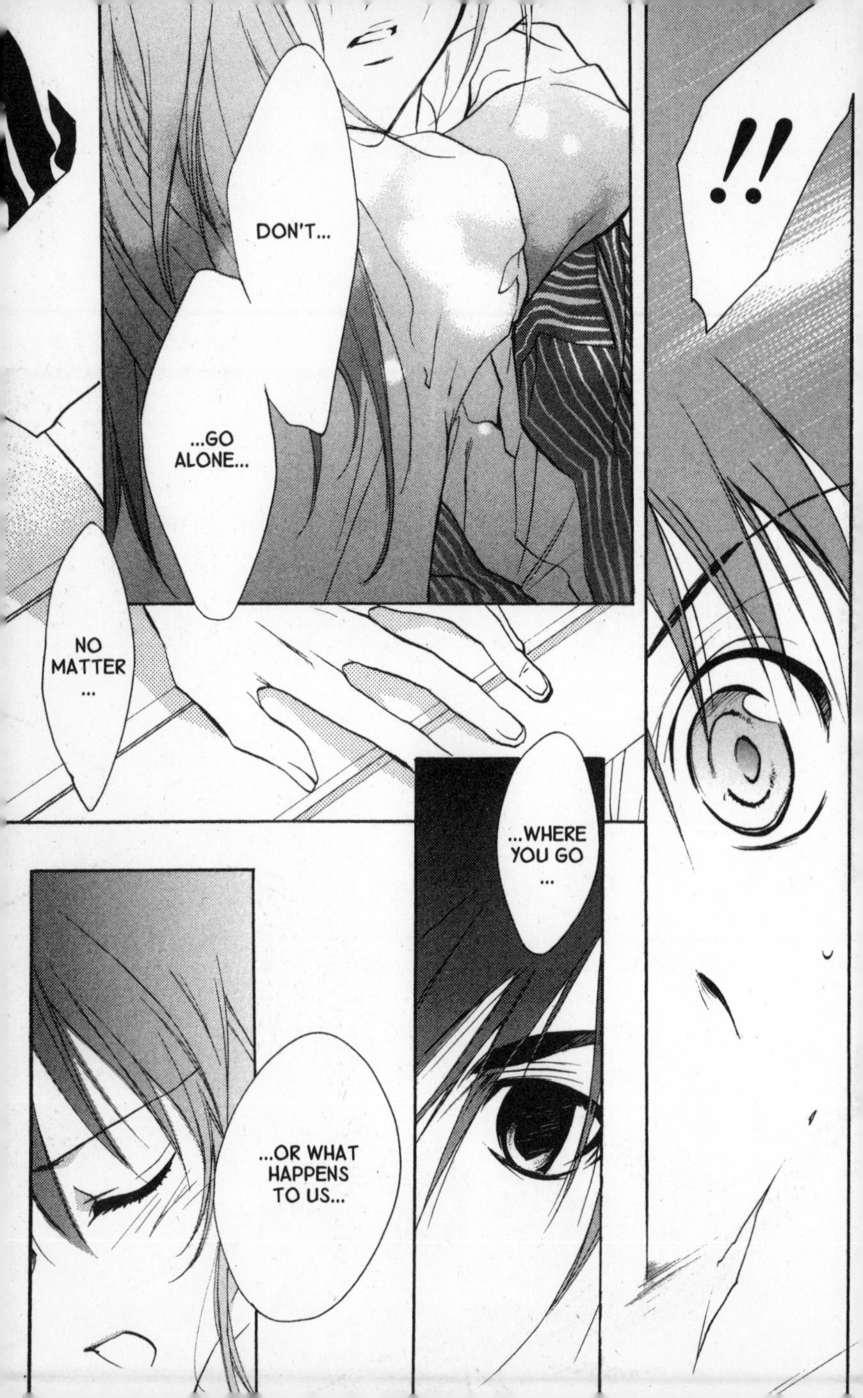
!!
DON'T...
...GO ALONE...
NO MATTER ...
...WHERE YOU GO ...
...OR WHAT HAPPENS TO US...

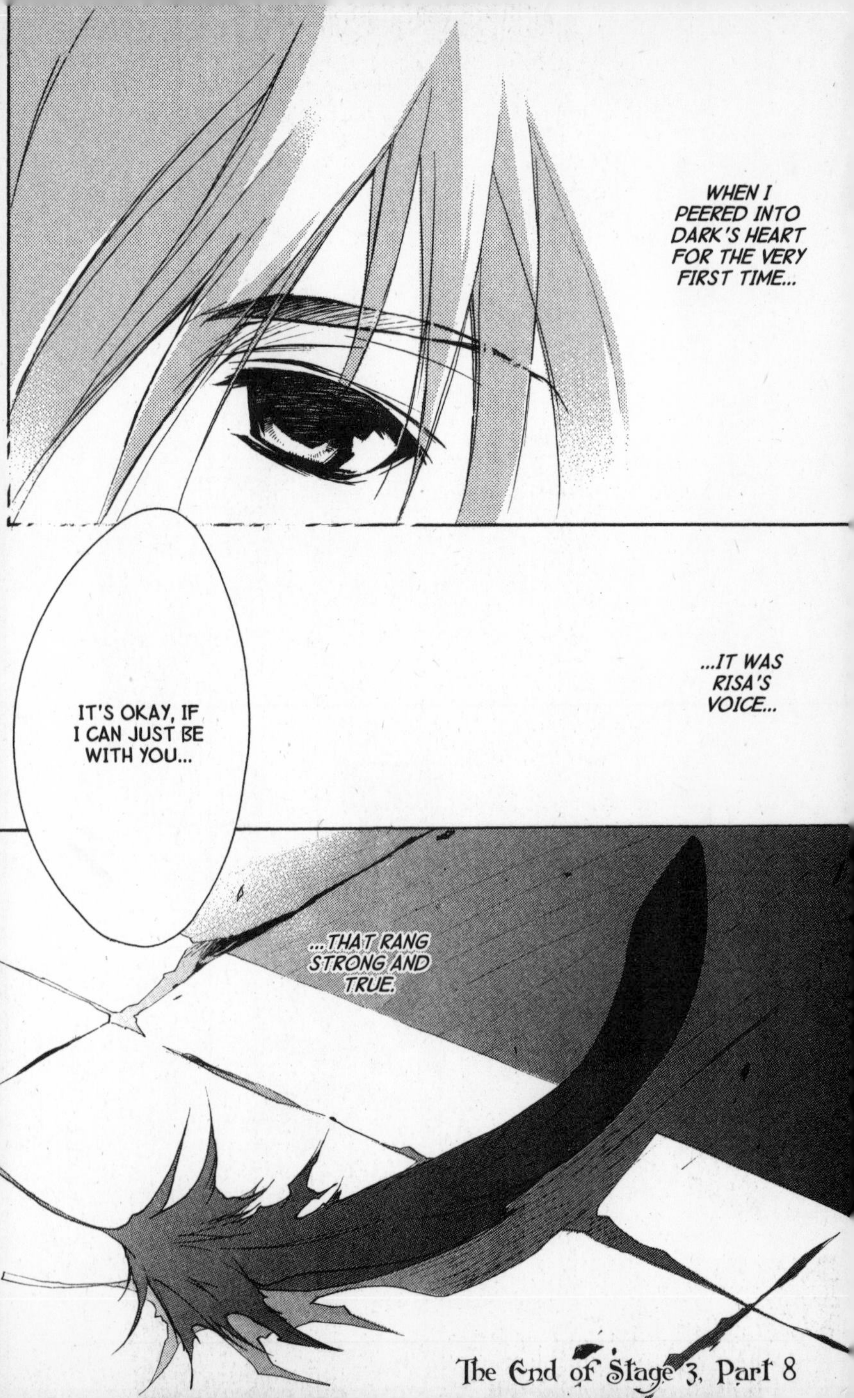
WHEN I PEERED INTO DARK'S HEART FOR THE VERY FIRST TIME...
...IT WAS RISA'S VOICE...
IT'S OKAY, IF I CAN JUST BE WITH YOU...
...THAT RANG STRONG AND TRUE.
The End of Stage 3, Part 8

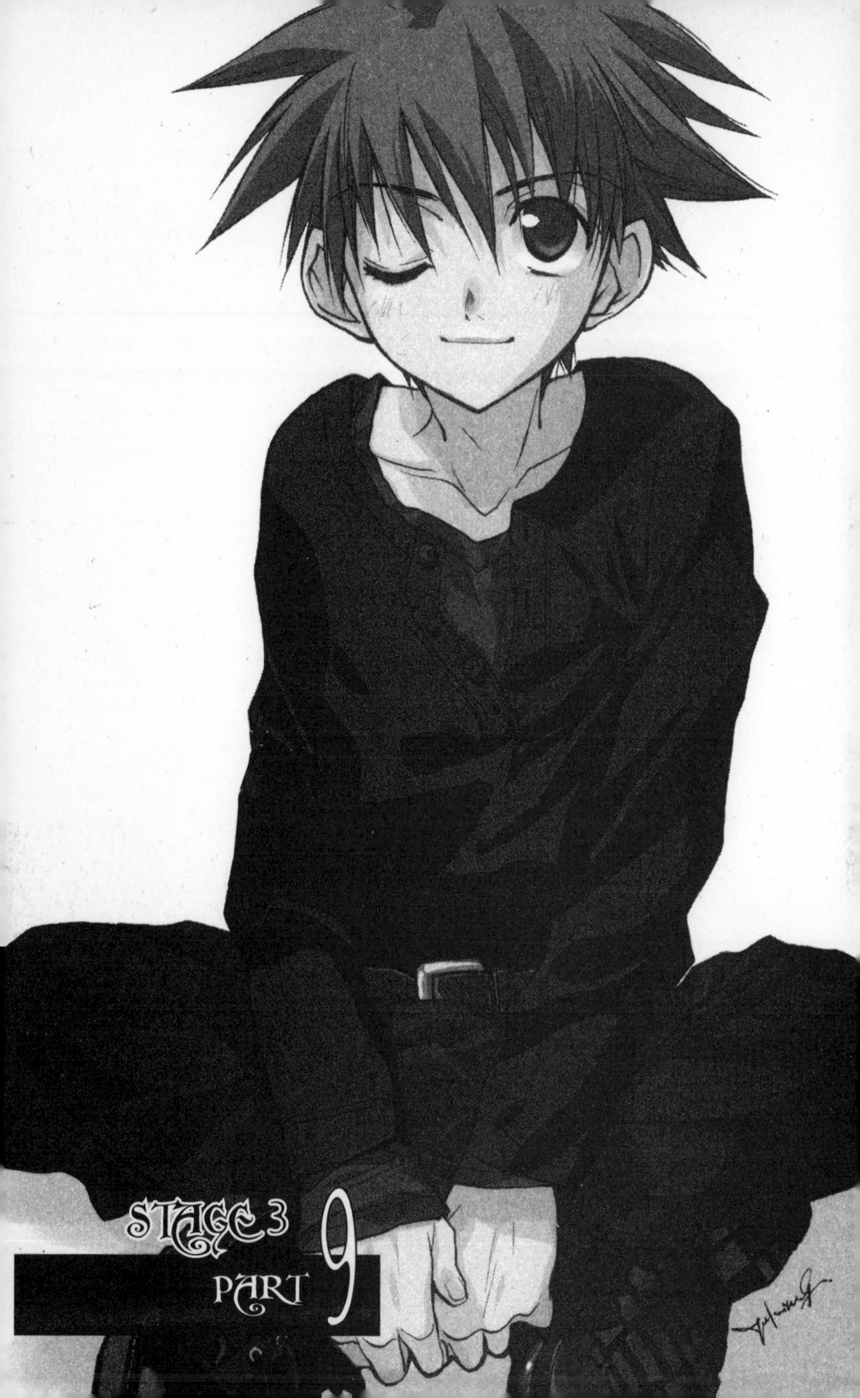
STAGE 3
PART 9

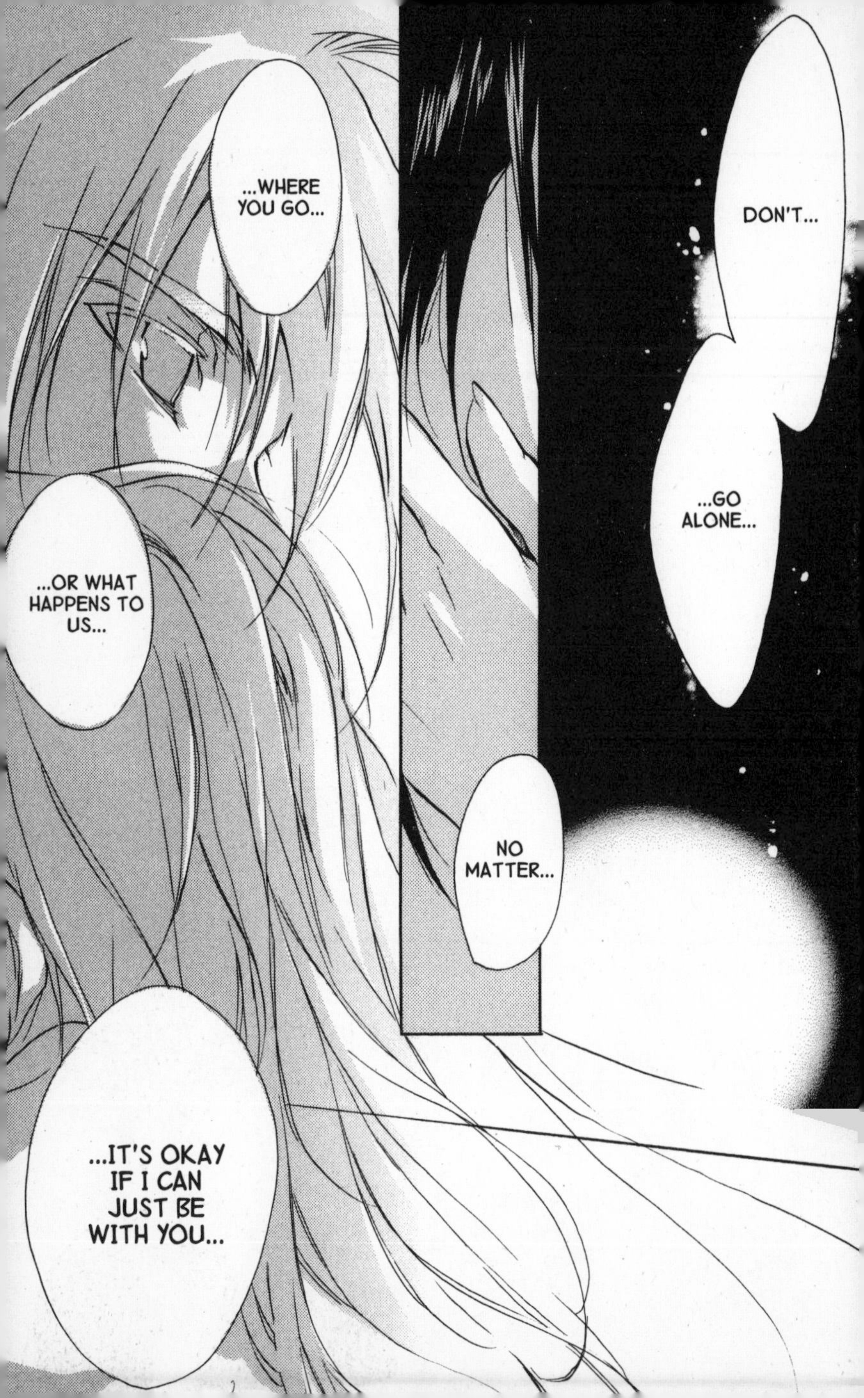
DON'T...
...GO ALONE...
NO MATTER...
...WHERE YOU GO...
...OR WHAT HAPPENS TO US...
...IT'S OKAY IF I CAN JUST BE WITH YOU...

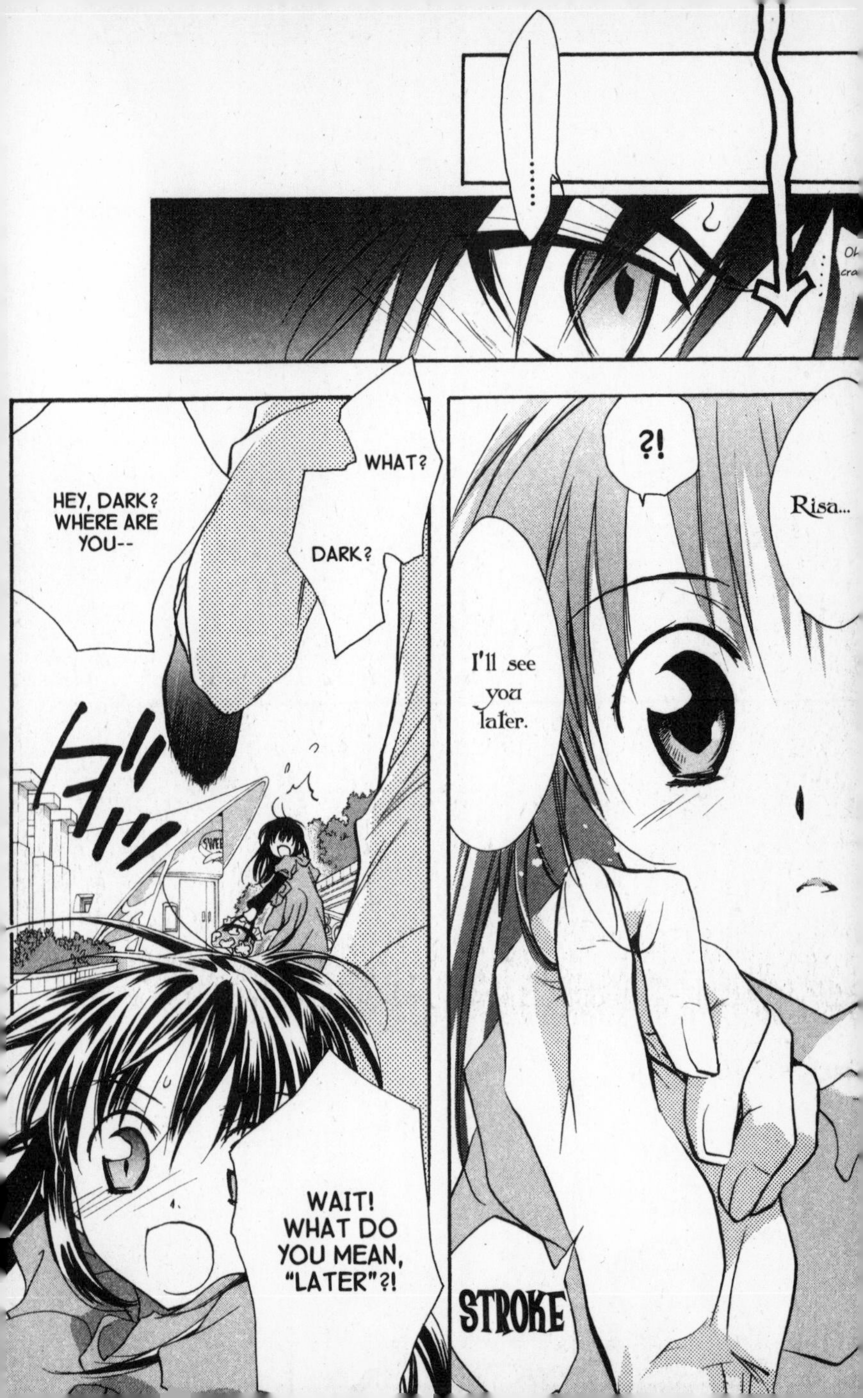
......
?!
Risa...
I'll see you later.
STROKE
WHAT?
DARK?
HEY, DARK? WHERE ARE YOU--
WAIT! WHAT DO YOU MEAN, "LATER"?!

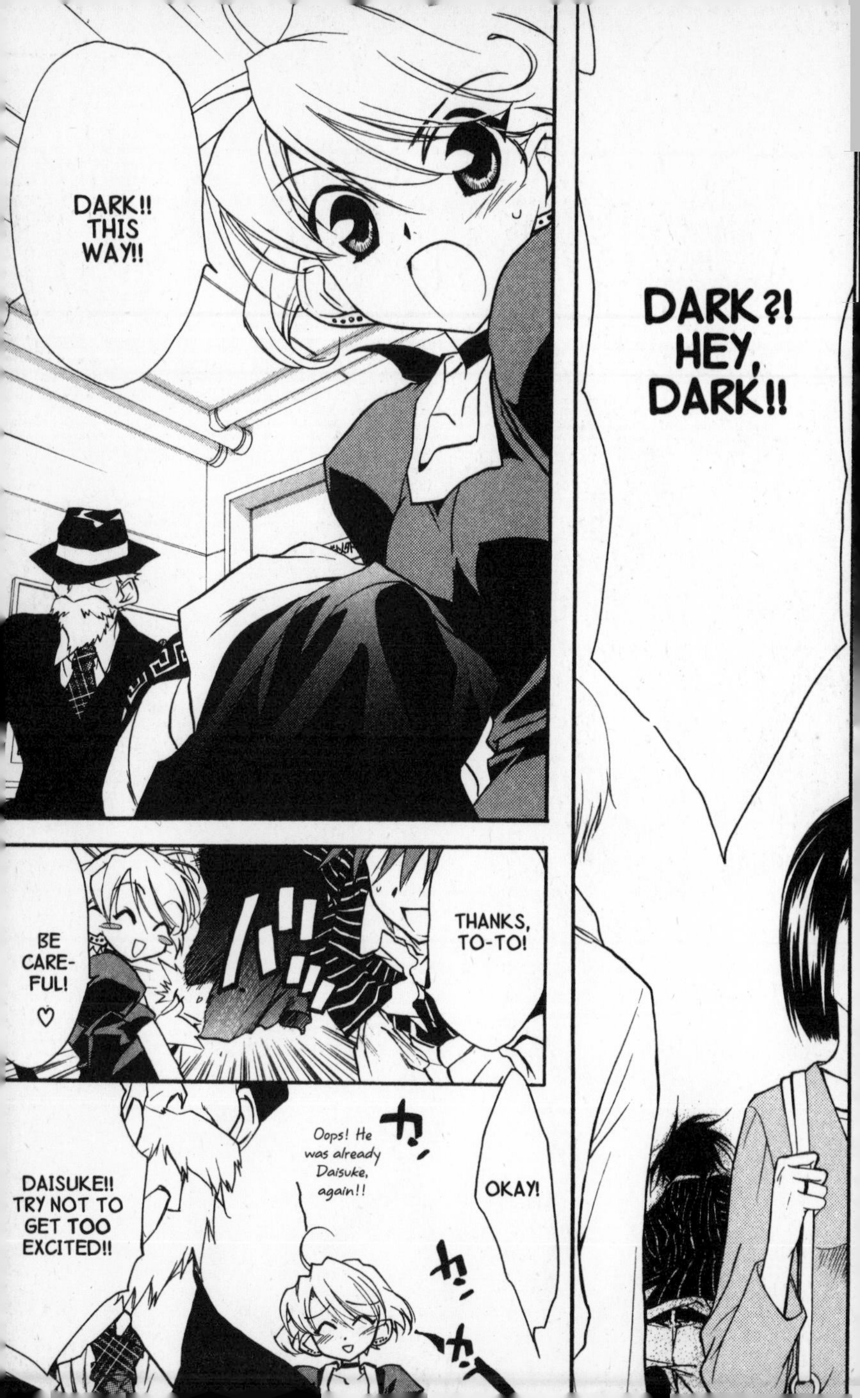
DARK?! HEY, DARK!!
DARK!! THIS WAY!!
THANKS, TO-TO!
BE CARE-FUL! ♡
OKAY!
Oops! He was already Daisuke, again!!
DAISUKE!! TRY NOT TO GET TOO EXCITED!!

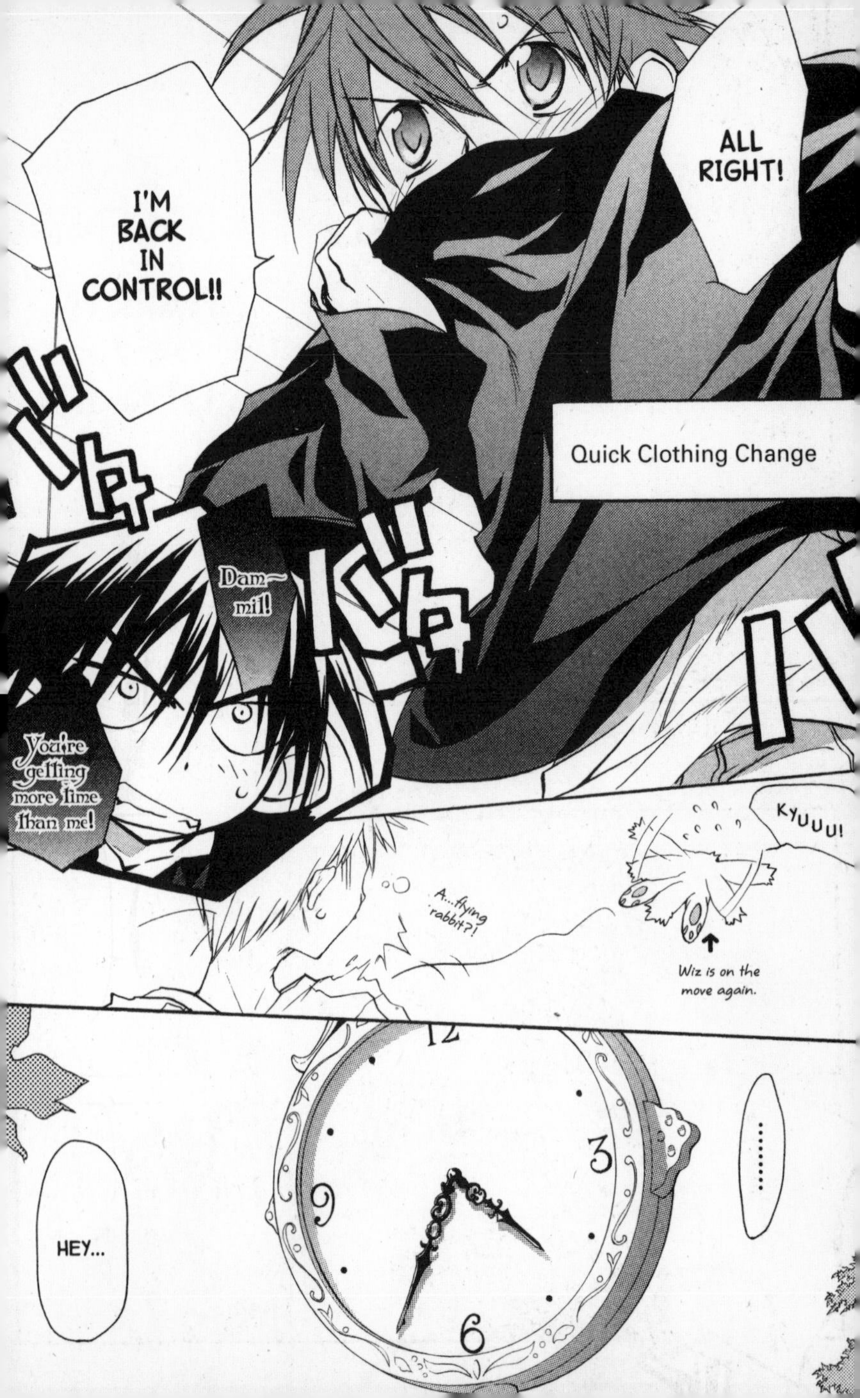
ALL RIGHT!
I'M BACK IN CONTROL!!
Quick Clothing Change
Dam~mit!
You're getting more time than me!
KYUUU!
A...flying rabbit?!
Wiz is on the move again.
......
HEY...

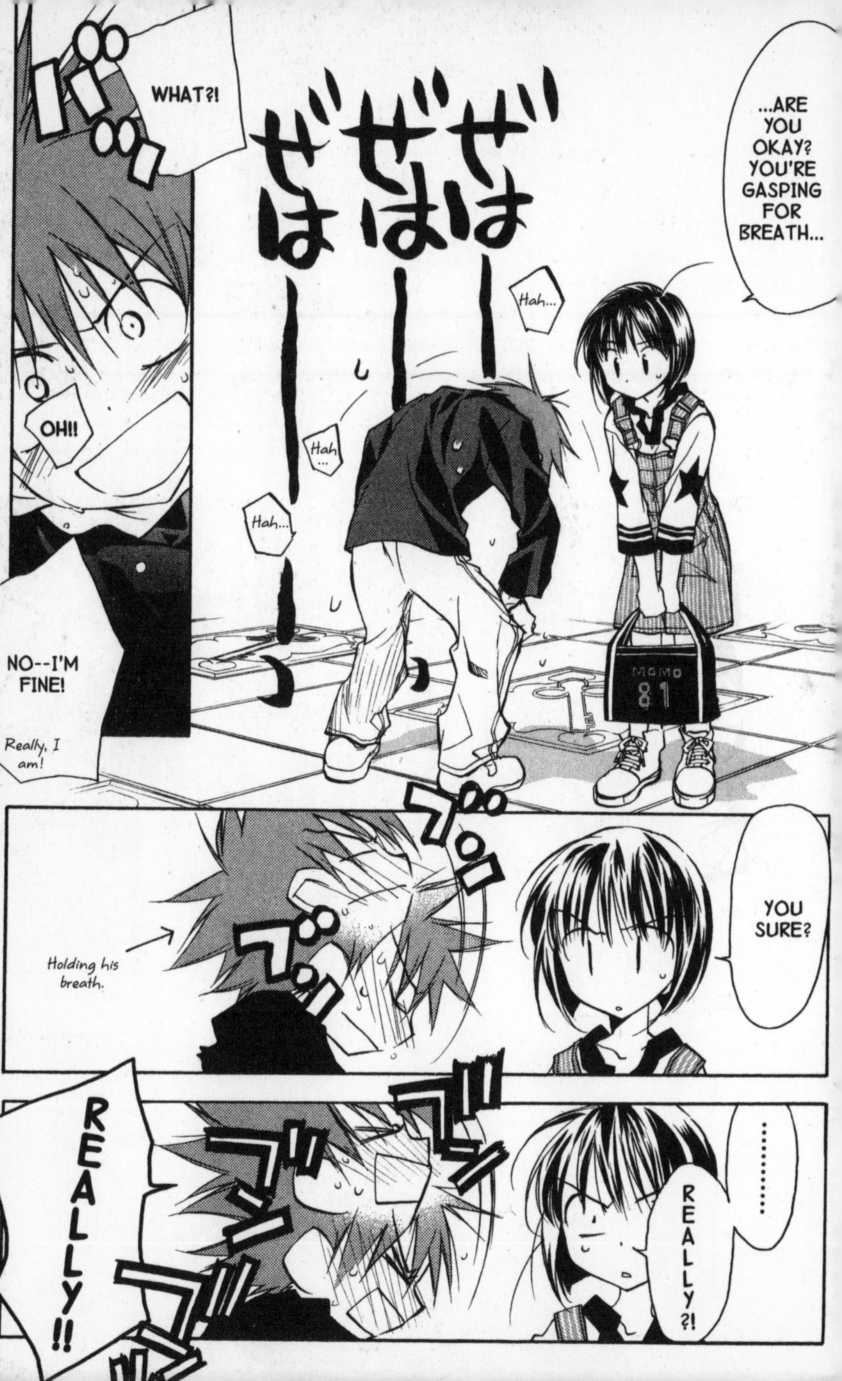
...ARE YOU OKAY? YOU'RE GASPING FOR BREATH...
ぜはー
ぜはー
ぜはー
Hah...
Hah...
Hah...
WHAT?!
OH!!
NO--I'M FINE!
Really, I am!
YOU SURE?
Holding his breath.
....
REALLY?!
REALLY REALLY!!

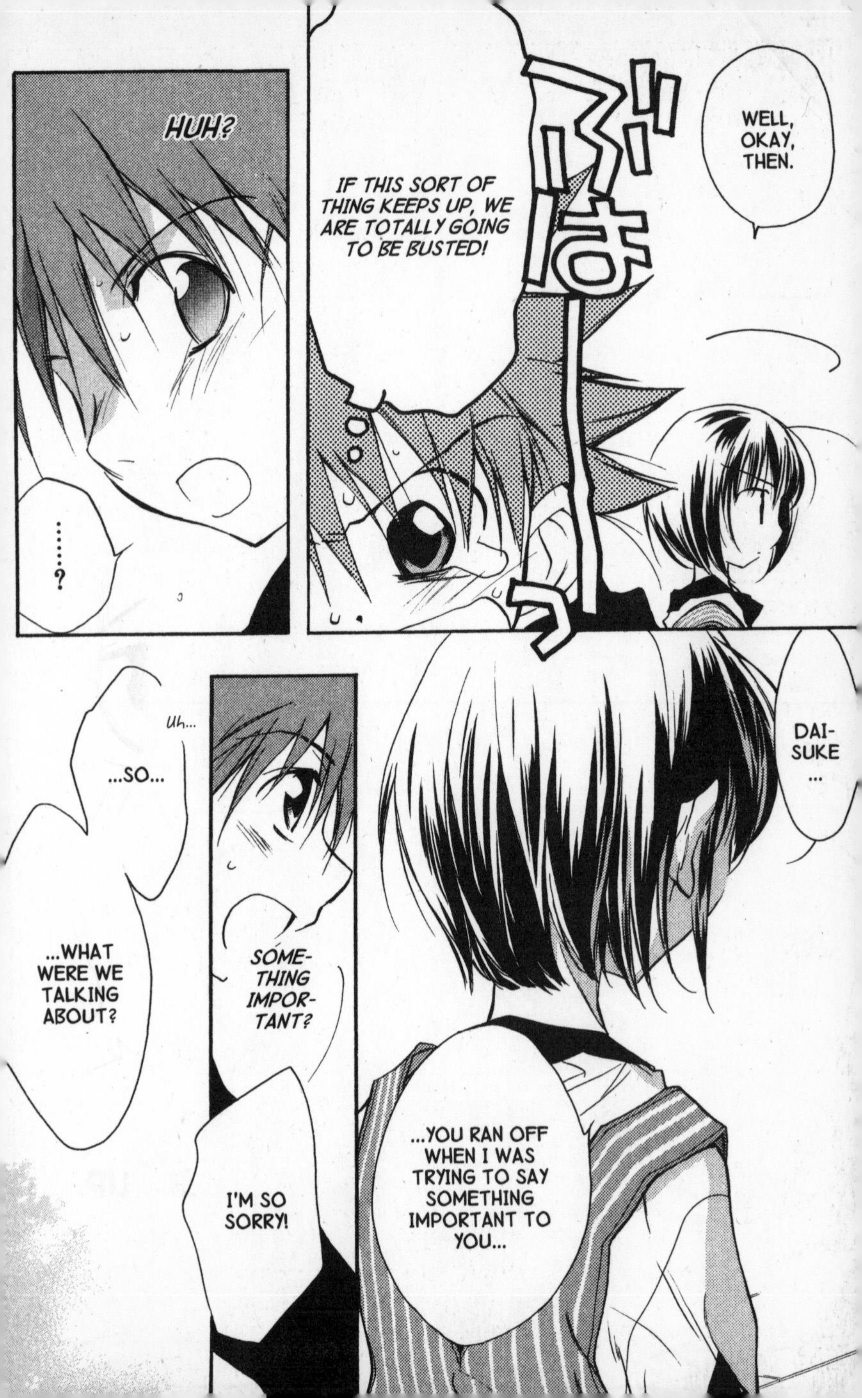
WELL, OKAY, THEN.
ぶはーっ
IF THIS SORT OF THING KEEPS UP, WE ARE TOTALLY GOING TO BE BUSTED!
HUH?
......?
DAI-SUKE ...
...YOU RAN OFF WHEN I WAS TRYING TO SAY SOMETHING IMPORTANT TO YOU...
SOME-THING IMPOR-TANT?
I'M SO SORRY!
Uh...
...SO...
...WHAT WERE WE TALKING ABOUT?

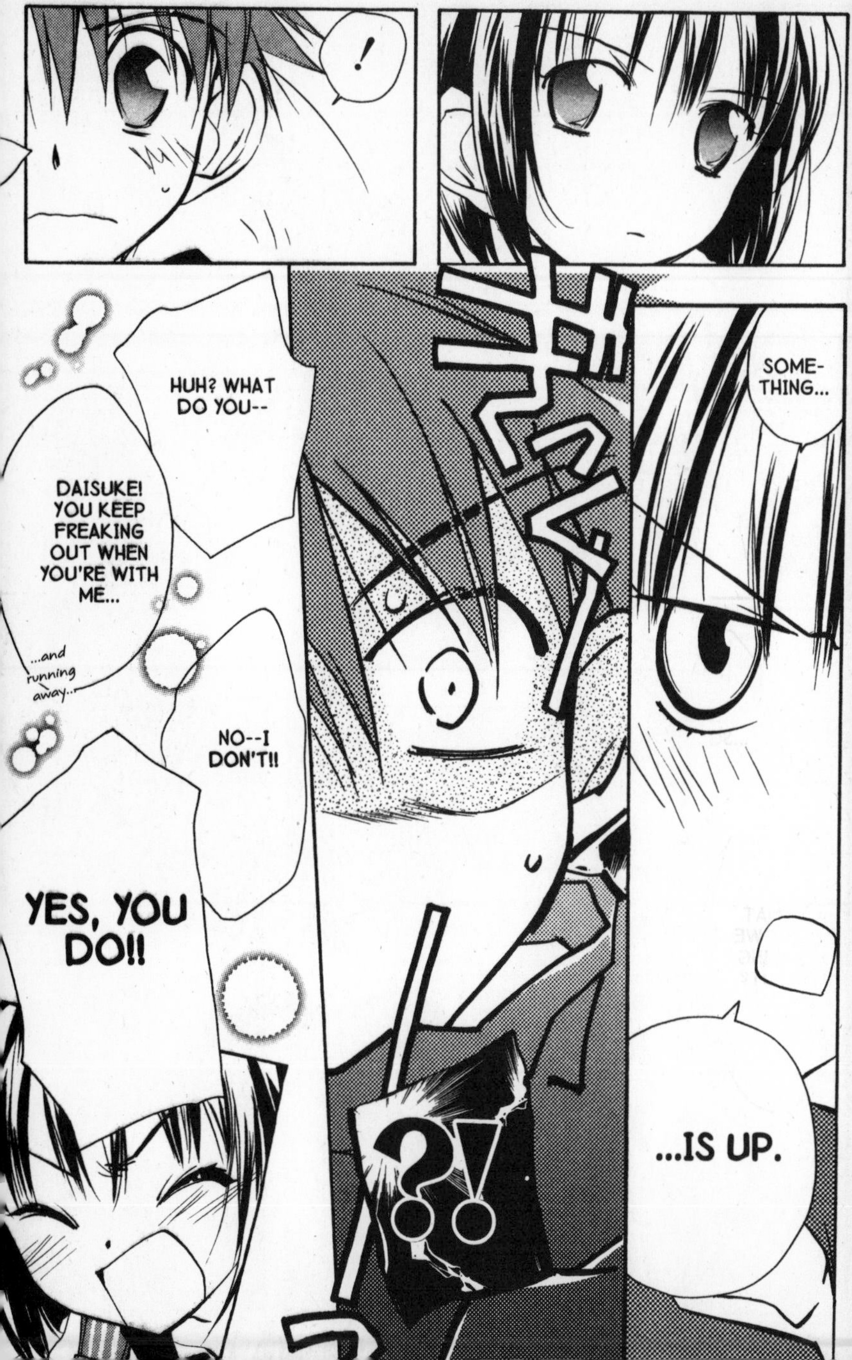
!
SOME-THING...
...IS UP.
?!
HUH? WHAT DO YOU--
DAISUKE! YOU KEEP FREAKING OUT WHEN YOU'RE WITH ME...
...and running away...
NO--I DON'T!!
YES, YOU DO!!

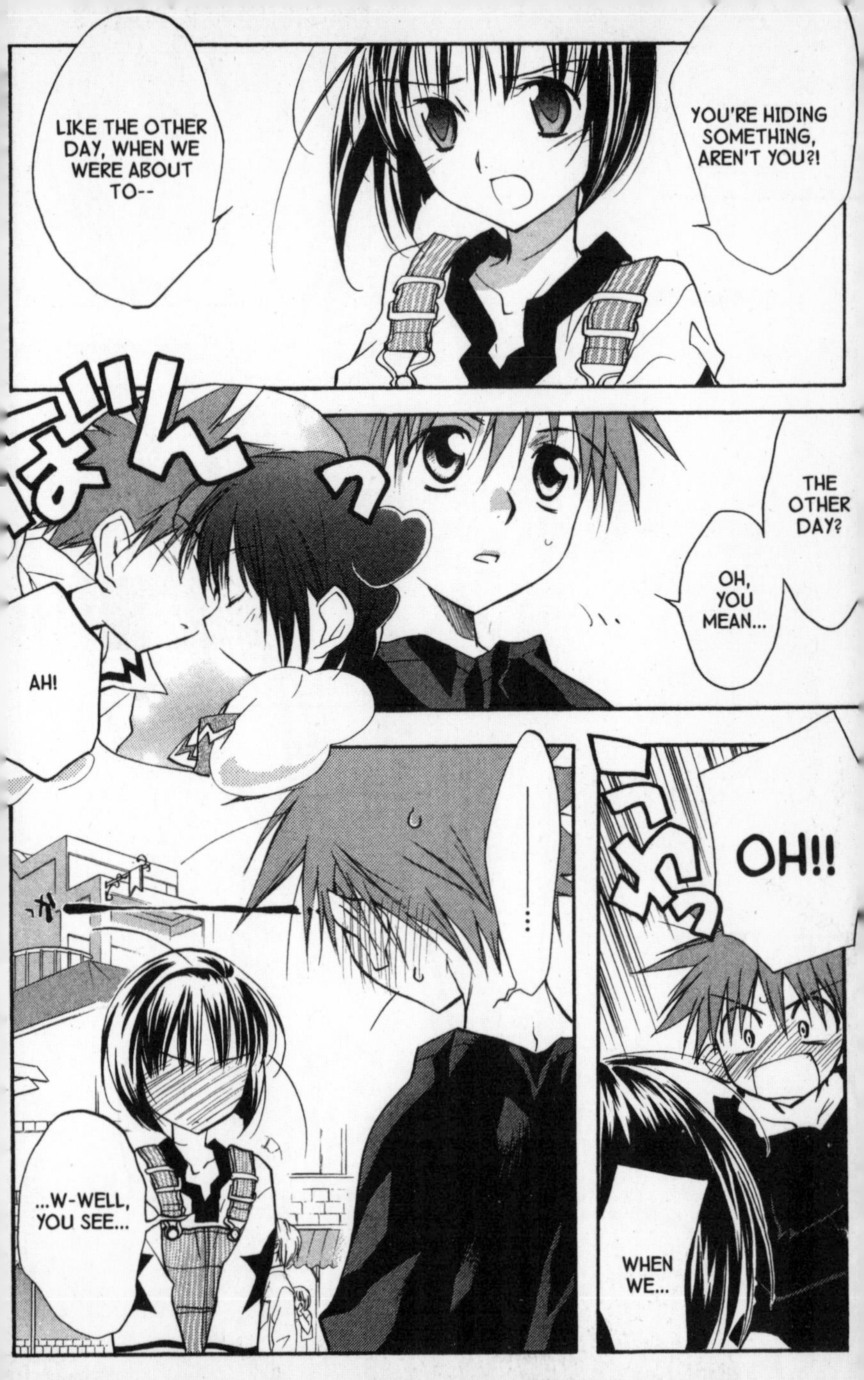
YOU'RE HIDING SOMETHING, AREN'T YOU?!
LIKE THE OTHER DAY, WHEN WE WERE ABOUT TO--
THE OTHER DAY?
OH, YOU MEAN...
AH!
OH!!
WHEN WE...
...
...W-WELL, YOU SEE...

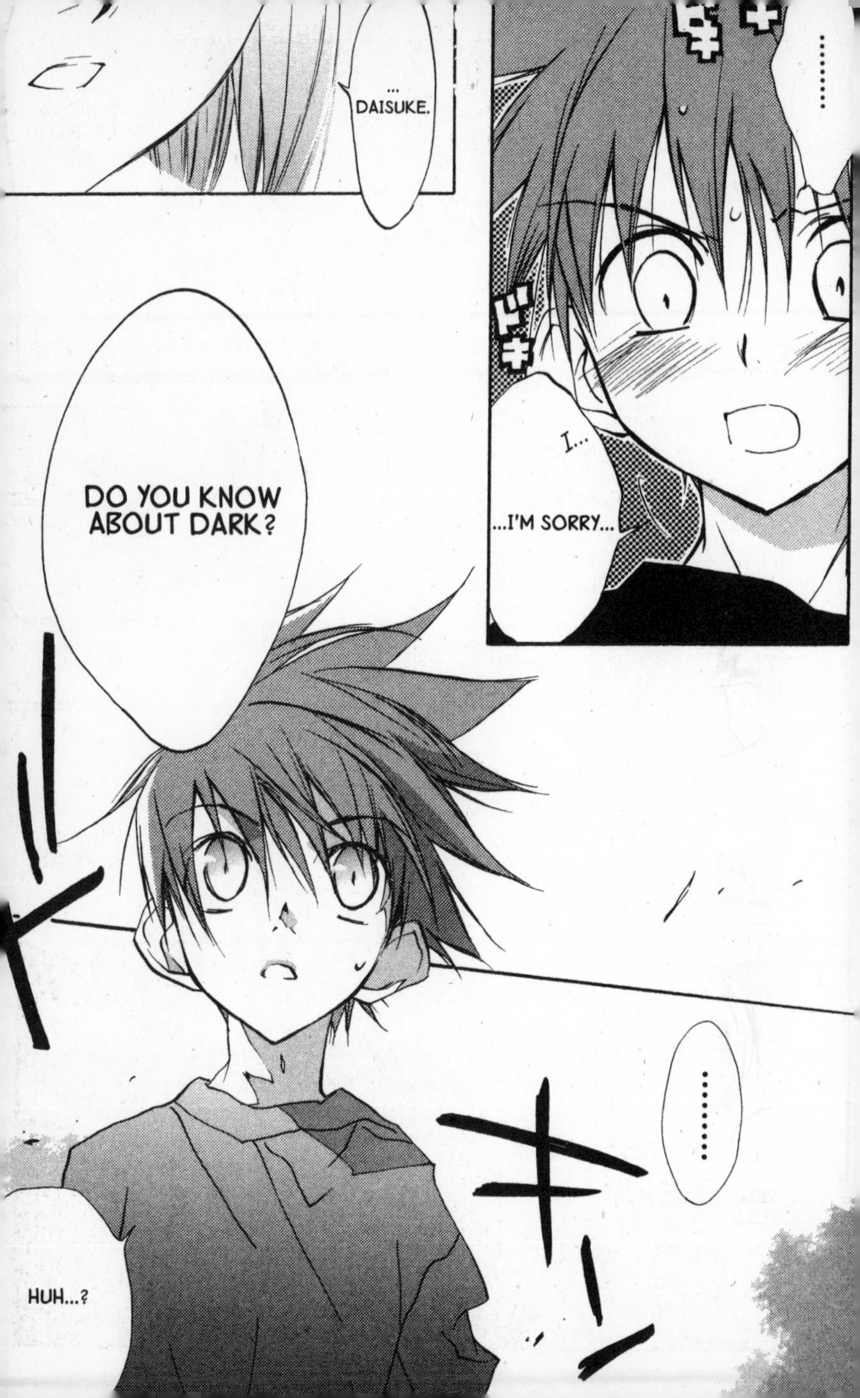
......
I...
...I'M SORRY...
... DAISUKE.
DO YOU KNOW ABOUT DARK?
....
HUH...?

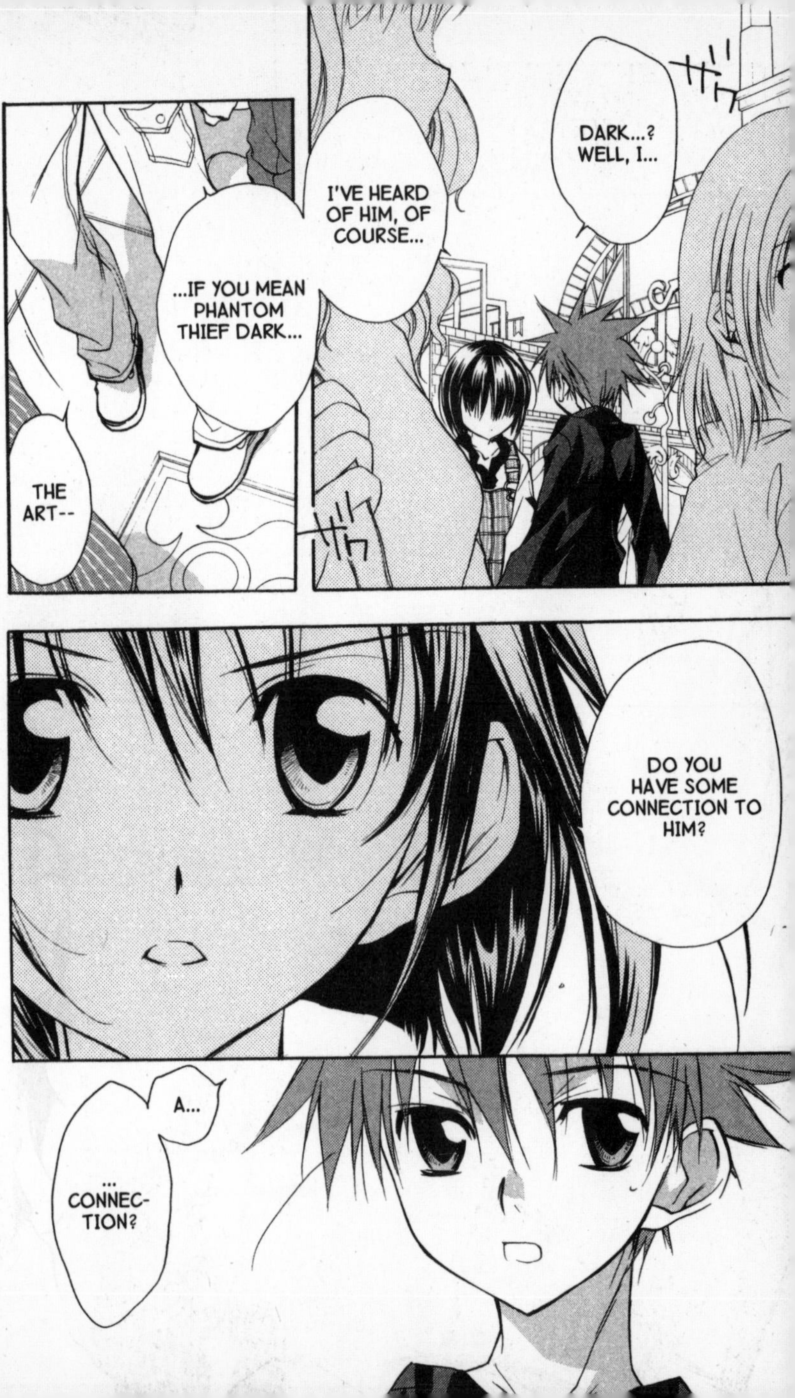
DARK...? WELL, I...
I'VE HEARD OF HIM, OF COURSE...
...IF YOU MEAN PHANTOM THIEF DARK...
THE ART--
DO YOU HAVE SOME CONNECTION TO HIM?
A...
... CONNEC-TION?

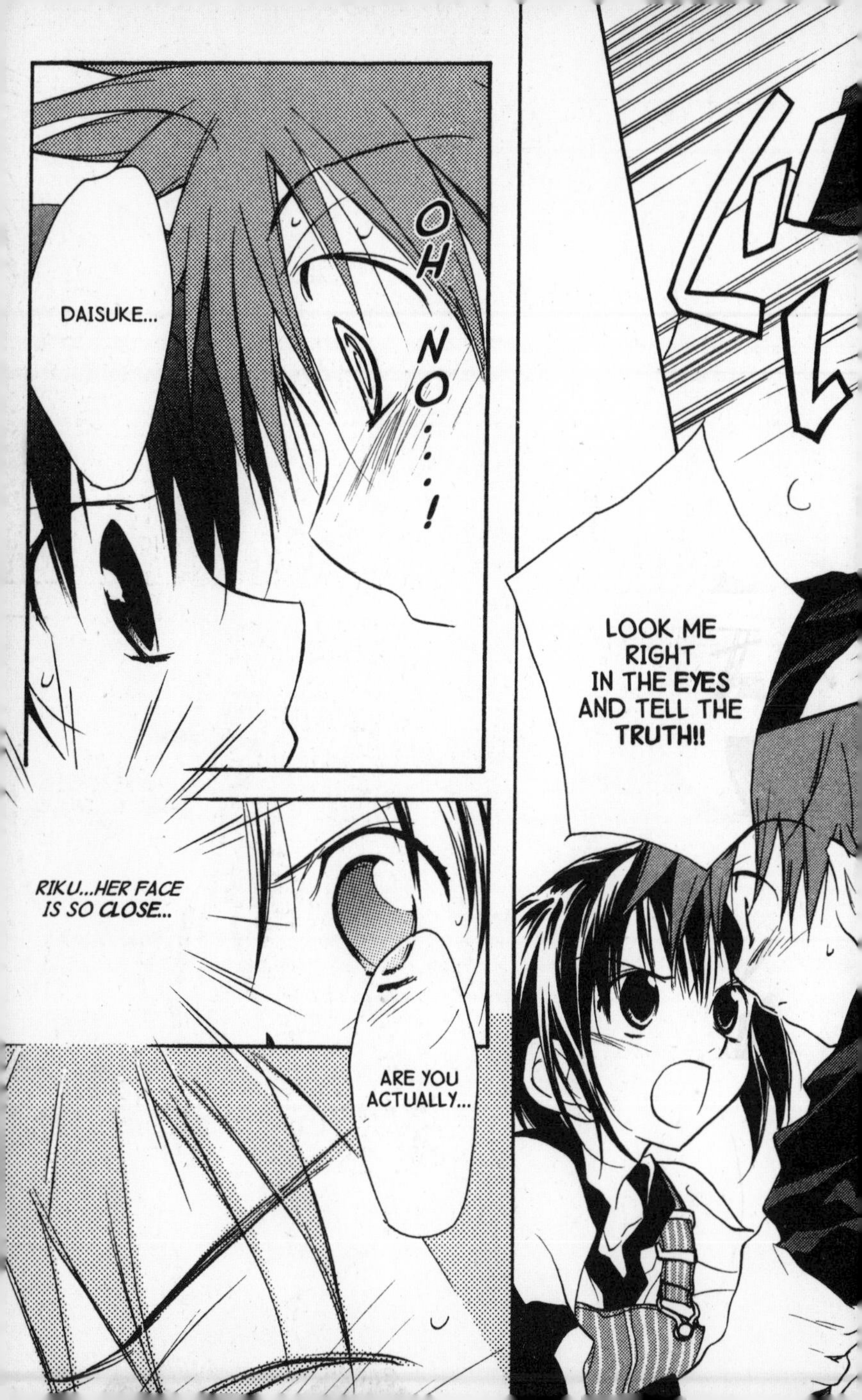
LOOK ME RIGHT IN THE EYES AND TELL THE TRUTH!!
DAISUKE...
OH NO...!
RIKU...HER FACE IS SO CLOSE...
ARE YOU ACTUALLY...

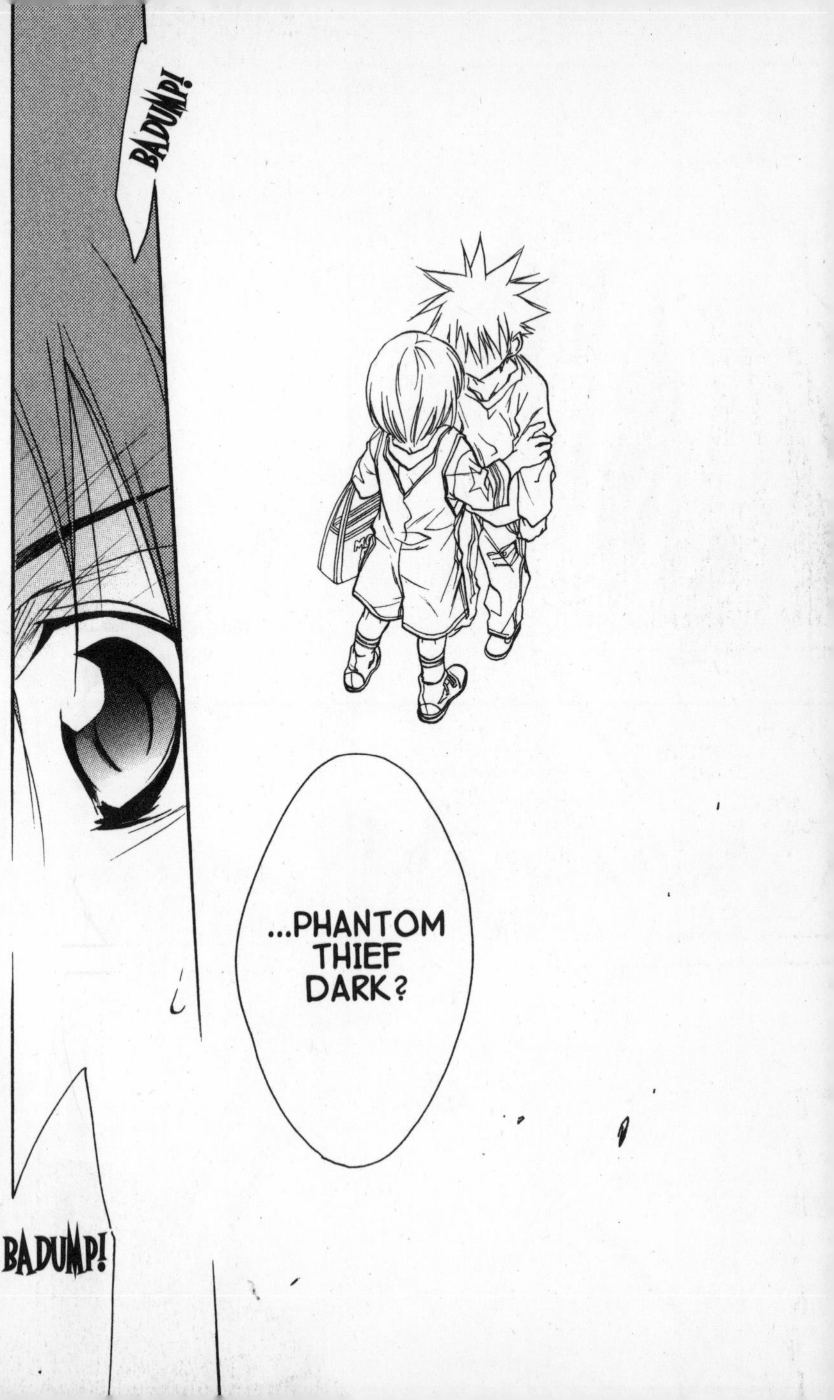
BADUMP!
...PHANTOM THIEF DARK?
BADUMP!

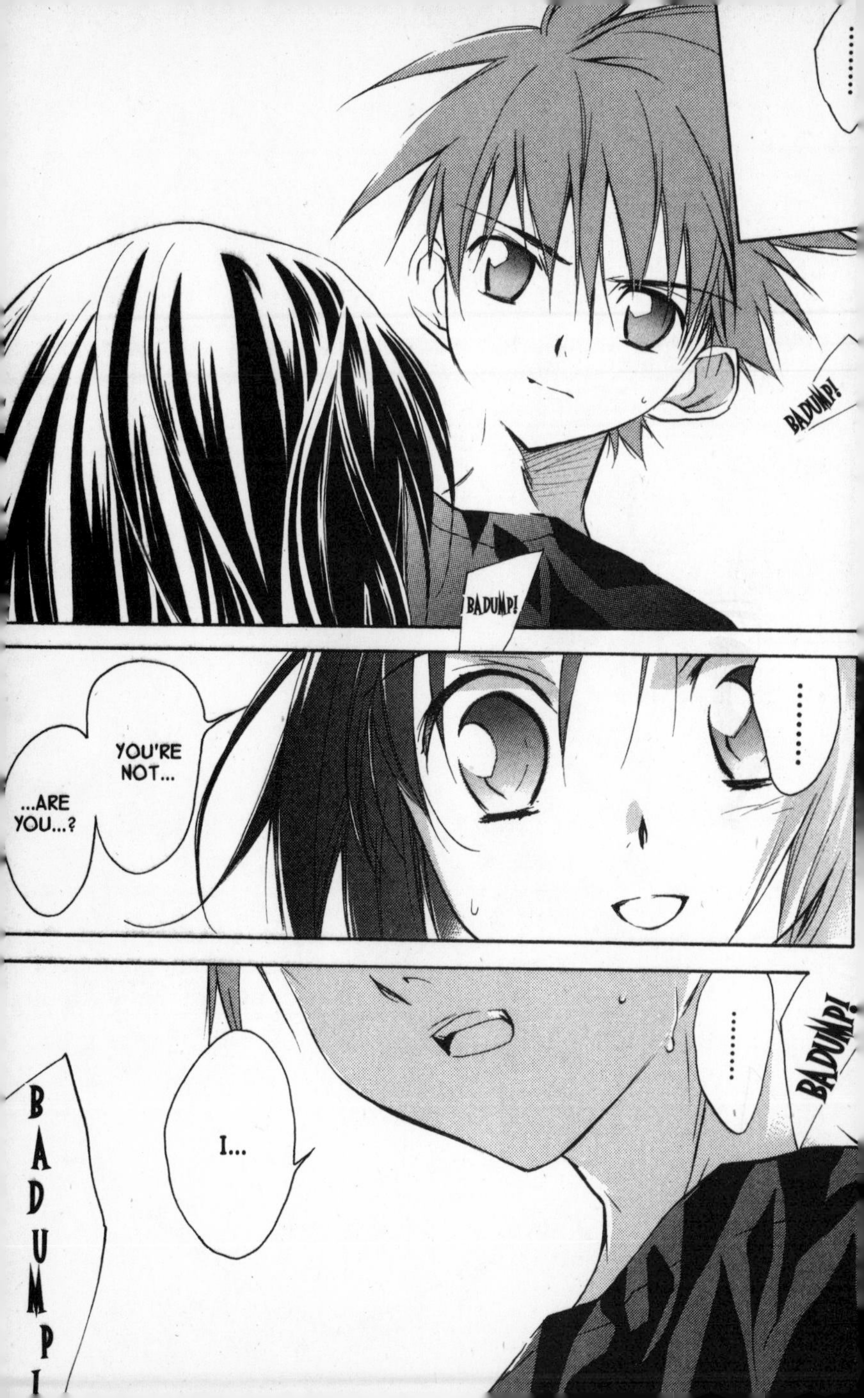
......
BADUMP!
BADUMP!
......
YOU'RE NOT...
...ARE YOU...?
BADUMP!
......
I...
BADUMP!

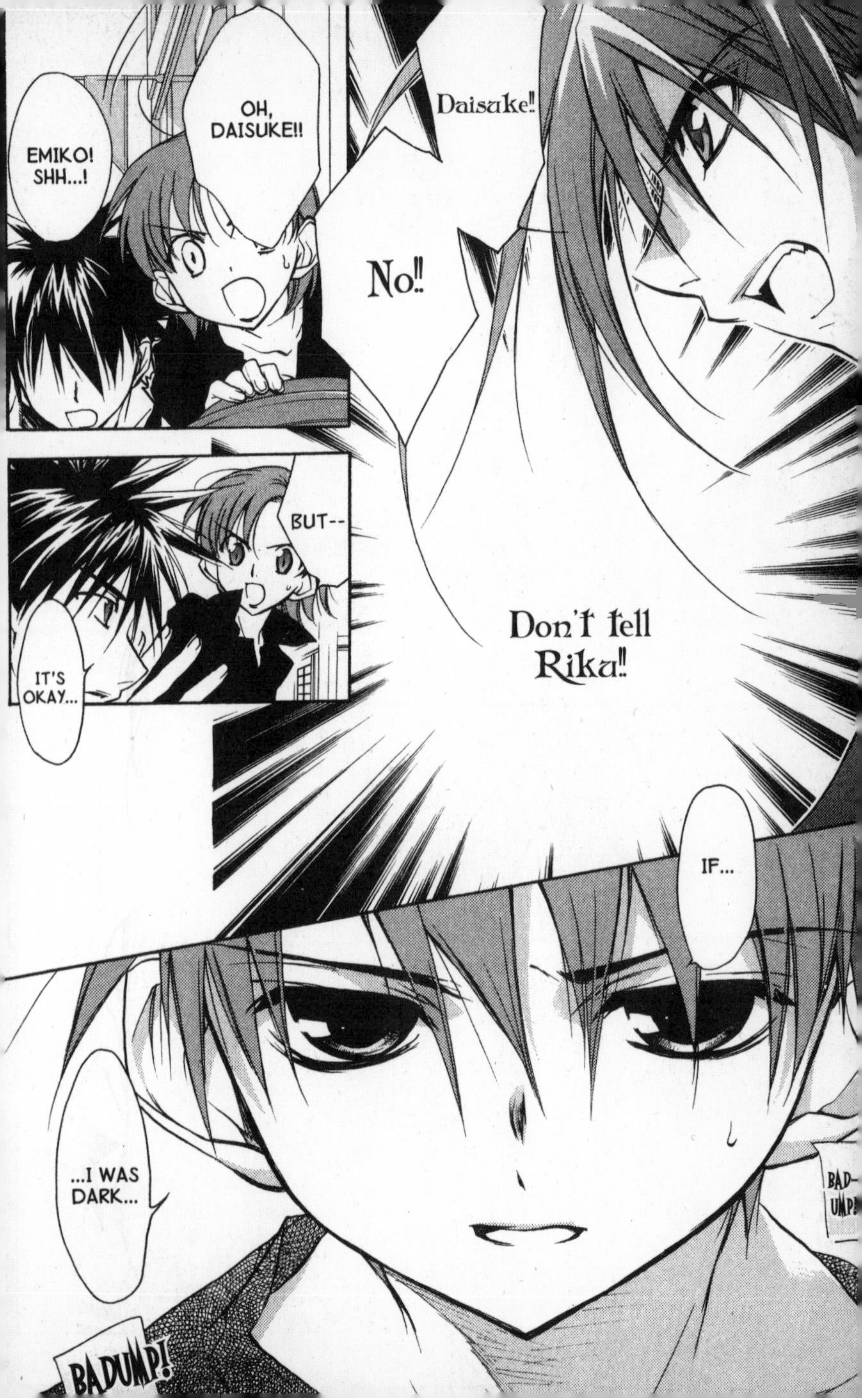
Daisuke!!
No!!
Don't tell Riku!!
OH, DAISUKE!!
EMIKO! SHH...!
BUT--
IT'S OKAY...
IF...
...I WAS DARK...
BAD-UMP!
BADUMP!

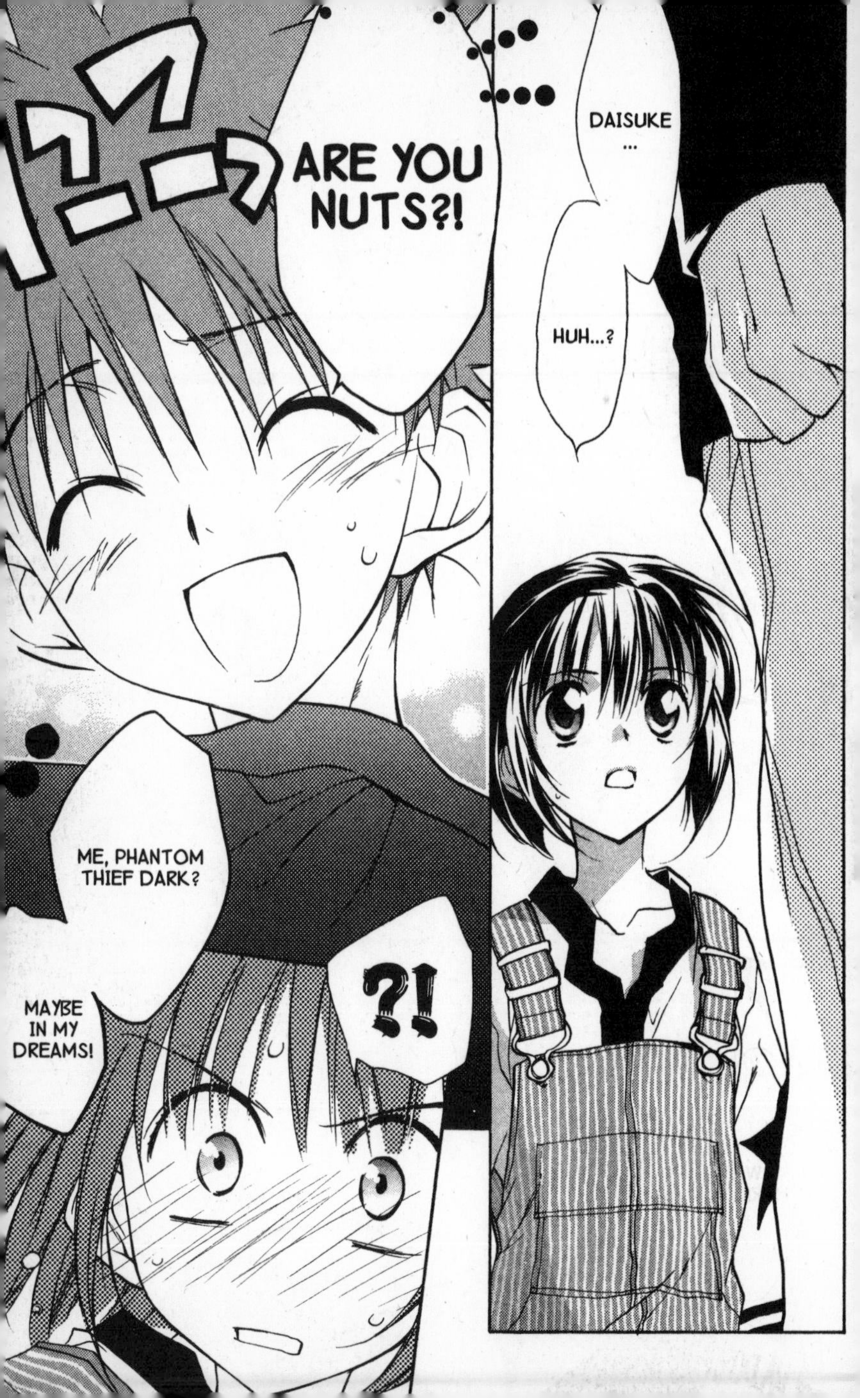
DAISUKE
...
HUH...?
ARE YOU NUTS?!
ME, PHANTOM THIEF DARK?
MAYBE IN MY DREAMS!
?!

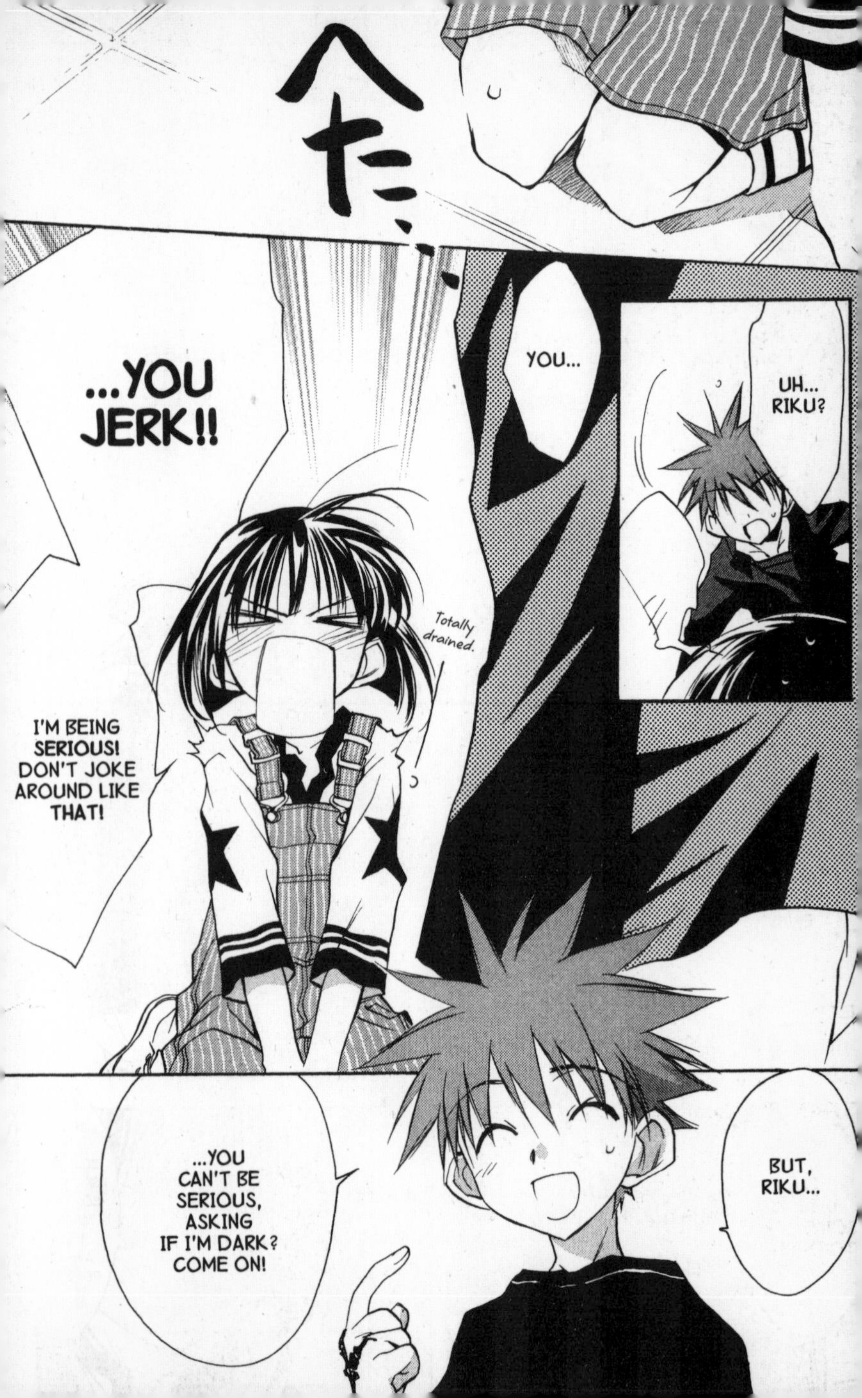
へた
UH... RIKU?
YOU...
...YOU JERK!!
Totally drained.
I'M BEING SERIOUS! DON'T JOKE AROUND LIKE THAT!
BUT, RIKU...
...YOU CAN'T BE SERIOUS, ASKING IF I'M DARK? COME ON!

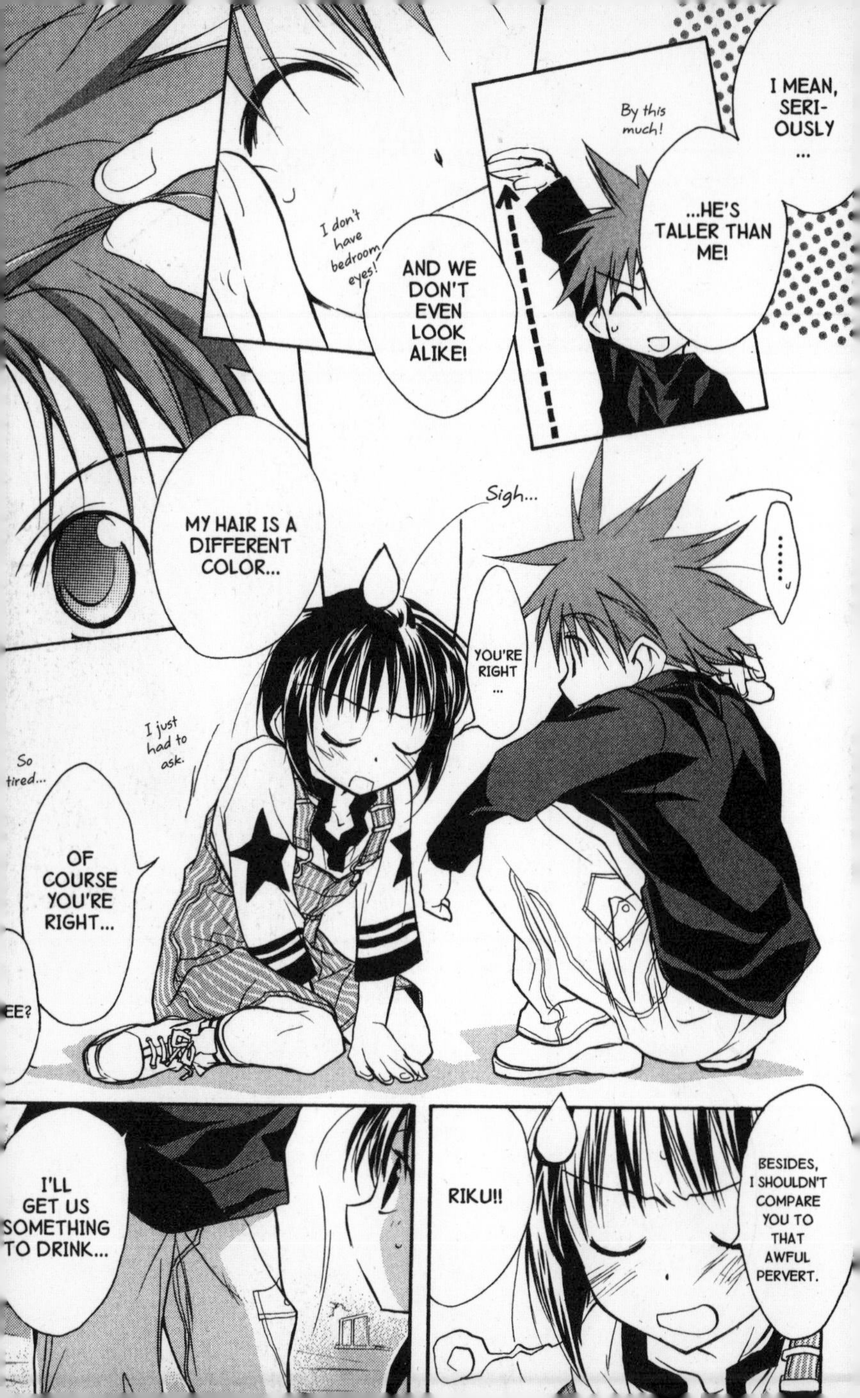
I MEAN, SERI-OUSLY ...
...HE'S TALLER THAN ME!
By this much!
AND WE DON'T EVEN LOOK ALIKE!
I don't have bedroom eyes!
MY HAIR IS A DIFFERENT COLOR...
Sigh...
......
YOU'RE RIGHT ...
I just had to ask.
So tired...
OF COURSE YOU'RE RIGHT...
EE?
BESIDES, I SHOULDN'T COMPARE YOU TO THAT AWFUL PERVERT.
RIKU!!
I'LL GET US SOMETHING TO DRINK...

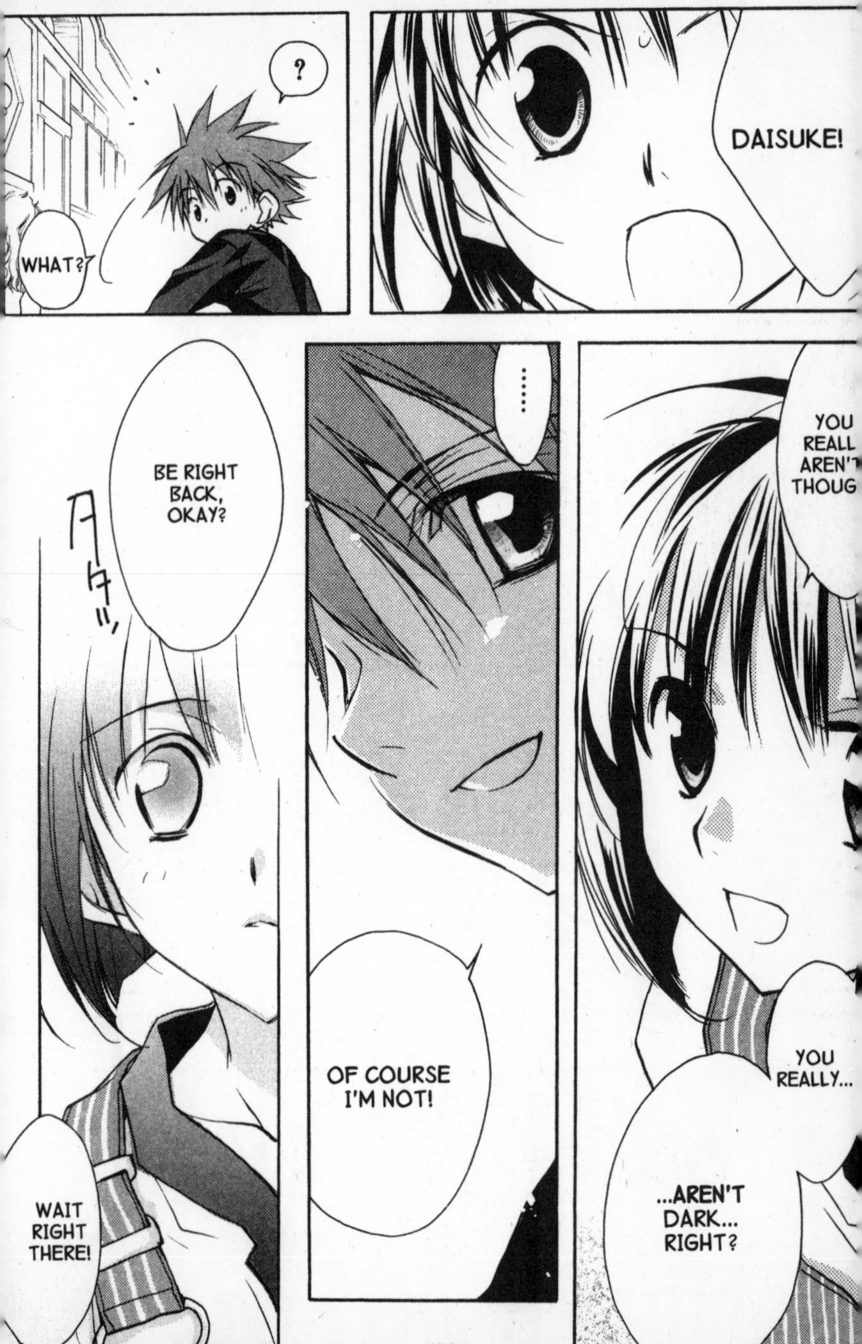

DAISUKE!
?
WHAT?
YOU REALL AREN'T THOUG
YOU REALLY...
...AREN'T DARK... RIGHT?
......
OF COURSE I'M NOT!
BE RIGHT BACK, OKAY?
タタッ
WAIT RIGHT THERE!

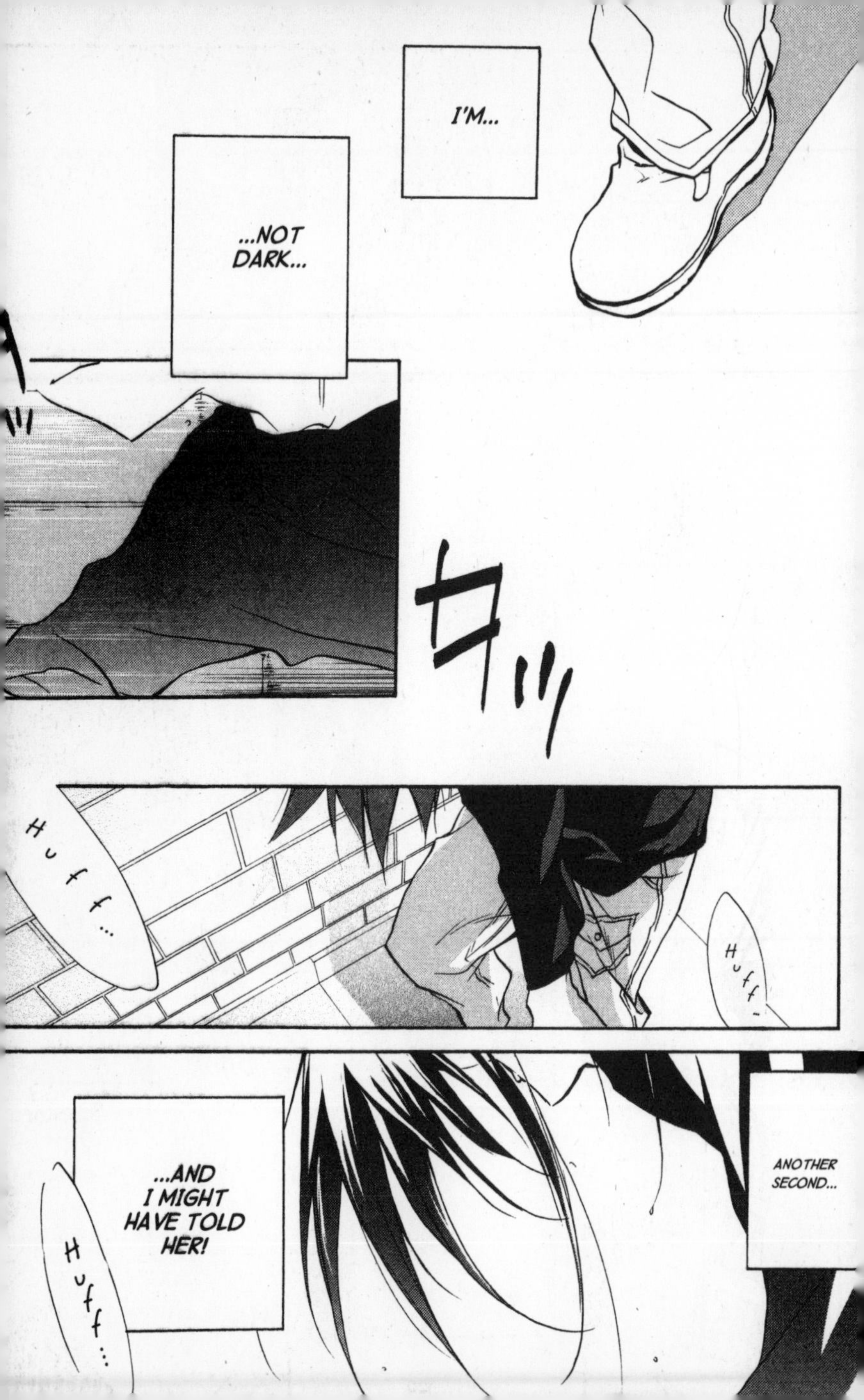
I'M...
...NOT DARK...
カッ
Huff...
Huff...
ANOTHER SECOND...
...AND I MIGHT HAVE TOLD HER!
Huff...

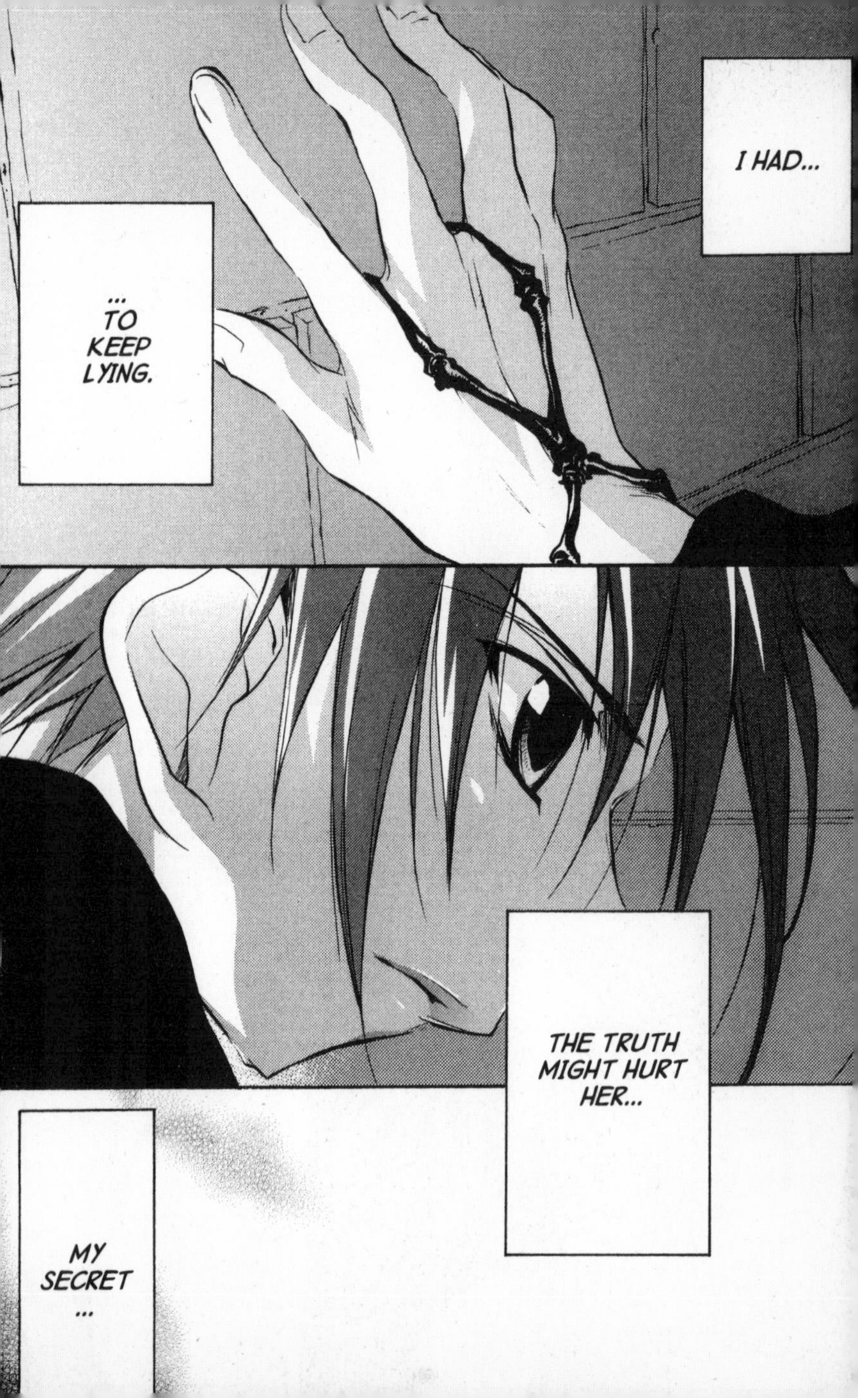
I HAD...
... TO KEEP LYING.
THE TRUTH MIGHT HURT HER...
MY SECRET ...

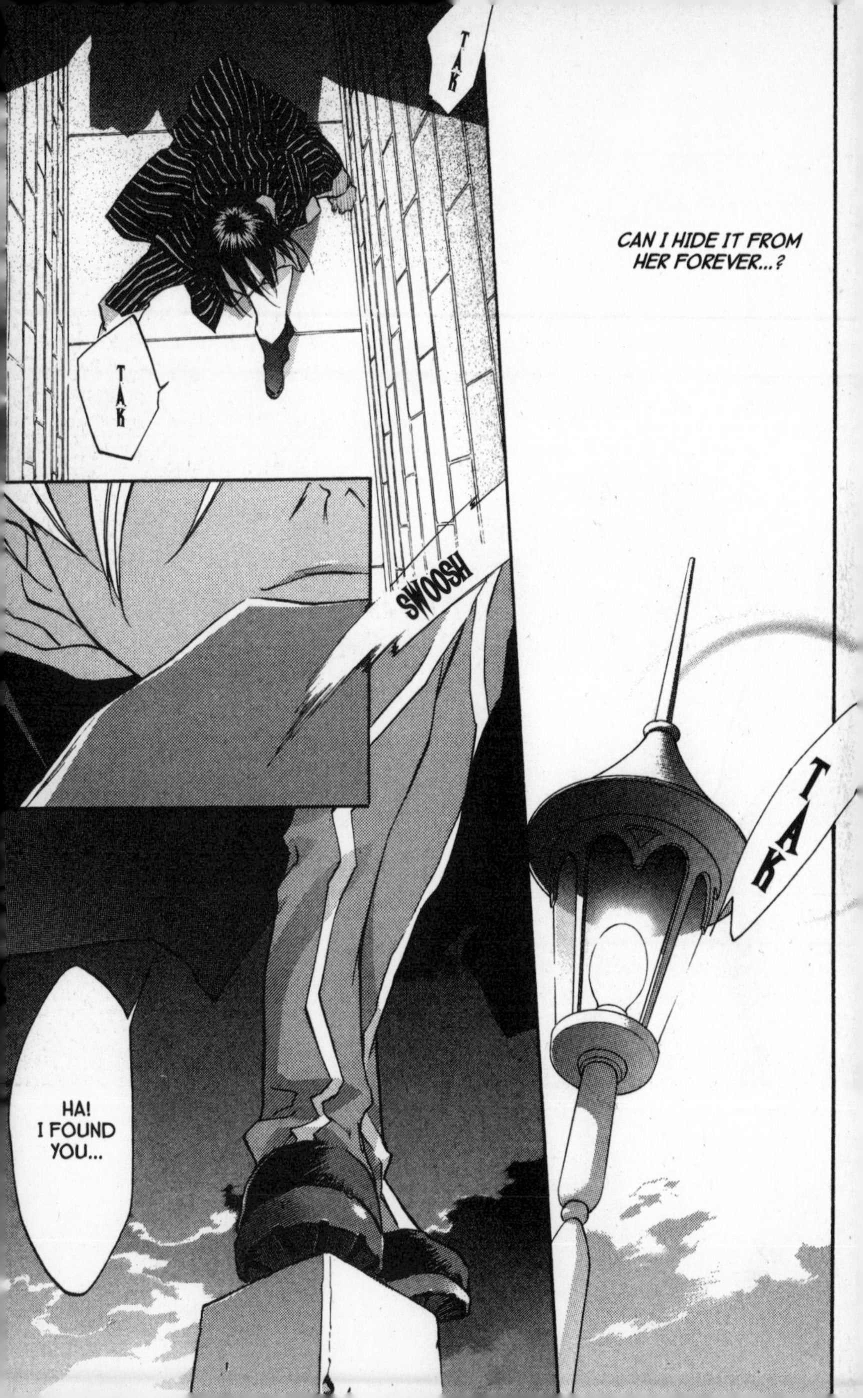
CAN I HIDE IT FROM HER FOREVER...?
TAK
TAK
TAK
SWOOSH
HA! I FOUND YOU...

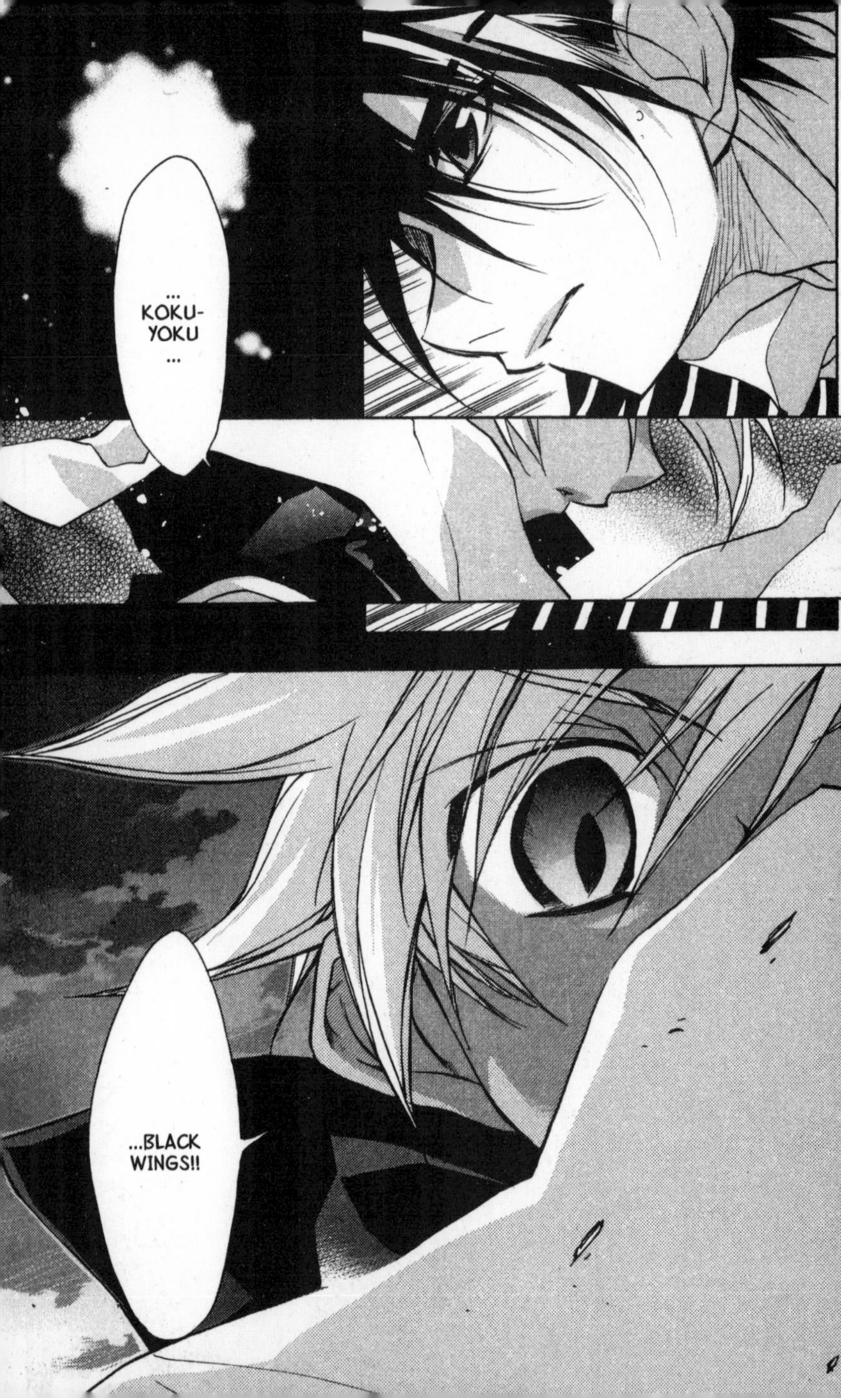
...KOKU-YOKU...
...BLACK WINGS!!

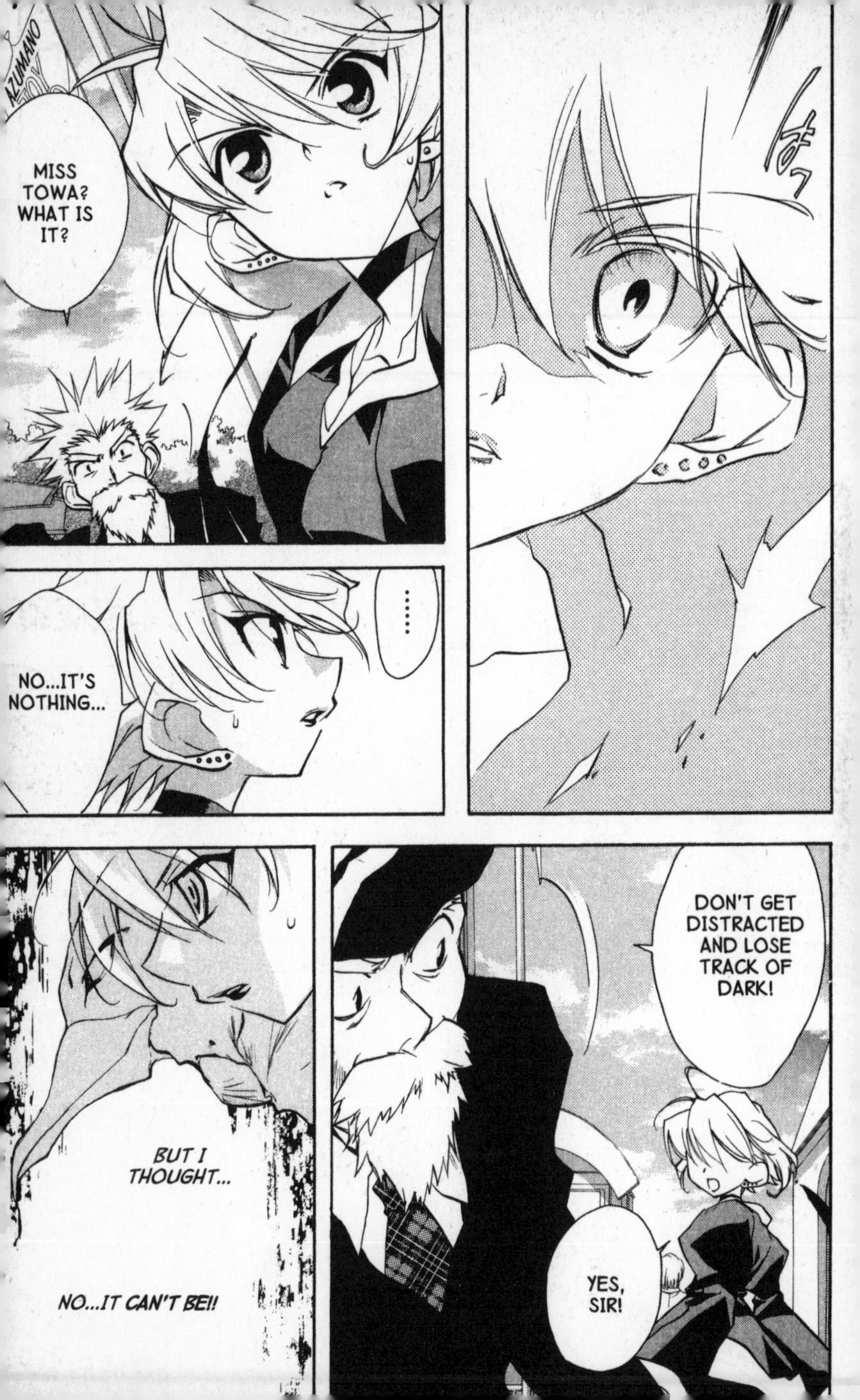
はっ
AZUMANO TOY
MISS TOWA? WHAT IS IT?
......
NO...IT'S NOTHING...
DON'T GET DISTRACTED AND LOSE TRACK OF DARK!
YES, SIR!
BUT I THOUGHT...
NO...IT CAN'T BE!!

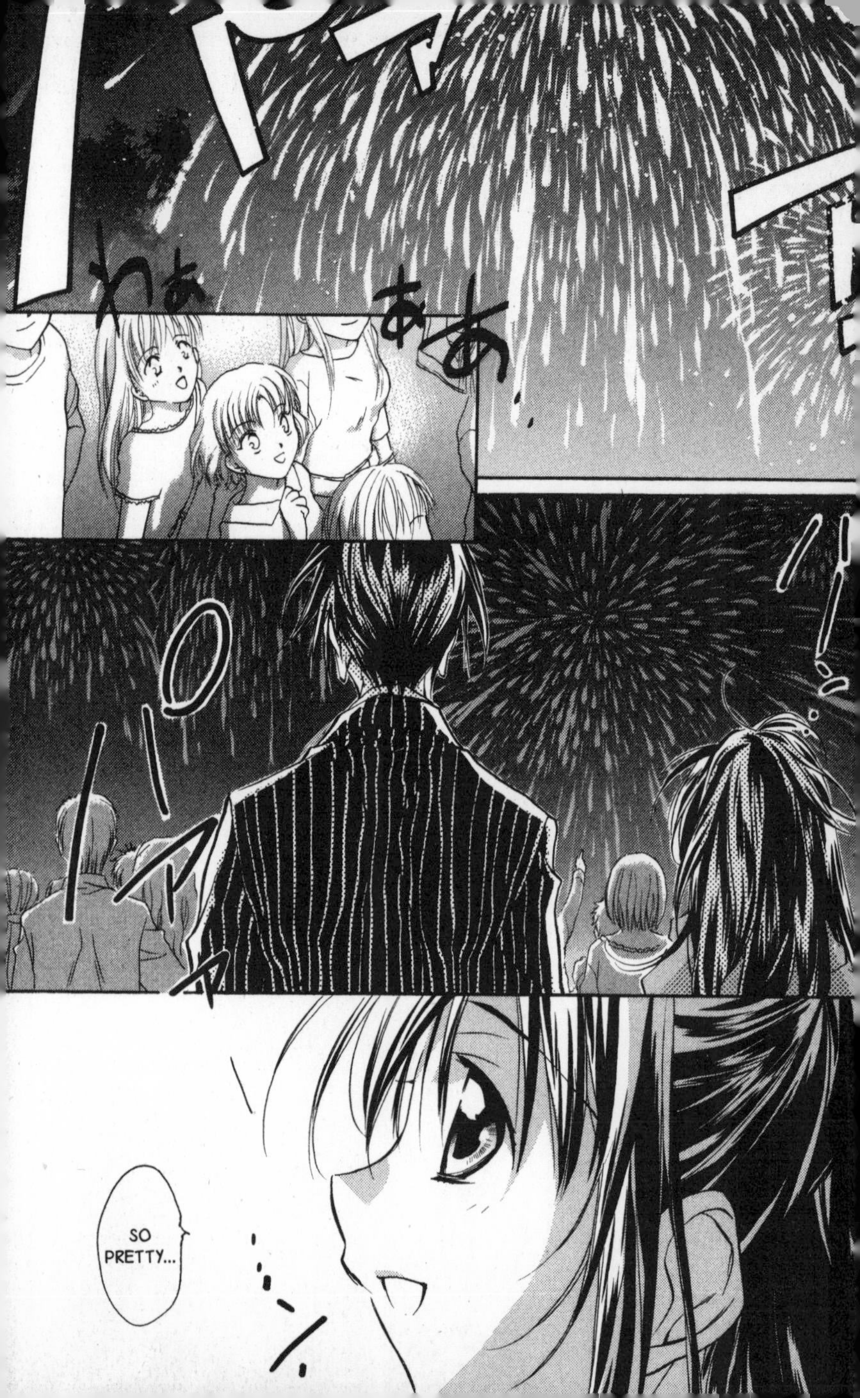
わあああ
SO PRETTY...

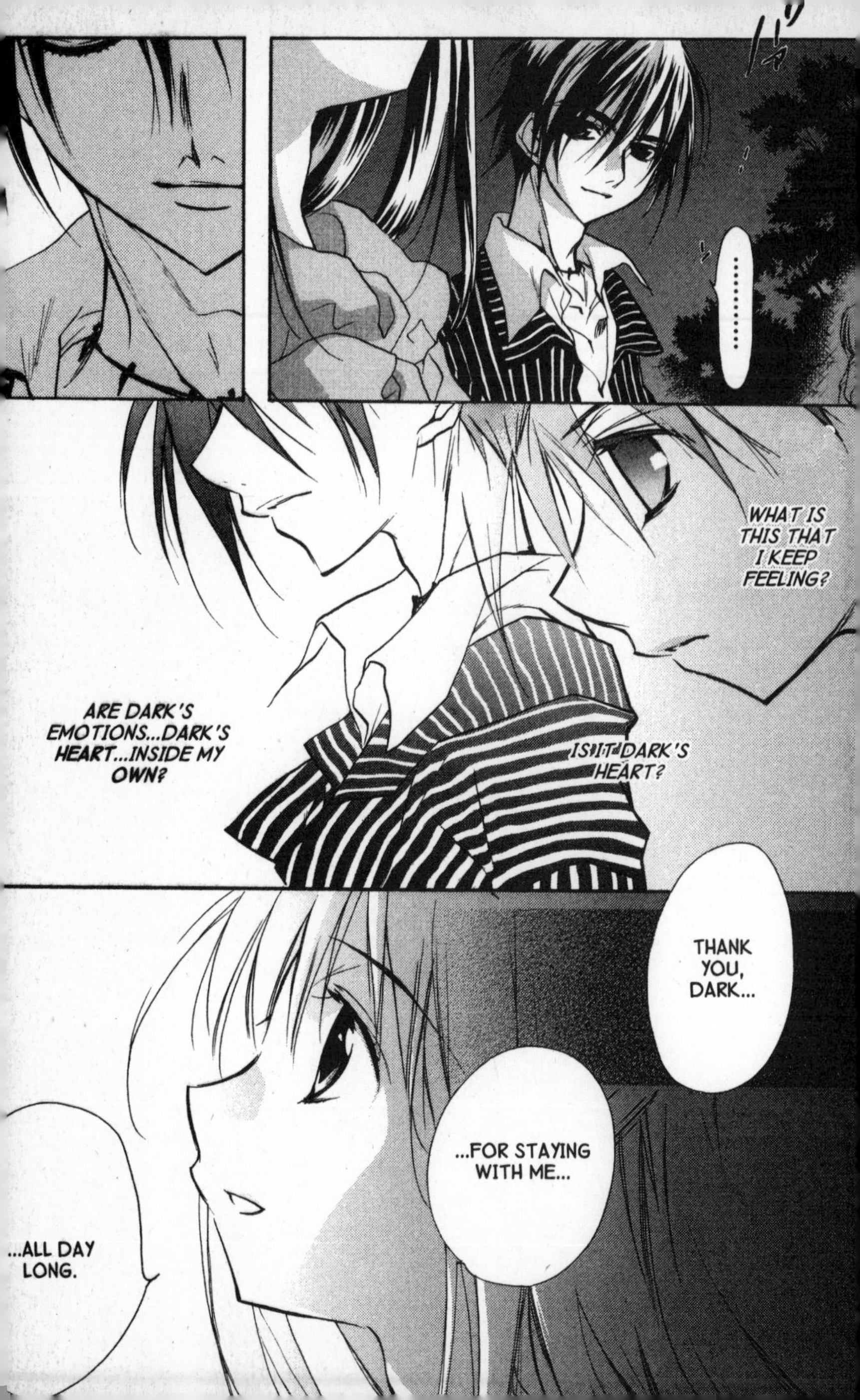
......
WHAT IS THIS THAT I KEEP FEELING?
IS IT DARK'S HEART?
ARE DARK'S EMOTIONS...DARK'S HEART...INSIDE MY OWN?
THANK YOU, DARK...
...FOR STAYING WITH ME...
...ALL DAY LONG.

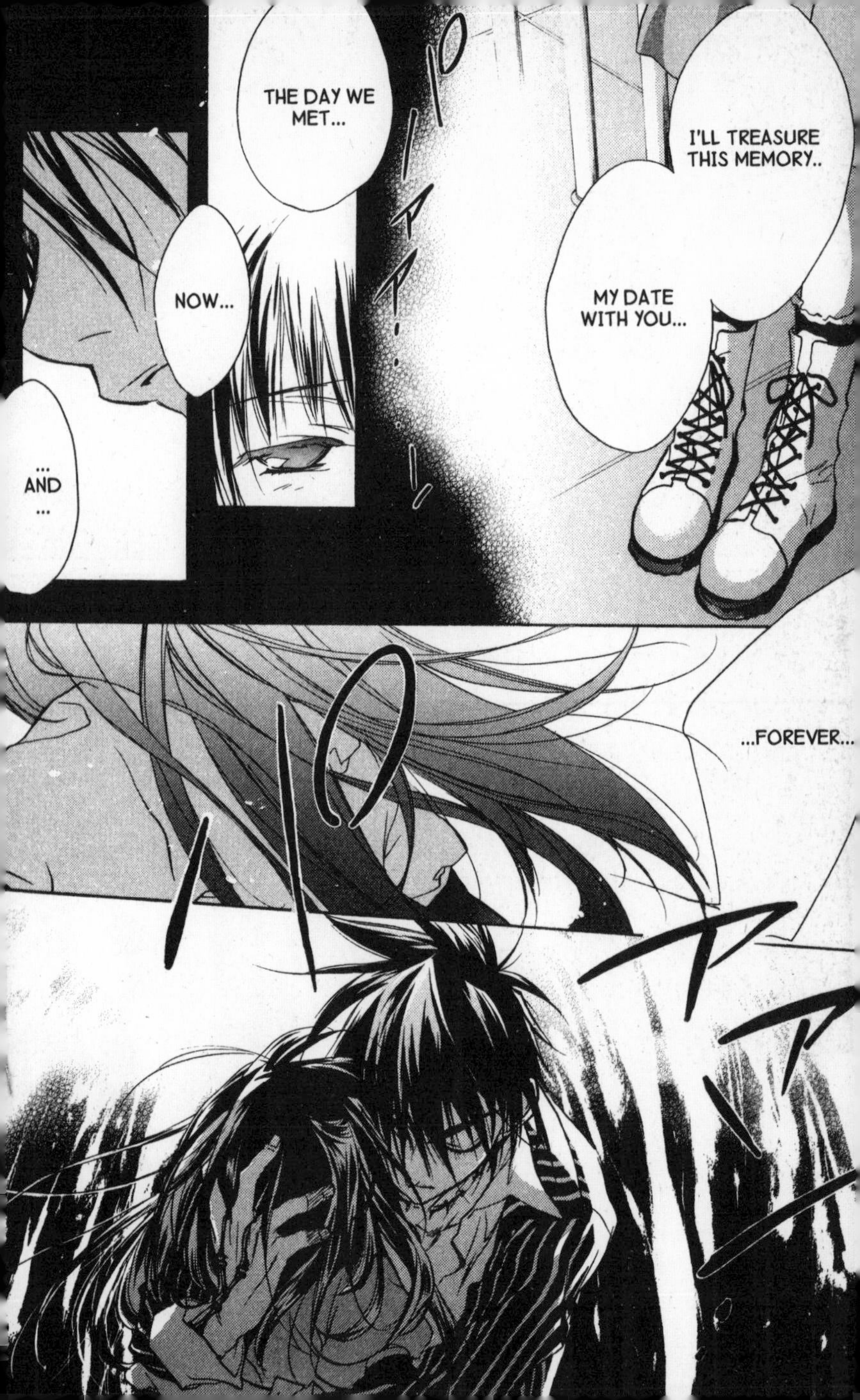
I'LL TREASURE THIS MEMORY..
MY DATE WITH YOU...
THE DAY WE MET...
NOW...
... AND ...
...FOREVER...

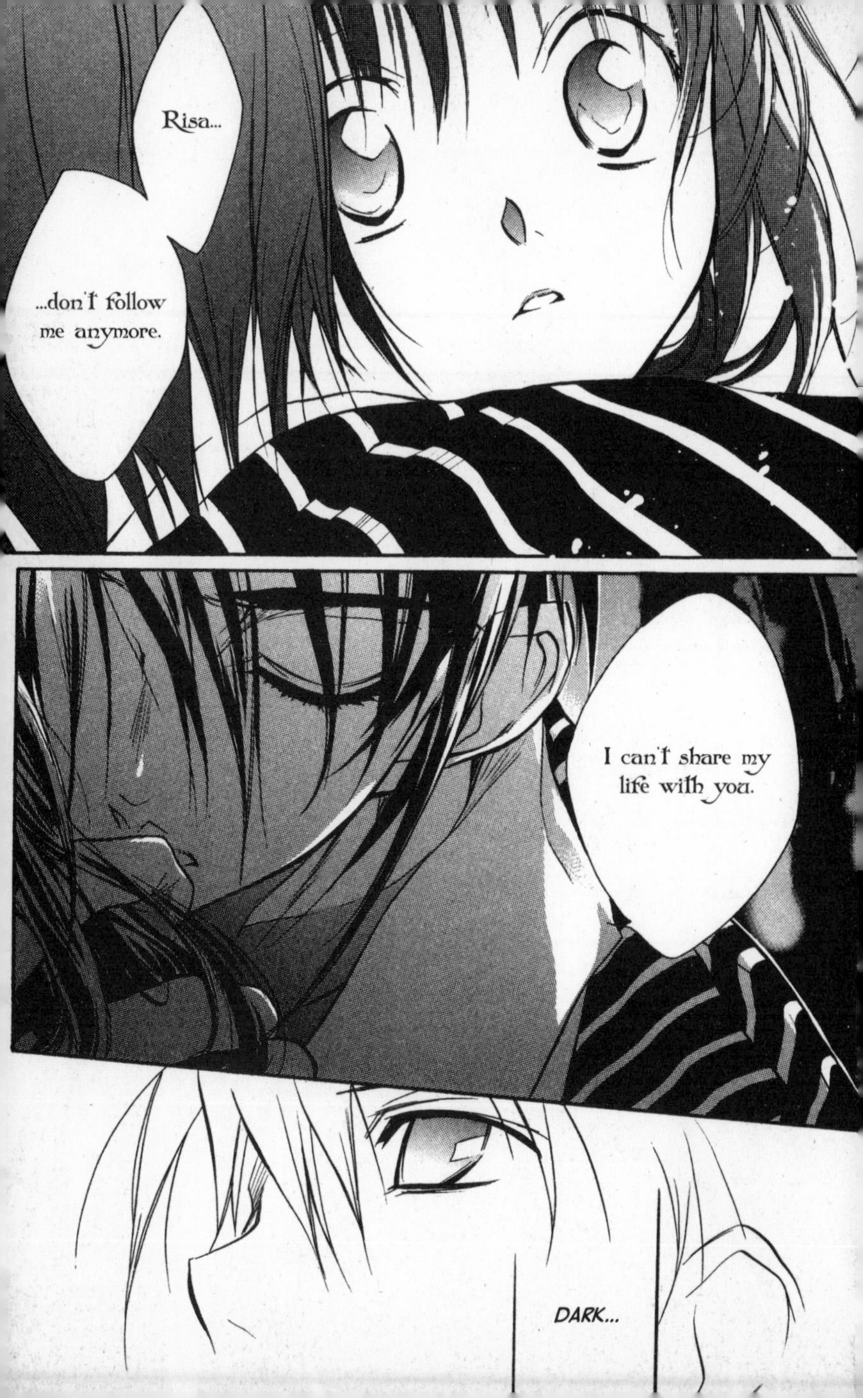
Risa...
...don't follow me anymore.
I can't share my life with you.
DARK...

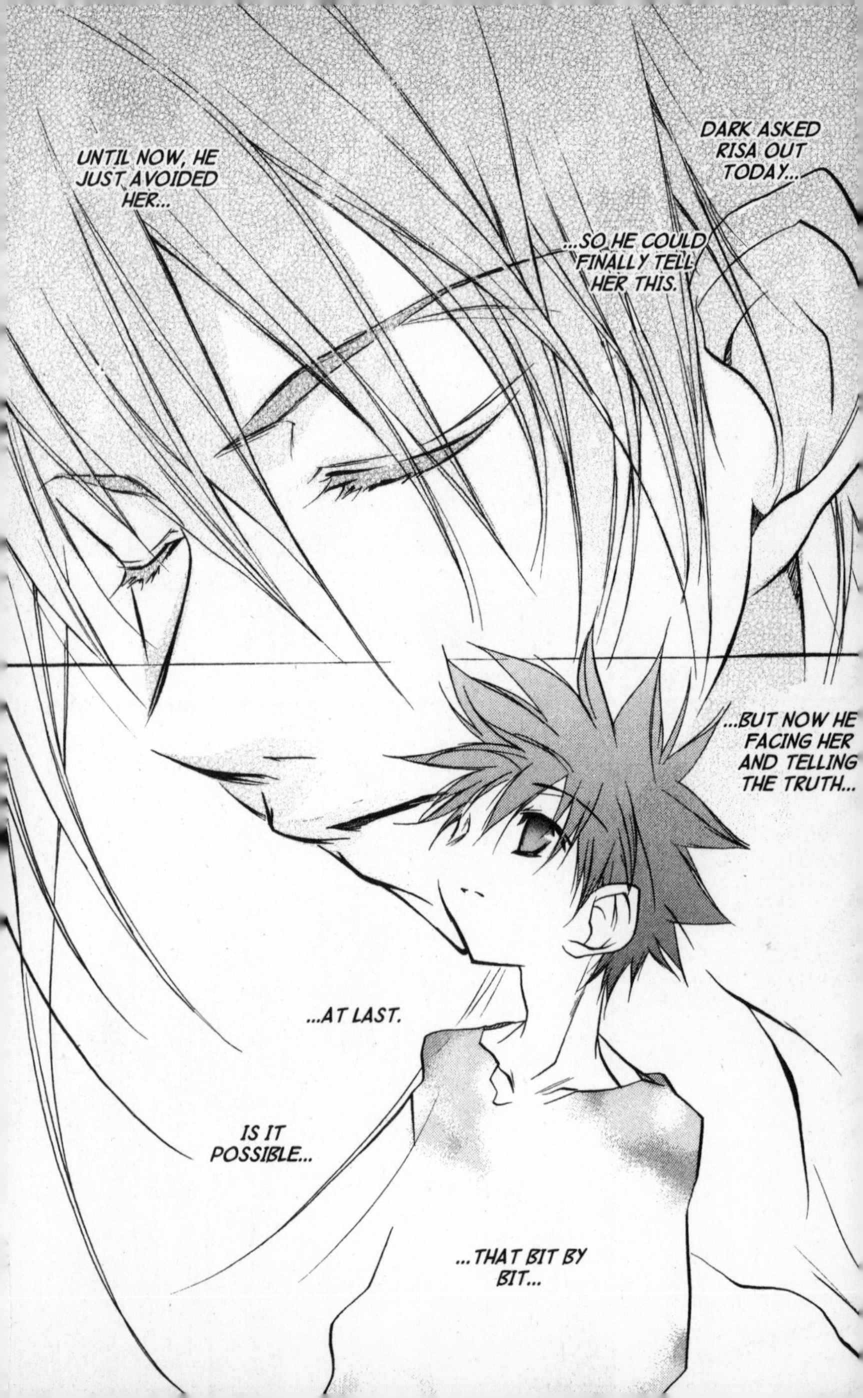
DARK ASKED RISA OUT TODAY...
...SO HE COULD FINALLY TELL HER THIS.
UNTIL NOW, HE JUST AVOIDED HER...
...BUT NOW HE FACING HER AND TELLING THE TRUTH...
...AT LAST.
IS IT POSSIBLE...
...THAT BIT BY BIT...

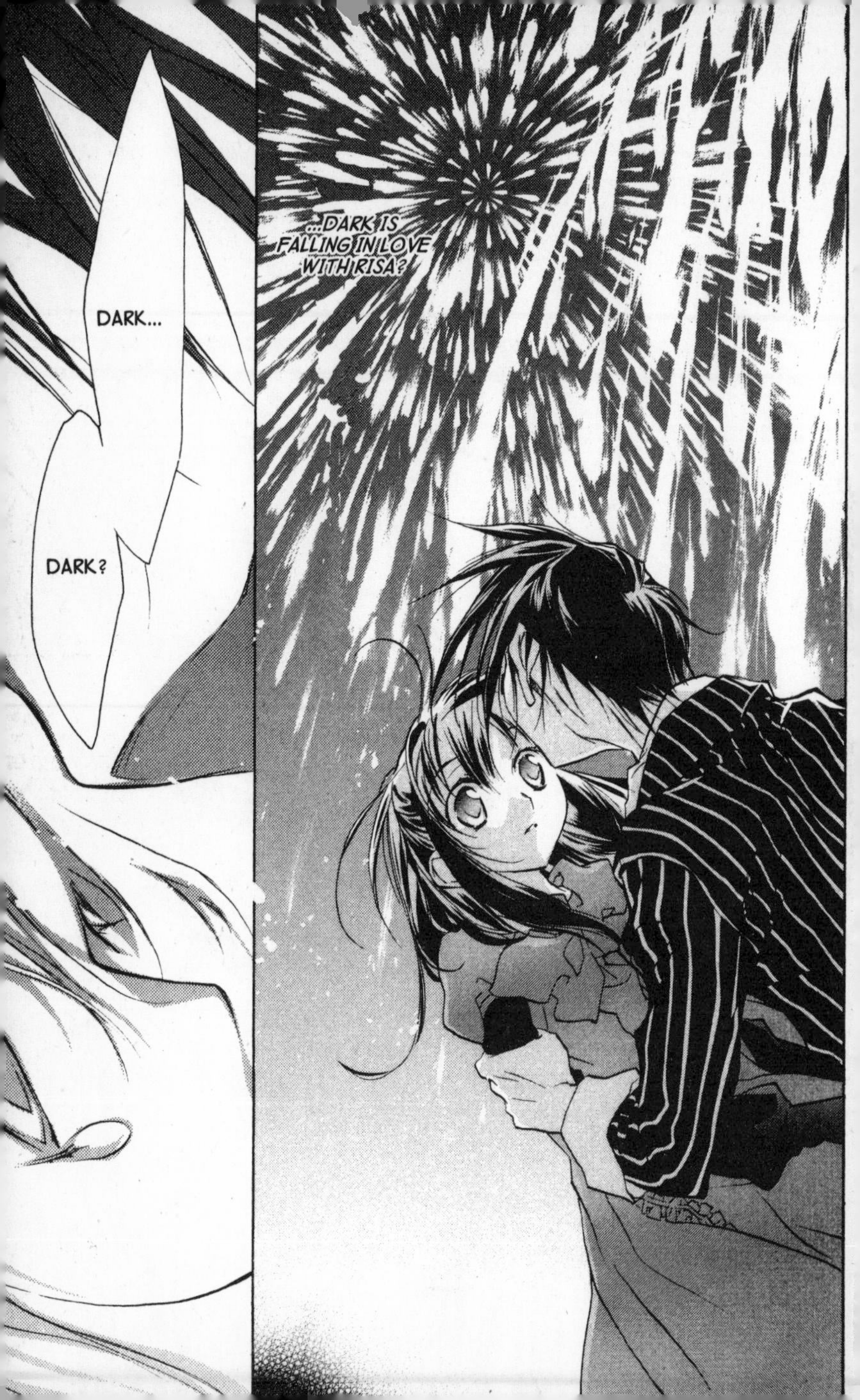
...DARK IS FALLING IN LOVE WITH RISA?
DARK...
DARK?

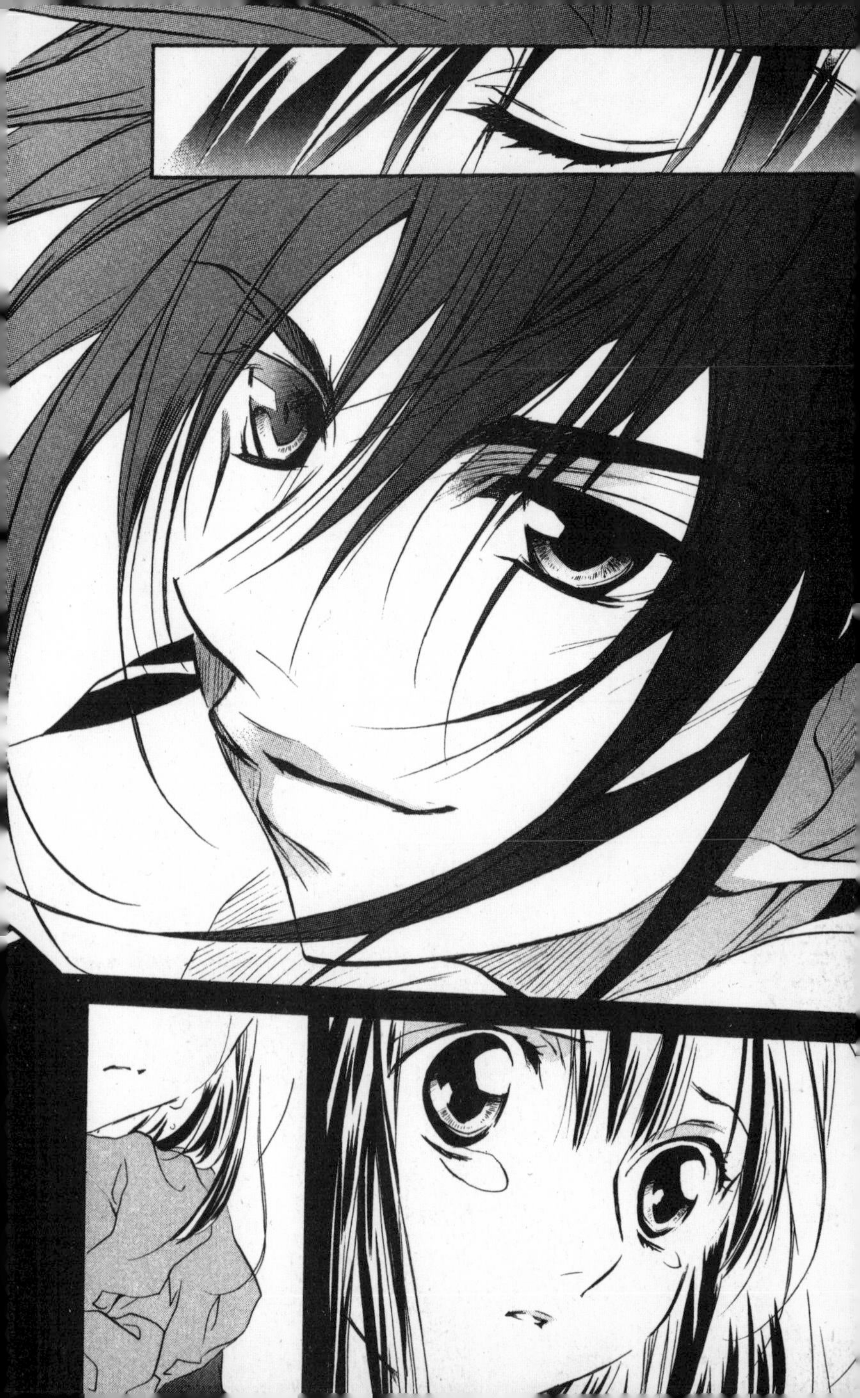

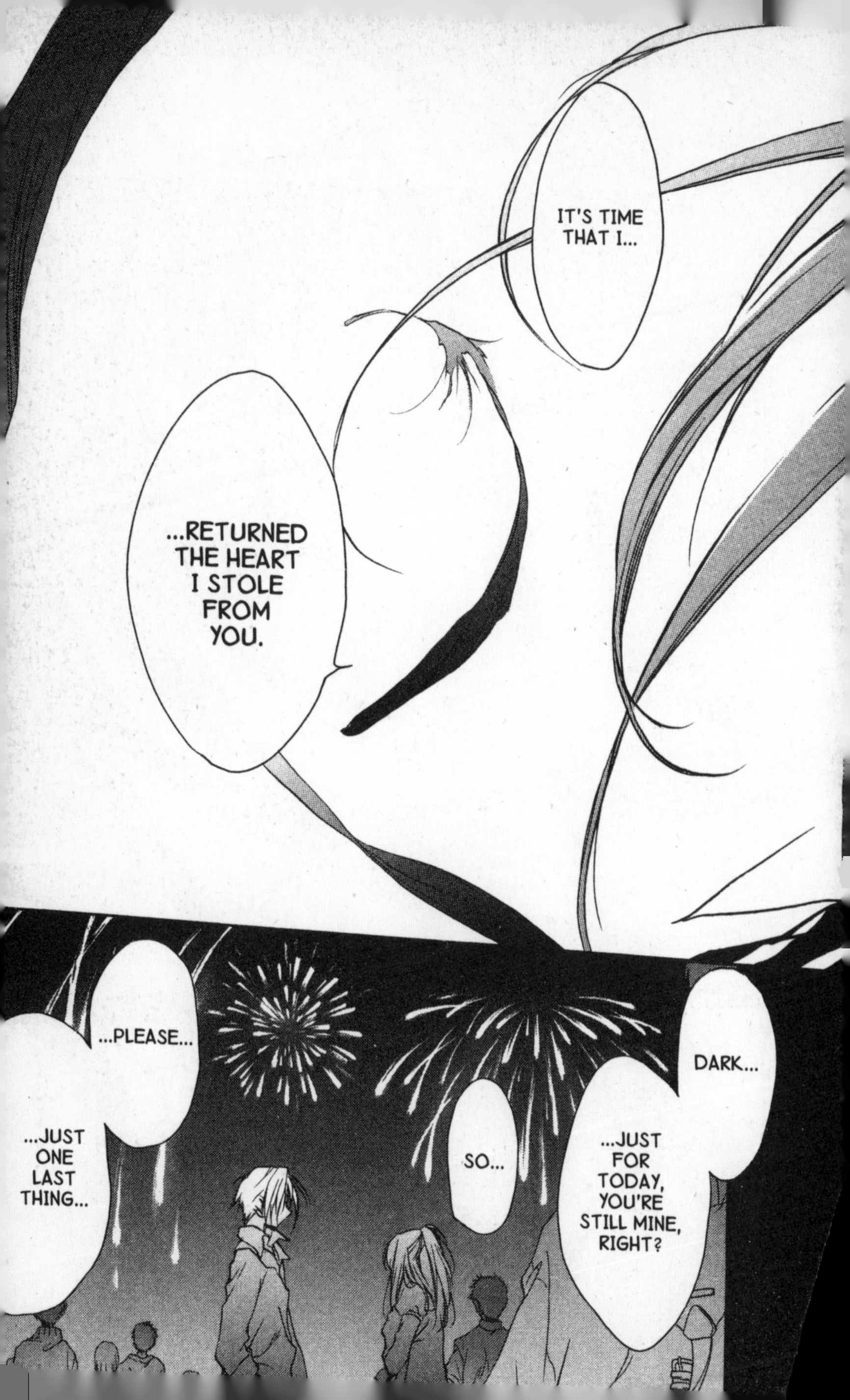
IT'S TIME THAT I...
...RETURNED THE HEART I STOLE FROM YOU.
DARK...
...JUST FOR TODAY, YOU'RE STILL MINE, RIGHT?
SO...
...PLEASE...
...JUST ONE LAST THING...

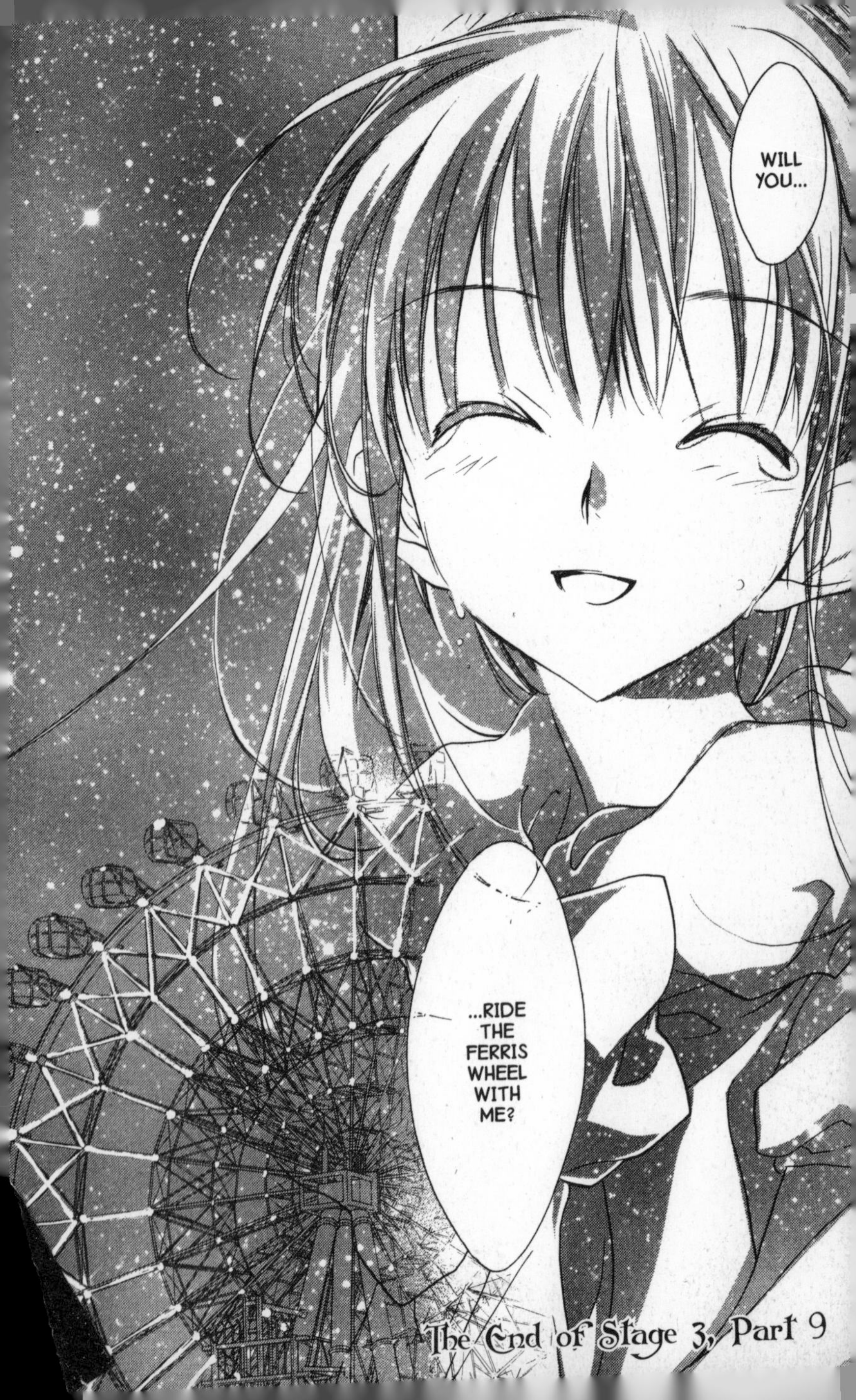
WILL YOU...
...RIDE THE FERRIS WHEEL WITH ME?
The End of Stage 3, Part 9

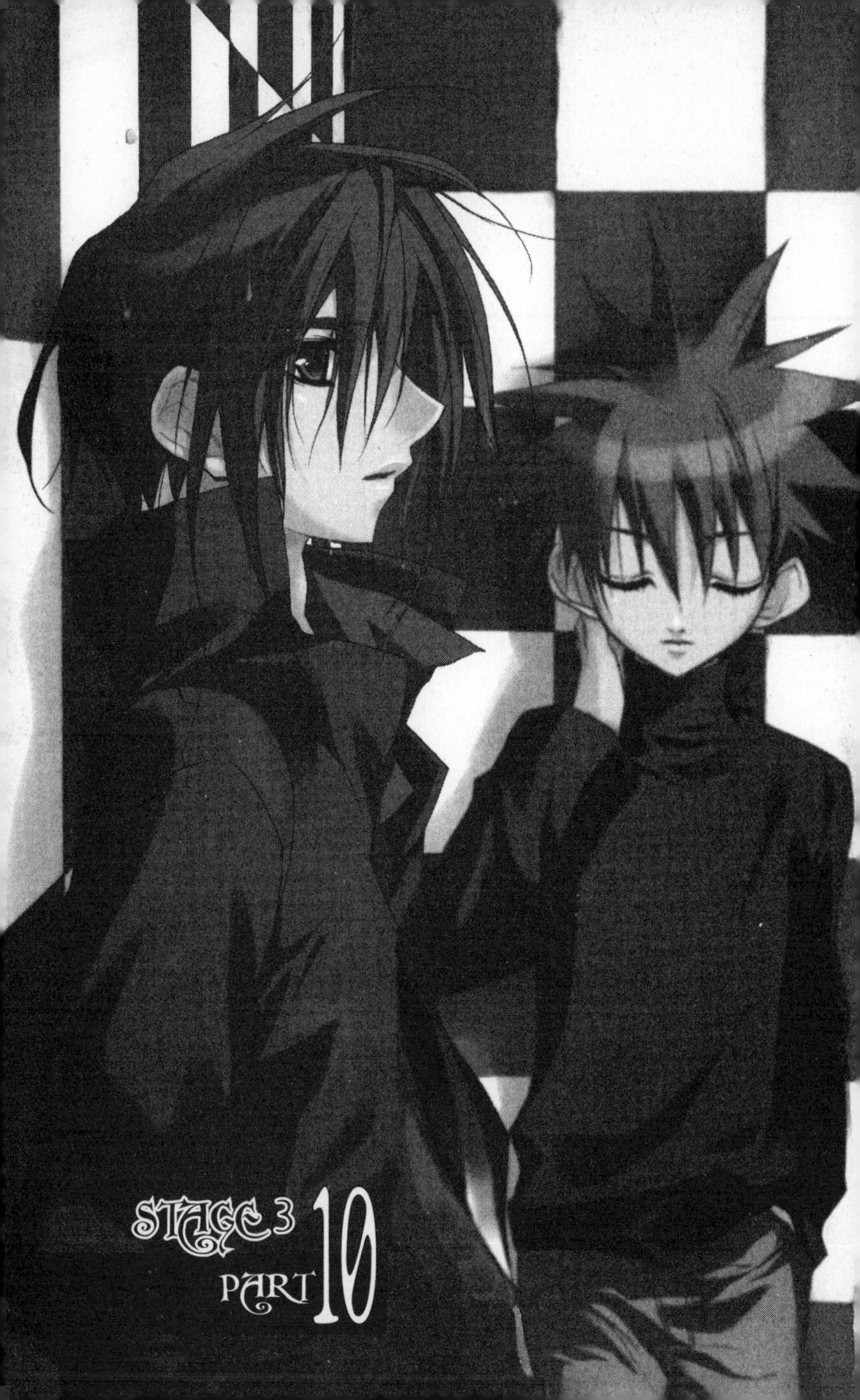
STAGE 3
PART 10

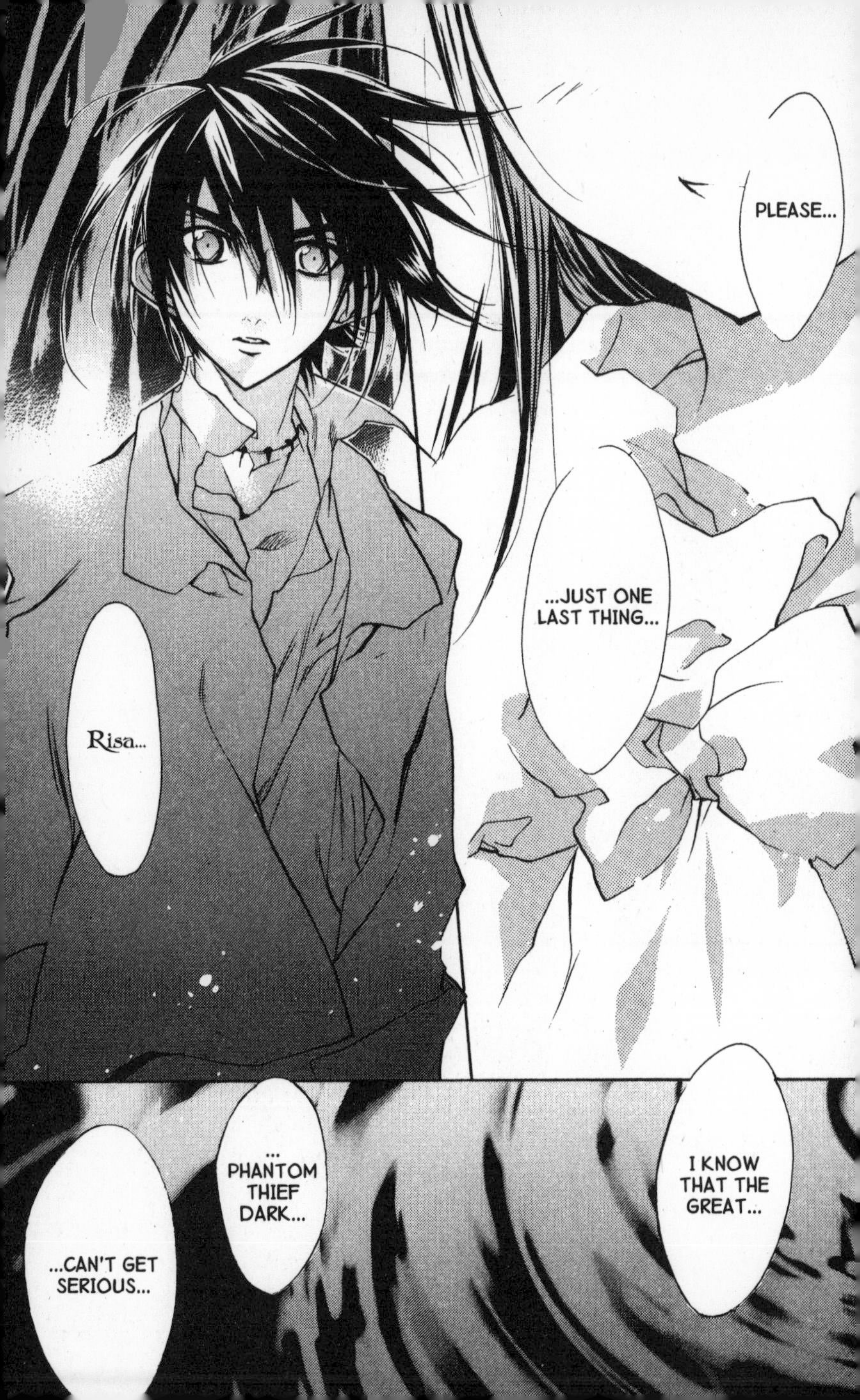
PLEASE...
...JUST ONE LAST THING...
Risa...
I KNOW THAT THE GREAT...
...PHANTOM THIEF DARK...
...CAN'T GET SERIOUS...

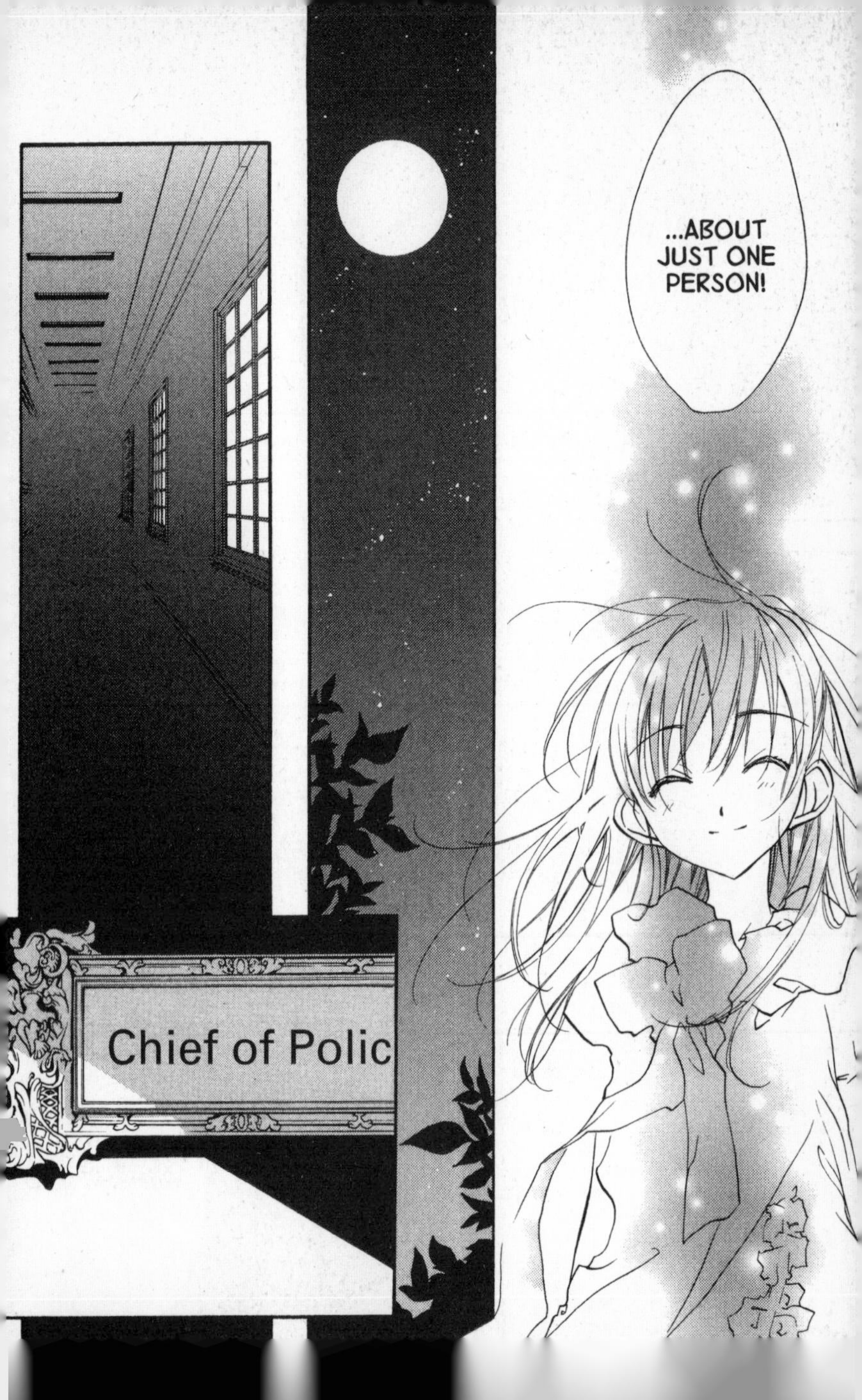
...ABOUT JUST ONE PERSON!
Chief of Polic

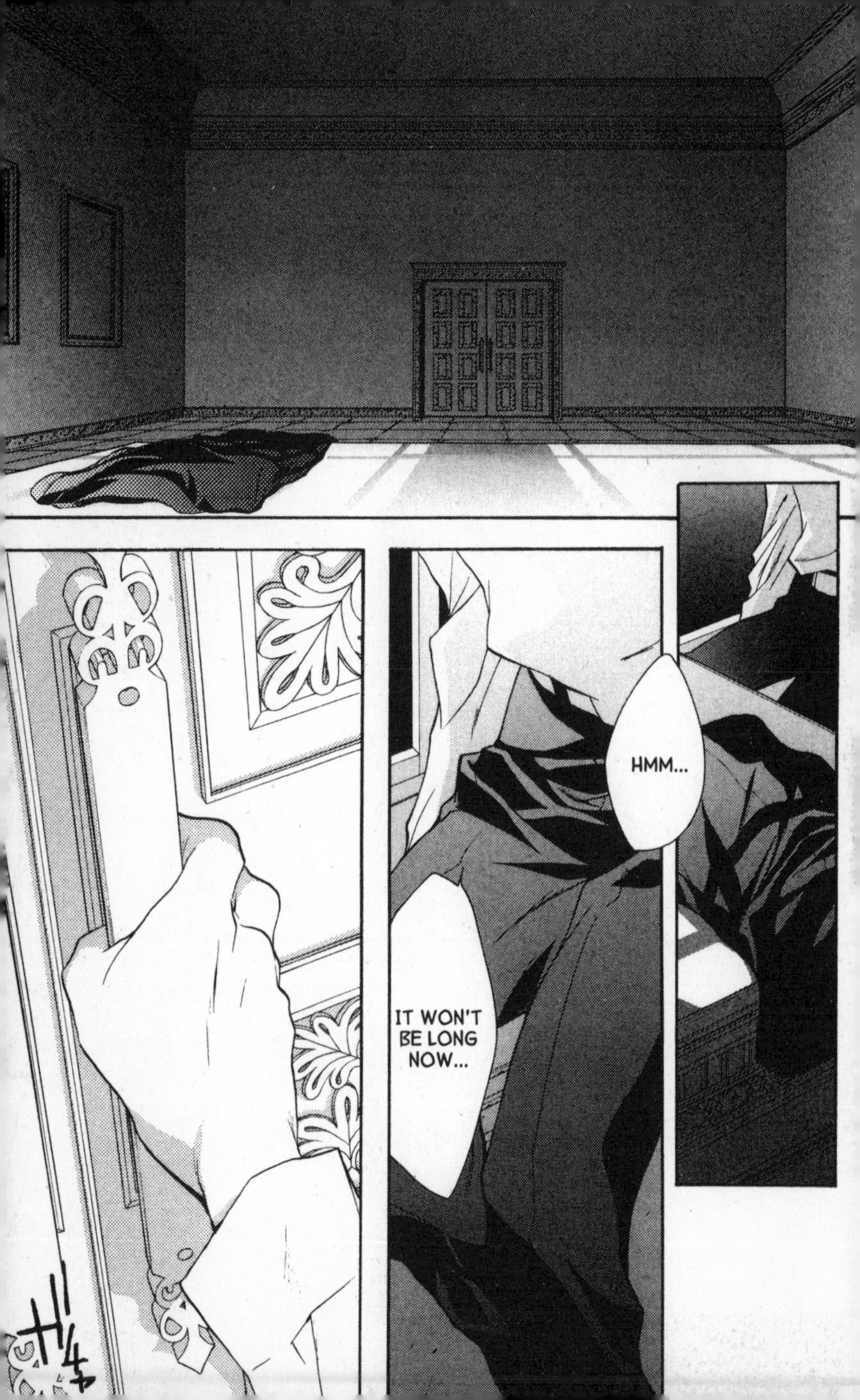
HMM...
IT WON'T BE LONG NOW...

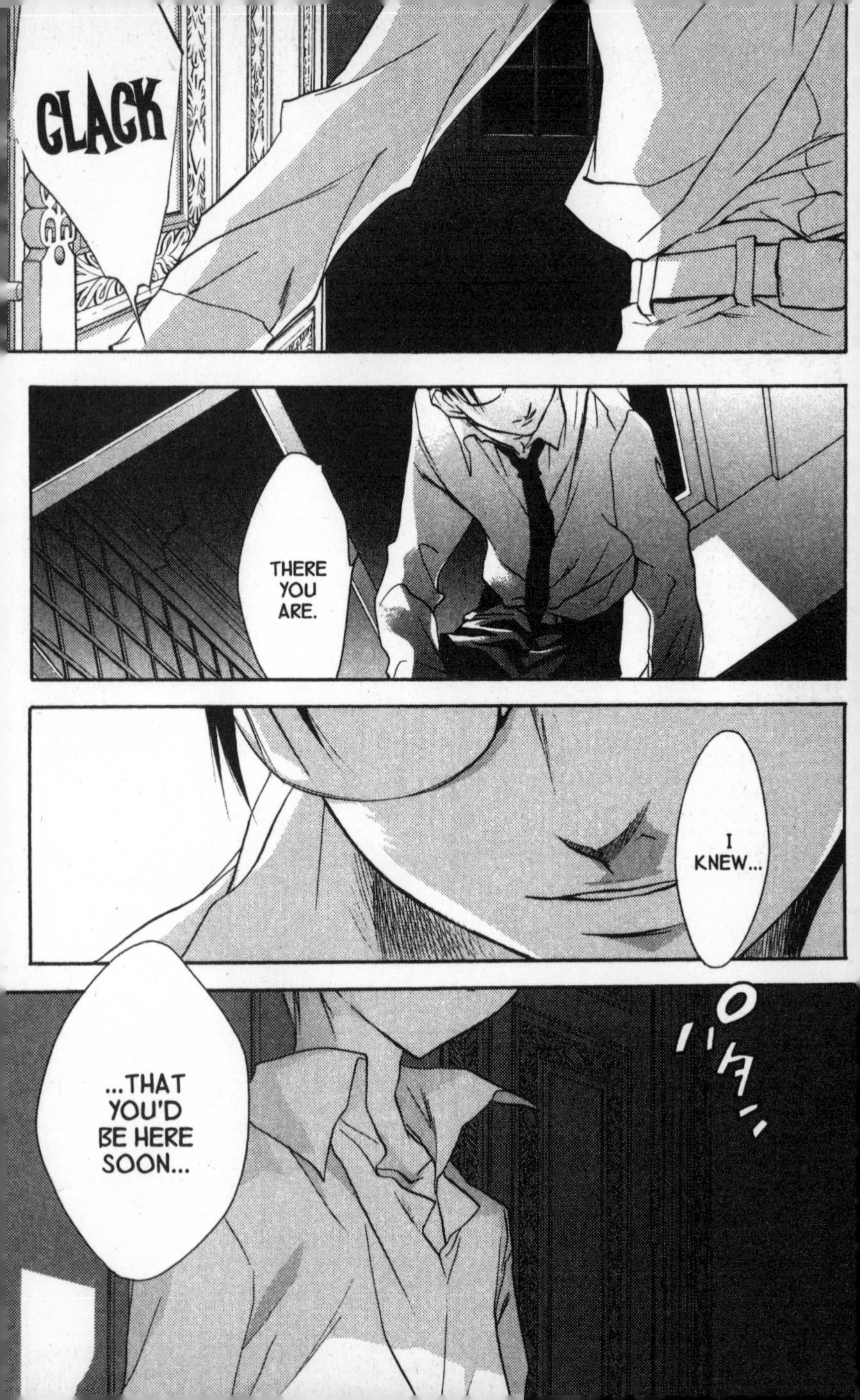
CLACK
THERE YOU ARE.
I KNEW...
...THAT YOU'D BE HERE SOON...

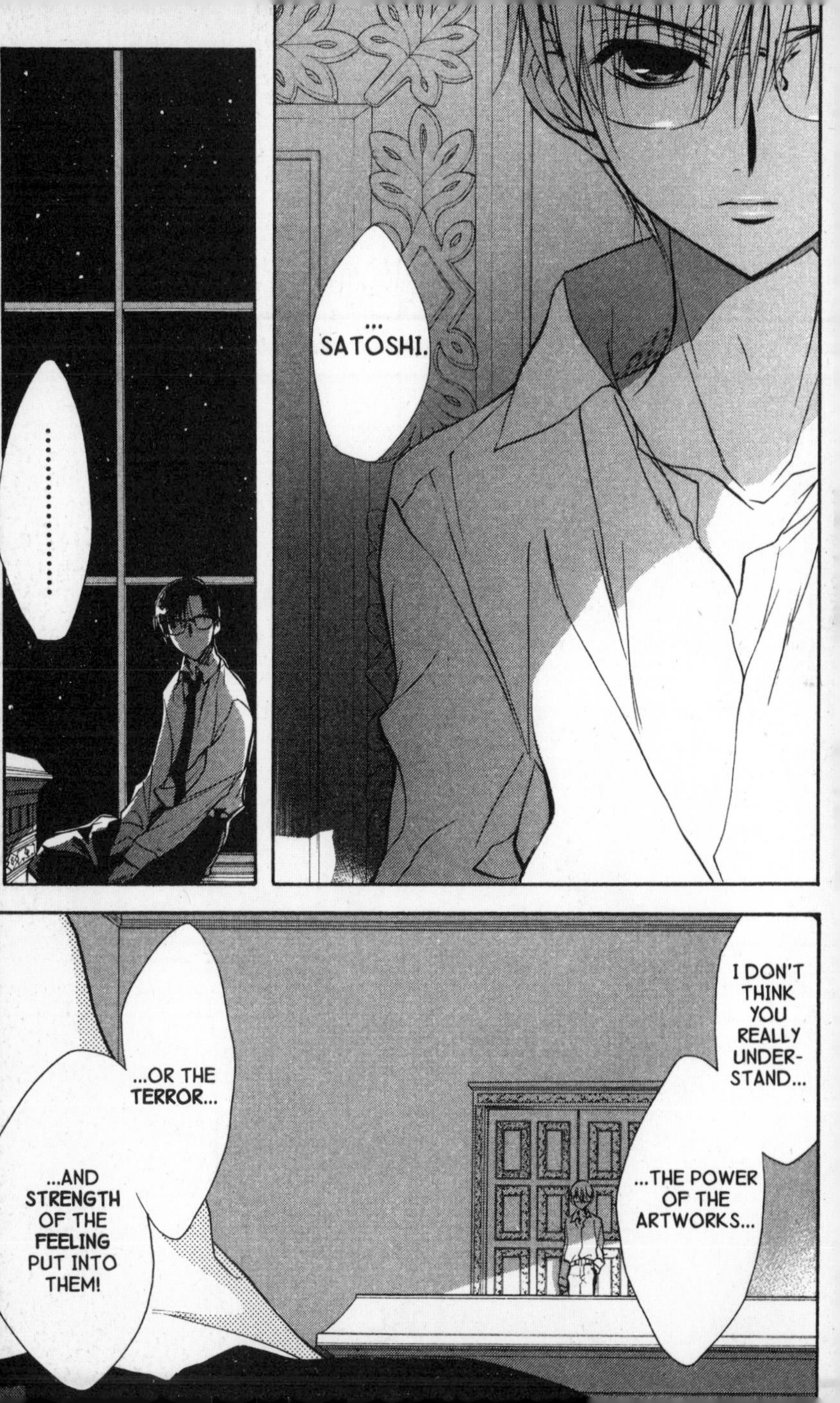
...SATOSHI.
......
I DON'T THINK YOU REALLY UNDERSTAND...
...THE POWER OF THE ARTWORKS...
...OR THE TERROR...
...AND STRENGTH OF THE FEELING PUT INTO THEM!

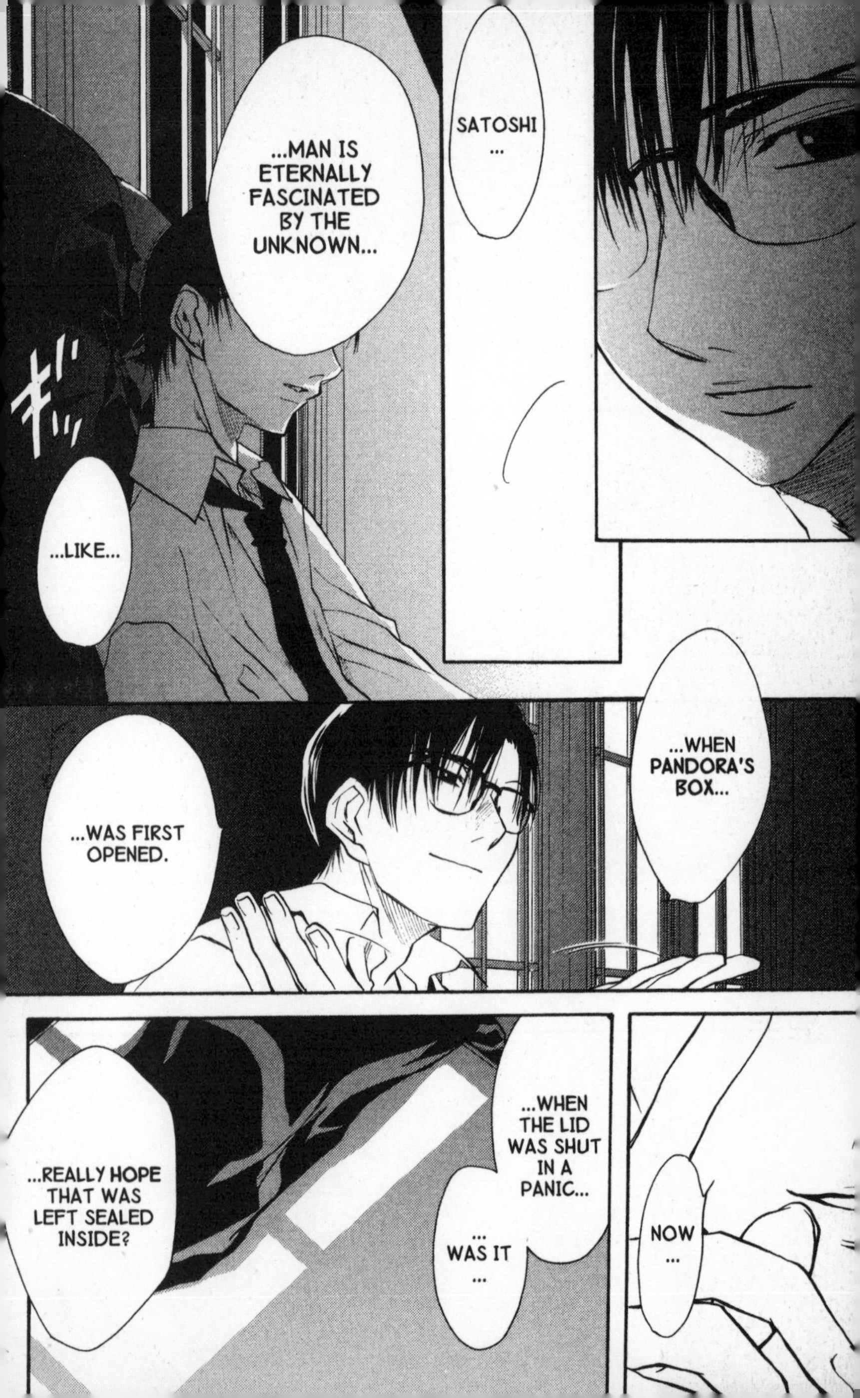
SATOSHI ...
...MAN IS ETERNALLY FASCINATED BY THE UNKNOWN...
...LIKE...
...WHEN PANDORA'S BOX...
...WAS FIRST OPENED.
NOW ...
...WHEN THE LID WAS SHUT IN A PANIC...
... WAS IT ...
...REALLY HOPE THAT WAS LEFT SEALED INSIDE?

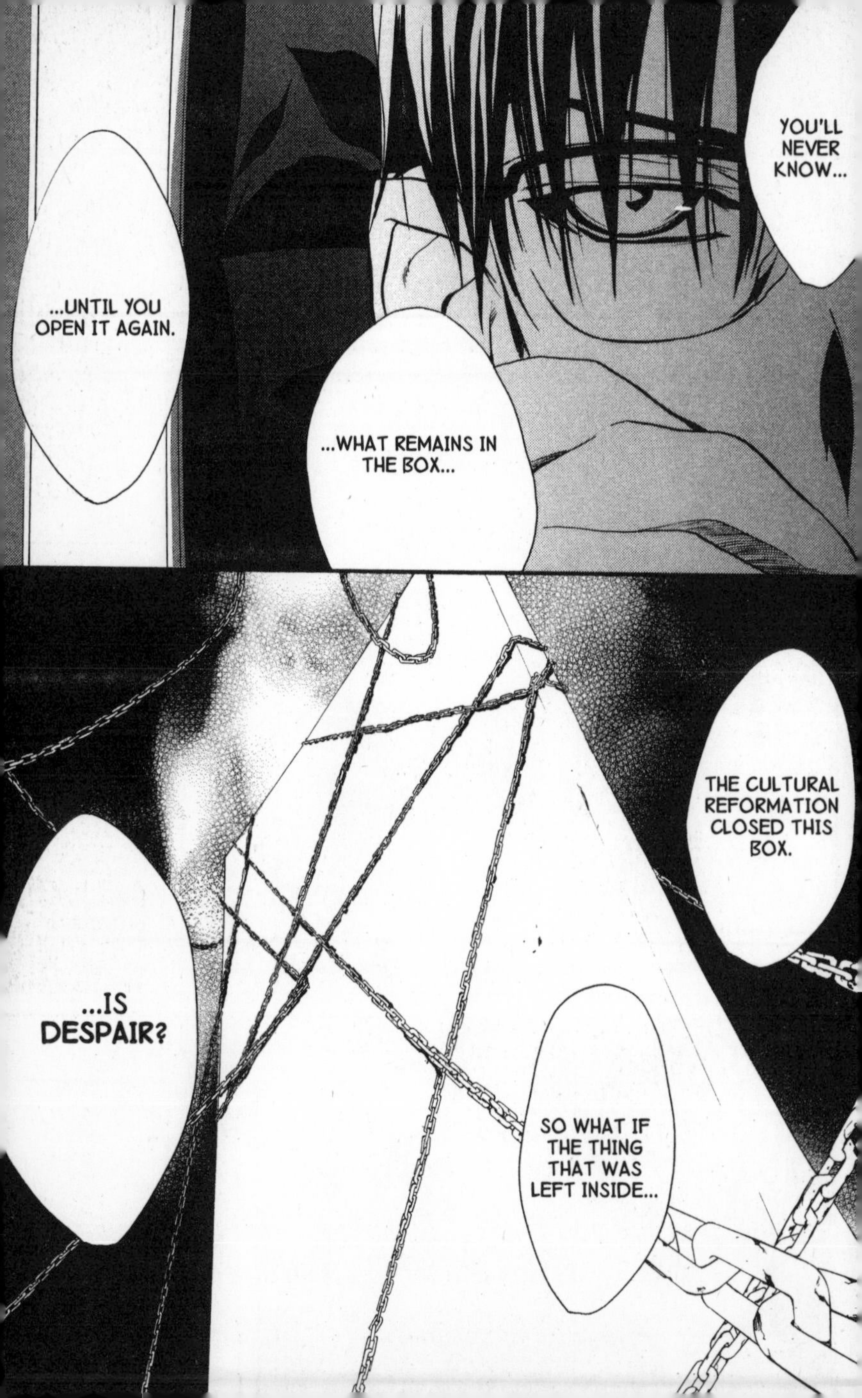
YOU'LL NEVER KNOW...
...WHAT REMAINS IN THE BOX...
...UNTIL YOU OPEN IT AGAIN.
THE CULTURAL REFORMATION CLOSED THIS BOX.
SO WHAT IF THE THING THAT WAS LEFT INSIDE...
...IS DESPAIR?

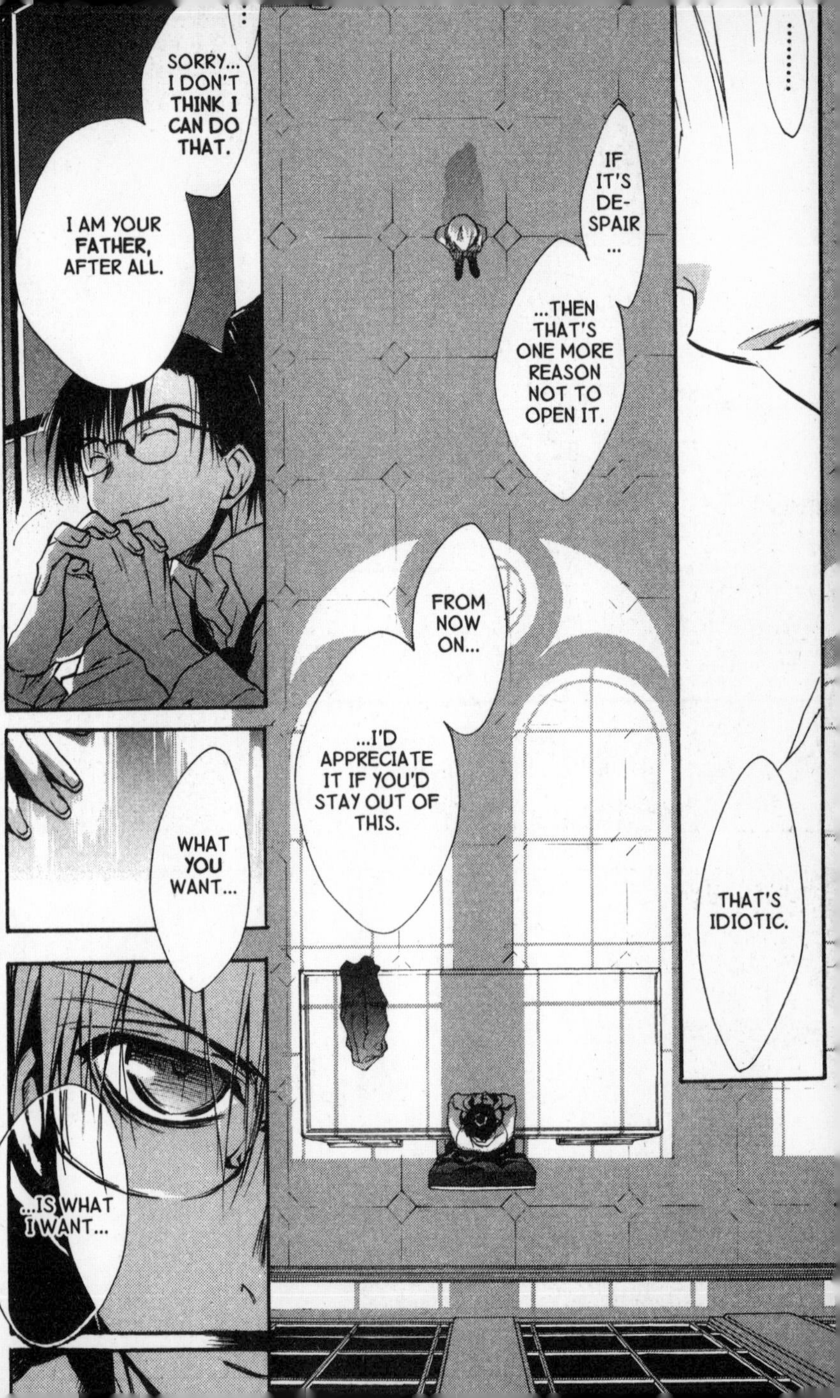

......
THAT'S IDIOTIC.
IF IT'S DE-SPAIR...
...THEN THAT'S ONE MORE REASON NOT TO OPEN IT.
FROM NOW ON...
...I'D APPRECIATE IT IF YOU'D STAY OUT OF THIS.
...
SORRY... I DON'T THINK I CAN DO THAT.
I AM YOUR FATHER, AFTER ALL.
WHAT YOU WANT...
...IS WHAT I WANT...

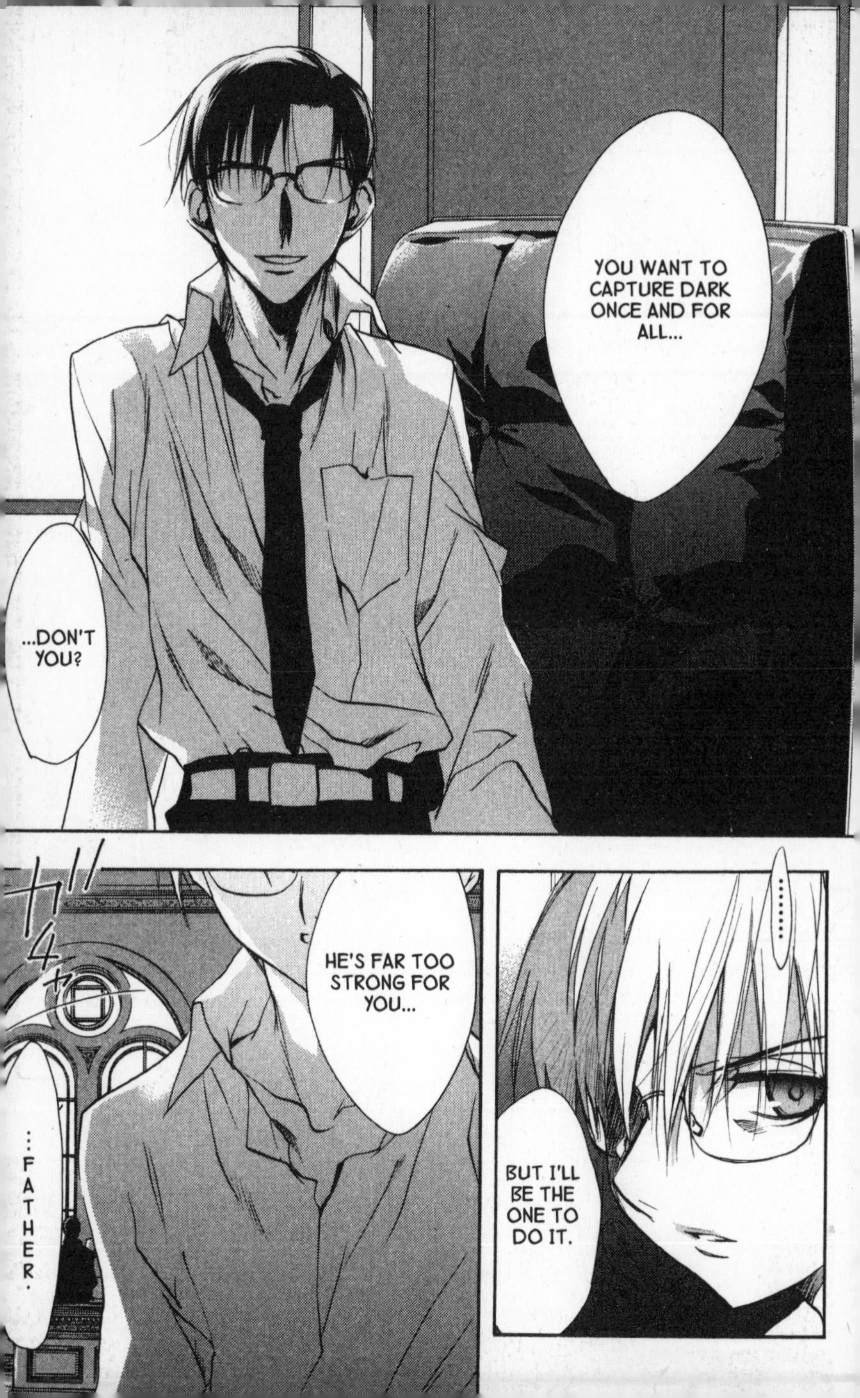
YOU WANT TO CAPTURE DARK ONCE AND FOR ALL...
...DON'T YOU?
......
BUT I'LL BE THE ONE TO DO IT.
HE'S FAR TOO STRONG FOR YOU...
...FATHER.

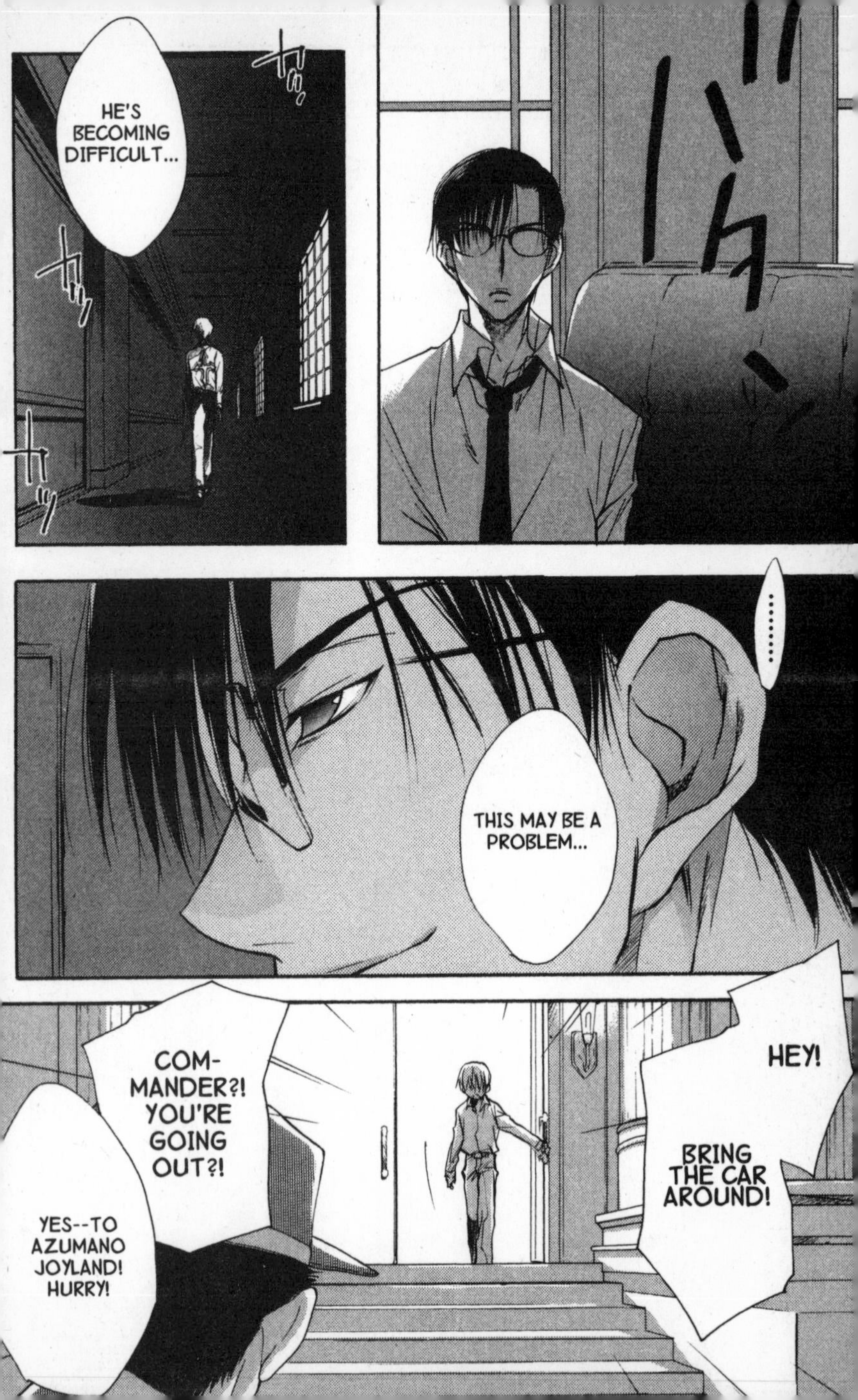
HE'S BECOMING DIFFICULT...
......
THIS MAY BE A PROBLEM...
HEY!
BRING THE CAR AROUND!
COM-MANDER?! YOU'RE GOING OUT?!
YES--TO AZUMANO JOYLAND! HURRY!

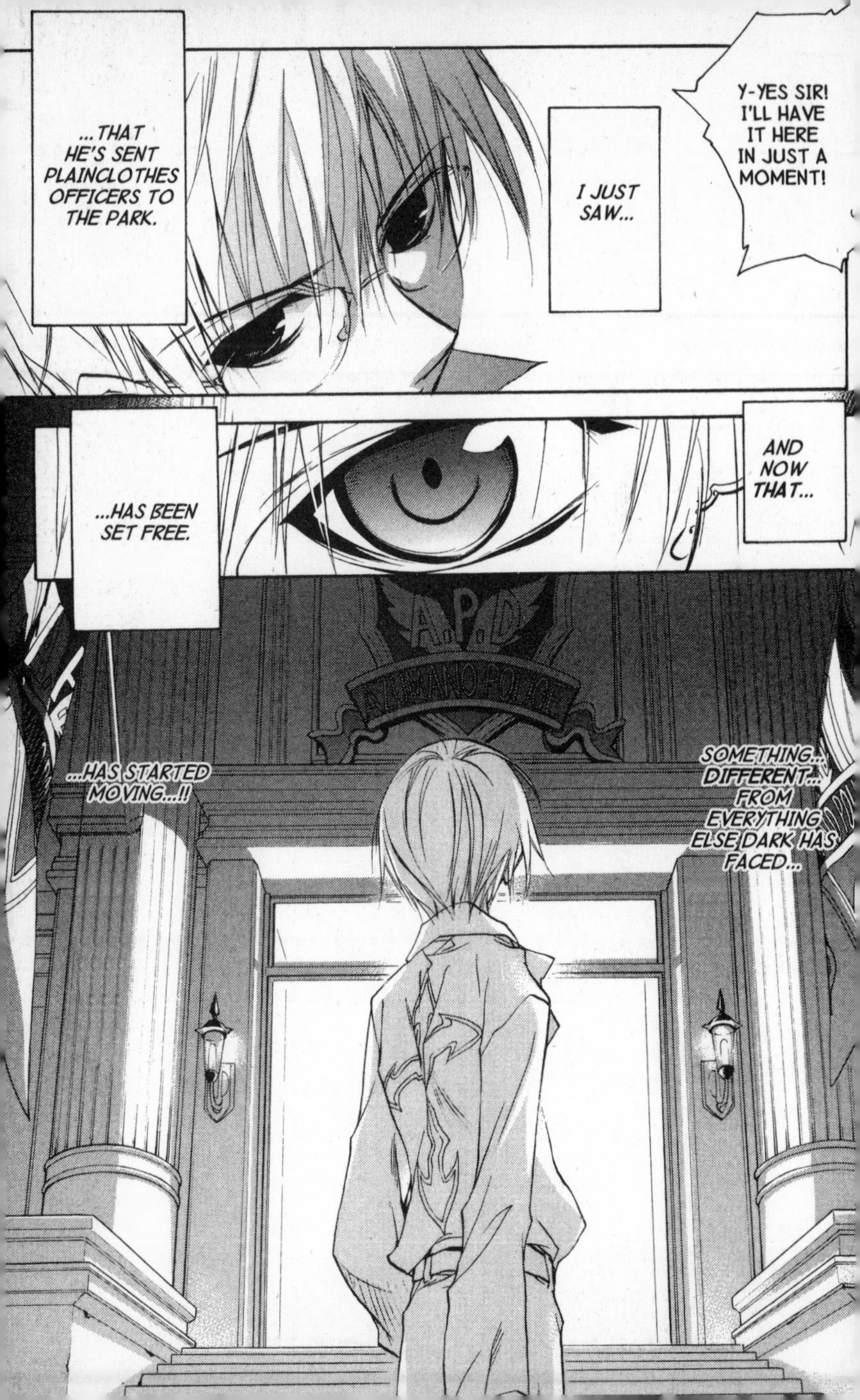
Y-YES SIR! I'LL HAVE IT HERE IN JUST A MOMENT!
I JUST SAW...
...THAT HE'S SENT PLAINCLOTHES OFFICERS TO THE PARK.
AND NOW THAT...
...HAS BEEN SET FREE.
SOMETHING... DIFFERENT... FROM EVERYTHING ELSE DARK HAS FACED...
...HAS STARTED MOVING...!!

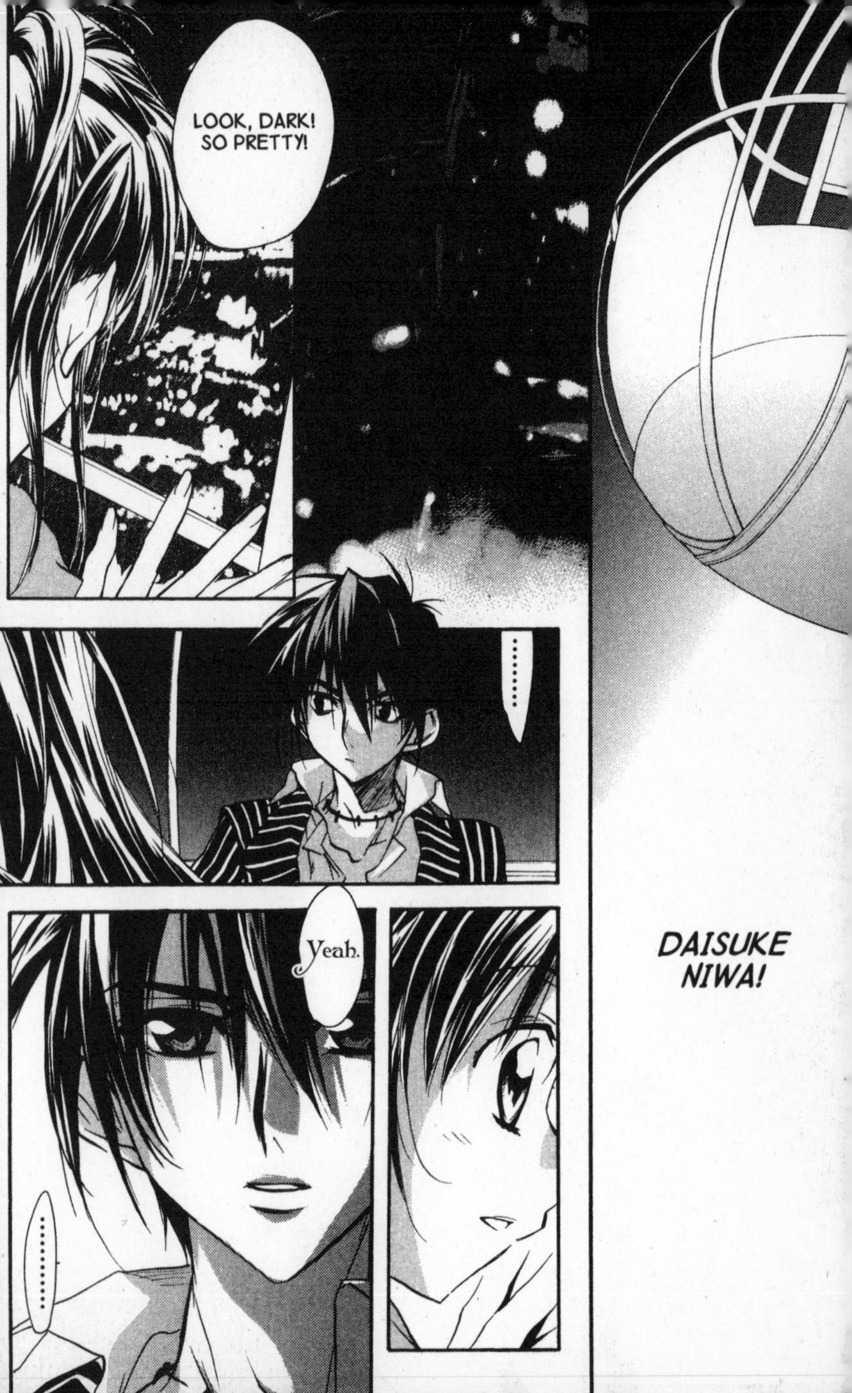
DAISUKE NIWA!
LOOK, DARK! SO PRETTY!
......
Yeah.
......

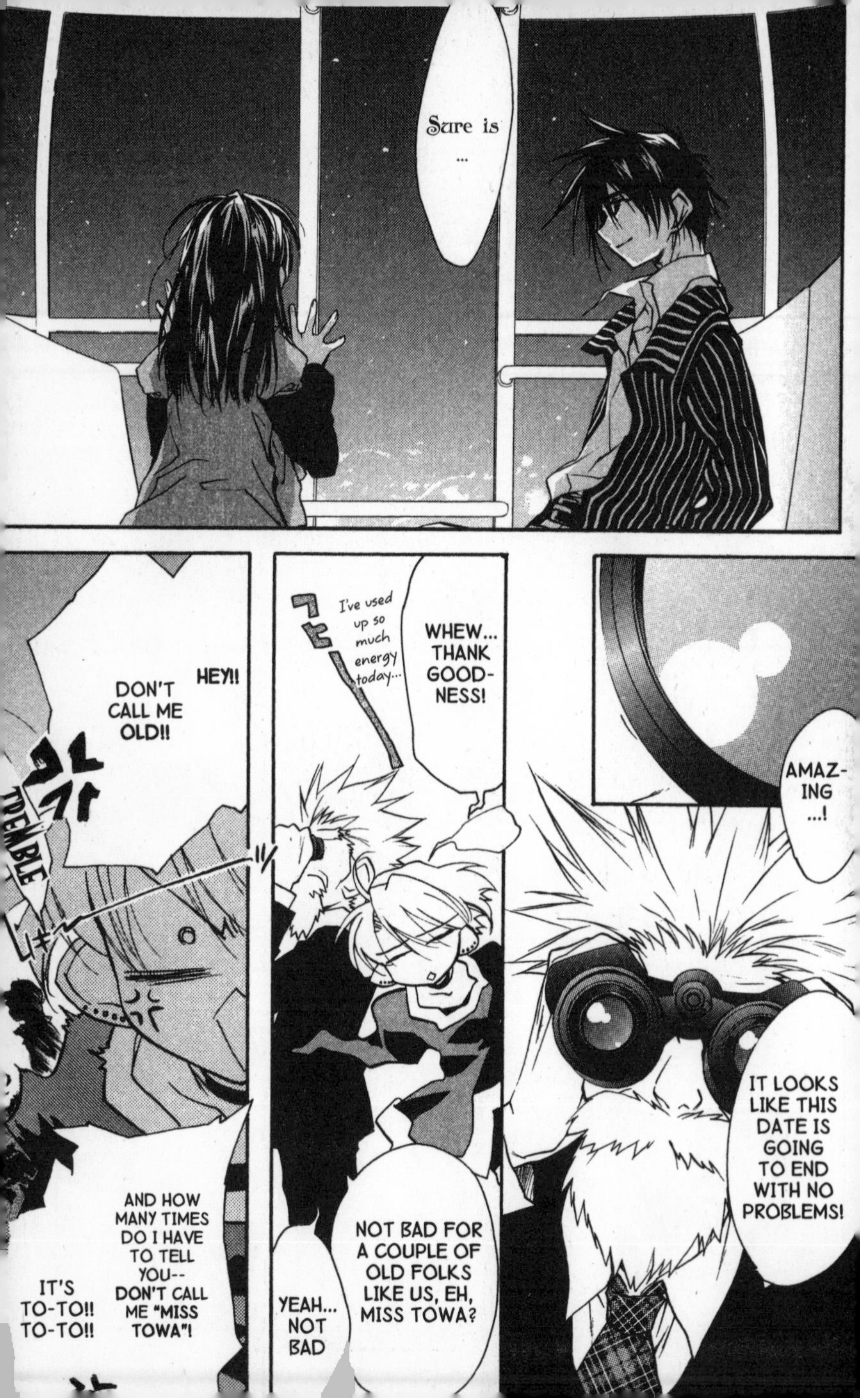
Sure is ...
AMAZ-ING ...!
IT LOOKS LIKE THIS DATE IS GOING TO END WITH NO PROBLEMS!
WHEW... THANK GOOD-NESS!
I've used up so much energy today...
NOT BAD FOR A COUPLE OF OLD FOLKS LIKE US, EH, MISS TOWA?
YEAH... NOT BAD
HEY!!
DON'T CALL ME OLD!!
TREMBLE
AND HOW MANY TIMES DO I HAVE TO TELL YOU-- DON'T CALL ME "MISS TOWA"!
IT'S TO-TO!! TO-TO!!

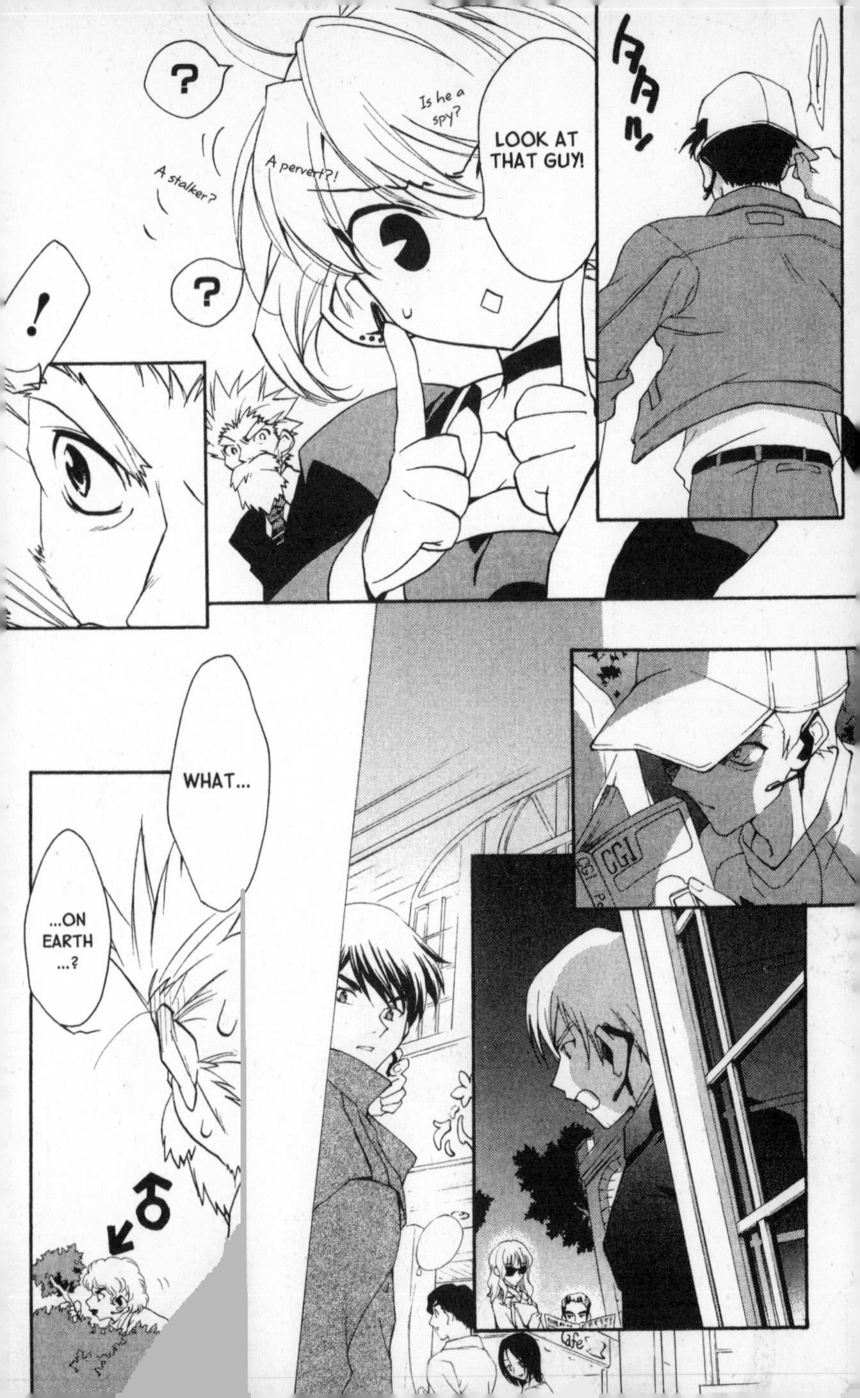
!
LOOK AT THAT GUY!
Is he a spy?
A pervert?!
A stalker?
?
?
!
Cafe
WHAT...
...ON EARTH ...?

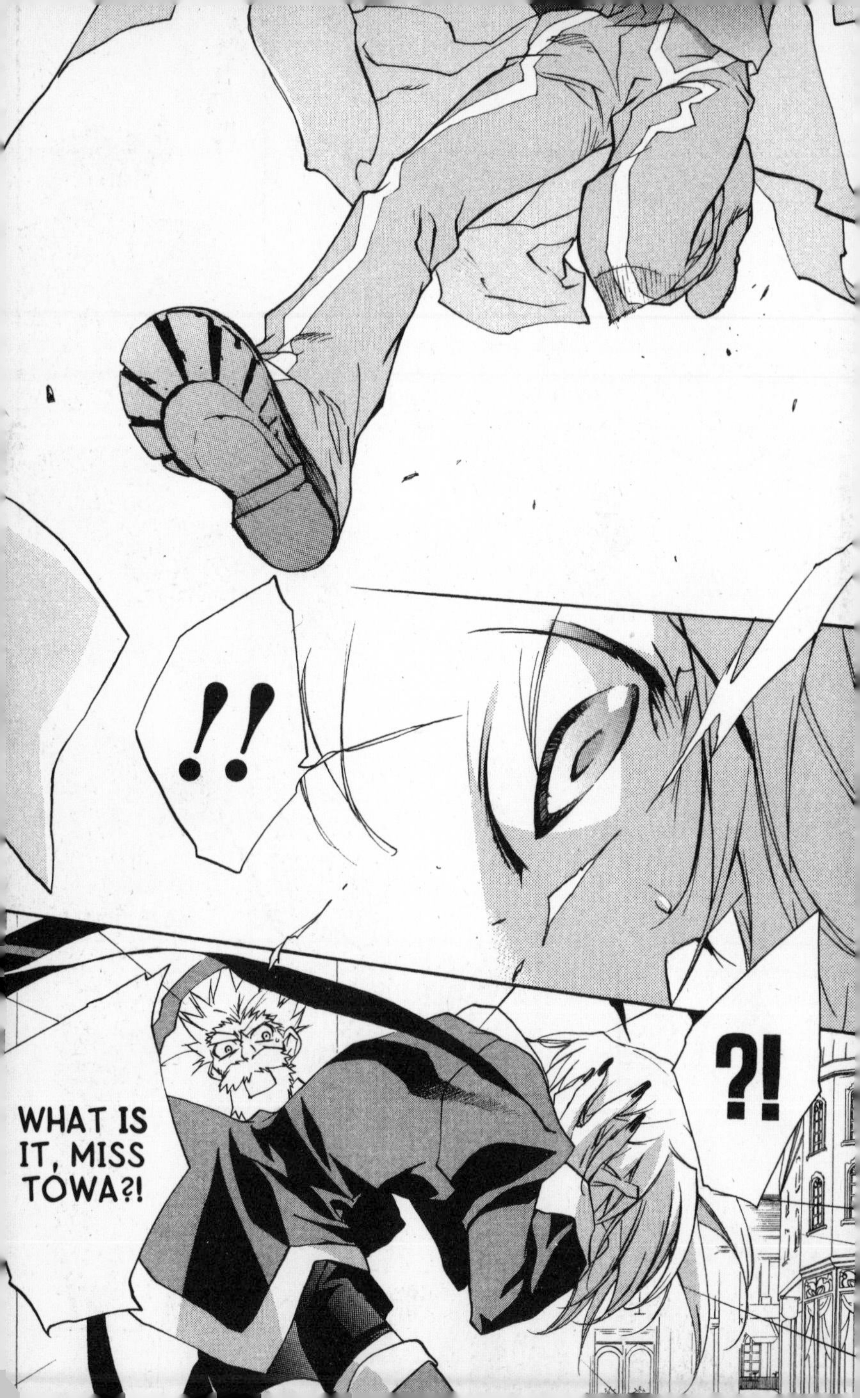
!!
?!
WHAT IS IT, MISS TOWA?!

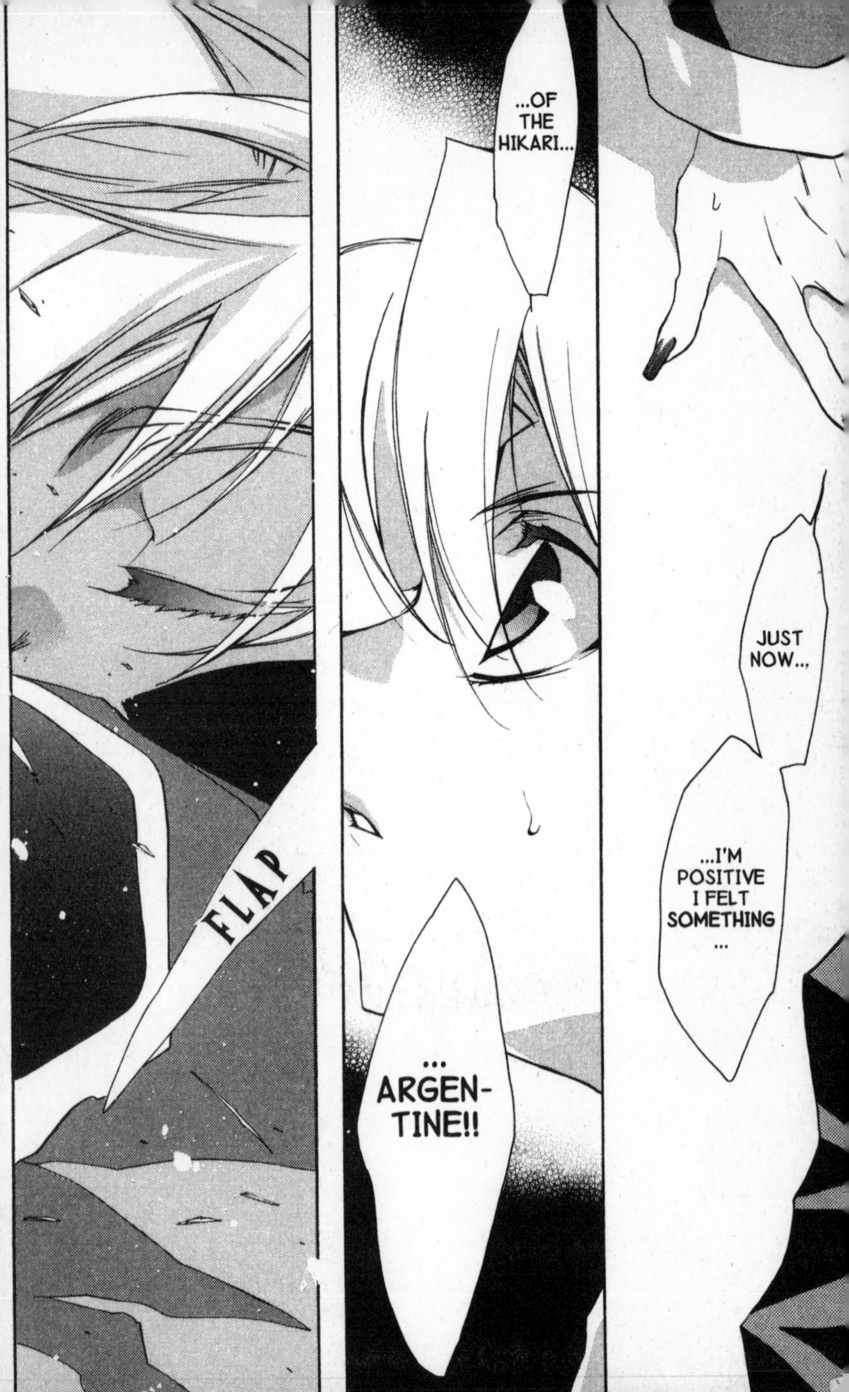
JUST NOW...
...I'M POSITIVE I FELT SOMETHING...
...OF THE HIKARI...
...ARGEN-TINE!!
FLAP

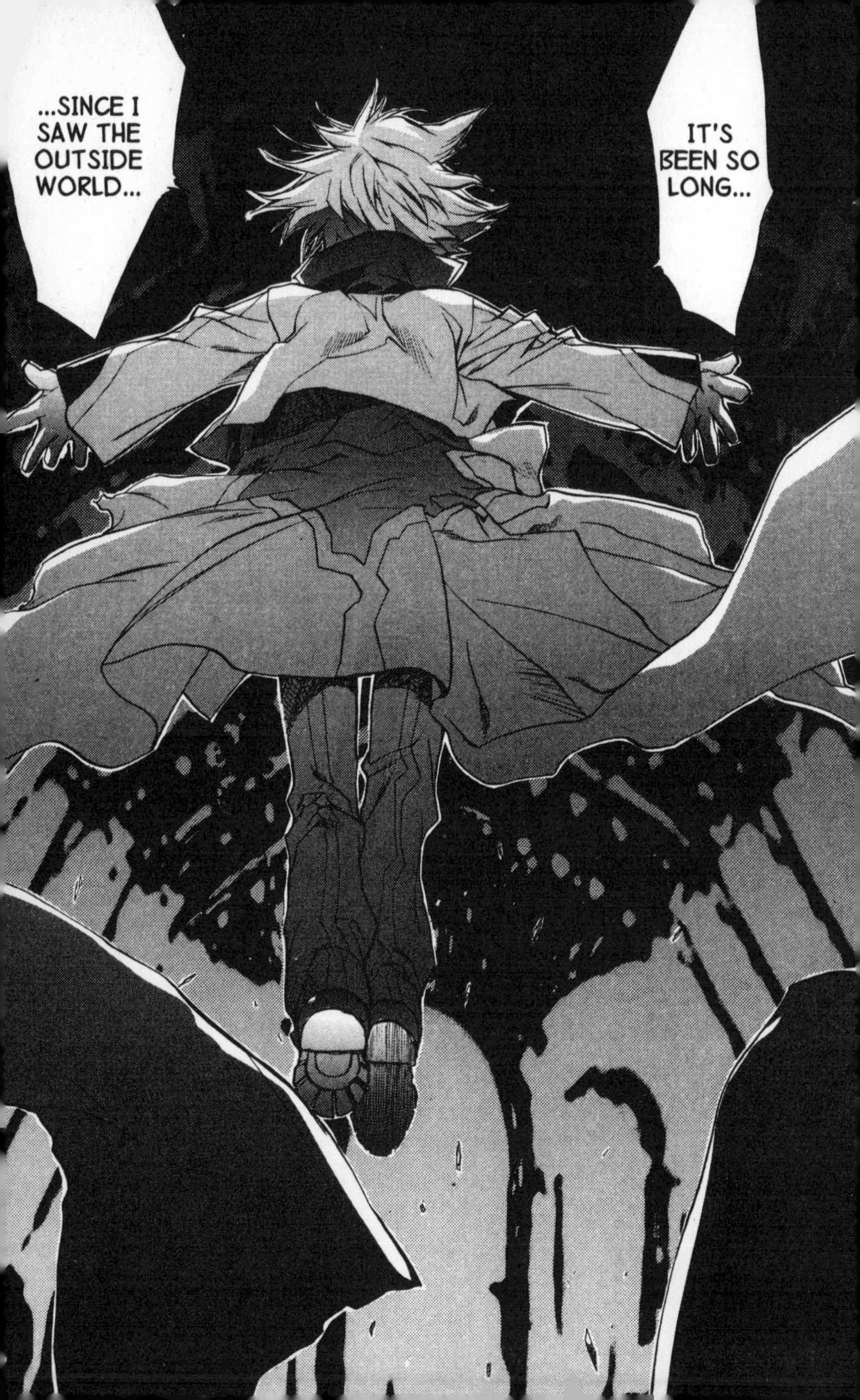
IT'S BEEN SO LONG...
...SINCE I SAW THE OUTSIDE WORLD...

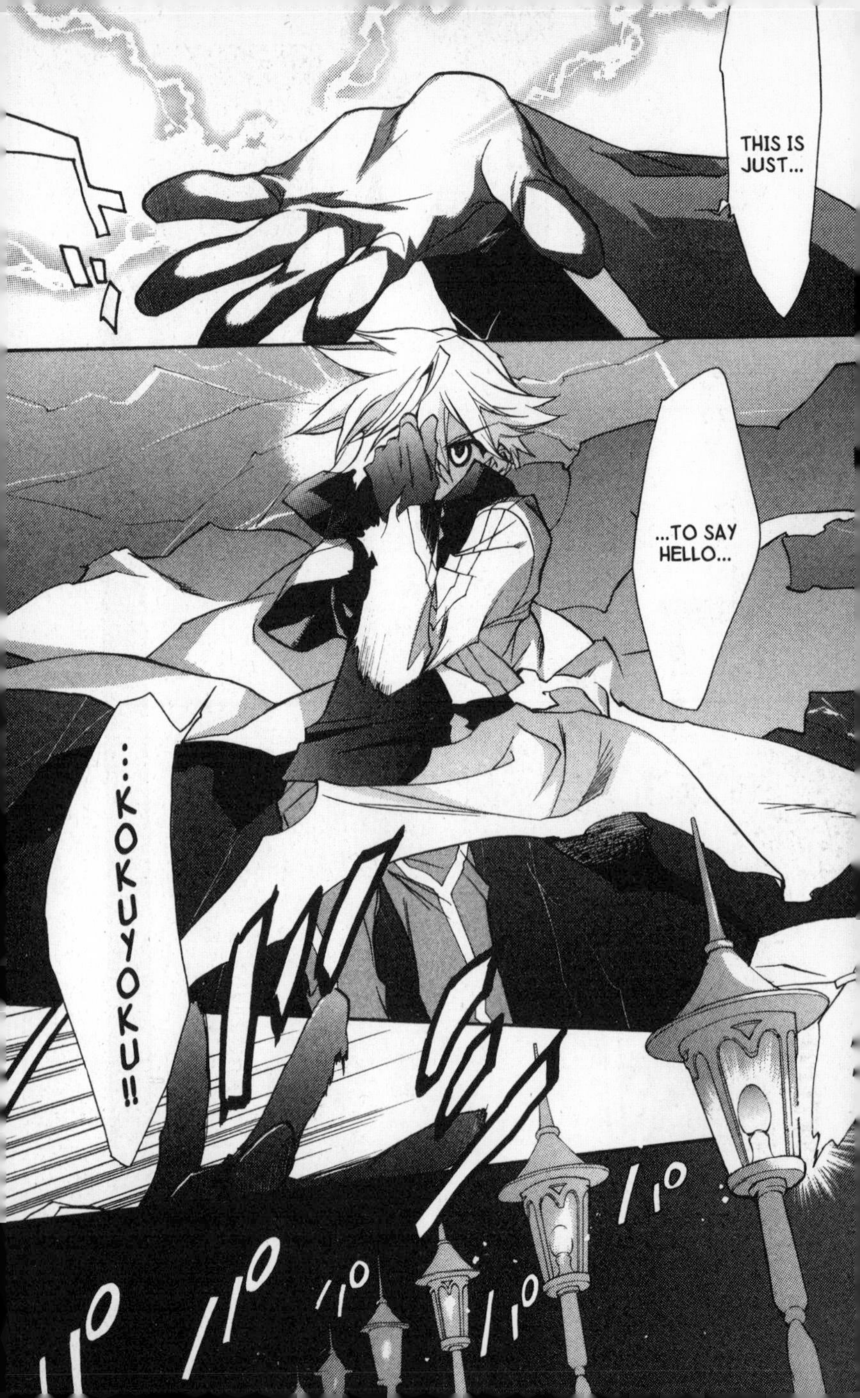
THIS IS JUST...
...TO SAY HELLO...
...KOKUYOKU!!

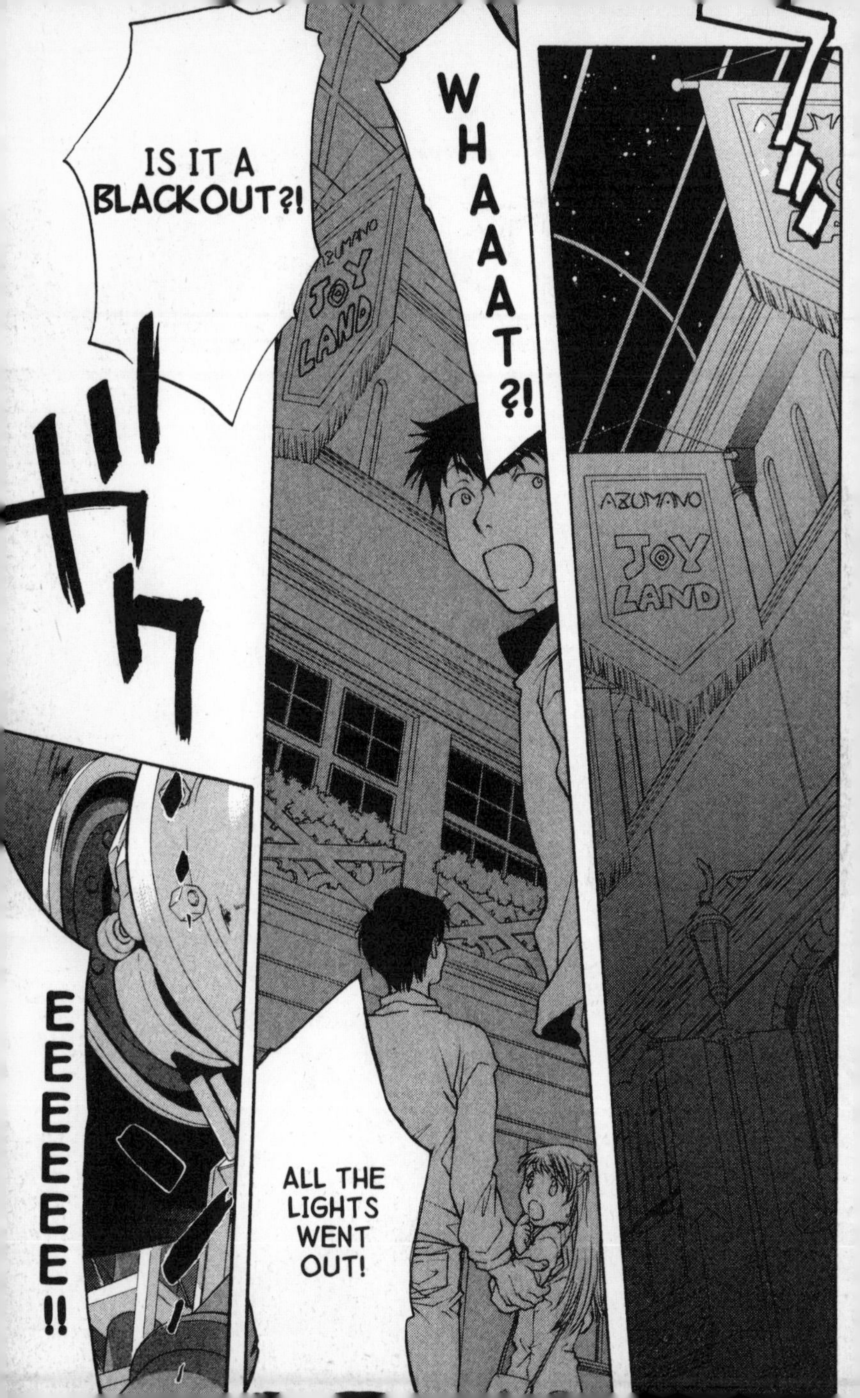
AZUMANO JOY LAND
WHAAAT?!
ALL THE LIGHTS WENT OUT!
IS IT A BLACKOUT?!
EEEEEEE!!

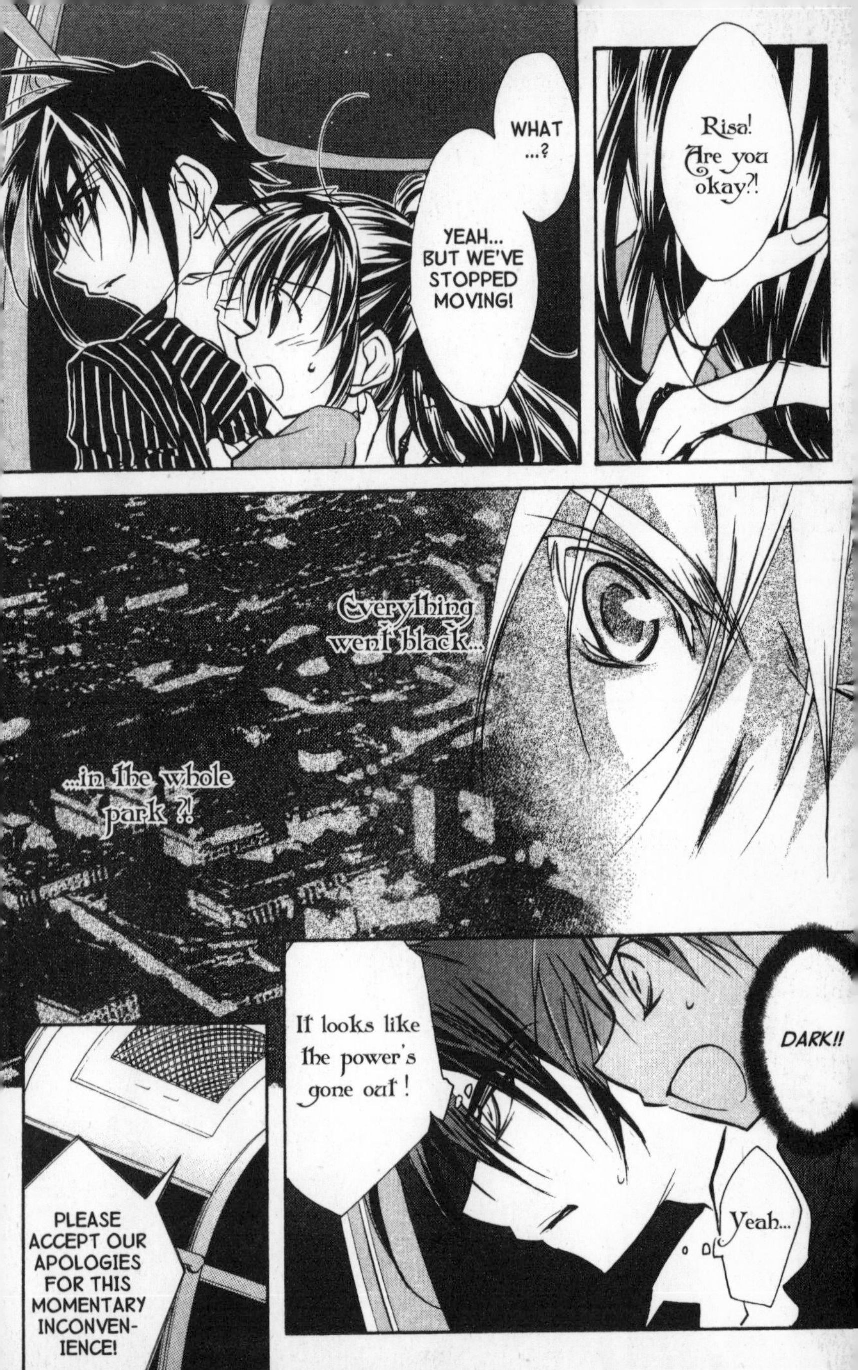
Risa! Are you okay?!
WHAT ...?
YEAH... BUT WE'VE STOPPED MOVING!
Everything went black...
...in the whole park ?!
DARK!!
It looks like the power's gone out !
Yeah...
PLEASE ACCEPT OUR APOLOGIES FOR THIS MOMENTARY INCONVEN-IENCE!

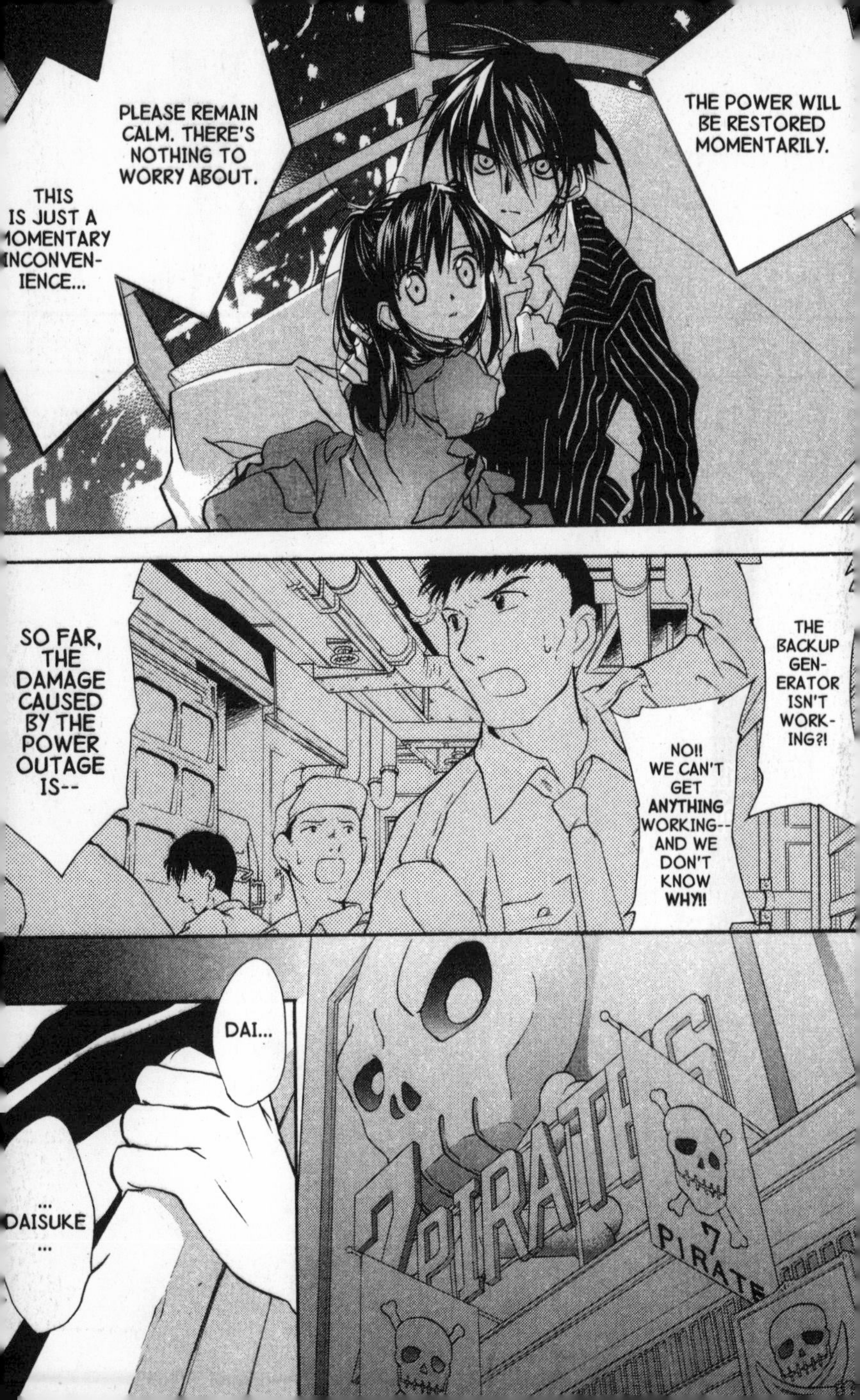
THE POWER WILL BE RESTORED MOMENTARILY.
PLEASE REMAIN CALM. THERE'S NOTHING TO WORRY ABOUT.
THIS IS JUST A MOMENTARY INCONVENIENCE...
THE BACKUP GENERATOR ISN'T WORKING?!
NO!! WE CAN'T GET ANYTHING WORKING-- AND WE DON'T KNOW WHY!!
SO FAR, THE DAMAGE CAUSED BY THE POWER OUTAGE IS--
7 PIRATE
7 PIRATE
DAI...
...DAISUKE...

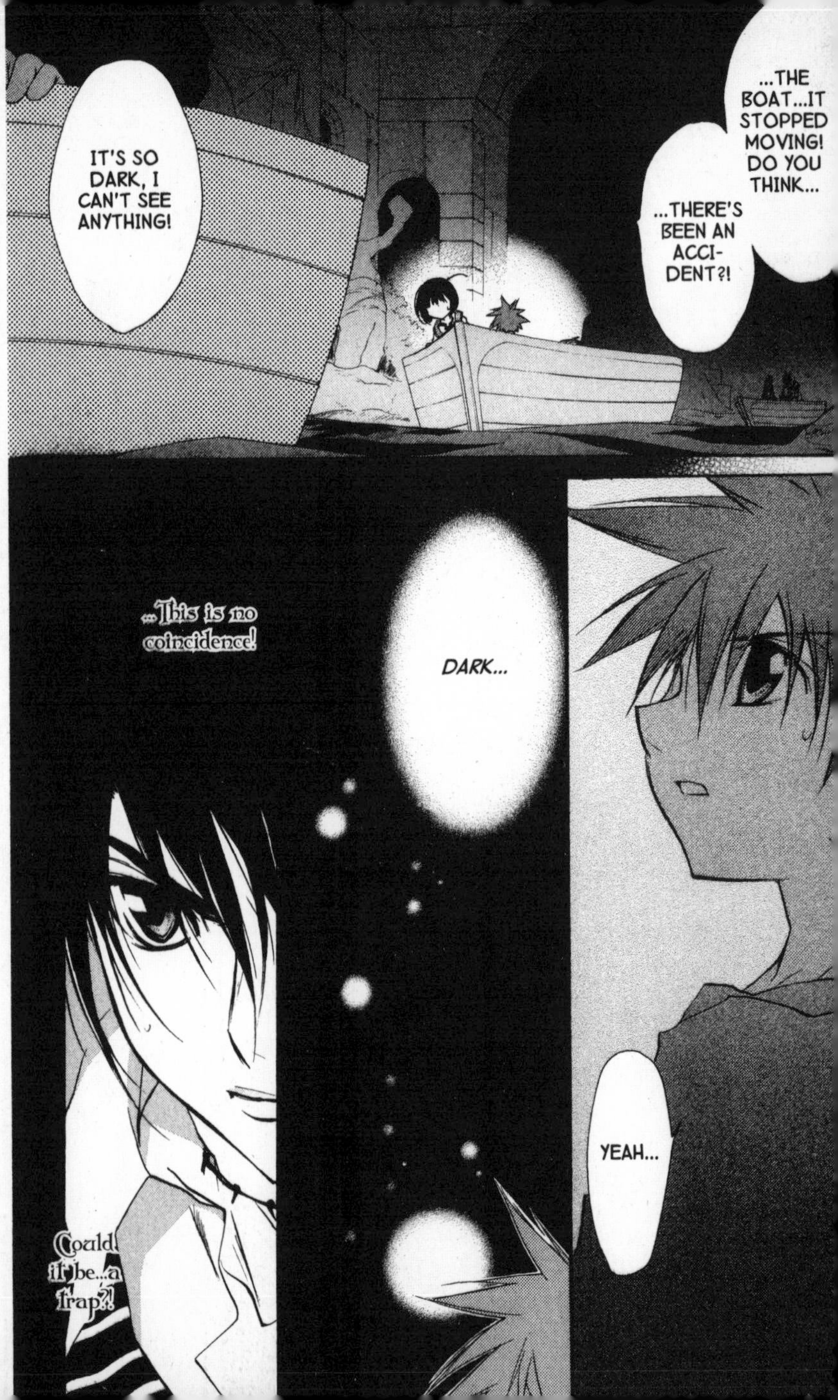
...THE BOAT...IT STOPPED MOVING! DO YOU THINK...
...THERE'S BEEN AN ACCIDENT?!
IT'S SO DARK, I CAN'T SEE ANYTHING!
YEAH...
DARK...
...This is no coincidence!
Could it be...a trap?!

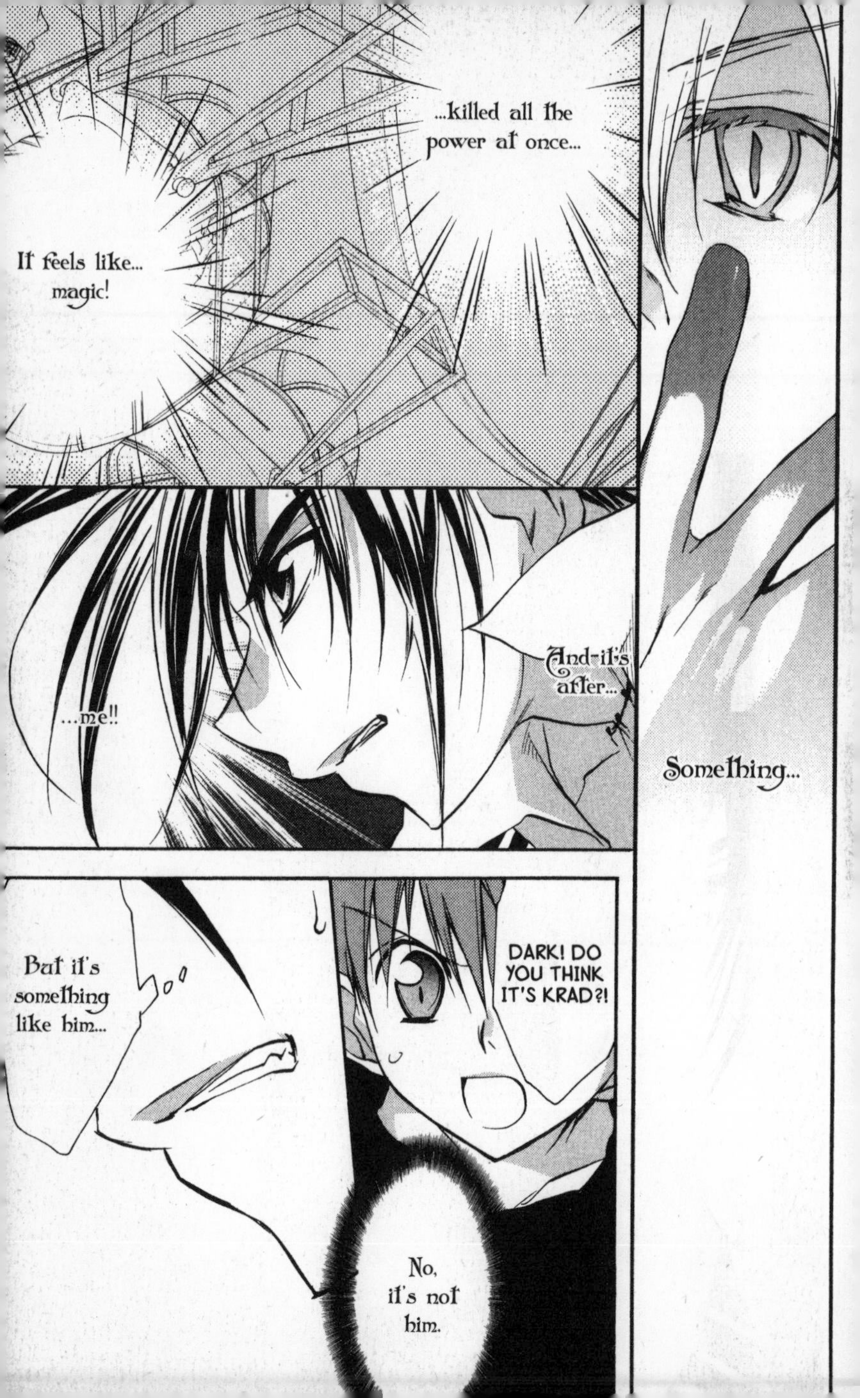
Something...
...killed all the power at once...
It feels like... magic!
And it's after...
...me!!
DARK! DO YOU THINK IT'S KRAD?!
But it's something like him...
No, it's not him.

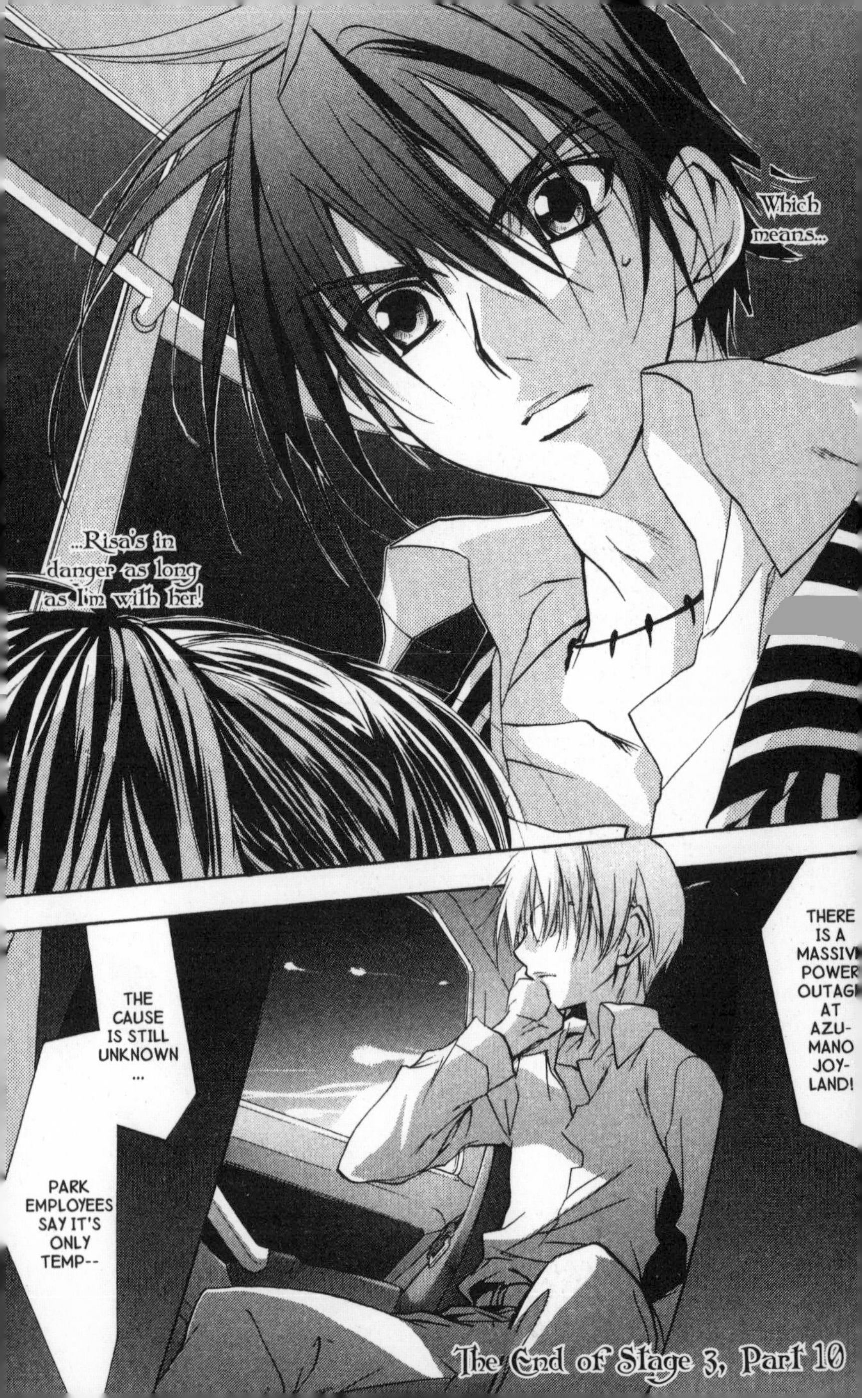
Which means...
...Risa's in danger as long as I'm with her!
THERE IS A MASSIV POWER OUTAG AT AZU-MANO JOY-LAND!
THE CAUSE IS STILL UNKNOWN ...
PARK EMPLOYEES SAY IT'S ONLY TEMP--
The End of Stage 3, Part 10

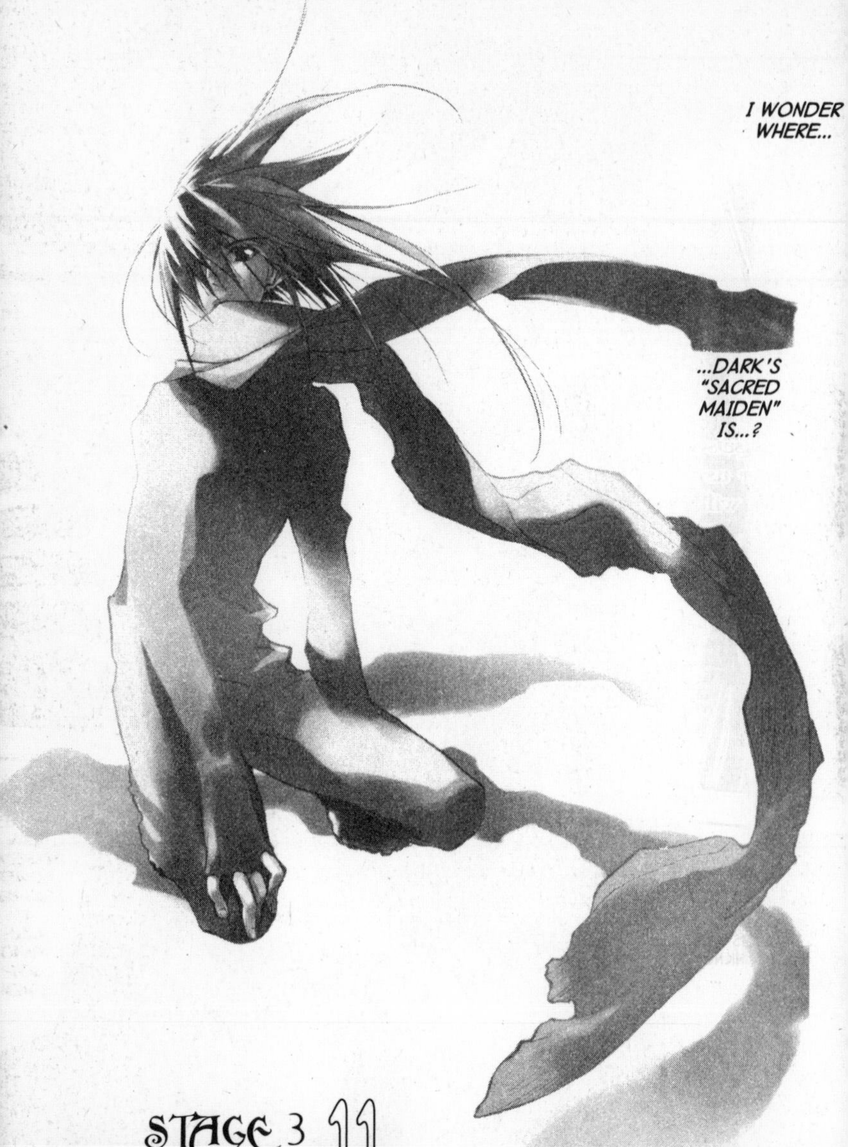
I WONDER WHERE...
...DARK'S "SACRED MAIDEN" IS...?

STAGE 3 PART 11

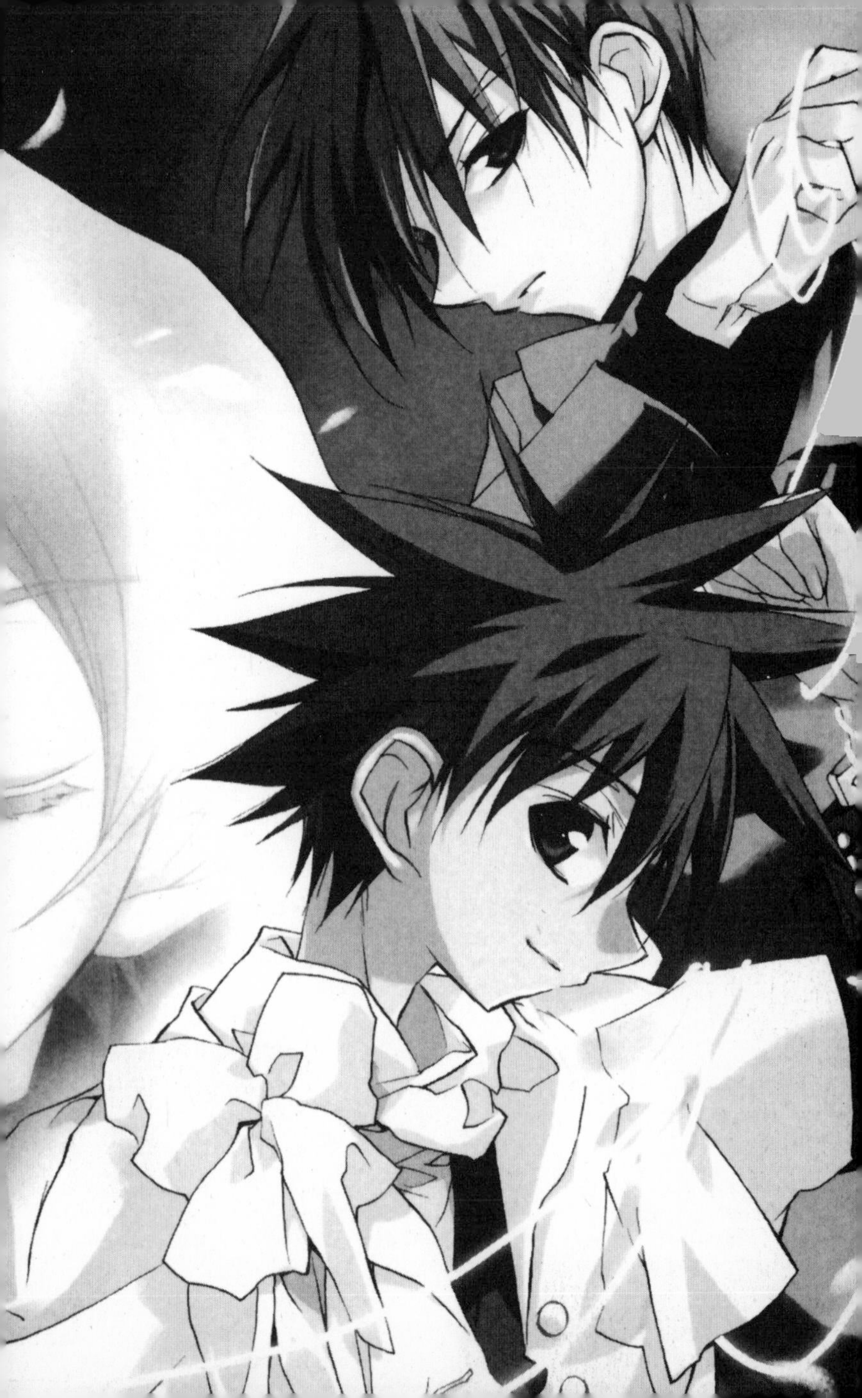

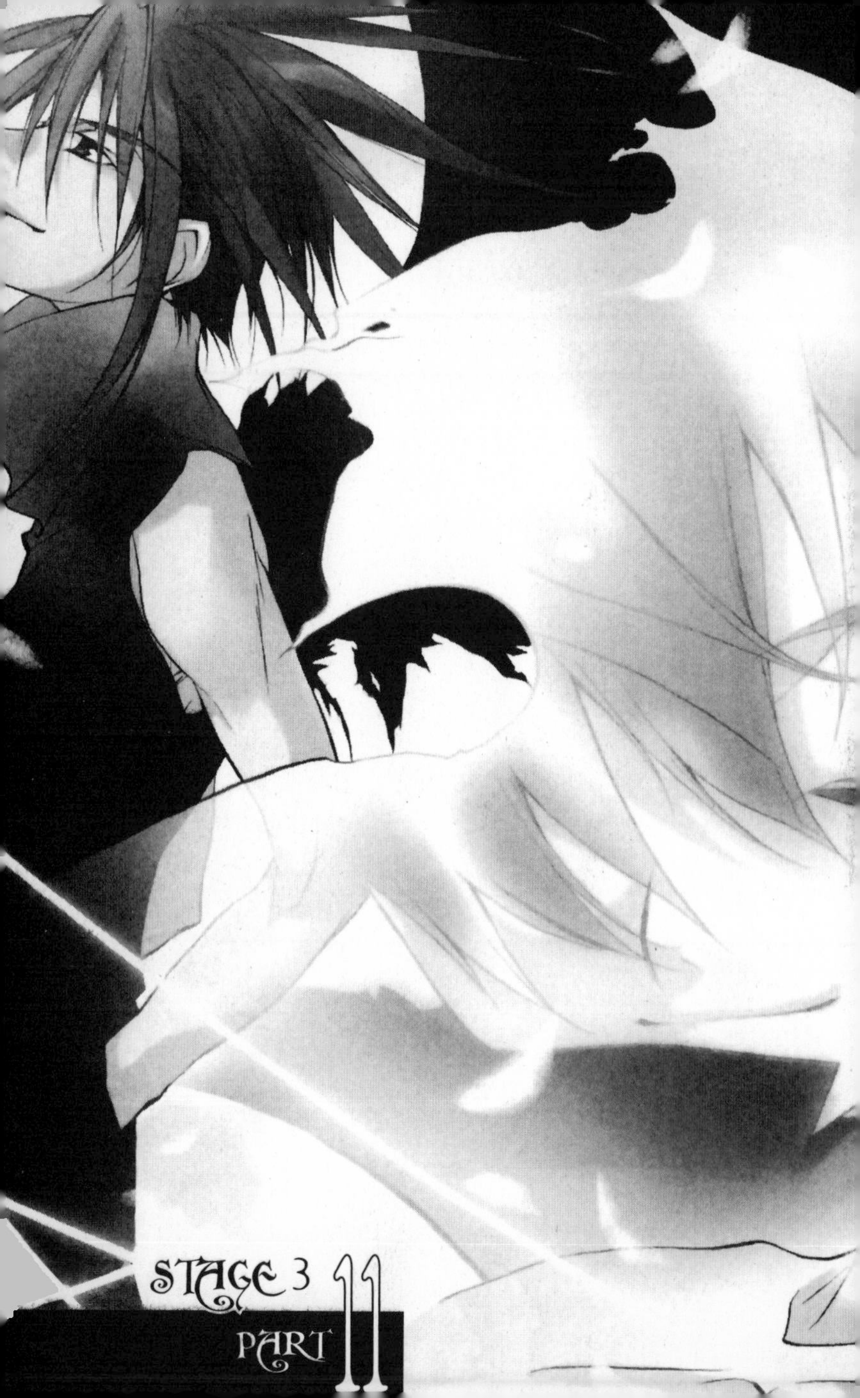
STAGE 3
PART 11

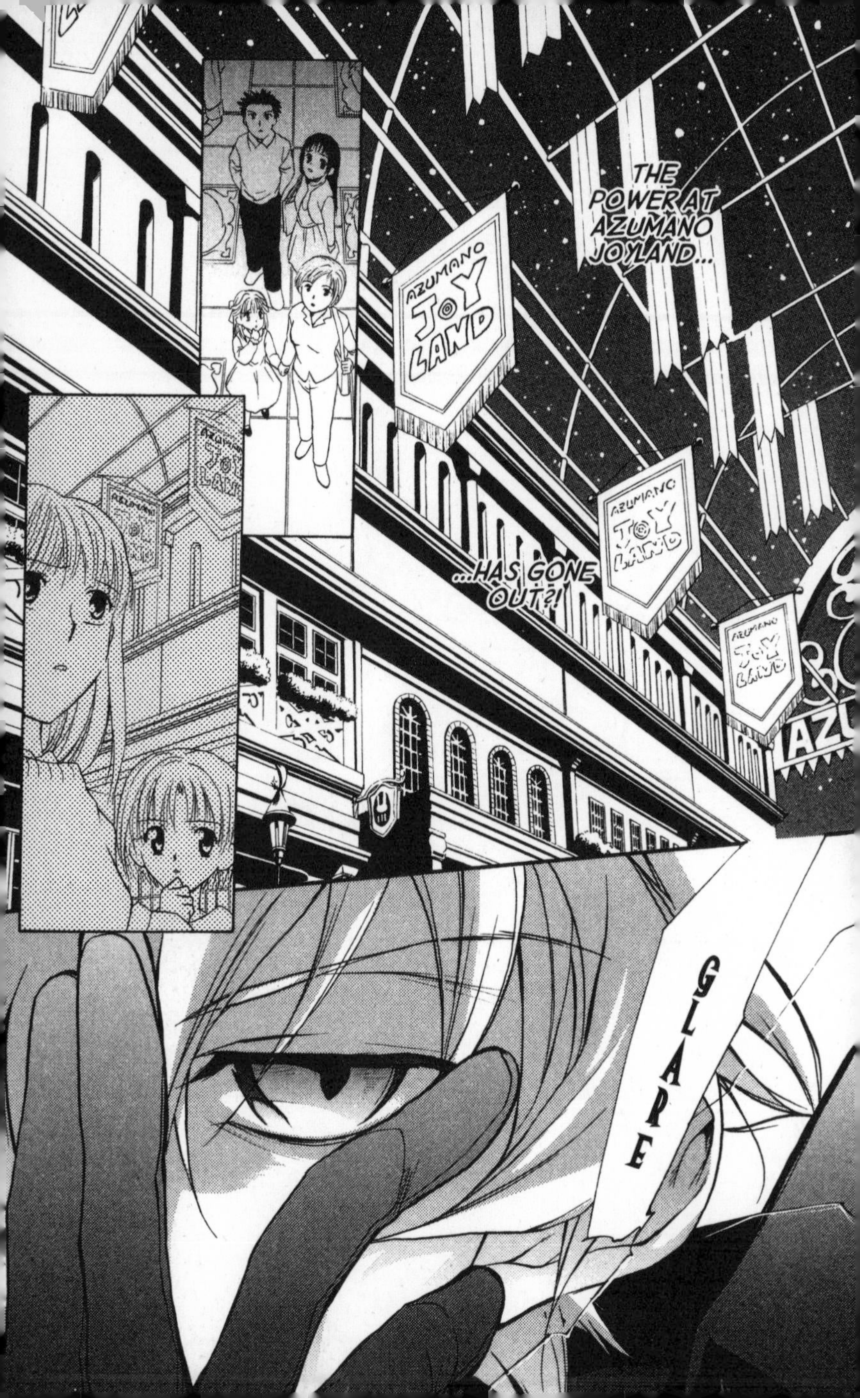
THE POWER AT AZUMANO JOYLAND...
AZUMANO JOY LAND
...HAS GONE OUT?!
AZUMANO JOY LAND
AZUMANO JOY LAND
GLARE

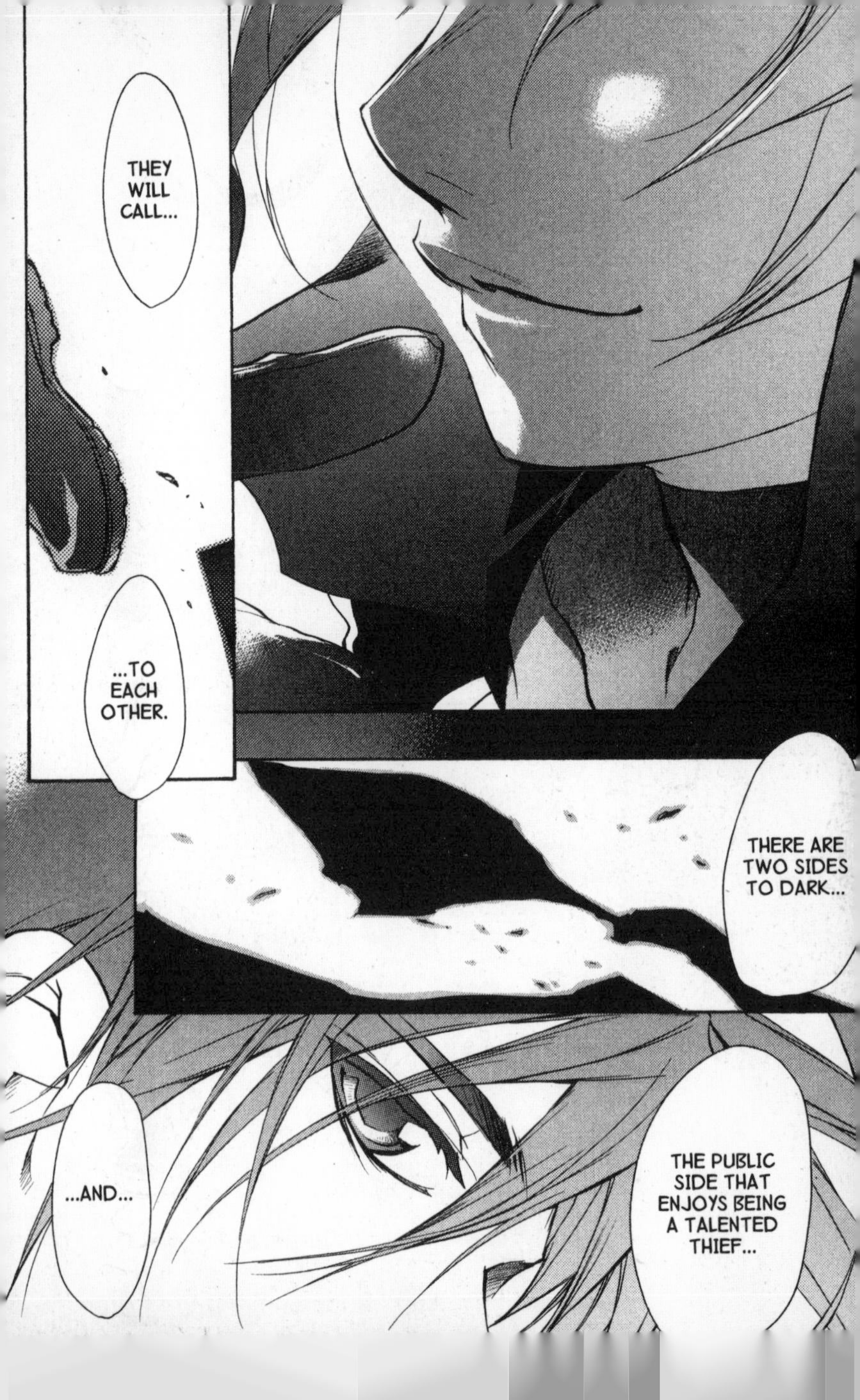
THEY WILL CALL...
...TO EACH OTHER.
THERE ARE TWO SIDES TO DARK...
THE PUBLIC SIDE THAT ENJOYS BEING A TALENTED THIEF...
...AND...

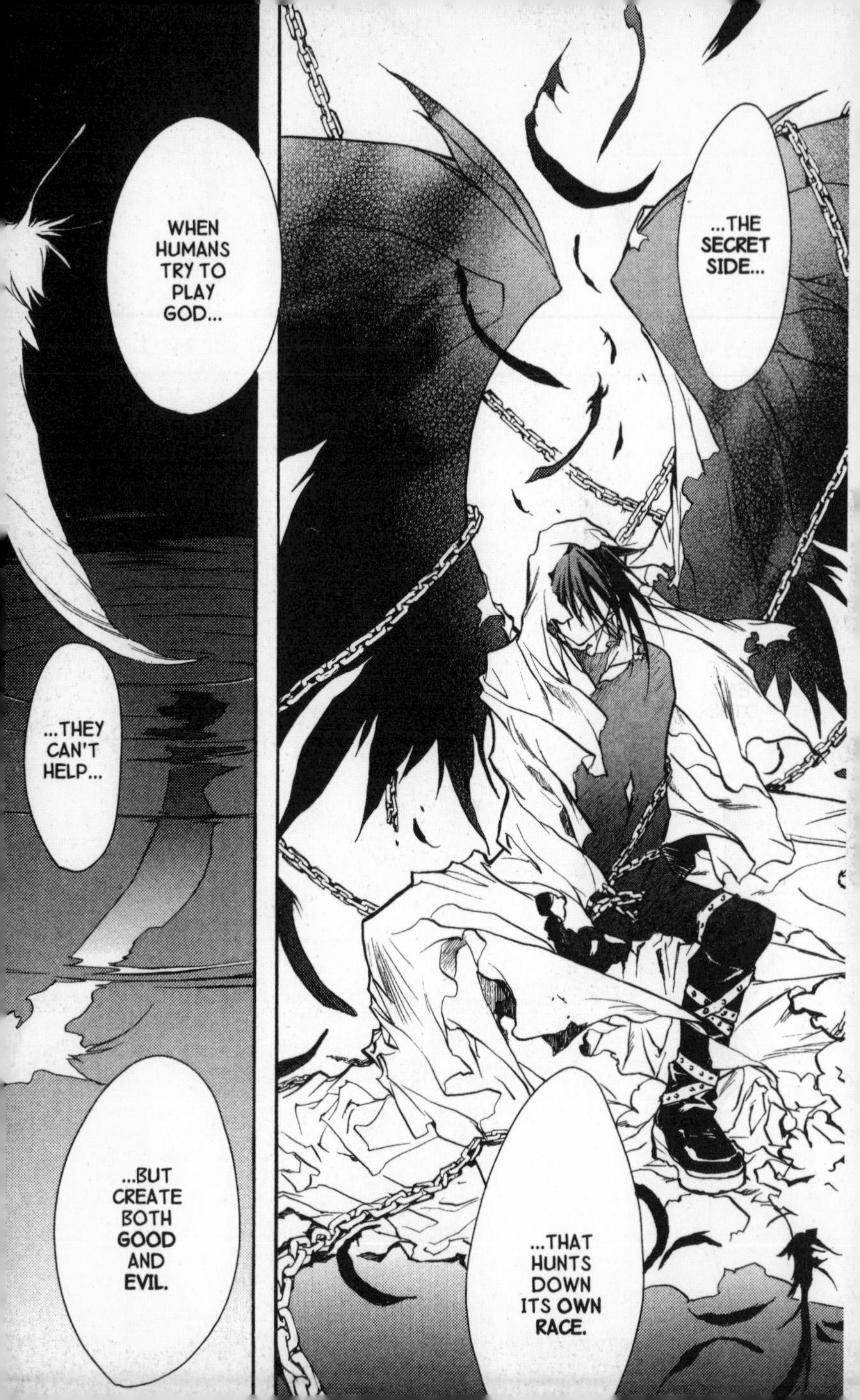
...THE SECRET SIDE...
...THAT HUNTS DOWN ITS OWN RACE.
WHEN HUMANS TRY TO PLAY GOD...
...THEY CAN'T HELP...
...BUT CREATE BOTH GOOD AND EVIL.

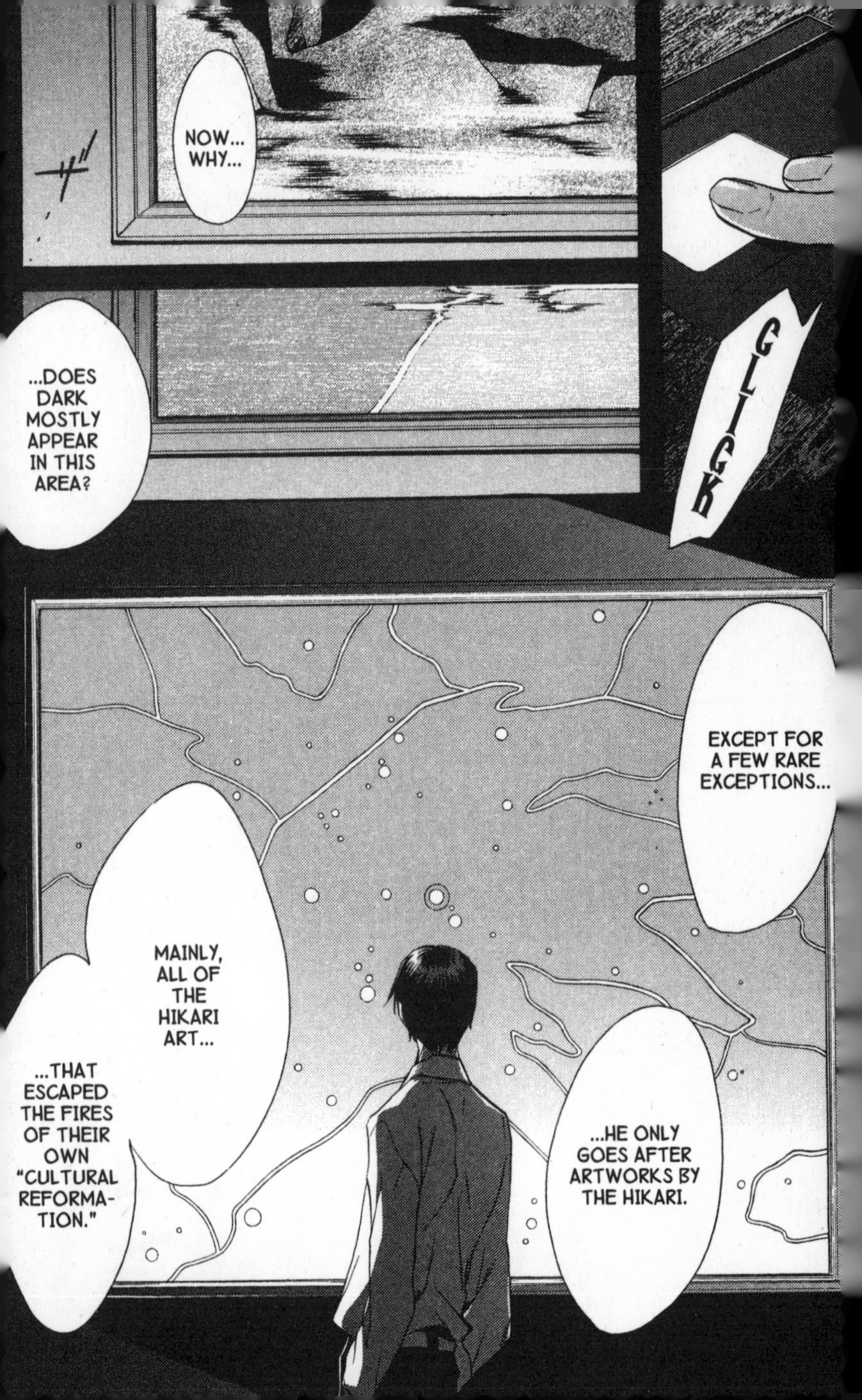
CLICK
NOW... WHY...
...DOES DARK MOSTLY APPEAR IN THIS AREA?
EXCEPT FOR A FEW RARE EXCEPTIONS...
...HE ONLY GOES AFTER ARTWORKS BY THE HIKARI.
MAINLY, ALL OF THE HIKARI ART...
...THAT ESCAPED THE FIRES OF THEIR OWN "CULTURAL REFORMATION."

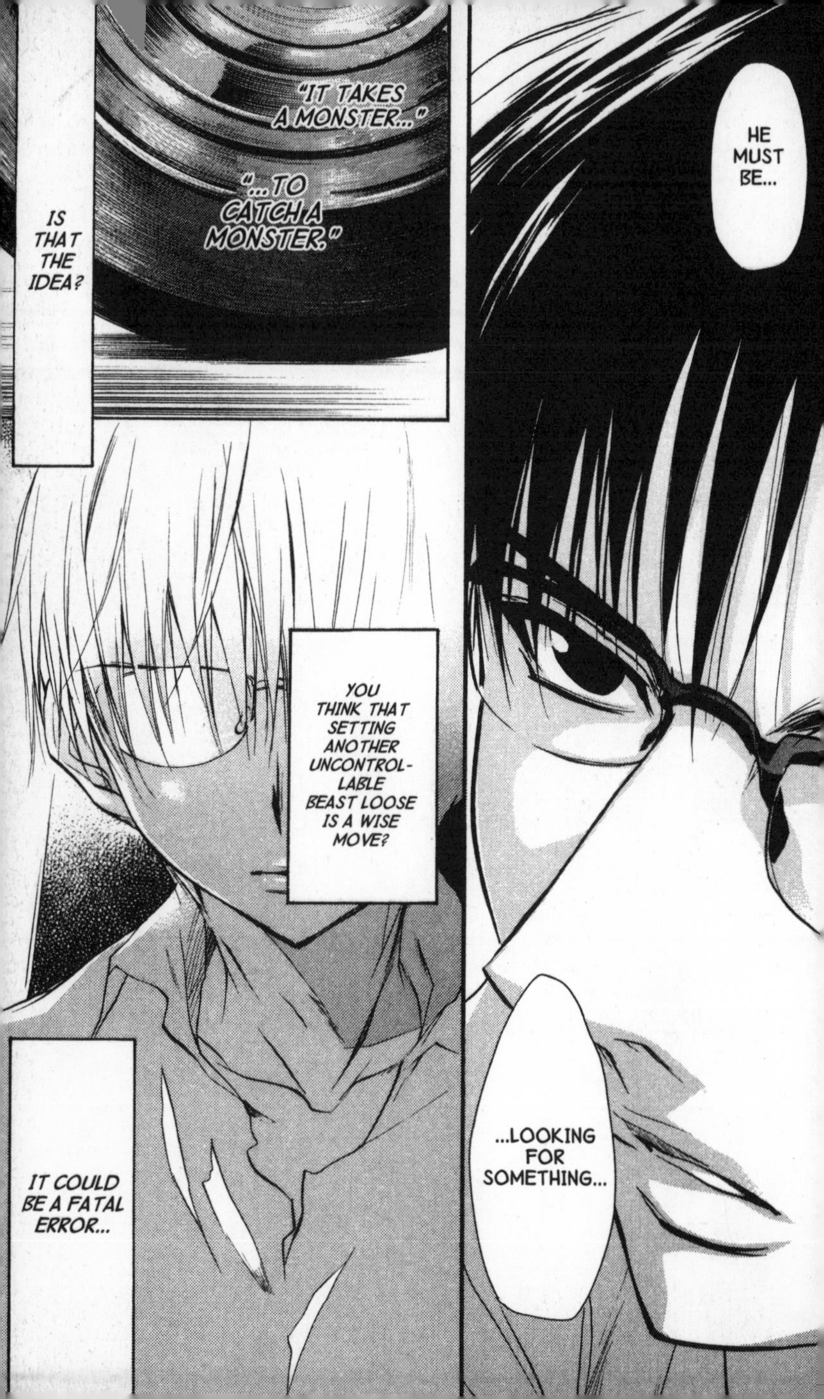
HE MUST BE...
...LOOKING FOR SOMETHING...
"IT TAKES A MONSTER..."
"...TO CATCH A MONSTER."
IS THAT THE IDEA?
YOU THINK THAT SETTING ANOTHER UNCONTROL-LABLE BEAST LOOSE IS A WISE MOVE?
IT COULD BE A FATAL ERROR...

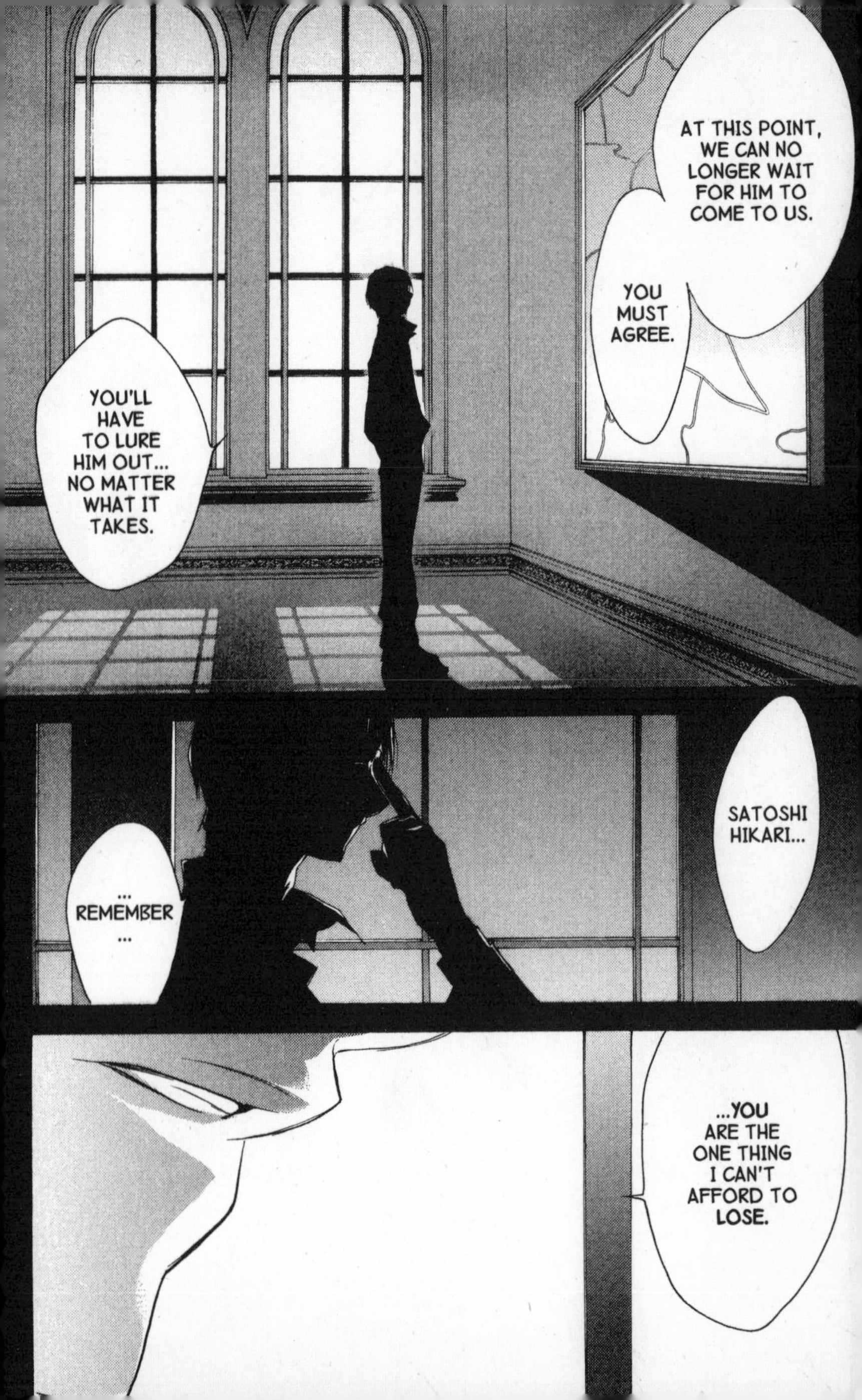
AT THIS POINT, WE CAN NO LONGER WAIT FOR HIM TO COME TO US.
YOU MUST AGREE.
YOU'LL HAVE TO LURE HIM OUT... NO MATTER WHAT IT TAKES.
SATOSHI HIKARI...
...REMEMBER...
...YOU ARE THE ONE THING I CAN'T AFFORD TO LOSE.

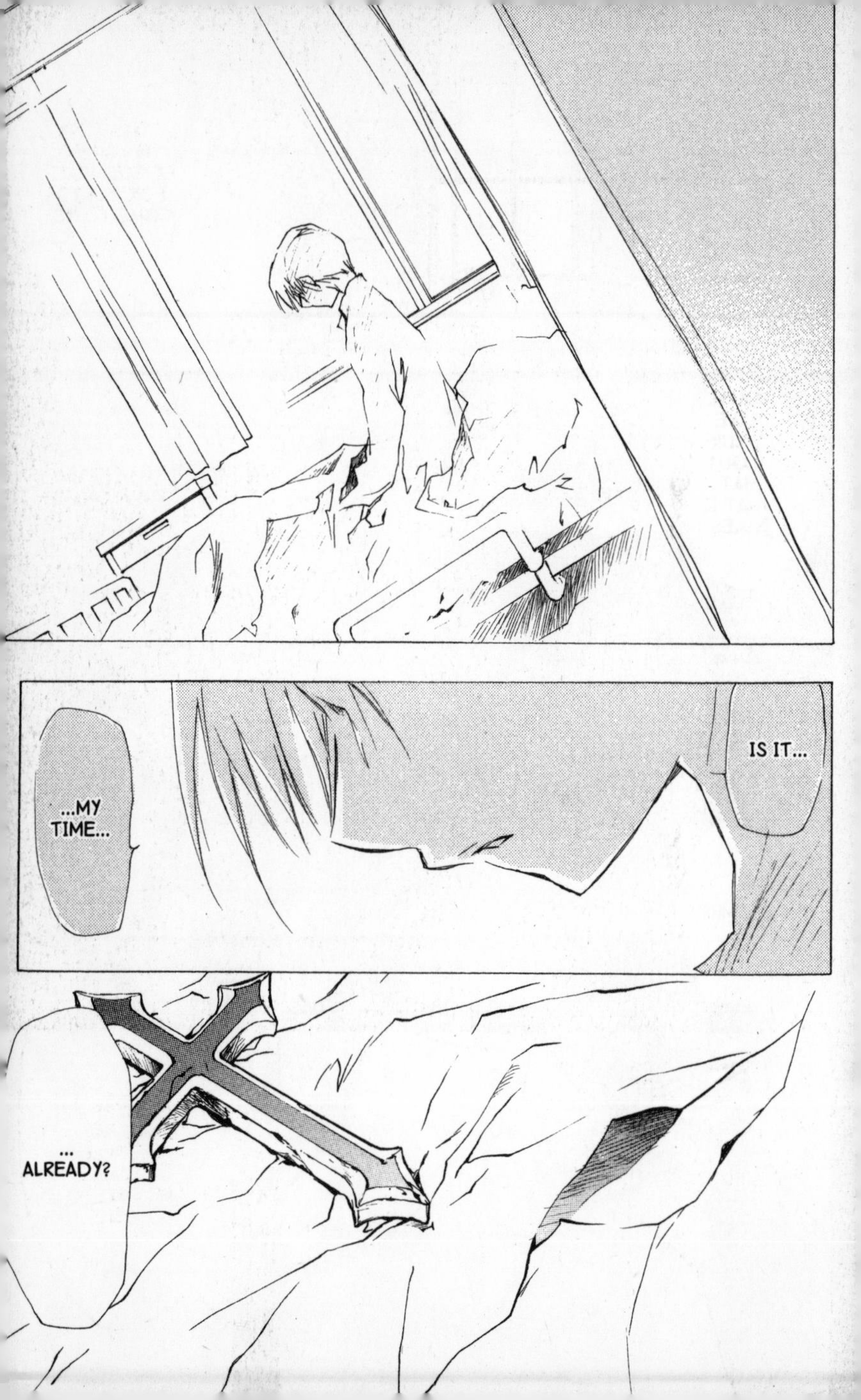

IS IT...
...MY TIME...
... ALREADY?

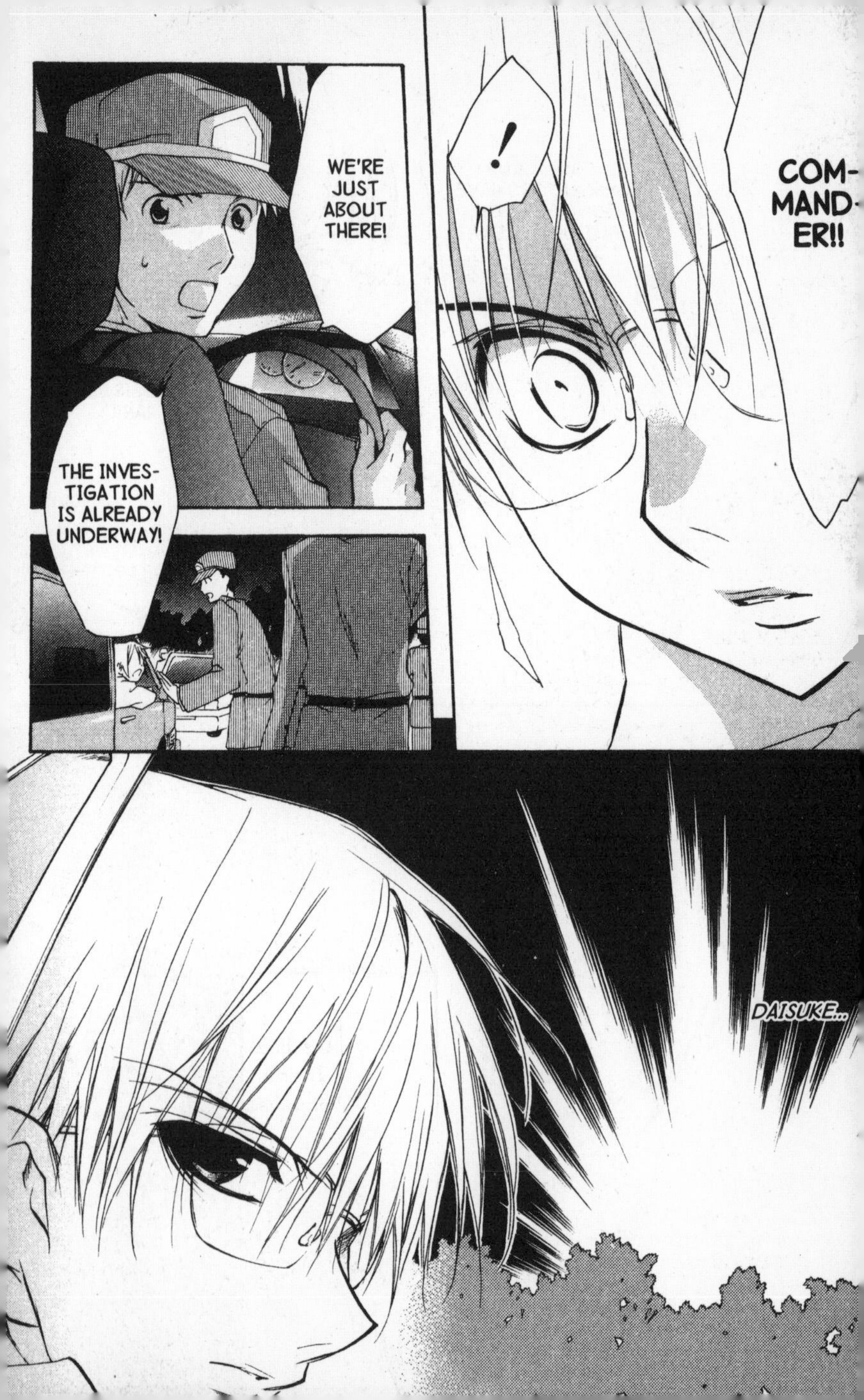
COM-MAND-ER!!
!
WE'RE JUST ABOUT THERE!
THE INVES-TIGATION IS ALREADY UNDERWAY!
DAISUKE...

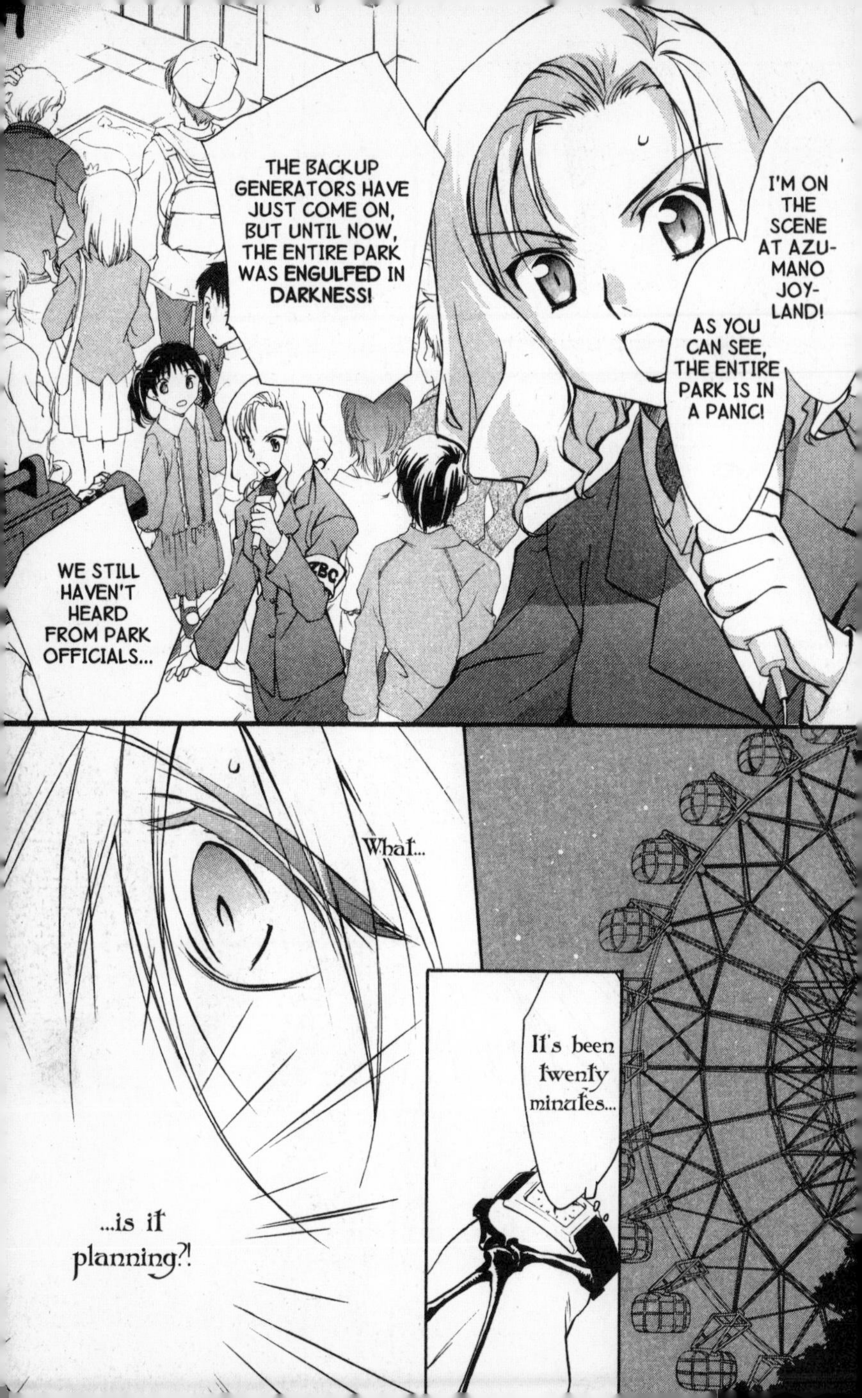
I'M ON THE SCENE AT AZUMANO JOYLAND!
AS YOU CAN SEE, THE ENTIRE PARK IS IN A PANIC!
THE BACKUP GENERATORS HAVE JUST COME ON, BUT UNTIL NOW, THE ENTIRE PARK WAS ENGULFED IN DARKNESS!
WE STILL HAVEN'T HEARD FROM PARK OFFICIALS...
It's been twenty minutes...
What...
...is it planning?!

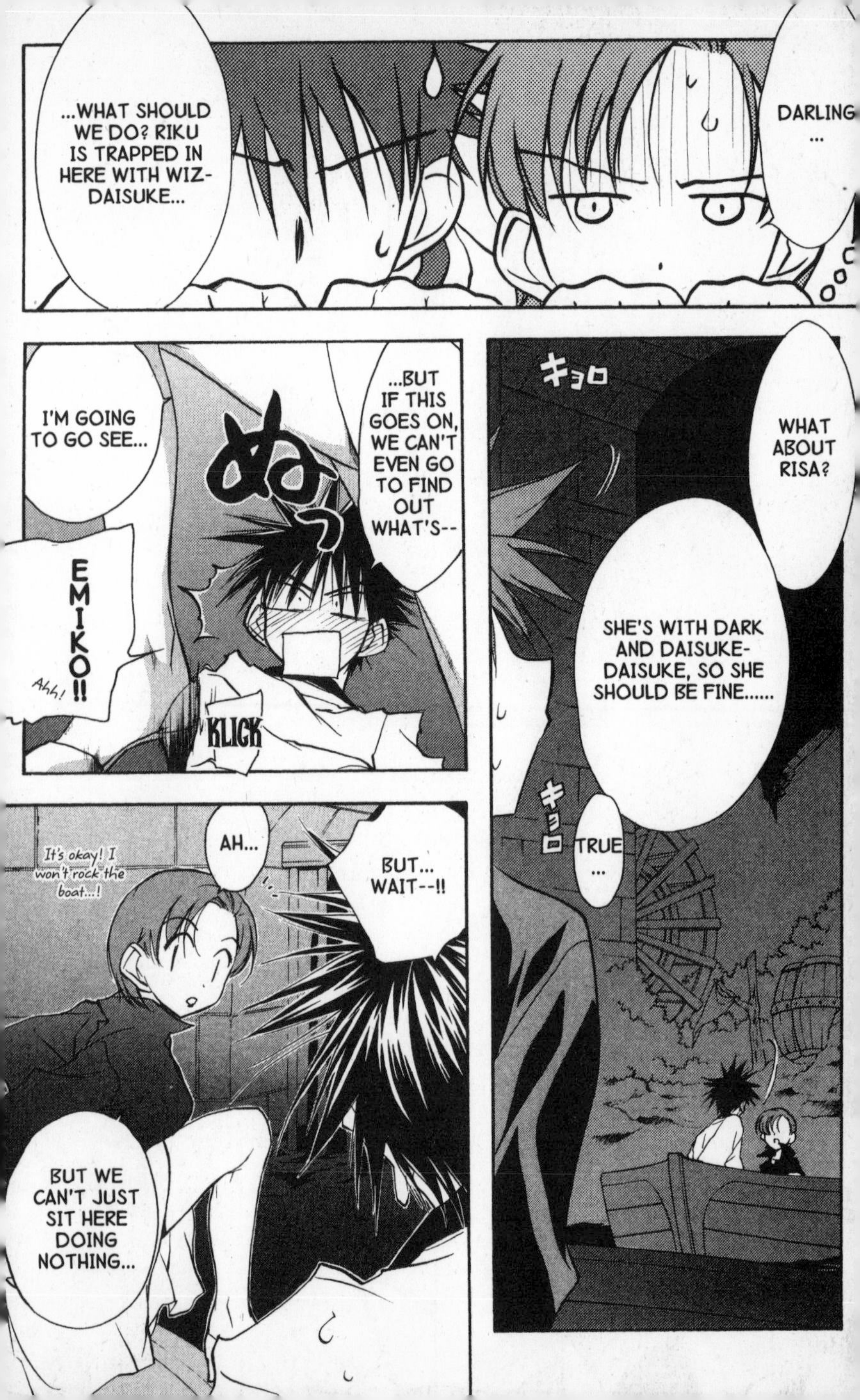
DARLING ...
...WHAT SHOULD WE DO? RIKU IS TRAPPED IN HERE WITH WIZ-DAISUKE...
キョロ
WHAT ABOUT RISA?
SHE'S WITH DARK AND DAISUKE-DAISUKE, SO SHE SHOULD BE FINE......
キョロ
TRUE ...
...BUT IF THIS GOES ON, WE CAN'T EVEN GO TO FIND OUT WHAT'S--
ぬっ
I'M GOING TO GO SEE...
EMIKO!!
Ahh!
KLICK
AH...
BUT... WAIT--!!
It's okay! I won't rock the boat...!
BUT WE CAN'T JUST SIT HERE DOING NOTHING...

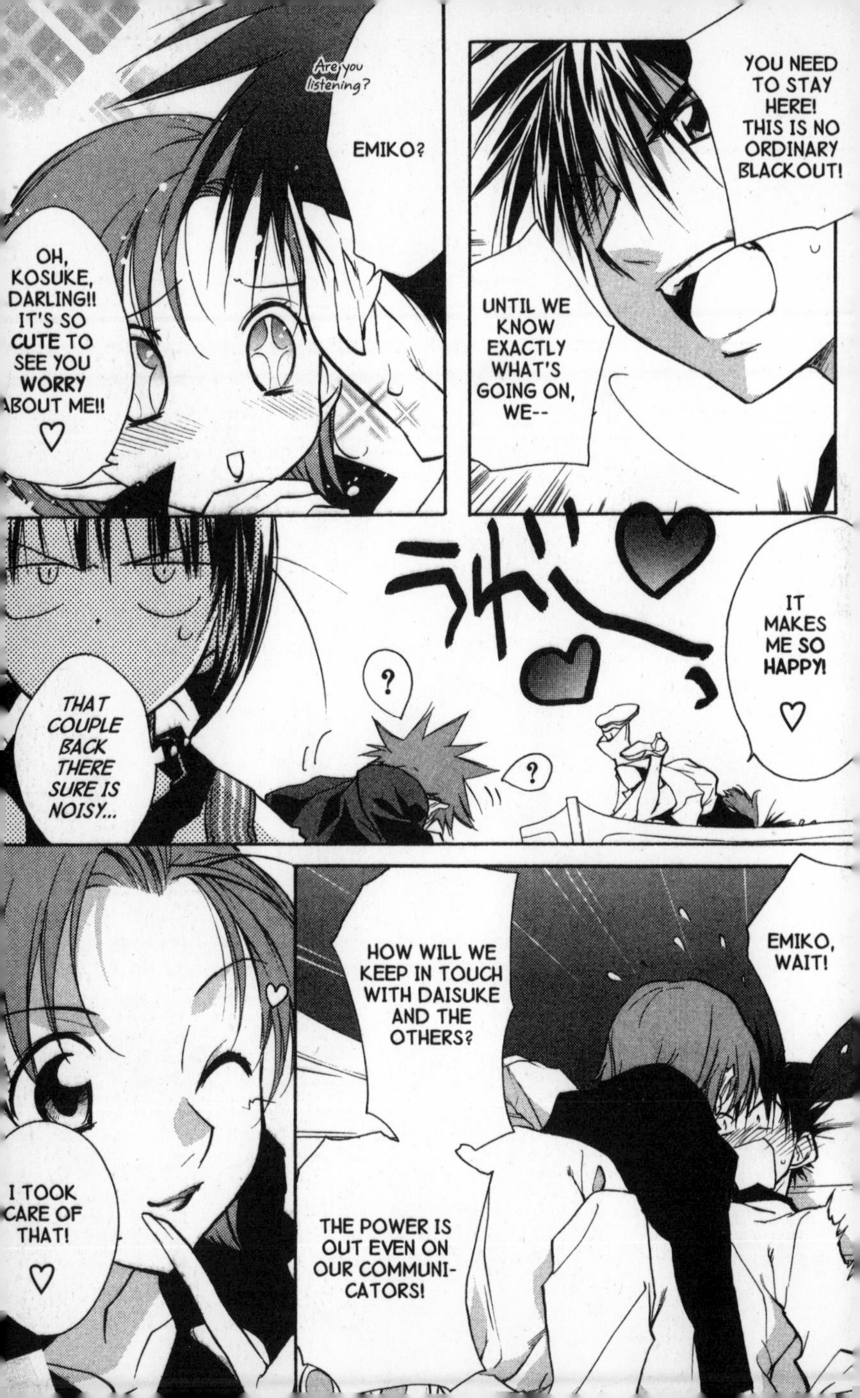
YOU NEED TO STAY HERE! THIS IS NO ORDINARY BLACKOUT!
UNTIL WE KNOW EXACTLY WHAT'S GOING ON, WE--
Are you listening?
EMIKO?
OH, KOSUKE, DARLING!! IT'S SO CUTE TO SEE YOU WORRY ABOUT ME!! ♡
IT MAKES ME SO HAPPY! ♡
?
?
THAT COUPLE BACK THERE SURE IS NOISY...
EMIKO, WAIT!
HOW WILL WE KEEP IN TOUCH WITH DAISUKE AND THE OTHERS?
THE POWER IS OUT EVEN ON OUR COMMUNICATORS!
I TOOK CARE OF THAT! ♡

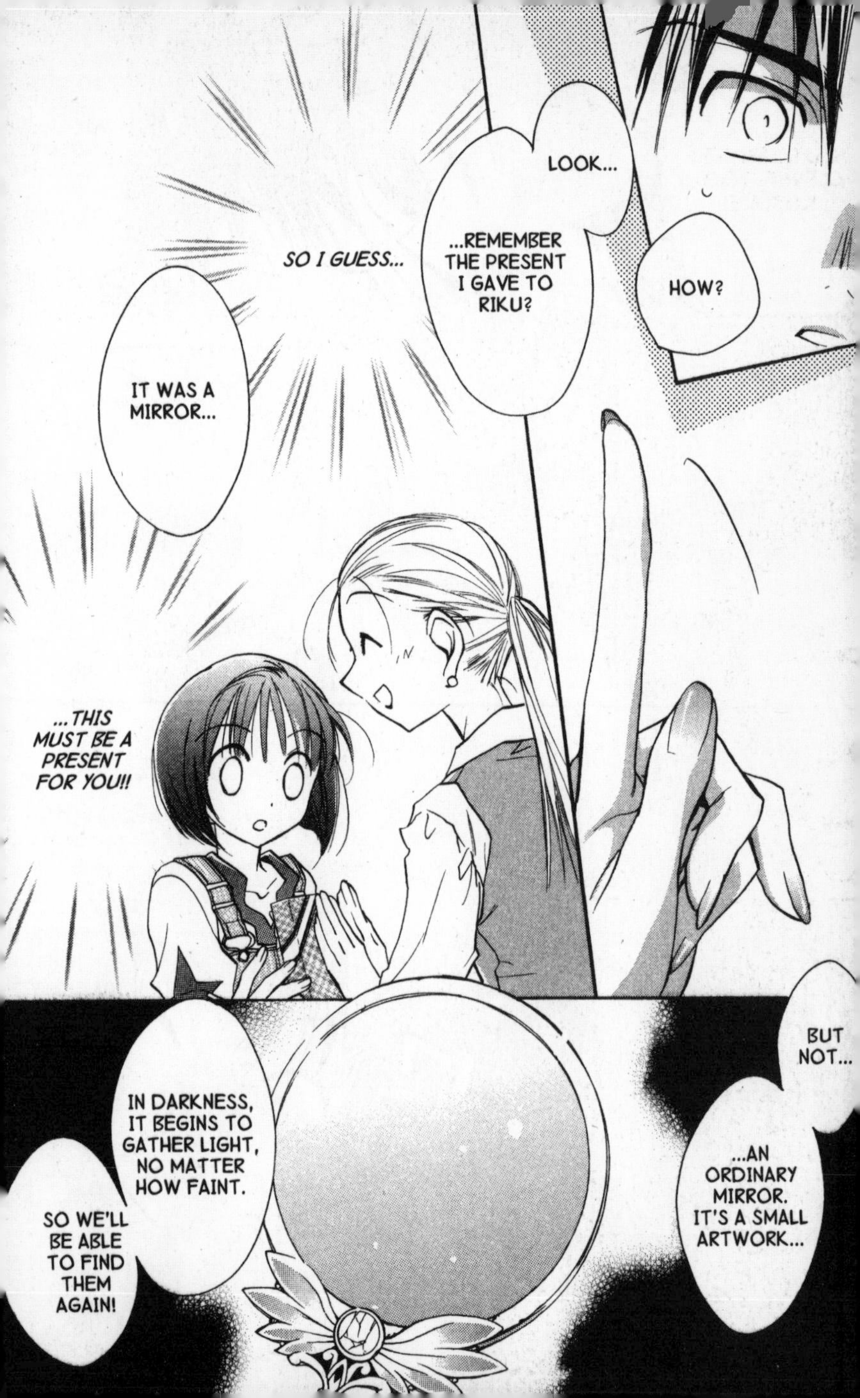
LOOK...
...REMEMBER THE PRESENT I GAVE TO RIKU?
HOW?
SO I GUESS...
IT WAS A MIRROR...
...THIS MUST BE A PRESENT FOR YOU!!
BUT NOT...
...AN ORDINARY MIRROR. IT'S A SMALL ARTWORK...
IN DARKNESS, IT BEGINS TO GATHER LIGHT, NO MATTER HOW FAINT.
SO WE'LL BE ABLE TO FIND THEM AGAIN!

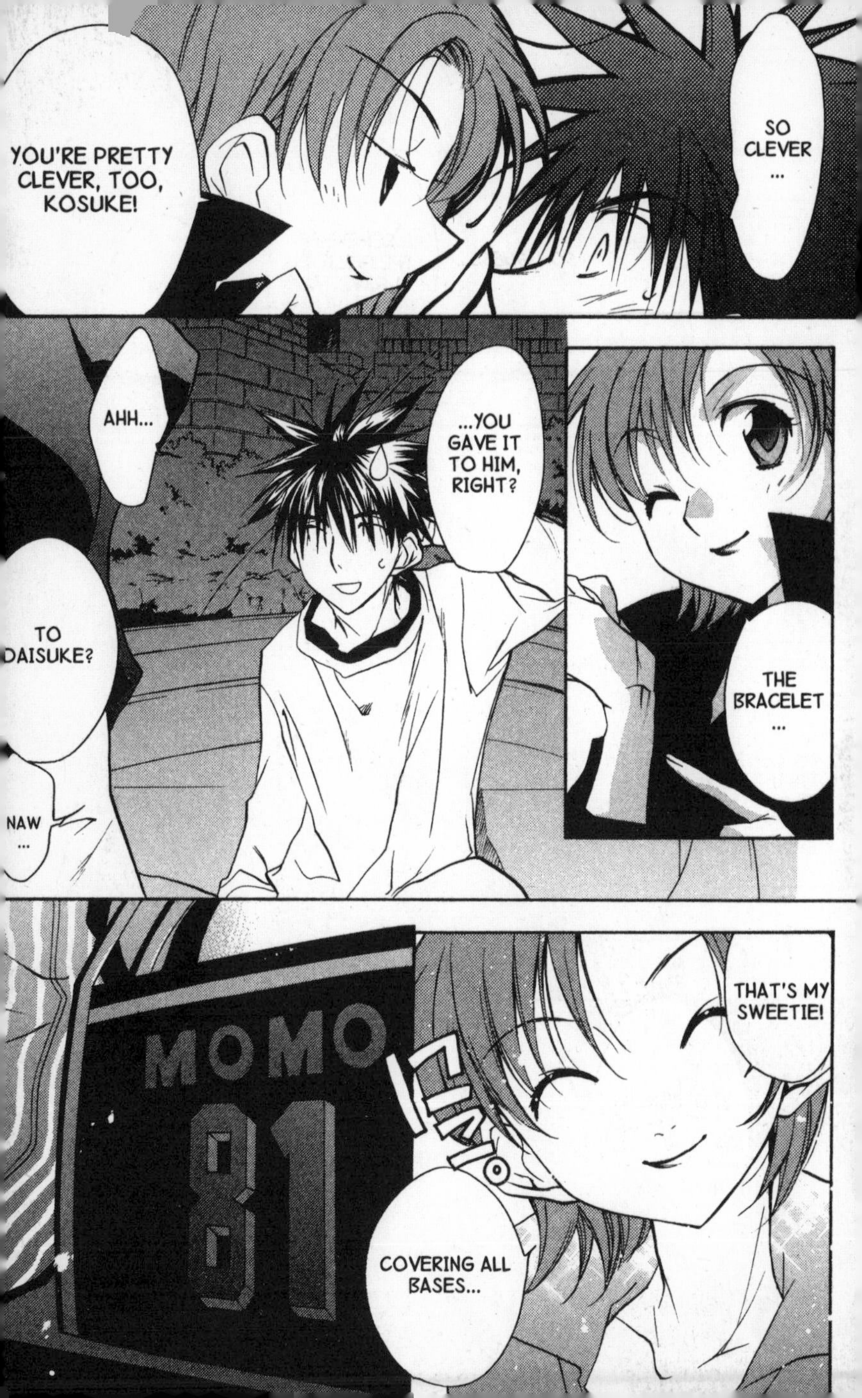
SO CLEVER ...
YOU'RE PRETTY CLEVER, TOO, KOSUKE!
THE BRACELET ...
...YOU GAVE IT TO HIM, RIGHT?
AHH...
TO DAISUKE?
NAW ...
THAT'S MY SWEETIE!
COVERING ALL BASES...
MOMO
81

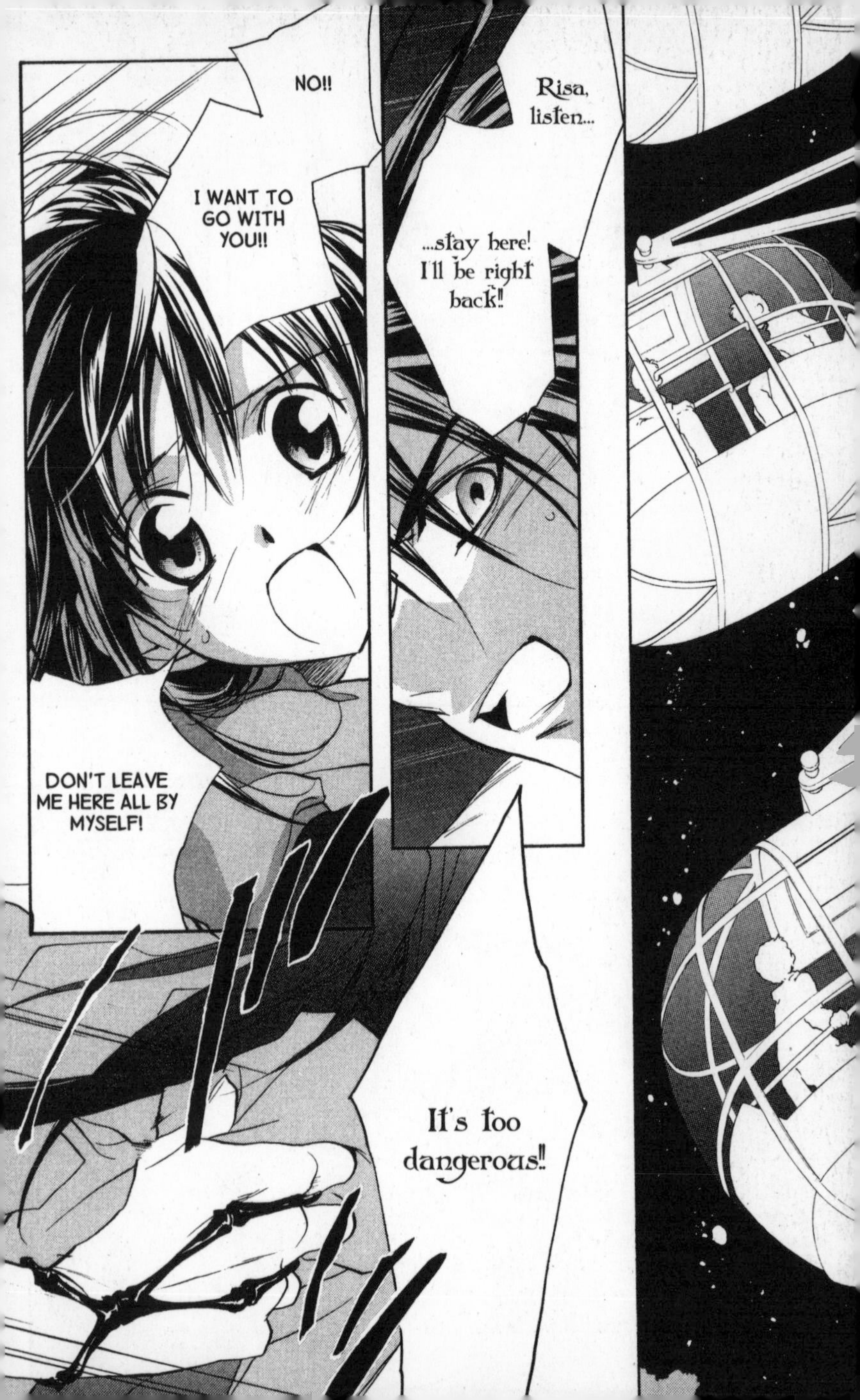
Risa, listen...
...stay here! I'll be right back!!
It's too dangerous!!
NO!!
I WANT TO GO WITH YOU!!
DON'T LEAVE ME HERE ALL BY MYSELF!

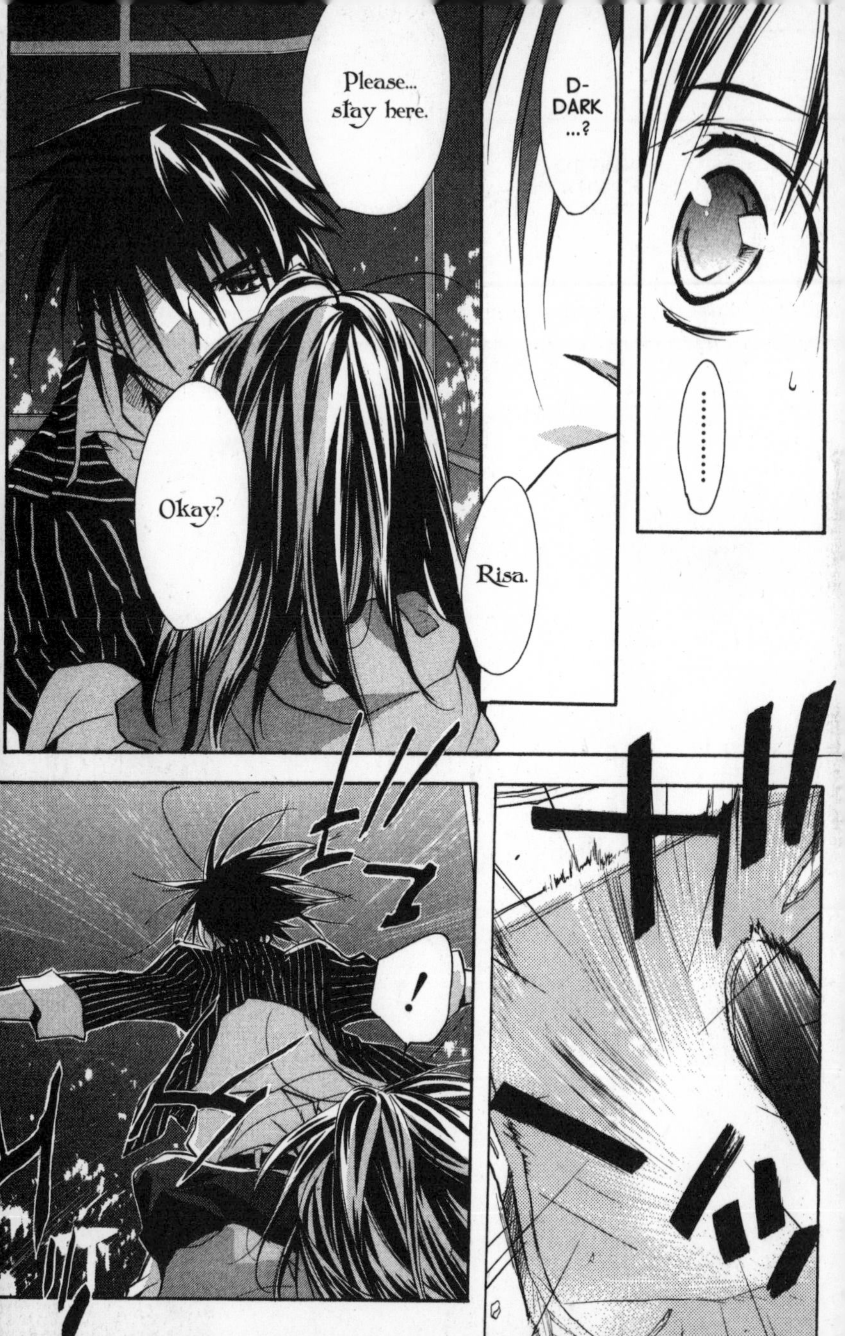
......
D-DARK ...?
Risa.
Please... stay here.
Okay?
!

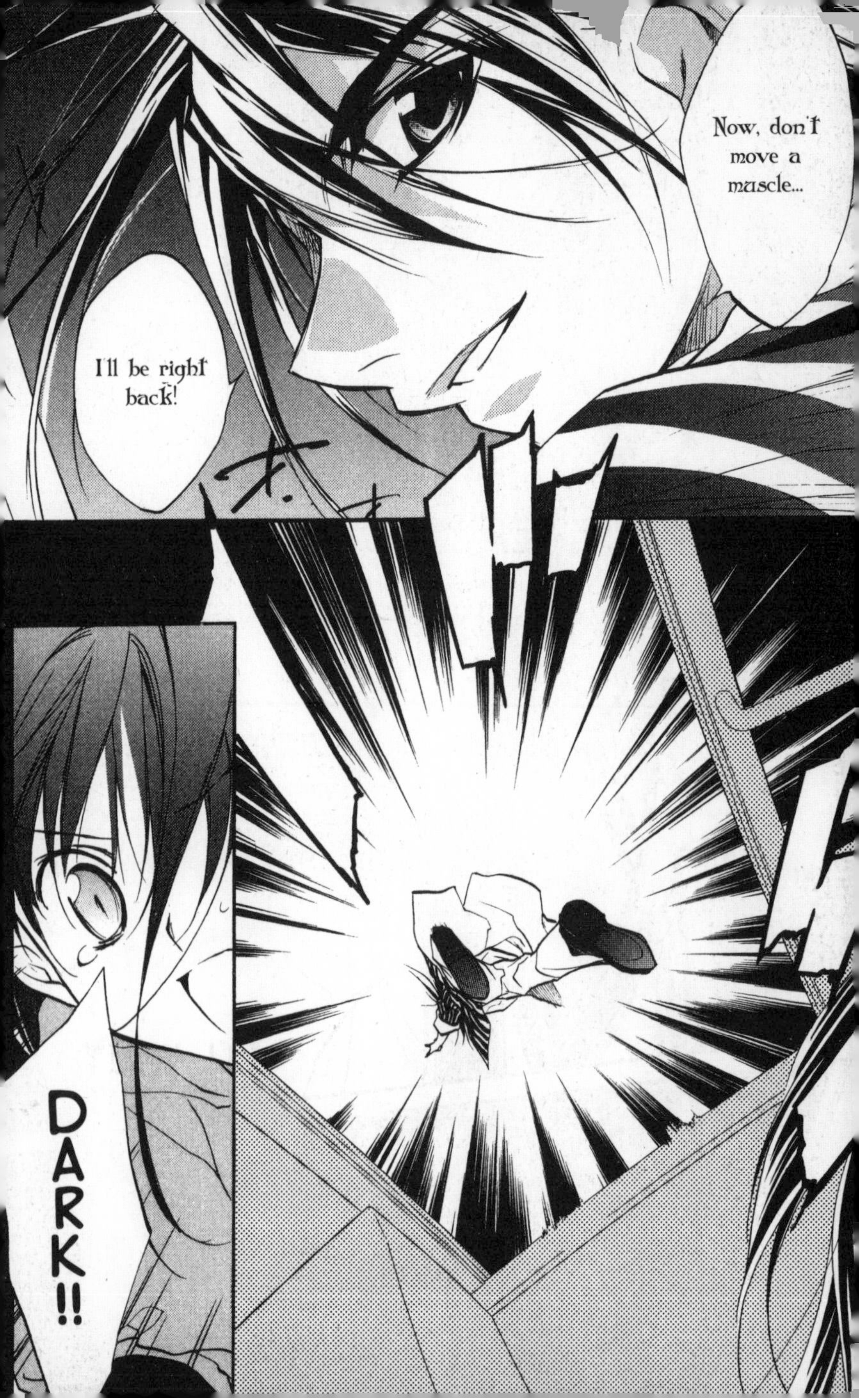
Now, don't move a muscle...
I'll be right back!
DARK!!

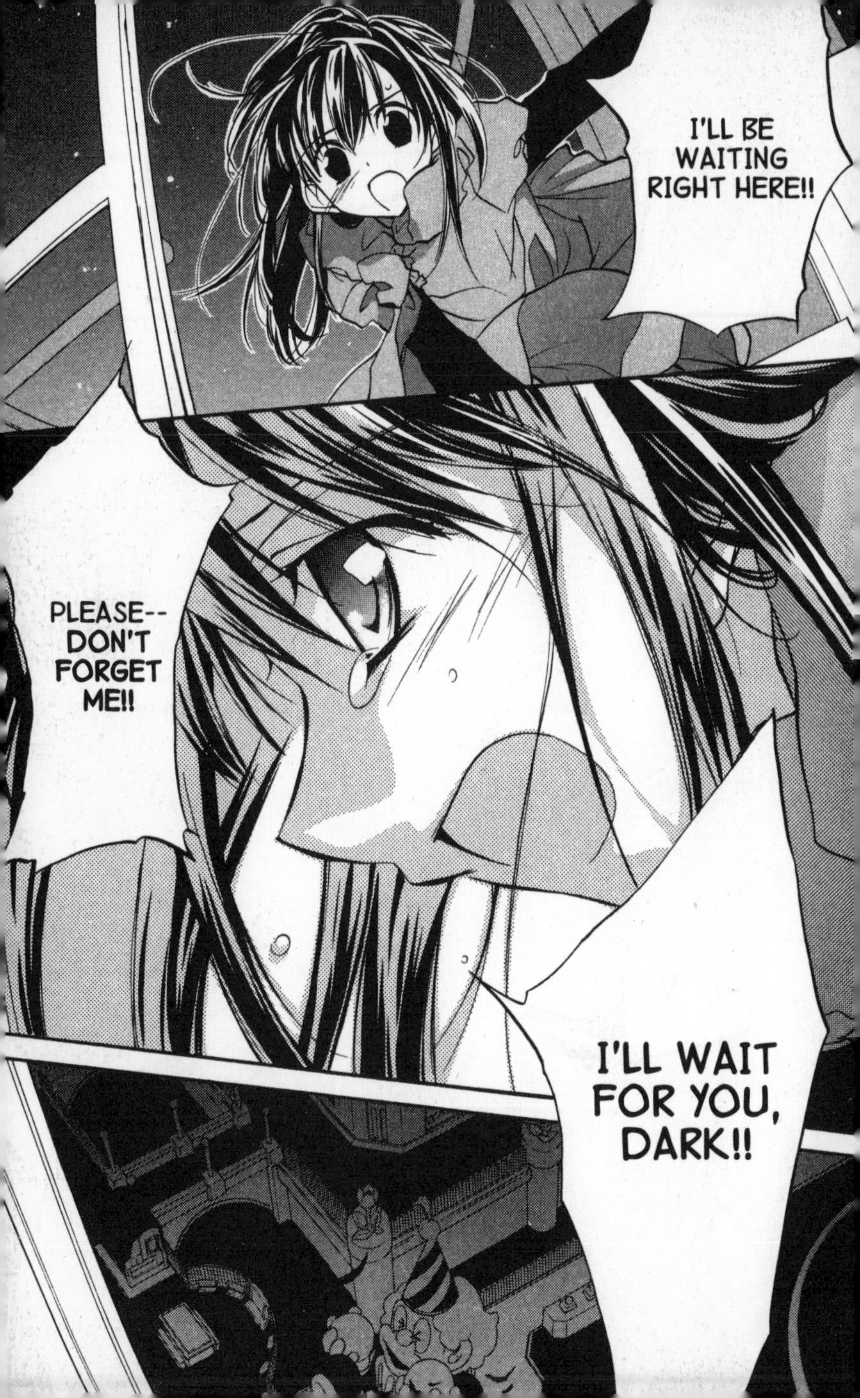
I'LL BE WAITING RIGHT HERE!!
PLEASE-- DON'T FORGET ME!!
I'LL WAIT FOR YOU, DARK!!

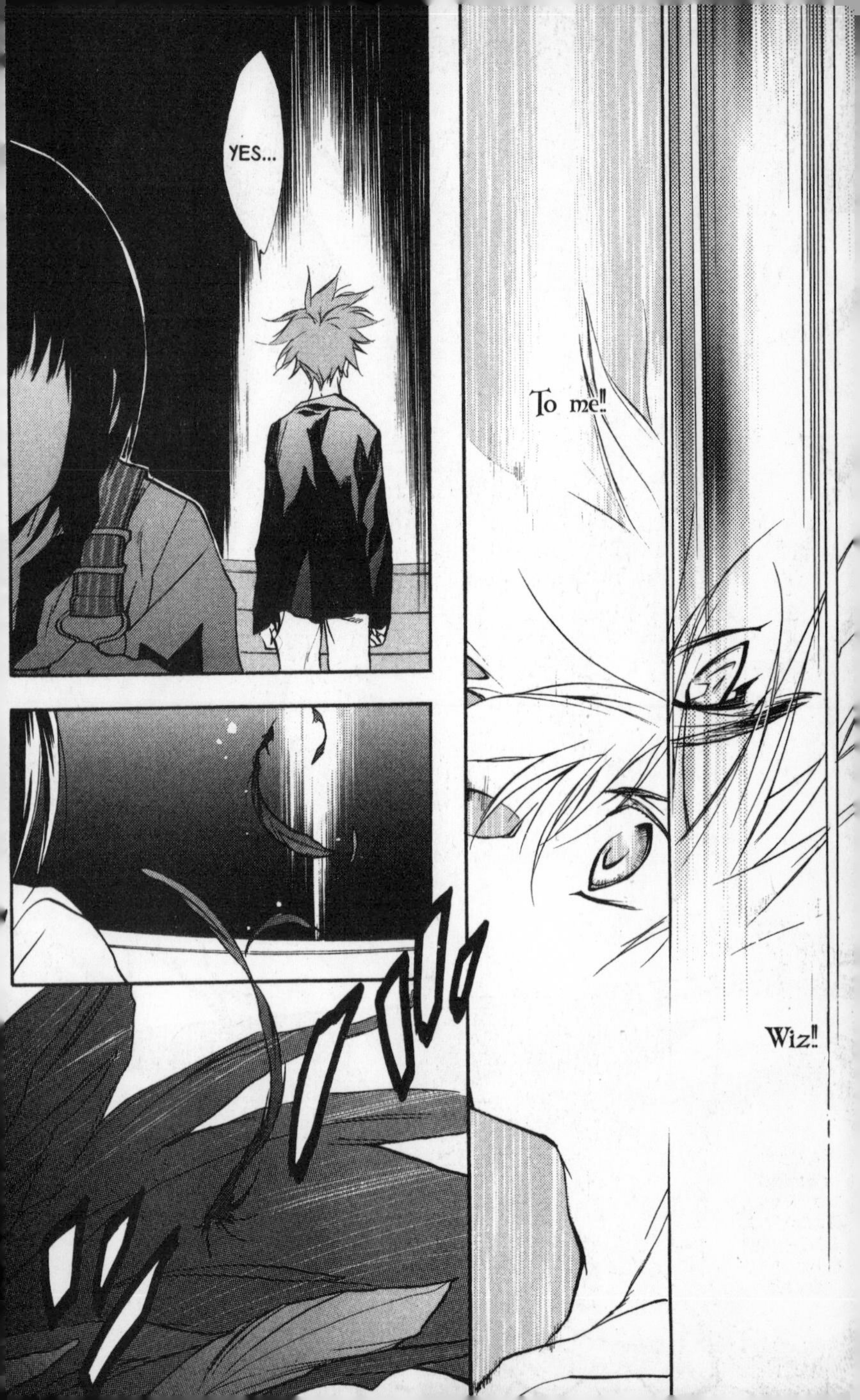
To me!!
Wiz!!
YES...

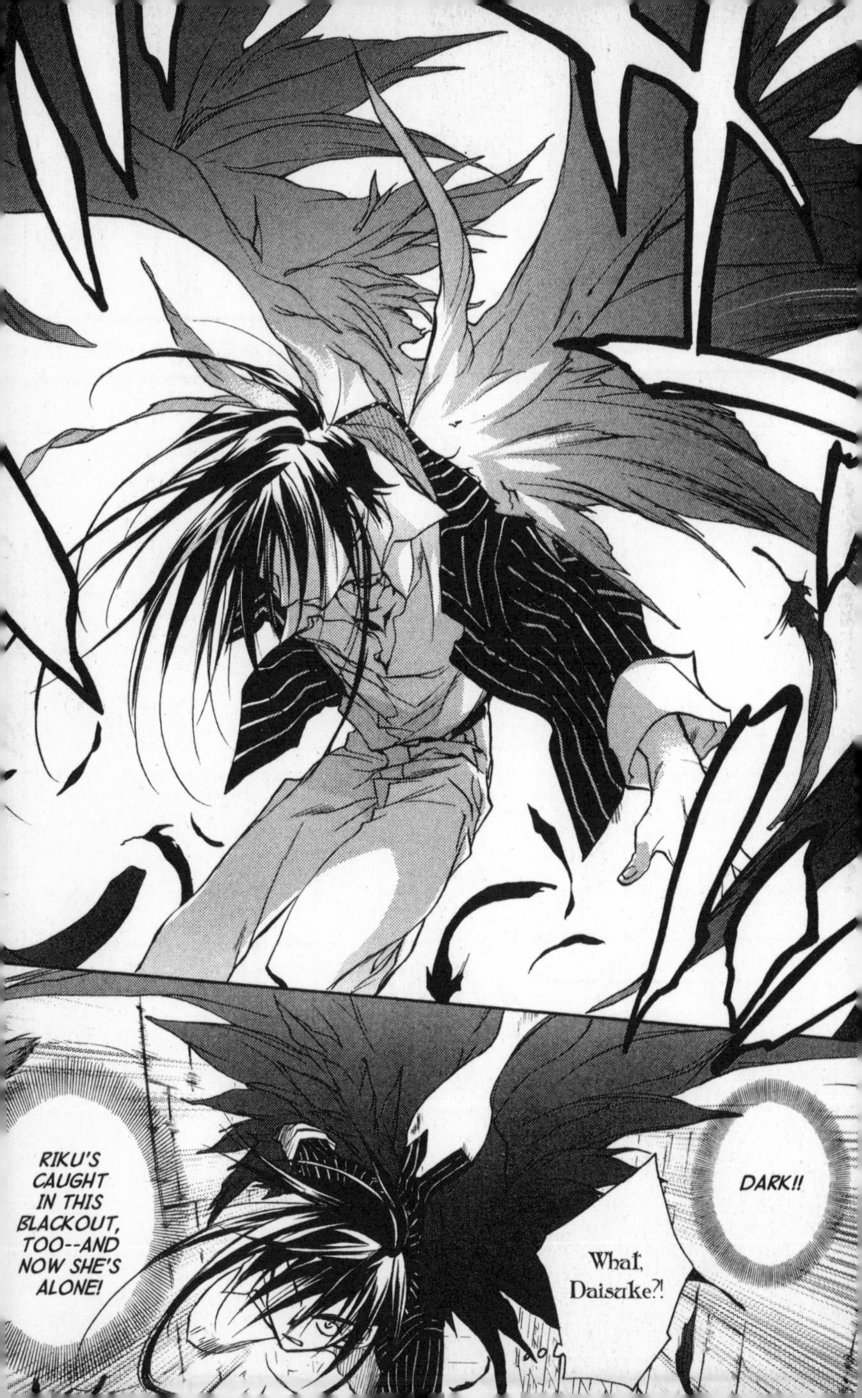
DARK!!
What, Daisuke?!
RIKU'S CAUGHT IN THIS BLACKOUT, TOO--AND NOW SHE'S ALONE!

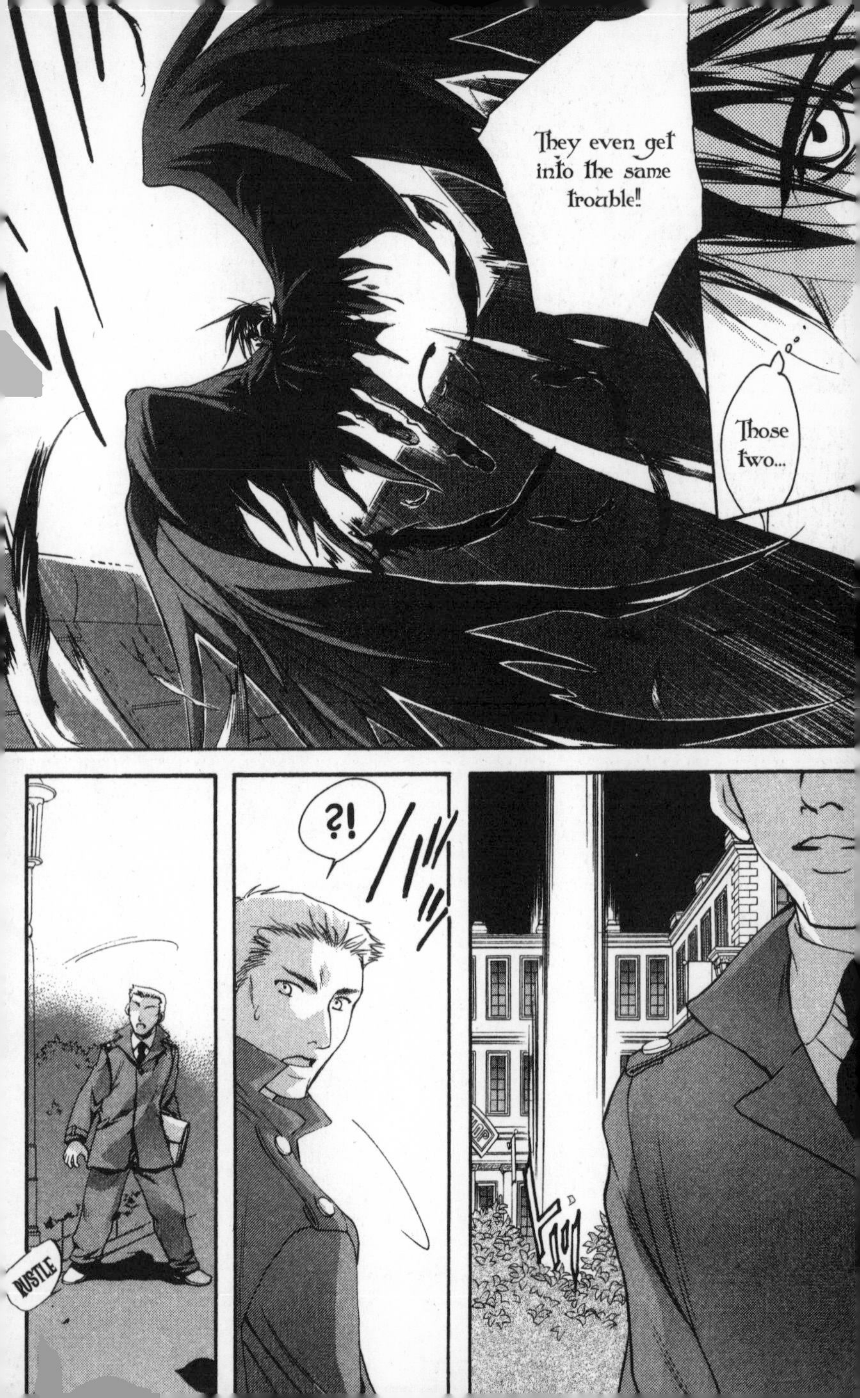
Those two...
They even get into the same trouble!!
?!
RUSTLE

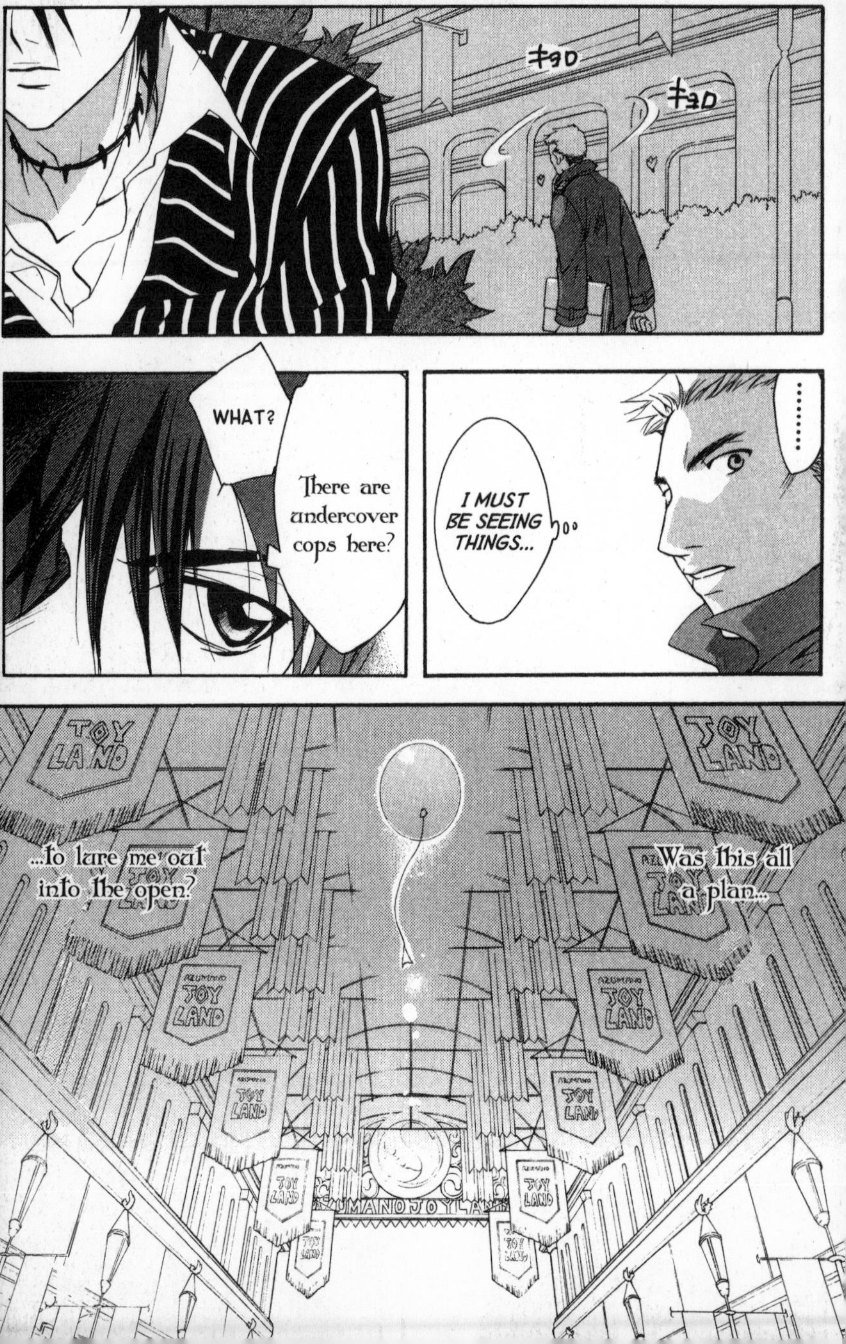

キョロ
キョロ
......
I MUST BE SEEING THINGS...
WHAT?
There are undercover cops here?
Was this all a plan...
...To lure me out into the open?
TOY LAND

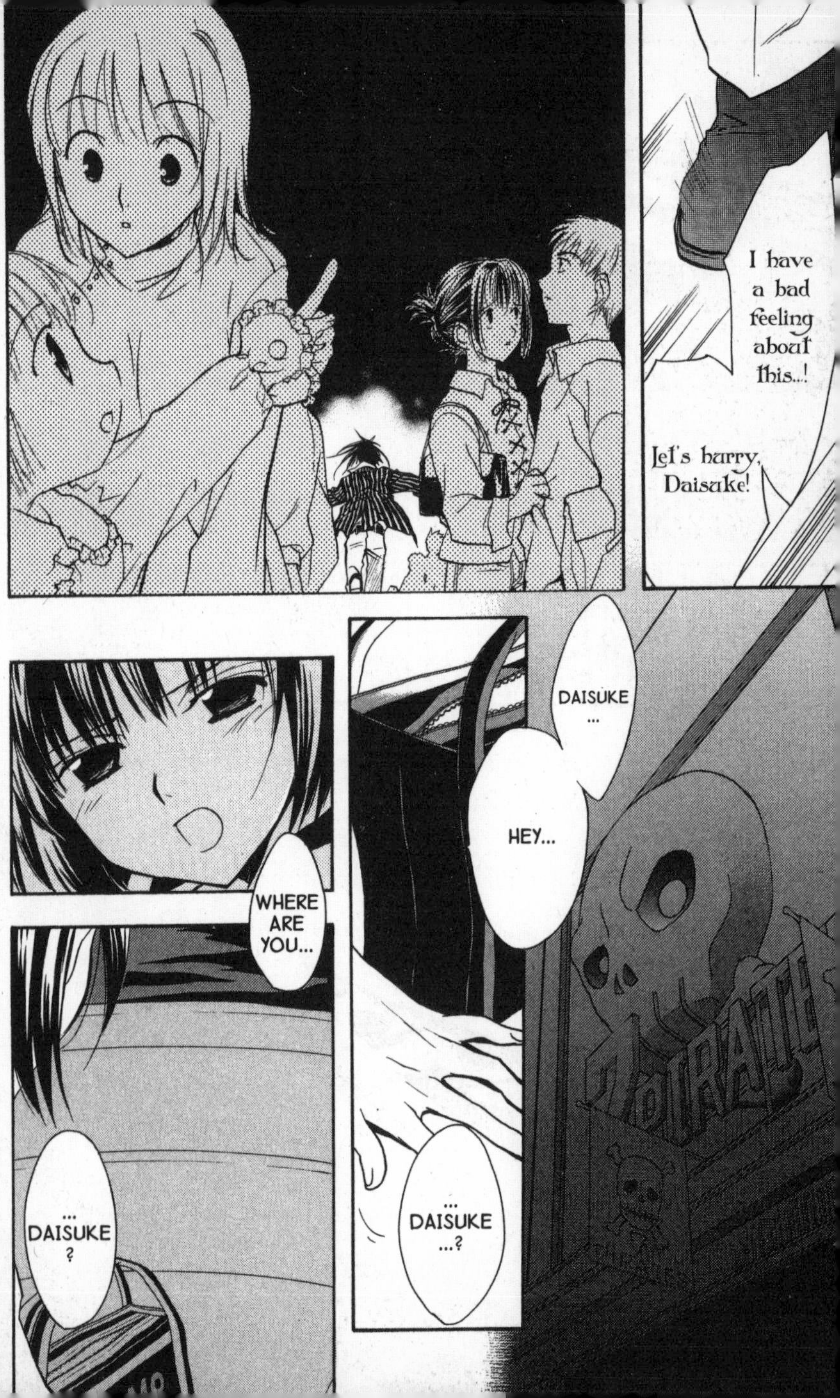
I have a bad feeling about this...!
Let's hurry, Daisuke!
DAISUKE ...
HEY...
... DAISUKE ...?
WHERE ARE YOU...
... DAISUKE ?

OH, NO...! PLEASE ANSWER ME, DAISUKE!

DAISUKE!!

AGH!!

I KNOCKED MY BAG OVER...

!!

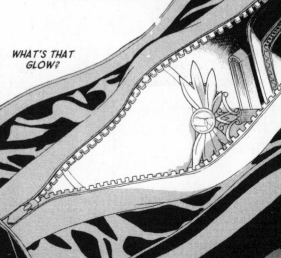

WHAT'S THAT GLOW?

IT'S...THE MIRROR...

...DAISUKE GAVE ME...

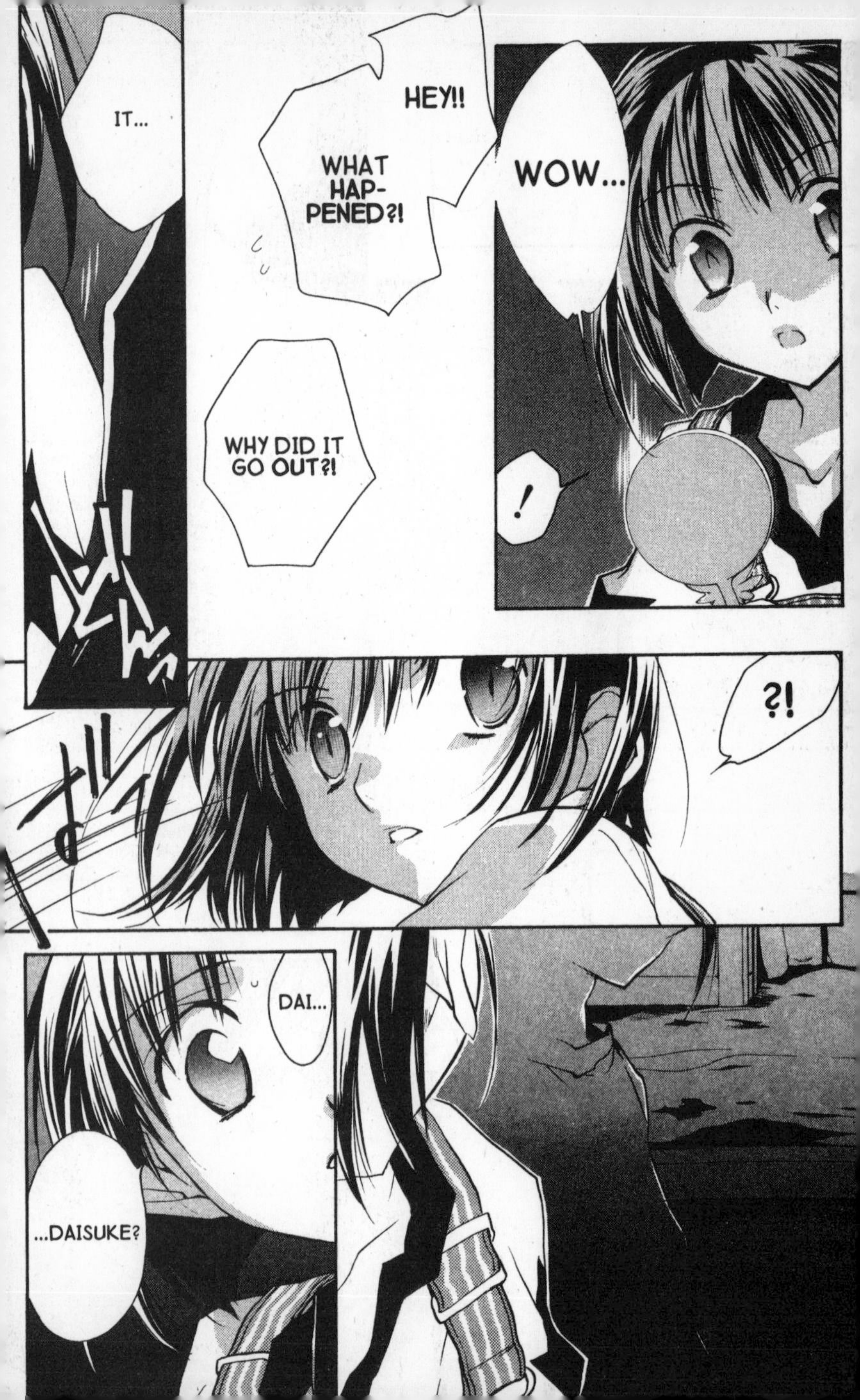
WOW...
!
HEY!!
WHAT HAP-PENED?!
WHY DID IT GO OUT?!
IT...
?!
DAI...
...DAISUKE?

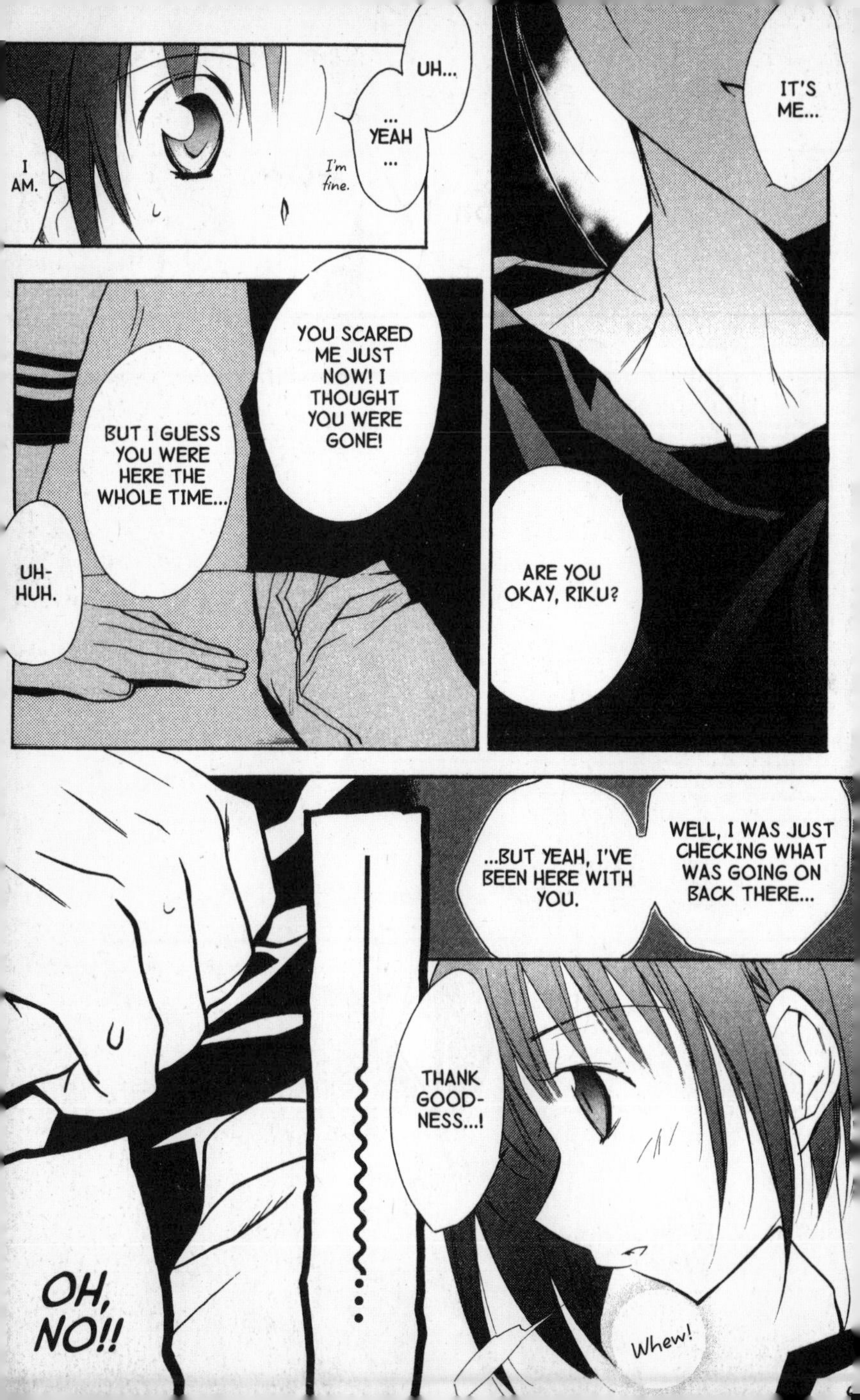
IT'S ME...
ARE YOU OKAY, RIKU?
UH...
...YEAH...
I'm fine.
I AM.
YOU SCARED ME JUST NOW! I THOUGHT YOU WERE GONE!
BUT I GUESS YOU WERE HERE THE WHOLE TIME...
UH-HUH.
WELL, I WAS JUST CHECKING WHAT WAS GOING ON BACK THERE...
...BUT YEAH, I'VE BEEN HERE WITH YOU.
THANK GOODNESS...!
Whew!
OH, NO!!

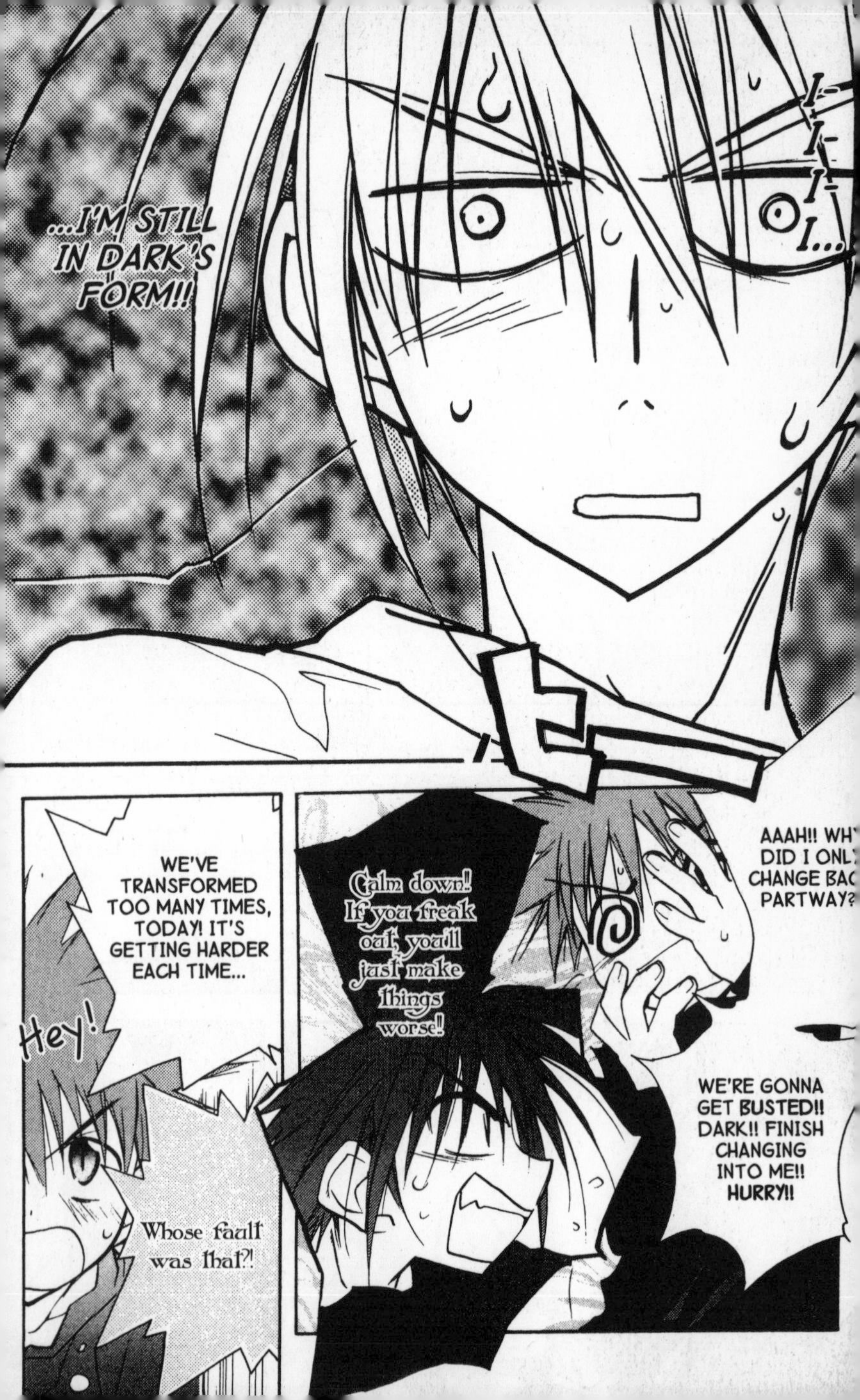
I-I-I-I...
...I'M STILL IN DARK'S FORM!!
AAAH!! WH DID I ONL CHANGE BAC PARTWAY?
Calm down!! If you freak out, you'll just make things worse!!
WE'RE GONNA GET BUSTED!! DARK!! FINISH CHANGING INTO ME!! HURRY!!
WE'VE TRANSFORMED TOO MANY TIMES, TODAY! IT'S GETTING HARDER EACH TIME...
Hey!
Whose fault was that?!

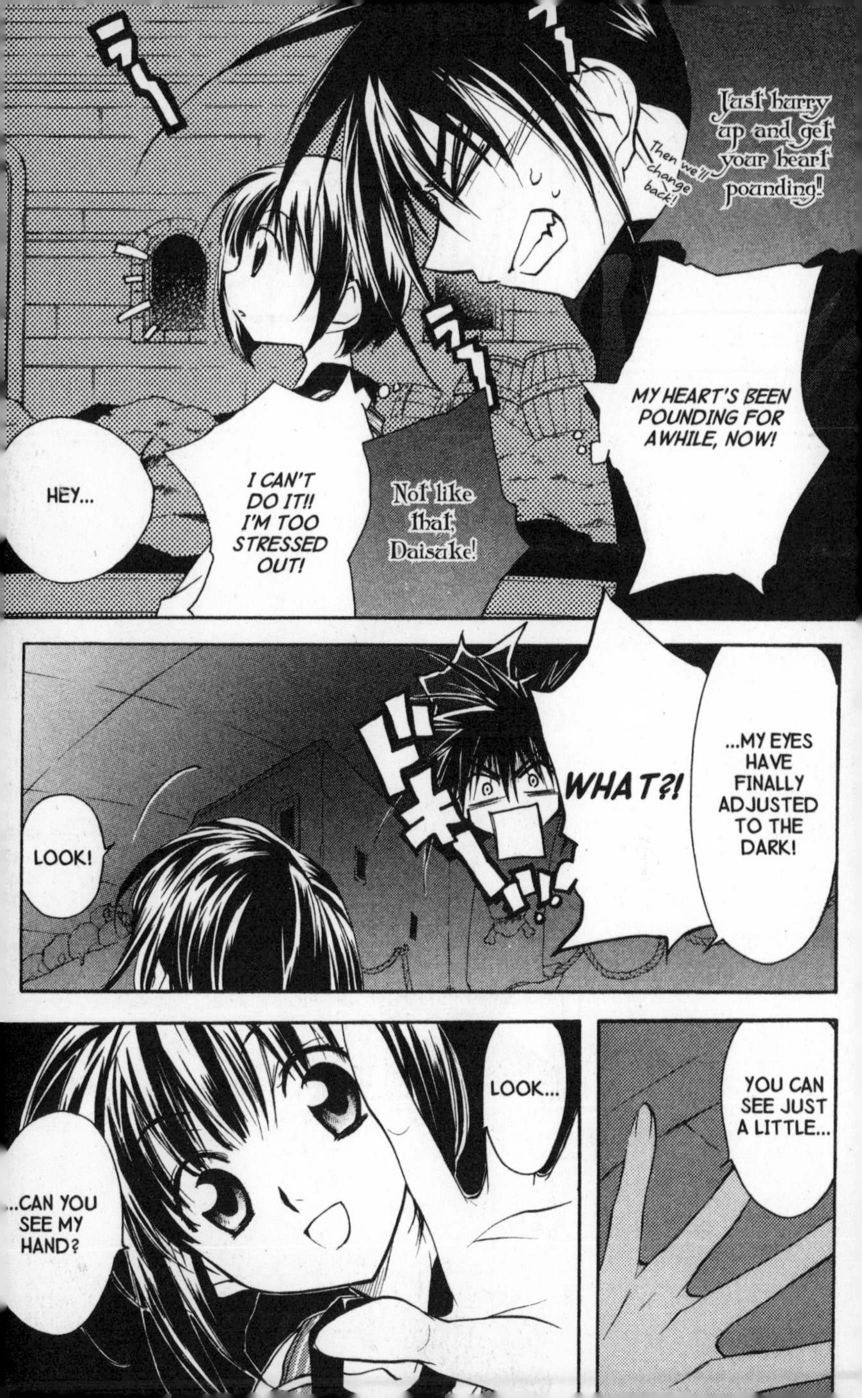
Just hurry up and get your heart pounding!!
Then we'll change back!
MY HEART'S BEEN POUNDING FOR AWHILE, NOW!
Not like that, Daisuke!
I CAN'T DO IT!! I'M TOO STRESSED OUT!
HEY...
...MY EYES HAVE FINALLY ADJUSTED TO THE DARK!
WHAT?!
LOOK!
YOU CAN SEE JUST A LITTLE...
LOOK...
...CAN YOU SEE MY HAND?

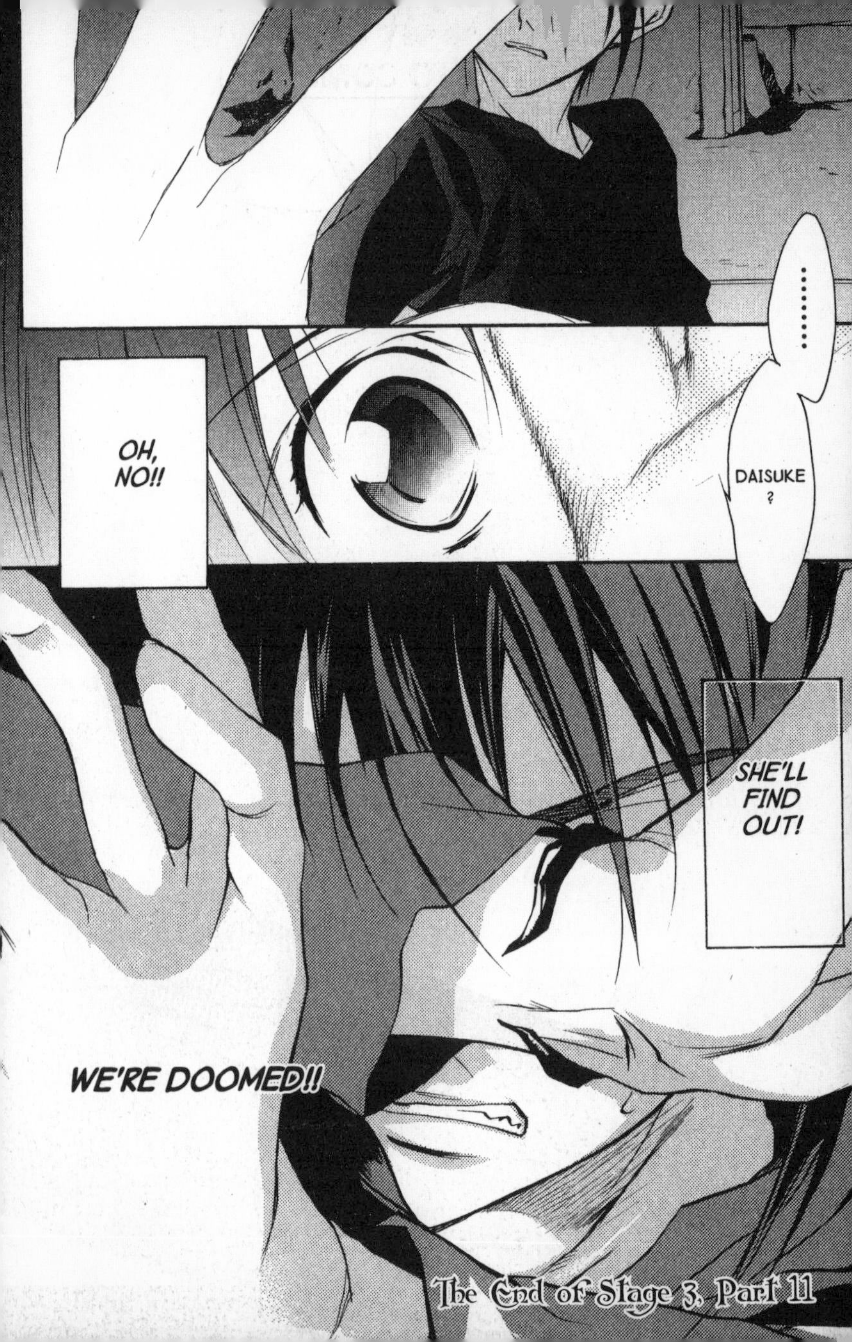
......
DAISUKE?
OH, NO!!
SHE'LL FIND OUT!
WE'RE DOOMED!!

The End of Stage 3, Part 11

D•N•ANGEL
THINGS TO COME...

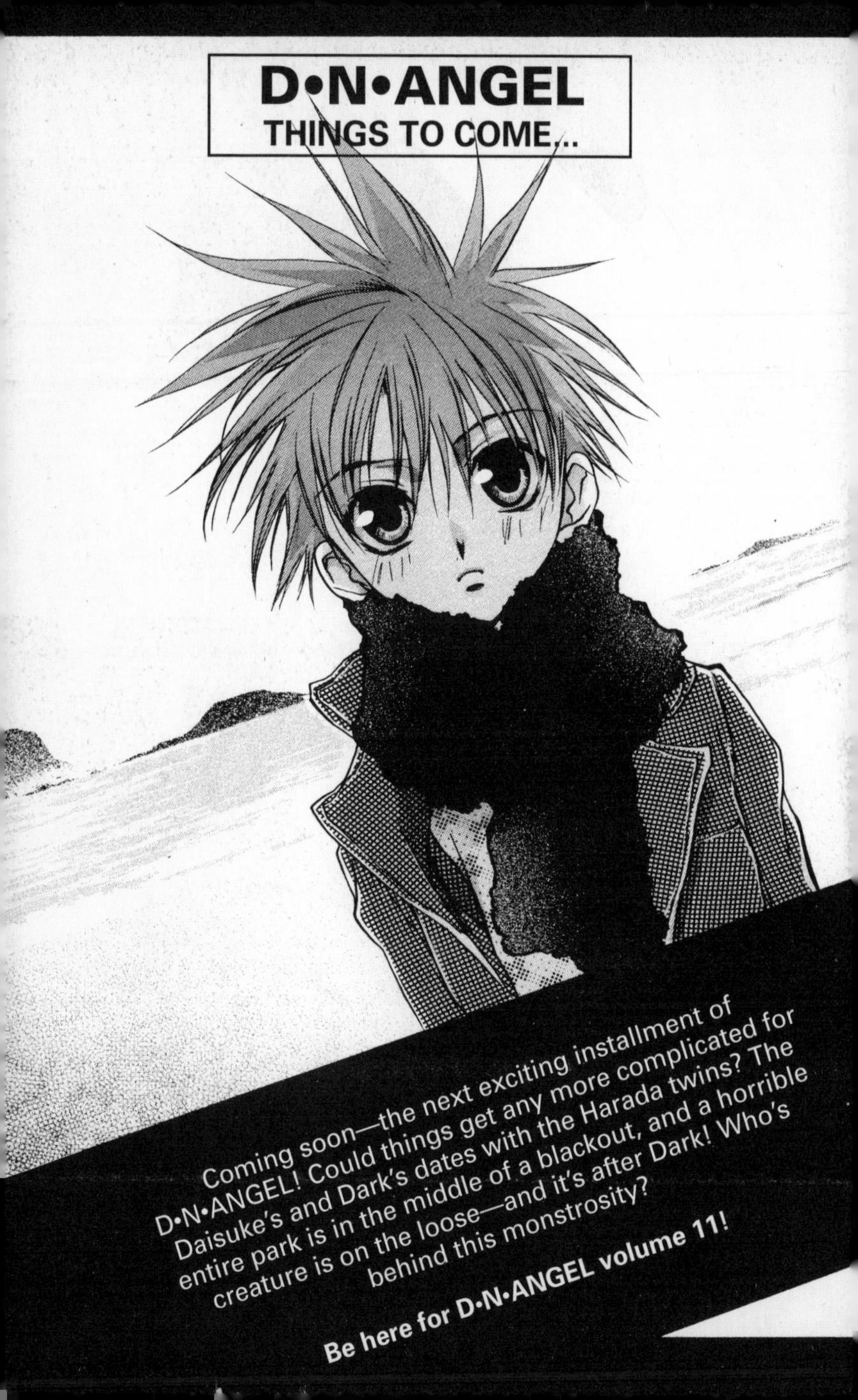

Coming soon—the next exciting installment of D•N•ANGEL! Could things get any more complicated for Daisuke's and Dark's dates with the Harada twins? The entire park is in the middle of a blackout, and a horrible creature is on the loose—and it's after Dark! Who's behind this monstrosity?

Be here for D•N•ANGEL volume 11!

TOKYOPOP SHOP

WWW.TOKYOPOP.COM/SHOP

HOT NEWS!
Check out the
TOKYOPOP SHOP!
The world's best
collection of manga in
English is now available
online in one place!

A Midnight Opera
and other hot titles are
available at the store
that never closes!

MARK OF THE SUCCUBUS

JUSTICE N MERCY
{A TOKYOPOP EXCLUSIVE ARTBOOK}

A MIDNIGHT OPERA

WWW.TOKYOPOP.COM/SHOP

- LOOK FOR SPECIAL OFFERS
- PRE-ORDER UPCOMING RELEASES
- COMPLETE YOUR COLLECTIONS

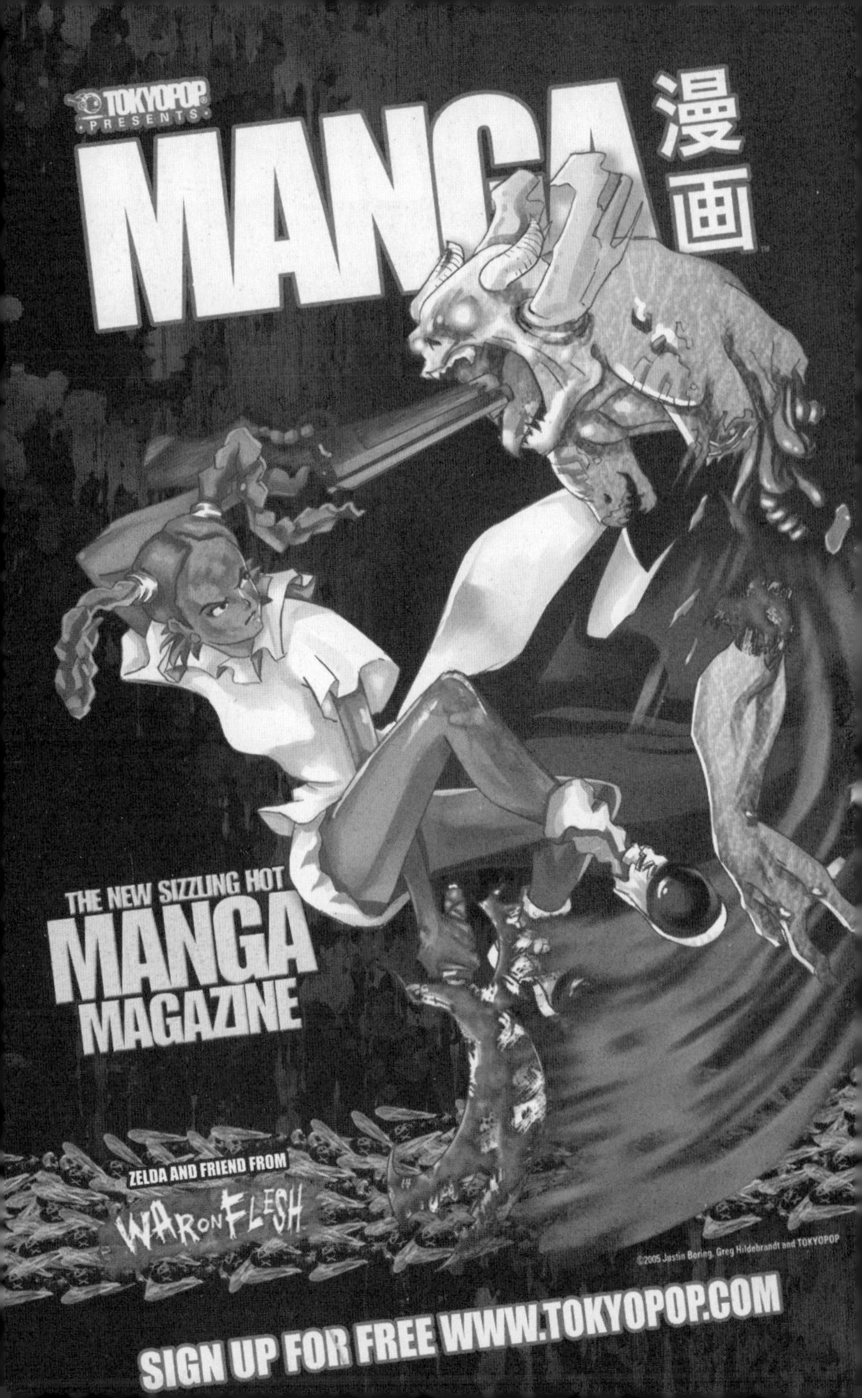
TOKYOPOP PRESENTS
MANGA 漫画
THE NEW SIZZLING HOT
MANGA
MAGAZINE
ZELDA AND FRIEND FROM
WAR ON FLESH
©2005 Justin Boring, Greg Hildebrandt and TOKYOPOP
SIGN UP FOR FREE WWW.TOKYOPOP.COM

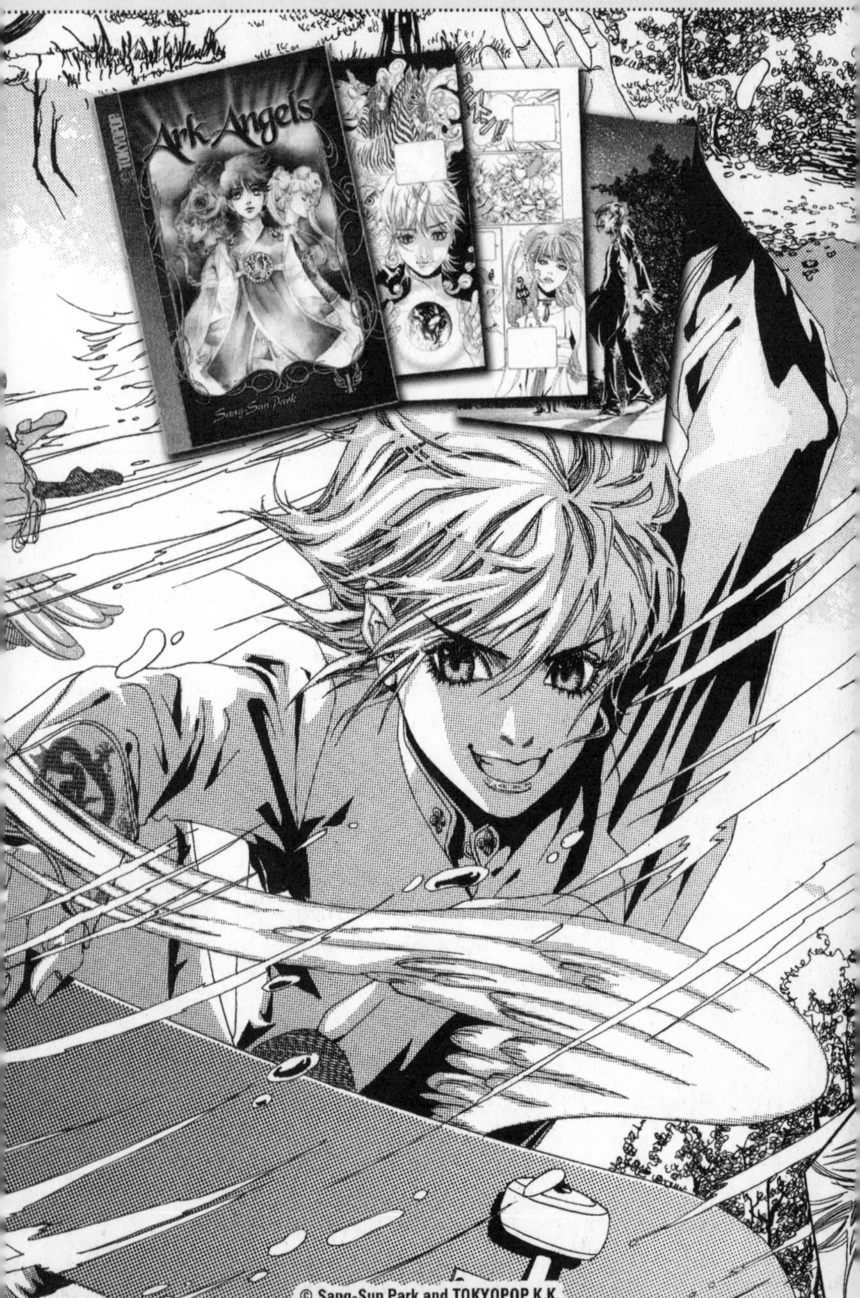
TOKYOPOP
Ark Angels
Sang-Sun Park

Ark Angels ™

Girls just wanna have fun—while saving the world.

From a small lake nestled in a secluded forest far from the edge of town, something strange has emerged: Three young girls—Shem, Hamu and Japheth—who are sisters from another world. Equipped with magical powers, they are charged with saving all the creatures of Earth from extinction. However, there is someone or something sinister trying to stop them. And on top of trying to save our world, these sisters have to live like normal human girls: They go to school, work at a flower shop, hang out with friends and even fall in love!

FROM THE CREATOR OF THE TAROT CAFÉ!

T
TEEN
AGE 13+

Read the entire first chapter online for free: www.TOKYOPOP.com/ArkAngels

SPOTLIGHT

TOKYOPOP MANGA SUPPLEMENT

THE DREAMING

BY QUEENIE CHAN

ALL OF THEM VANISHED...WITHOUT A TRACE.

When twin sisters Amber and Jeanie enroll in an Australian boarding school, they soon uncover a dark, unexplained secret: Students have been known to walk off into the surrounding bushlands, where they have vanished completely! Few know how the girls disappeared...fewer yet know why. Amber and Jeanie soon realize that the key to unlocking a secret that has been hidden for years may lie in the world of their dreams!

SUSPENSE-HORROR SHOJO FROM THE CREATOR OF THE HIT WEB MANGA *BLOCK 6*

© Queenie Chan and TOKYOPOP, Inc.

FOR MORE INFORMATION VISIT: WWW.TOKYOPOP.COM/THEDREAMING

TOKYOPOP®
· P R E S E N T S ·

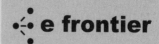

e frontier

MANGA STUDIO™ 3.0

WHAT WILL *YOU* CREATE?

The Best Software For Digital Manga Creation

e frontier's Manga Studio lets you draw, ink, tone and letter your manga in the computer. A library of **1800 digital tones** uses vector technology for moiré-free results. Automated drawing tools speed the process of creating your sequential art. Twelve types of layers keep your work organized and easy to edit. Scan in existing artwork and finish it in the computer, saving time and money on materials. Manga Studio's 1200-dpi resolution ensures professional-quality files that can be saved in several popular formats.

For more information or to purchase, visit:
www.e-frontier.com/go/tokyopop

SPECIAL INTRODUCTORY PRICE FOR MANGA STUDIO 3.0 DEBUT:
$49.99

CALL OFF YOUR MONSTERS, ADONETTE.

VAN VON HUNTER™

Copyright © 2005 e frontier America, Inc. and © 2003-2005 CelSys, Inc. Manga images from Van Von Hunter © 2005 Pseudomé Studio LLC. TOKYOPOP is a registered trademark and Van Von Hunter is a trademark of TOKYOPOP Inc. All other logos, product names and company names are trademarks or registered trademarks of their respective owners.

VAN VON HUNTER **MANGA CREATED WITH MANGA STUDIO.**

STOP!

This is the back of the book.
You wouldn't want to spoil a great ending!

This book is printed "manga-style," in the authentic Japanese right-to-left format. Since none of the artwork has been flipped or altered, readers get to experience the story just as the creator intended. You've been asking for it, so TOKYOPOP® delivered: authentic, hot-off-the-press, and far more fun!

DIRECTIONS

If this is your first time reading manga-style, here's a quick guide to help you understand how it works.

It's easy... just start in the top right panel and follow the numbers. Have fun, and look for more 100% authentic manga from TOKYOPOP®!

CROOK COUNTY LIBRARY
175 N. W. MEADOW LAKES DR.
PRINEVILLE, OR 97754
541-447-7978

100% AUTHENTIC MANGA